Distance, Rating Systems and Enterprise Finance

T0358899

In response to the credit crunch during the global financial crisis of 2007–2008, many have called for the re-establishment of regional banks in the UK and elsewhere. In this context, Germany's regional banking system, with its more than 1,400 small and regional savings banks and cooperative banks, is viewed as a role model in the financing of small and medium-sized enterprises (SMEs). However, in line with the 'death of distance' debate, the universal application of ICT-based scoring and rating systems potentially obviates the necessity for proximity to reduce information asymmetries between banks and SMEs, calling into question the key advantage of regional banks.

Utilising novel ethnographic findings from full-time participant observation and interviews, this book presents intimate insights into regional savings banks and compares their SME lending practices with large, nationwide-operating commercial banks in Germany. The ethnographic insights are contextualised by concise description of the three-pillar German banking system, covering bank regulation, structural and geographical developments, and enterprise finance. Furthermore, the book advances an original theoretical approach that combines classical banking theories with insights from social studies of finance on the (ontological) foundation of new realism. Ethnographic findings reveal varying distances of credit granting depending on the rating results, i.e. large banks allocate considerable credit-granting authority to local staff and therefore challenge the proximity advantages of regional banks. Nevertheless, by presenting case studies of lending to SMEs, the book demonstrates the ability of regional banks to capitalise on proximity when screening and monitoring financially distressed SMEs and explains why the suggestion that ICT can substitute for proximity in SME lending has to be rejected.

Franz Flögel is a researcher at the Institute for Work and Technology (Westfälische Hochschule Gelsenkirchen, Germany). He studied geography and economics in Germany and the United Kingdom and conducted his PhD at Catholic University of Eichstätt-Ingolstadt. His key research interest lies in finance and regional development.

Routledge International Studies in Money and Banking

For more information about this series, please visit www.routledge.com/series/SE0403

Distance, Rating Systems and Enterprise Finance

Ethnographic Insights from a Comparison of Regional and Large Banks in Germany

Franz Flögel

Routledge
Taylor & Francis Group

LONDON AND NEW YORK

First published 2019
by Routledge
2 Park Square, Milton Park, Abingdon, Oxon OX14 4RN

and by Routledge
52 Vanderbilt Avenue, New York, NY 10017, USA

First issued in paperback 2020

Routledge is an imprint of the Taylor & Francis Group, an informa business

This work has been accepted as *Dissertation* (PhD thesis) at the Catholic University of Eichstätt-Ingolstadt in 2017.

British Library Cataloguing-in-Publication Data
A catalogue record for this book is available from the British Library

Library of Congress Cataloging-in-Publication Data
Names: Flèogel, Franz, author.
Title: Distance, rating systems and enterprise finance : ethnographic
    insights from a comparison of regional and large banks in Germany /
    Franz Flèogel.
Description: Abingdon, Oxon ; New York, NY : Routledge, 2018. |
Series: Routledge international studies in money and banking | Includes
    bibliographical references and index.
Identifiers: LCCN 2018014832 | ISBN 9780815367970 (hardback) | ISBN
    9781351256124 (ebook)
Subjects: LCSH: Banks and banking—Germany. | Banks and banking,
    German. | Financial institutions—Germany.
Classification: LCC HG3048 .F64 2018 | DDC 332.10943—dc23
LC record available at https://lccn.loc.gov/2018014832

ISBN 13: 978-0-367-58823-6 (pbk)
ISBN 13: 978-0-8153-6797-0 (hbk)

Typeset in Times New Roman
by Apex CoVantage, LLC

Contents

Figures

Maps

Boxes

Tables

Preface

As a result of the introduction of modern information and communication technologies and various regulatory requirements, banks' decision-making procedures have changed profoundly in the past two decades. By using computer-assisted standardised instruments, in particular credit scoring (in the private customer business) and credit rating (in case of corporate customers), at the extreme a fully automated credit decision is possible nowadays. This automation allows remote lending; thus, also in continental Europe, which traditionally has been dominated by trusting *Hausbank* relationships, various providers have for some time been granting loans in the private client business using only electronic and telephone contact. In business with small and medium-sized enterprises (SMEs), in contrast, spatial proximity to a personal contact at the bank remains important as matters stand.

From both a banking business, i.e. managerial, and a regional economic development point of view, the increasing standardisation of lending is highly controversial. On the one hand, standardisation leads to an objectification of lending decisions and enables efficiency increases, from which clients can, in principle, benefit. On the other hand, local competence is reduced in highly standardised decision-making processes, which eliminates local knowledge and so-called soft information from lending decisions. In addition, financial models, like rating algorithms, can be manipulated, as was the case for the FICO consumer score in the USA, and research has shown that models are able to develop performative effects, thus promoting uniform action and hence reinforcing a volatile economy.

Despite these well-known problems, the importance of model-based risk controlling has even tended to increase in the aftermath of the financial crisis. As this study by Franz Flögel shows, standardisation and model-based risk controlling not only affect large international banks but also the small and regional German savings and cooperative banks, which are considered to be the *Hausbanken* and patient lenders of SMEs. Considering the importance of these regional banks for access to finance, especially in peripheral and structurally weak regions, the question of whether standardisation undermines regional banks' ability to consider local knowledge and soft information is relevant not only for research but also for practice.

Franz Flögel tackles this question by comparing the lending practices of regional savings banks and large banks in Germany. His ethnographic study unfolds the everyday work of a regional savings bank to the reader and demonstrates the inadequacy of making credit decisions only on the basis of rating scores in the messy business of lending to small firms. The in-depth comparison with a large bank demonstrates that despite standardisation and the binding use of rating systems, regional banks still capitalise on proximity and consider soft information when lending to SMEs. This finding has been taken for granted in research but has actually not been tested before. It is desirable that this and other key results of the study will be taken up by a broad professional audience and stimulate more research on banking, space and (uneven) regional development.

Eichstätt, January 2018 Hans-Martin Zademach

Acknowledgements

The ethnographic study in hand takes the reader into the 'society' of banks and SMEs. The conducted participant observation enabled intimate insights into the everyday work of bank employees and their clients. I am very grateful to all participants, observed or interviewed, who permitted the insights into their professional life. I hope that the more than 60 individuals involved, who cannot be named for obvious reasons, find their everyday business 'society' accurately depicted. If you will allow me the personal comment, I did not find a 'society' of 'greedy' bankers, neither in the savings bank nor in the big bank studied in-depth, but rather a 'society' of pragmatic cooperation, tough competitions, restricting hierarchies, feeling of responsibility and caring supervisor. A 'society' quite familiar to me after more than six years in the sciences. My special thanks go to the more than 60 individuals of the banks and organisations studied as well as to the 'door openers' Franz-Josef Arndt and Thorsten Wehber from the respective banking associations who provided me with the information necessary to produce this work.

I owe an exceptional debt to my academic teachers Hans-Martin Zademach and Stefan Gärtner who supported the research project at any time. Their profound effort for critical reflections and comments as well as contacts, inspiration and motivation fuelled this work. Furthermore, I would like to acknowledge Reinhard H. Schmidt for agreeing to be the *Korreferent*, or second assessor, of this work and for his supportive advice. I owe the colleagues from the Institute for Work and Technology gratitude for their diverse range of support and encouragement, especially Martina Brandt, Anna Butzin, Chantal Lang, Carmen Lehmbeck, Timo Schenkhorst, Tim Stegmann, Karin Weishaupt and Kristin Wordel. Many thanks to Katharine Thomas, Michelle Paschen and Stefanie Flick for excellent proofreading.

A range of useful advice, comments and discussions from presentations on conferences and workshops advanced the work at different stages. Let me only name the repeated workshops: the workshop financial geography, the working group on qualitative research hosted at Technical University of Dortmund and the postgraduate network *Raumaneignung*. Two research stays – one at the Catholic University of Eichstätt-Ingolstadt in the winter of 2015 and one at the Centre for Urban and Regional Development Studies of Newcastle University in the summer of 2016 – provided welcome changes of scenery and stimulated crucial writing phases. Many thanks go to the hosts Hans-Martin Zademach and Jane Pollard and their teams for support and instructive comments on my research. Furthermore, the team from Catholic University of Eichstätt-Ingolstadt accompanied me during the four years of research. I would also like to acknowledge the financial and ideational support of the *Studienstiftung des deutschen Volkes* that granted me the freedom to conduct the research I wanted to do.

Specific thanks go to my aunt Petra Krause who introduced me to the 'society' of savings banks from childhood on and supported the research with her insights and networks. I would not have thought that she would be unable to witness the completion of this work. Finally let me acknowledge the support of my family, my parents Birgitt and Dietmar Flögel as well as my four brothers and sisters. Especially my sister Anna and her husband Martin Flögel accompanied this work with comments and corrections. I owe my wife Caroline great thanks for two reasons. Firstly, for her support, corrections and comments, during all stages of research, and secondly, for being with me through all the ups and downs of this work.

Gelsenkirchen, February 2018 Franz Flögel

Abbreviations

BaFin	*Bundesanstalt für Finanzdienstleistungsaufsicht* (English: Federal Financial Supervisory Authority)
Bn	Billion
BWA	*Betriebswirtschaftliche Auswertung* (English: business assessment)
DCF	Discounted cash-flow
DSGV	*Deutscher Sparkassen- und Giroverband* (English: German Savings Banks Association)
ECB	European Central Bank
HIC	High-income countries
ICT	Information and communication technologies
IRA	*Interner Ratingansatz* (English: internal rating–based approach)
KSA	*Kreditrisikostandardansatz* (English: credit risk standardised approach)
KWG	*Gesetz über das Kreditwesen* (English: German Banking Act)
LMIC	Low- and middle-income countries
LGD	Loss given default
MaRisk	*Mindestanforderungen an das Risikomanagement* (English: minimum requirements for risk management)
OSPlus	OneSystemPlus (ICT system of the Savings Banks Financial Group)
PD	Probability of default
SMEs	Small and medium-sized enterprises
SolvV	*Solvabilitätsverordnung* (English: Solvency Regulation)
SSoF	Social studies of finance
VoC	Varieties of capitalism

1 Introduction

Germany evoked several surprises during the global financial crisis of 2008. The high level of engagement of Germany's banking sector in US securities and the consequently substantial losses contradict the common view of a domestic-oriented, bank-based German financial system. Between 2007 and 2010, German banks wrote off 2% of their assets. Only the USA, the country where the financial crisis originated, topped this (Hardie et al. 2013: 12). Even more surprisingly, it was not only the big globally operating banks like Deutsche Bank and Commerzbank that needed to write off many US securities, but also government-owned banks like IKB and a range of *Landesbanken* (Hardie and Howarth 2013a, 2013b). This observation sharply contradicts the widespread view that Germany's bank-based financial system, with its domestic-oriented government-owned banks, remains rather disentangled from global finance (Beyer 2009; Hardie and Howarth 2013b).

Yet despite these heavy losses, the financial crisis hardly affected the financial sector in total or lending to firms in particular (Gärtner 2009a, 2009c; Gärtner and Flögel 2013; Hardie and Howarth 2013b). No bank run occurred and lending to domestic firms decreased only moderately (Gärtner and Flögel 2015). Furthermore, the crisis only temporarily affected the German economy, which quickly returned to growth, while the unemployment rate remained low (Bruff and Horn 2012). In fact, public debates see the German model as a 'winner' of the crisis and prime example of a competitive economy (Kirchner et al. 2012; The Economist 14.04.2012). This represents a remarkable turnaround of public and academic perceptions, as Germany was seen as the *Kranker Mann Europas*, or sick man of Europe, a decade ago (e.g. Die Welt 06.01.2003; Kitschelt and Streeck 2004; Bruff and Horn 2012; Audretsch and Lehmann 2016).

A range of factors explain the positive performance of the German economy during the crisis: the strong manufacturing sector in relation to the financial sector; the high competitiveness of Germany's small and medium-sized enterprises (SMEs), especially the so-called hidden champions; the beneficial euro exchange rates; and the coordinated labour market organisation which enabled the implementation of short-time work under the short-time allowance scheme (Beck and Scherrer 2013). Furthermore, Gärtner (2009a) and others argue that the decentralised banking system ideally supported Germany's firms during the crisis and also accounts for the success of the German model (e.g. Hardie and Howarth 2013b).

Germany's banking system shows several special features in comparison to the banking systems of other OECD countries. The public- and cooperative-owned banks preserve a significant market share in Germany and compete as universal banks with their private-owned peers (Hackethal et al. 2006; Klagge 2009). From a geographical point of view, the more than 1,400 regional (mainly cooperative and savings) banks hallmark the decentralised German banking system. These banks are regional because as independent banks they operate in regionally designated market areas. Thus, the so-called *Regionalprinzip*, or regional principle, obliges savings banks to run branches only in the area of their dedicated municipalities (cities, towns or counties) and to lend to the institutions, companies and private individuals of their municipalities first. Cooperative banks apply this regional segregation in a similar way (Bülbül et al. 2013). Gärtner (2009a, 2011) and others argue that especially the regional savings and cooperative banks continued handing out credits during the financial crisis (Hardie and Howarth 2013b; Gärtner and Flögel 2015). Because of this lending, German firms experienced few financial constraints and overcame global economic weakening rather well, rendering the firms particularly competitive once the economy recovered (Abberger et al. 2009).

Figure 1.1 supports this argument. From the peak in 2008 to the lowest value in 2010, all banks reduced overall lending to German non-financial firms and the self-employed by €47 billion (bn). The so-called German big banks and especially the *Landesbanken* greatly reduced credits granted. In the same period, the more than 1,400 regional savings and cooperative banks actually increased credit volume by €5.7 bn and €8 bn, respectively, and thus attenuated the overall credit cutdown. In fact, in 2015 all savings banks together handed out the most credits to firms, followed by the cooperative banks. These banking groups have increased credits almost steadily since 2007, whereas big banks and, since the financial crisis also *Landesbanken*, have cut down lending. Therefore, the regional savings and cooperative banks contribute to the favourable credit supply in Germany, especially during the financial crisis.

This line of argumentation assumes (implicitly) that the regional savings and cooperative banks operate differently from the centralised big banks and *Landesbanken*. Disentangled from global finance, regional banks preserve close relationships to their SME customers and were willing and able to support their SMEs during the crisis. The book in hand scrutinises this widespread assumption. Against the background of homogenising bank regulation and the standardisation of processes, especially the use of rating systems by all modern banks, the study investigates if lending to SMEs by regional savings and cooperative banks still differs from such lending by large banks. Put differently: What differences exist in the credit-granting processes to SMEs between regional and large banks?

To this end, the credit-granting processes of regional and large banks are compared in this book. In detail the book describes and contrasts the organisation of

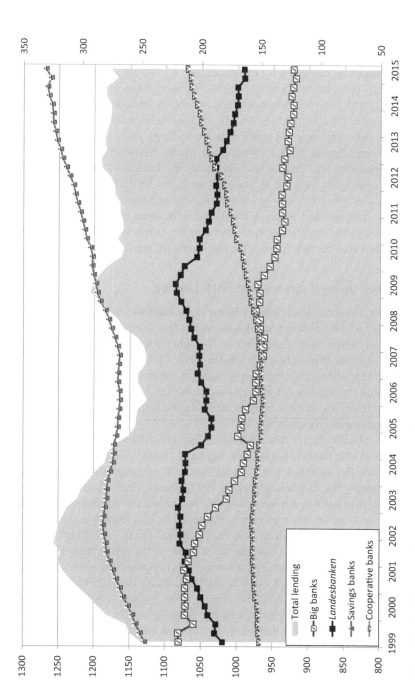

Figure 1.1 Credits to non-financial firms and the self-employed by banking groups in bn euros

Source: author's figure based on Deutsche Bundesbank 2015

credit decision making to SMEs of one savings bank and one German big bank by utilising ethnographic findings from participant observation during a two-month, full-time internship in the regional savings bank and expert interviews with employees from the big bank. In the big bank, a branch in the same region as the savings bank that competes for the same SME clients was analysed. Furthermore, the study relates these findings to eight additional banking cases (examined in less detail) and analyses documents and secondary statistics to estimate the generalisability of the empirical results. The analysis focuses on the differences in the geographical organisation of credit decision making.

The following section of this introduction places this work in the research field of the geography of finance and introduces the classification of decentralised versus centralised banking, which represents the conceptual starting point of this study (Section 1.1). Section 1.2 sketches the influence of credit decisions for economic development, indicates the impact of distance on lending and problematises a simplistic understanding of distance in modern banking. Section 1.3 clarifies the research contributions of the book and outlines its proceedings.

1.1 The geography of finance and SME lending

More than two decades ago Richard O´Brien (1992) declared "the end of geography". Because of the development of information and communication technologies (ICT) and deregulation, "geographical location no longer matters in finance, or matters much less than hitherto" (O'Brien 1992: 1). Local banking and financial markets were important in the past because co-location was vital for the communication and transmission of information. However, with the advancement of ICT and the lessening of regulatory boundaries the importance of co-location decreased and global finance arose.

The internationalisation of finance is now a fact. Nevertheless, partly provoked by O'Brien's (1992) claim (Martin 1994; Pike and Pollard 2010), a geographical line of research has emerged that studies the role of geographical proximity in finance (Schamp 1993; Leyshon and Thrift 1997; Klagge 1995; Martin 1999). On the one hand, proximity to certain customers in fact lost its importance because of advances in distance communication technologies, like telephone and online banking (Marshall and Richardson 1996; Leyshon and Thrift 1999; Martin 1999; Leyshon and Pollard 2000). Yet, on the other hand, proximity to other financial actors such as competitors, service providers, public bodies and other business partners remained important or even gained relevance (Thrift 1994; Lo 2003; Clark 2005; Hall and Appleyard 2009; Wójcik 2009; Schamp 2009). The financial sector thus tends to concentrate in global financial centres and offtake from certain peripheral regions and districts (e.g. Leyshon and Thrift 1995; Marshall and Richardson 1996; Pollard 1999; Martin 1999).

Scholars assess this logic of spatial concentration in finance – at the risk of oversimplification – in two opposing ways. On the one hand, they explore and explain the development of global and national financial centres (Taylor et al. 2003; Lo 2003; Grote 2004; König et al. 2007; Hall and Appleyard 2009; Schamp

2009; Dörry 2015). Thus, knowledge spillovers and other agglomeration economies explain the innovativeness and competitiveness of financial centres. In line with territorial innovation models (Maskell and Malmerg 1999; Rehfeld 1999; Bathelt et al. 2004), financial centres possess specific atmospheres that boost the innovativeness of the clustering financial sector (comparable to clusters of high-tech firms). An innovative and large financial sector, in turn, fosters economic growth (King and Levine 1993; Levine 2005), wherefore the spatial concentration of finance positively impacts economic growth.

On the other hand, scholars evaluate the development of global finance centres critically. The world city/global city research direction expresses this criticism (Friedmann and Wolff 1982; Friedmann 1986; Sassen 2001; Therborn 2011). According to this line of research, a handful of interconnected global cities with massive financial sectors execute immense power and control over the world economy. In peripheral regions the spatial concentration of finance leads to losses of autonomy and poor capital provision, which reinforces polarised economic development (Chick and Dow 1988; Klagge and Martin 2005; Gärtner 2009b, 2013). Furthermore, the research line of financialisation observes "the growing influence of capital markets, their intermediaries, and processes" (Pike and Pollard 2010: 29) and critically assesses their global spread (Leyshon and Thrift 2007; French et al. 2011). The short-term profit orientation of a financialised financial sector hampers economic development in the long run (Froud et al. 2000; Aglietta and Breton 2001; Epstein 2005; Theurillat et al. 2010). Thus, the spatial concentration of finance negatively impacts economic growth.

Both views expect a further spatial concentration of the finance sector. Yet, this development is not mandatory. Thus, Wójcik and MacDonald-Korth (2015) and Gärtner and Flögel (2017) actually show that the spatial concentration of banking and finance (in terms of financial employees) did not increase in Germany between 2002 and 2012. In this light it is posited that the same argumentation which explains why the financial sector tends to concentrate (information advantages in financial centres) also explains why finance stays decentralised (Gärtner 2011). If spatial proximity between financial intermediaries and clients remains important in terms of gaining information, then instead of concentration, a distribution across space which follows the spatial distribution of its customers is to be expected. And in fact Sternberg and Litzenberger (2004) and Titze et al. (2011) show that retail finance remains decentralised in Germany, whereas auxiliary services to finance tend to concentrate in space.

The research direction of small firm financing supports notions of the usefulness of decentralised banking. Small and regional banks have advantages in processing proprietary information in comparison to centralised large banks. Therefore, they are better off when financing informationally opaque SMEs (Stein 2002; Berger et al. 2005; Udell 2008, 2009; Alessandrini 2009a; Wray 2010; Behr et al. 2013). Thus, a decentralised financial system with many regional banks tends to yield advantages in SME financing, especially in peripheral regions, and balances regional economic disparities (Chick and Dow 1988; Gärtner 2009b).

Klagge (1995) proposed a classification of decentralised and centralised banking and also applied this to other financial intermediaries (Klagge and Martin 2005; see also Verdier 2002). With the global financial crisis of 2008 this topic gained new attention (Gärtner 2009a, 2011; Gärtner and Flögel 2013, 2014; Wójcik and MacDonald-Korth 2015; Klagge et al. 2017), because the decentralised German banking system with its more than 1,400 regional savings and cooperative banks attenuated a credit crunch. Two reasons potentially explain why regional banks were able to extend lending to firms during the financial crisis (Gärtner and Flögel 2015). Firstly, regional banks refinance their lending from regional savings, which make them independent of global finance; in this way regional banks did not face a funding gap during the crisis. Secondly, regional banks grant credit to regional customers at short distance, which gives them informational advantages. Therefore, the credit risk assessment of these banks was superior and they faced fewer write-offs during the crisis.

Although this argumentation in favour of decentralised banking appears conclusive, open questions remain if one considers the actual business practices of modern banks. Standardisation of banks' credit-granting processes and bank regulations tend to centralise credit decisions, despite the regional independency of banks (Leyshon and Thrift 1999; Degryse et al. 2009; Gärtner and Flögel 2013; Dixon 2014). Therefore, the predicted end of geography in finance (O'Brien 1992) remains a current issue (Petersen and Rajan 2002; Pieper 2005). Addressing the issue, Degryse et al. (2009: 182) ask provocatively, "Is distance [in banking] dead? Or will it die another day?".

In Germany all regional savings banks use the same rating systems, centrally developed by an affiliated company of the German Savings Banks Association (DSGV), to assign rating scores to their business clients (Sparkassen Rating and Risikosysteme GmbH 2010). As the rating score is key information for credit decisions, expressing the probability of default, it is questionable if savings banks gain informational advantages from short metric distance to firms (Gärtner and Flögel 2013, 2014). In other words, does the widespread assumption that regional banks decide at a shorter distance to their SME clients than large banks and thus gain information advantages in SME lending hold true? The study in hand tackles this question empirically by comparing the credit decision-making processes of regional and large banks in Germany.

Analysing SME lending processes and the practices of banks is not only the next step with regard to a classification of decentralised versus centralised banking, but also helps to fill a more general research gap. More than 10 years ago Pollard (2003: 430) argued "that firm finance is something of a 'black box' in economic geography, a largely taken-for-granted aspect of production". She called for "detailed analysis [of firm finance], not simply to 'add' to our knowledge [. . .], but in order to further develop and refine our understanding of uneven development" (Pollard 2003: 430). To date, scholars have analysed the link between SMEs and financial intermediaries from a geographical perspective, mainly in the field of venture capital (Martin et al. 2005; Zademach 2009; Wallisch 2009; Klagge and Peter 2009; Scheuplein 2013), but also for bank-based

SME lending (Handke 2011; Panzer-Krause 2011). Yet, to the author's knowledge, there has been no in-depth study of banks' decision making practices in SME lending from a geographical perspective. Therefore, more than 10 years after Pollard's (2003) call, the need for more research on banking and firm financing continues (e.g. Appleyard 2013; Baumeister and Zademach 2013; Gärtner and Flögel 2013; Hall 2013).

1.2 Credit decisions and rating systems

Banks and other financial intermediaries such as venture capital firms and investment funds influence economic development based on their decisions as to which firms and projects receive external capital (e.g. loans, equity capital). Depending on the success of these (credit) investment decisions, economic development and decline is co-determined by finance; e.g. banks finance innovative and successful firms or inflate asset bubbles. To conduct credit decisions, banks and other financial intermediaries collect private and public information about potential borrowers. Furthermore, they monitor borrowers and execute corporate governance. By doing so, banks and other financial intermediaries facilitate capital allocation and overcome information asymmetries between borrowers and lenders (Levine 1997; Engerer and Schrooten 2004; Klagge 2009; Beck et al. 2009; Turner 2010).

Research of distance and small firm financing argues that the lending decisions of banks are geographical rather than neutral. Distance influences lending, as more distant banks receive less knowledge about borrowers than banks that conduct lending decisions at a short distance to borrowers (Stein 2002; Alessandrini et al. 2009a; Behr et al. 2013). However, short geographical distance is neither necessary nor sufficient to facilitate knowledge exchange (Boschma 2005; Torre and Rallet 2005; Torre 2008; Bathelt and Henn 2014). This argument has special importance in lending to SMEs, because in contrast to high finance (Vopel 1999; Lo 2003; Hall and Appleyard 2009) banks have standardised most processes in the SME retail business (Pieper 2005; Riese 2006). Furthermore, several employees are involved in the credit decisions of banks to SMEs as bank regulation instructs (BaFin 2012a). Thus, to understand the role of distance in modern banks' credit decisions, the interplay of a range of actors and the standardisation of processes must be taken into consideration.

Rating systems in particular standardise the credit decision processes of banks. Banks use internal rating systems to assess the creditworthiness of SMEs, i.e. to calculate their default probability. The use of rating systems tends to shift the credit decisions from banks' local staff (that execute the interviews with the customers) to the algorithms of the rating systems (Leyshon and Thrift 1999; Martin 1999; Leyshon and Pollard 2000). As the rating scores represent key information in the credit decision processes of banks, an analysis of banks' lending decisions must take rating systems into account. Interestingly, Berger et al. (2011) show for the USA that not only large banks but also regional banks rely on rating scores for credit decisions. This observation contradicts the assumption that regional banks decide SME credits at a shorter distance to their customers and therefore achieve informational advantages. It is known that regional savings and cooperative banks use rating systems in SME lending in Germany, too (Behr et al. 2013). However, the extent to which rating systems influence lending remains unclear. The study in hand aims to answer this question empirically by explicitly considering the influence of rating systems in the credit-granting processes of banks. Pursuing this aim requires conceptual work, as economic theories on distance and small firm finance tend to neglect rating systems and only consider the human actors – e.g. customer advisors, customer relationship managers, supervisors, bank CEOs – of the credit-granting processes. Therefore, one aim of this work is to elaborate a conceptualisation of decision making in bank-based (SME) lending which explicitly considers rating systems as non-human actors that influence credit decisions. Three strands of theory inform the conceptualisation:

- Firstly, the social studies of finance (SSoF) and especially the theory on the performativity of economic theories and models help to trace the influence of rating systems on credit decisions (Callon 1998; MacKenzie 2006).
- Secondly, on the metatheoretical level, actor-network theory (ANT) captures the power of non-human actors to influence and constrain human actions (Callon 1999; Latour 2005).
- Thirdly, this study builds on the new realist ontology (Gabriel 2013, 2015) to incorporate these strands of rather anti-realist theory with theories on distance and small firm finance that rely on a realist perspective.

With these three strands of theory this study conceptualises rating systems as (asymmetric) non-human actors that conduct credit decisions in cooperation with humans.

1.3 Research contributions and proceedings

Building on the classification of decentralised versus centralised banking and the research on distance and small firm finance, this book compares the SME credit-granting processes of regional and large banks in Germany. Germany's banking system tends to be a striking example of how decentralised banking smoothens SME financing and thus fosters the competitiveness of SMEs. It is seen as an alternative model to centralised banking systems, like the UK, with few international banks which are accused of offering insufficient support for domestic SMEs (The Economist 14.04.2012; Greenham and Prieg 2015). The book in hand aims to contribute to this discussion of alternative banking models with the comparison of regional and large banks. The comparison identifies differences in the organisation of credit-granting processes and discusses which effects these differences have on access to finance for SMEs. In this context, the question of whether regional banks decide credit at shorter distances than large banks and thus gain information advantages is addressed using the comparison of selected banks.

With this approach, the debate on distance and small firm finance is advanced. To the widespread assumption, regional banks gain informational advantages in lending at short distances to informationally opaque SMEs (Berger et al. 2005; Alessandrini 2009a; Behr et al. 2013). However, against the background of bank regulation, standardisation of processes and especially the use of rating systems, it remains unclear whether modern regional banks decide credits at a shorter distance to their SME clients than large banks. The comparison reveals varied distances of credit decision making; hence the big bank studied in-depth decides on certain SME credits at shorter distances than the observed savings bank. Nevertheless, the comparison suggests that the assumption of informational advantages for regional banks holds true.

Furthermore, the book contributes to the debate on geographical distance and knowledge transfer. It is well recognised that short geographical distance (e.g. co-location) between actors says little about their capacity to exchange knowledge (Boschma 2005; Torre 2008; Bathelt and Henn 2014). This work analyses information transmission in credit decision processes and discusses metric and non-metric aspects of distance between the actors involved and their interplay. According to the findings of the analysis, geographical distance tends to be subordinated to organisational embeddedness for information transmission in credit decisions of the banks studied. Nevertheless, face-to-face interaction plays a role for the reliable transmission of so-called soft information.

This book also contributes to the comparative financial systems studies on decentralised versus centralised banking systems, i.e. the geographical classification of banking systems. In line with the distance and small firm finance debate, scholars argue that proximity to customers is an important characteristic of decentralised banking and is associated with enhanced access to finance for SMEs (Klagge 1995; Gärtner and Flögel 2014, 2017). However, if regional banks do not reach credit decisions at a shorter distance to their clients than large banks, then the proximity argument for a geographical classification loses its validity. According to the findings from the comparison, the savings bank observed tends to decide at shorter distances than the big bank studied in-depth when soft information influences SME credit decisions most, indicating the explanation power of the proximity argument for the geographical classification. In this context, the book relates the geographical classification of banking to the debate on diversity in banking. Researchers commonly approach diversity by differentiating according to the ownership structure of the banks (Ayadi et al. 2009, 2010) and argue that diversity enhances the resilience of banking systems. This book argues that distance differences in the credit granting of regional and supraregional banks foster divergent lending decisions and hence diversity.

Finally, this book contributes to the research field of SME finance and (uneven) regional development (Chick and Dow 1988; Dow and Rodríguez-Fuentes 1997; Klagge 2003; Pollard 2003; Klagge and Martin 2005; Gärtner 2008). Despite several calls for research (Baumeister and Zademach 2013; Hall 2013), studies on the causalities between the centralisation of banks, firm finance and polarised regional economic development are still rare. The findings presented in this book support the notion of a positive association between decentralised banking and reduced credit rationing to SMEs.

The remainder of this book is structured in four chapters. Chapter 2 deduces the theory basis for the empirical comparison and is subdivided into four sections. Section 2.1 places this research in the broader field of financial system studies, outlining the potential of the geographical classification of decentralised and centralised banking to explore the impact of finance on economic development. Section 2.2 reviews theories and empirical studies that explain why distance matters in SME finance, and Section 2.3 critically advances the previous section by conceptualising rating systems as non-human actors that influence credit decisions. Taking these three sections into account, Section 2.4 outlines how distance in bank-based lending to SMEs is approached. Chapter 3 introduces the research object, the German banking system, and outlines the methodology. In this context, Section 3.1 justifies the selection of ethnography as the research methodology and explains the empirical execution of this study. Section 3.2 describes the German banking system, and Section 3.3 introduces the actual bank cases under study. Chapter 4 presents the empirical results of the study by contrasting the SME lending of regional and large banks in three parts. Section 4.1 outlines the informational sources that banks draw upon when conducting lending decisions, and Section 4.2 compares the organisation of lending processes between the regional and large banks by reviewing the human and non-human actors involved. Section 4.3 discusses the effects of the observed differences on SME finance. The conclusion is outlined in Chapter 5.

2 Financial systems, the geography of firm financing and rating systems

2.1 Financial systems and economic development

Following Schmidt and Tyrell (2004: 21ff), the financial sector is defined as:

> That part – or sector – of an economy which offers and provides financial services to the other sectors of the economy. It consists of the central bank, other banks, non-bank financial institutions, organized financial markets and the relevant regulatory and supervisory institutions.

The financial sector is one part of a financial system. A *financial system* in general is defined as "the interaction between the supply of and the demand for the provision of capital and other finance-related services" (Schmidt and Tyrell 2004: 21). In addition to the financial sector, a financial system also comprises the demands of the users of financial services (e.g. savings and investment preferences) and the state that demands and regulates finance. Furthermore, the flows of information and influence (or power) that mirror financial flows belong to a financial system (Schmidt and Tyrell 2004; Zademach 2014).

This chapter elaborates on the connections between financial systems and economic development and focuses on the institutional design of financial systems. It shows the need of structural classifications of financial systems in light of "too much finance" (Arcand et al. 2012) and outlines the rationales for a geographical classification of banking systems in the context of the diversity in banking debate. Section 2.1.1 reviews the finance–growth nexus. Section 2.1.2 considers the structure of financial systems and indicates that several structural variables influence economic development. Section 2.1.3 demonstrates that the geographical classification explains the varying lending practices of decentralised and centralised banks and tends to be one relevant structural variable of financial systems.

2.1.1 Finance–growth nexus

The importance of financial systems for economic development is contested. Whereas most scholars state that financial system development supports economic growth (Schmidt and Tyrell 2004; Klagge and Martin 2005; Beck 2012; Deller-Schneil 2012; Zademach 2014), other researchers claim its neutrality (Lucas 1988).

Capital allocation, i.e. the channelling of savings into productive investment, is recognised to be the primary function by which financial sectors impact economic development. The literature specifies this general function and elaborates catalogues of the functions of financial systems (Merton and Bodie 1995; Levine 2005; Turner 2010; Beck 2012). The selection and monitoring of capital investment represents the primary function of financial systems. Financial systems help to select quality investments ex ante by collecting information about potential investment projects/borrowers. The quality of this information influences investment decisions and thus the success of investments (Beck 2012). Monitoring, i.e. enforcing financial contracts, is related to the selection function. Financial systems monitor capital investment by executing corporate governance (Beck 2012). Both functions increase economic growth by supporting efficient capital allocation and thus capital accumulation (Pagano 1993; Sachverständigenrat zur Begutachtung der gesamtwirtschaftlichen Entwicklung 2008; Deller-Schneil 2012). With the risk, size and maturity transformation functions, financial systems stimulate savings and increase the rate of investment (Sachverständigenrat zur Begutachtung der gesamtwirtschaftlichen Entwicklung 2008). Developed financial systems manage to offer all savers products that fit their preferences (e.g. concerning risk–return mix) and supply borrowers with the funds they demand (Turner 2010). Thus, as illustrated in Figure 2.1, overall financial systems fuel economic growth by influencing the rate of investment and accumulation of capital.

Most researchers who question financial system influence on economic growth do not deny different functionalities between the financial systems of high-income countries (HIC) and low- and middle-income countries (LMIC). They rather argue that financial system development follows economic development (Merton and Bodie 1995), or as Robinson (1952, cited in Deller-Schneil 2012: 11) put it, "where enterprise leads, finance follows". Against this background, research on the finance–growth nexus must examine the direction of causality between the size of the financial sector and economic development (King and Levine 1993; Levine et al. 2000). This research has a long tradition, going back to Bagehot and Schumpeter (Stolbov 2013) and Goldsmith (1969), and has yielded extensive output (Levine 2005; Ang 2008; Beck 2012; Havránek et al. 2013; Zademach 2014). According to the meta-analysis of Havránek et al. (2013), ca. 50% of all reviewed estimations find a positive and significant correlation and about 10% report a negative and significant effect between the size of the financial sector and economic growth. Also the issue of causality is settled in favour of the finance–growth nexus (Havránek et al. 2013); the positive influence of financial system development on economic growth is accordingly taken largely for granted.

However, since the financial crisis of 2008, the finance–growth nexus has been revisited in light of "too much finance" (Arcand et al. 2012; Turner 2010;

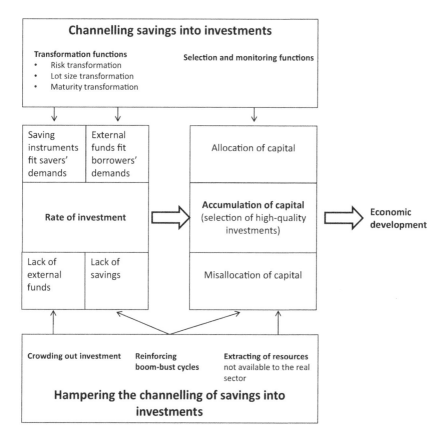

Figure 2.1 Functions and dysfunctions of financial systems and link to economic development

Source: author's figure following Sachverständigenrat zur Begutachtung der gesamtwirtschaftlichen Entwicklung (2008: 12) and Pagano (1993)

Capelle-Blancard and Labonne 2011; Epstein and Crotty 2013). Rousseau and Wachtel (2011) report that the positive association between finance and growth between 1960 and 1989 vanished in the period from 1990 to 2004. Arcand et al. (2012) argue that the causality between finance and growth is non-linear. The initially positive association between the size of the banking sector and economic growth vanishes at a certain level of financial deepening, i.e. when credit to the private sector reaches ca. 80% to 100% of gross domestic product (GDP). These new empirical findings indicate that large and active financial sectors hamper economic growth.

These findings are hardly new. Marx and Keynes pointed out the risk of excessive speculation caused by deep financial sectors (Harvey 1982; Tobin 1984).

Basically, the literature advances three related dysfunctions of large and complex financial systems that explain hampering effects on economic development (Turner 2010):

- Firstly, the extracting of resources dysfunction. At a certain point of financial deepening, the input of capital and labour into the financial sector far exceeds the social benefits this sector produces (Tobin 1984), causing a misallocation of resources from the non-financial sectors to finance (Sawyer 2014).
- Secondly, the reinforcing boom-bust cycles dysfunction. In their profit-generating manner, overlarge financial systems over- and underscore economic cycles and accelerate cyclicity (Minsky 1992). Large financial sectors enable highly leveraged investments and real estate price inflation that, in turn, cause unnecessarily high losses in bust phases (Brunnermeier et al. 2009; Turner 2010).
- Thirdly, the crowding out investments dysfunction. During economic boom cycles the danger exists that "exuberant lending will tend to crowd out that element of lending which is indeed related to the funding of marginal productive investments" (Turner 2010: 28). For example, it becomes difficult for SMEs to gain loans during a real-estate boom because banks gain profits in the mortgage business more easily. In this way, deep financial sectors paradoxically tend to cause a reduction of funds for firms, and thus diminish the rate of investment of an economy.

Against the background of the empirical findings and the dysfunctions of financial systems, the view that the growth of financial sectors always causes economic growth must be rejected. Especially in HIC more finance is no longer associated with economic growth (Arcand et al. 2012). Thus, other factors need to be taken into consideration to understand the finance–growth nexus, which brings the structure of financial systems into the spotlight of research.

2.1.2 *Financial systems' structure and economic development*

The distinction between bank-based and market-based financial systems represents the prominent structure classification (Allen and Gale 2000; Demirgüç-Kunt and Levine 2001; Hall and Soskice 2001; Krahnen and Schmidt 2004) and is applied in economics and other social sciences (Hardie et al. 2013). In the broader varieties of capitalism (VoC) classification, bank-based financial systems represent a key element of coordinated market economies (e.g. Germany, Japan), and market-based financial systems are an important pillar of liberal market economies (USA, UK) (Hall and Soskice 2001; Dixon 2012). VoC scholars point out complementarities between the institutions of the financial and economic systems (Hall and Soskice 2001; Schmidt and Tyrell 2004; Hackethal et al. 2006), and thus expect bank-based and market-based financial systems to persist.

In contrast to VoC, several scholars see the homogenisation of financial systems under the pressure of financialisation. *Financialisation* refers to the global development of contemporary capitalism towards financial market capitalism and is characterised by "the increasing role of financial motives, financial markets, financial actors and financial institutions in the operation of the domestic and international economies" (Epstein 2005: 3; see also Froud et al. 2000; Aglietta and Breton 2001; Epstein 2005; Windolf 2005; Corpataux et al. 2009; Beyer 2009; Leyshon and Thrift 2007; Pike and Pollard 2010; French et al. 2011). While financialisation has also changed liberal market economies (Epstein 2005), scholars expect the strongest transformation in coordinated market economies like Germany, where capital markets have been less important. Accordingly, the transformation of the German economy has attracted great academic interest (Deeg 2001; Schmidt et al. 2001; Beyer 2002; Krahnen and Schmidt 2004; Dixon 2012). The erosion of the close capital and personal interconnections of major German companies and large banks as well as a range of changes in German taxation, pension and finance regulation systems indicate the move towards market-based finance (Deeg 2001; Beyer 2002, 2009; Dixon 2012). In contrast to this, Schmidt et al. (2001; Hackethal et al. 2006) highlight that despite the changes for the large corporations, the majority of firms continue to gain finance from the banks they have long-term relationships with. Also, no major shifts between the three banking pillars arose (Hackethal et al. 2006), indicating persistence in the German financial system.

The homogenisation of national financial systems may have become evident with the global financial crisis of 2008 as it affected most market economies, which is naturally a challenge for VoC, which claims that differences between countries' financial and economic systems persist (Beyer 2009; Bruff and Horn 2012). A range of banks of the German bank-based financial system were hit surprisingly strongly by the financial crisis, including also the government-owned banks (e.g. *Landesbanken*) that were seen as the backbone of Germany's coordinated market economy (Beyer 2009). While not denying these developments, other authors argue that the traditional classification into bank-based and market-based financial systems is no longer sufficient to observe differences and call for alternative classifications of financial and banking systems (Hardie and Howarth 2013a; Gärtner and Flögel 2014; see Figure 2.2).

This section reviews established and alternative structural classifications of financial and banking systems and discusses the extent to which the structural differences explain economic development. Gärtner (2013b) lists five possible classifications of financial and banking systems (Figure 2.2). The first classification of Figure 2.2 refers to financial sector deepening, as discussed in Section 2.1.1. In the following sections the other classifications of Figure 2.2 are discussed, starting with the traditional classification in bank-based and market-based financial systems (Section 2.1.2.1). The other three classifications solely focus on the banking sector. This focus accords with Hardie et al.'s (2013) call to carefully distinguish within banking, rather than naïvely contrast bank-based

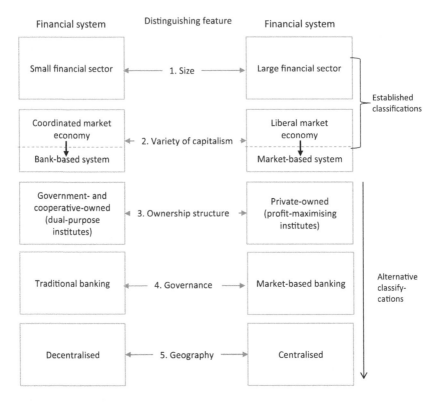

Figure 2.2 Established and alternative classifications of financial systems

Source: Gärtner 2013: 237 (translated and modified)

and market-based financial systems. The third classification looks at the owner-ship structure of banks and banking systems and discusses the pros and cons of dual-purpose banks versus profit-maximising banks (Section 2.1.2.2). The fourth classification builds on Hardie and Howarth's (2013a) concept of market-based banking and distinguishes between traditional and market-based banking (Section 2.1.2.3). Finally, the fifth classification – the conceptual foundation of this book – looks at the geographical organisation of banking systems and distinguishes between centralised and decentralised banking (Section 2.1.2.4).

2.1.2.1 Bank-based versus market-based financial systems

A considerable body of literature approaches financial systems according to the importance of banks (credits) versus capital markets (shares, bonds and venture capital) (Allen and Gale 2000; Krahnen and Schmidt 2004; Hackethal et al. 2006).

According to Allen and Gale (2000), a range of economists assume capital markets' superiority to banks because perfect markets lead to the optimal allocation of resources and to the model of perfect competition. However, Allen and Gale (2000) point out that financial markets appear to fit very poorly to the model of perfect markets – i.e. information asymmetries are high and agency problems apparent – arguing that banks and other financial intermediaries help to overcome market failures.

Actual financial systems usually consist of banks and organised capital markets and empirical comparison looks at the degree of usage of both institutions. In bank-based systems, SMEs and even large corporations are often owned by few associates, external finance is acquired through bank loans and savers hold their money predominantly as bank deposits. In market-based financial systems, banks also exist. However, large and even medium-sized firms are publicly listed, and private households invest their savings in shares and bonds, either directly or via institutional investors. Companies predominantly source external finance with stocks and bonds, and young and small firms acquire finance from private equity firms (Luintel et al. 2008; Hardie et al. 2013; Bijlsma and Zwart 2013).

The literature discusses several pros and cons of bank-based and market-based financial systems regarding their ability to deal with asymmetric information, regarding their ability to cope with risk and regarding their cooperative governance.

Organised capital markets and banks overcome informational asymmetries between savers and capital users in different ways (Allen and Gale 2000; Luintel et al. 2008; Beck 2012). On well-performing capital markets, the security prices comprise all (publicly) available information about companies instantly. In this way the price of shares and bonds reflects the diverse evaluations of companies by all market participants. Banks, in contrast, evaluate companies based on private information, too. Bank secrecy protects the dissemination of this information which hinders its circulation but encourages companies to reveal more private information as they do not have to fear that competitors, customers, suppliers etc. receive adverse information. In contrast, active financial markets tend to discourage information gathering because of the free rider problem; i.e. individual evaluations of companies are discouraged as the results quickly spread to all market participants (Stiglitz 1985; Allen and Gale 2000; Luintel et al. 2008).

Capital markets are deemed to be superior at coping with risk because they effectively diversify risk across actors, regions and sectors and develop tailor-made securities which fit the risk–return–maturity preferences of savers (Luintel et al. 2008). In contrast, Allen and Gale (2000) argue that banks perform an intertemporal smoothing of returns for deposit holders and offer constant and risk-free earnings to savers (mitigating intertemporal risk), "thus providing insurance to investors [savers] who would otherwise be forced to liquidate assets at disadvantageous prices" (11). Therefore, bank-based financial systems may be better placed to stimulate savings from risk-adverse savers. In this context, Turner

(2010) points out that the mechanisms of banks and markets with which they produce tailor-made investment opportunities tend to be quite similar as both produce saving opportunities that are relatively risk free (e.g. bank deposits and senior tranche securities) and assets which are risky and more profitable (e.g. bank shares and junior tranche securities).

In long-standing borrower relationships banks tend to execute cooperative governance more patiently than capital markets and hence reduce "short-termism" (Luintel et al. 2008: 5). However, banks "can stymie innovation by extracting informational rents and protecting firms with close bank-firm ties from competition [. . . and] may collude with firm managers against other creditors" (Levine 2002: 3 cited in Luintel et al. 2008). In the tradition of VoC research, several scholars point out complementarities between the institutions of the financial and the economic systems (Hall and Soskice 2001; Schmidt and Tyrell 2004; Hackethal et al. 2006). As patient lenders, banks optimally support the long-term orientation and incremental innovations (i.e. small improvements to current products) of coordinated market economies. In contrast, capital markets and venture capital firms optimally fuel the competition and radical innovations of liberal market economies. Thus, in addition to the abovementioned differences between banks and capital markets, both organisations possess the capability to optimally support their corresponding economic systems (Hall and Soskice 2001), suggesting similar overall growth rates of bank-based and market-based economies.

Determining the structure of financial systems empirically is not straightforward because of the strong effect of financial systems' overall development on bank-based and market-based indicators. Less developed financial systems are often bank based, as almost no capital market exists. Therefore, empirical classifications must control for overall financial system development. (Demirgüç-Kunt and Levine 2001). Using data from 2006, Bijlsma and Zwart (2013) present an empirical classification for the EU 27 countries, with the USA and Japan as benchmarks. They identify three clusters of countries in Europe: besides the bank-based and market-based financial systems, the Eastern European countries form a third cluster (Map 2.1).

Austria, Denmark, Germany, Greece, Italy, Portugal and Spain belong to the bank-based cluster. In these countries a larger fraction of household assets are deposits, and bank credits to firms are higher than in market-based systems (Bijlsma and Zwart 2013: 9). The Netherlands, the UK, Belgium, France, Finland and Sweden belong to the cluster of market-based financial systems, as they have large and active stock, venture capital and bond markets (Bijlsma and Zwart 2013). The Eastern Europe countries – Bulgaria, Czech Republic, Estonia, Hungary, Latvia, Lithuania, Poland, Romania, Slovakia and Slovenia – have low values for both bank-based and market-based indicators (Bijlsma and Zwart 2013).

Beck et al. (2001) analyse the impact of financial systems' structure on long-term economic growth for 48 countries from 1980 to 1995 and do not find an association between structure indicators and economic growth. Furthermore, the

Map 2.1 Classification of bank-based and market-based financial systems in Europe (2006)
Source: Bijlsma and Zwart 2013: 8 (modified)

authors analyse the impact of financial systems' structure on other economic performance indicators. Overall, Beck at al. (2001: 233) conclude:

> Financial structure is not an analytically useful way to distinguish among financial systems. More precisely, countries do not grow faster, financially dependent industries do not expand at higher rates, new firms are not created more easily, firms access to external finance is not easier, and firms do not grow faster in either market- or bank-based financial systems.

A range of studies reproduce these results with comparable empirical methods (Beck and Levine 2002; Luintel et al. 2008), supporting the VoC expectation of similar overall economic growth rates because of institutional complementarities between banks and capital markets and their corresponding economies.

Recent studies somewhat undermine the consensus. In their meta-analysis Havránek et al. (2013) show that indicators of financial market development have greater effects on economic growth than indicators of banking system development. Demirgüç-Kunt et al. (2013: 476) report this effect from 1980 to 2008 using a database of 72 countries. The authors observe that in the course of development "the association between an increase in economic output and an increase in bank development becomes smaller", whereas it becomes stronger for security market development. Peia and Roszbach (2013) report similar results in their country-by-country time series analysis for 26 developed countries from 1973 to 2011. Whereas banking system development is associated with economic growth only in Japan, stock market development shows a significant effect in 7 out of the 26 countries. The authors conclude that stock market rather than banking development triggers economic growth for HIC. The results suggest that financial structure matters in HIC as capital market growth becomes more important for economic development. However, one striking limitation must be highlighted. As indicated in Section 2.1.1, in the last decade banking system development (measured in private credits/GDP) has lost its association with economic development in most HIC. Therefore, instead of indicating the superiority of market-based financial systems for HIC, the study results tend to reproduce the observed effect of "too much finance", suggesting the need for qualitative indicators of banking system development.

2.1.2.2 Government- and cooperative-owned versus private-owned banks

The ownership structure of banks is discussed as a range of politicians and economists perceive deviances from the assumed normal form of private-owned (large) commercial banks as a distortion of competition (Schmidt 2009; Nguyen et al. 2012). Two alternative ownership forms are popular in banking despite the private ownership: (1) government-owned banks that the national state and/or regional/ municipal government or related entities own and (2) cooperative-owned banks that have *Genossen* with restricted property rights as owners (Schmidt 2009). According to Schmidt (2009), the distinctive characteristic of government- and cooperative-owned banks is their dual bottom line and dual-purpose orientation. Dual-purpose institutes are obliged by their owners to pursue other (social) goals as well as profit maximising; e.g. German savings banks were founded to serve the poor (Gärtner 2008; Schmidt 2009). The literature indicates mixed results regarding the pros and cons of dual-purpose versus profit-maximising banks (Beck et al. 2009; Nguyen et al. 2012). Discussion focuses especially on the stability aspect and, to a lesser degree, on the effects on economic development (social benefits). Table 2.1 summarises the pros and cons regarding these two aspects.

With respect to stability it is argued that government- and cooperative-owned banks are more stable because their owners push less towards profit maximisation and rather have very long-term goals, e.g. preserving capital for future generations (Beck et al. 2009). Less pressure to pay high dividends further enables these banks to create reserves in good times and unlock them in crisis times, which allows risk to be mitigated intertemporally and smoothes business cycles (Allen

Table 2.1 Pros and cons of government-/cooperative-owned and private-owned banks

		Stability	*Effects (social benefits)*
Dual-purpose banks (government- and cooperative-owned)	Pros	Less profit pressure Long-term orientation and prudency to preserve capital for future generations (especially cooperative banks) Mitigating intertemporal risk Diversity	Ensuring banking services (to less affluent. customers) Promoting economic development SME finance
	Cons	High risk taking for social goals (e.g. promoting the economy) Political capture and cronyism (especially government banks) Less-skilled bankers Inefficiency because of poor monitoring of management and implicit government guarantees	Misallocation of capital due to: o Financing inefficient companies/delaying insolvency o Political capture and cronyism o Inefficiency
Profit-maximising banks (private owned)	Pros	Superior banking skills	Effective allocation of capital Promoting innovation and structural change
	Cons	Risk taking to maximise profit, especially if shareholders are concentrated and can pressure management effectively to accept profitable but risky business models Short-termism Too big to fail for large institutions	No or poor service for less-profitable customers ('cherry picking') Higher conflicts of interest with customers (profit maximising vs. reliable high-quality services at a low price)

Source: author's table following Gärtner 2008; Taboada 2011; Schmidt 2009; Nguyen et al. 2012

and Gale 2000; Schmidt 2009). However, a range of scholars argue that banks which focus on maximising social goals rather than profits have higher risks (La Porta et al. 2002; Beck et al. 2009; Taboada 2011; Nguyen et al. 2012). If banks strive to promote economic development, e.g. local firms, the risk of bad loans is apparent. Furthermore, government-owned banks are prone to harmful political control; e.g. governments may misuse control power to benefit supporters and pursue their own goals (La Porta et al. 2002; Nguyen et al. 2012). Also, government and the *Genossen* may monitor banks' management less strictly and private banks employ more professional bankers, use more sophisticated risk-controlling technologies and have superior banking knowledge (Taboada 2011). In addition, government guarantees for public banks (even if implicit) tend to further motivate poor management, although the financial crisis has demonstrated that governments also implicitly guarantee for large private banks – because of the too-big-to-fail problem (Stern and Feldman 2003).

Turning to the effects, the literature highlights the dual purpose of government- and cooperative-owned banks, e.g. to ensure banking services for everyone and to promote economic development (Gärtner 2008; Schmidt 2009). Cooperative- and government-owned banks have a mandate to improve access to finance. On the other hand, a range of authors view this intervention in capital allocation as a disadvantage of dual-purpose banks, as it triggers inefficient capital allocation (La Porta et al. 2002; Taboada 2011; Nguyen et al. 2012). In contrast to dual-purpose banks, profit-maximising banks – it is argued – push their corporate customers to innovate and facilitate structural changes (La Porta et al. 2002). On the con side, private-owned banks have an incentive to serve less profitable customers poorly and are under suspicion of 'cherry picking' (Cole et al. 2004), leaving unprofitable customers to their dual-purpose competitors. Profit pressure and strong incentives to sell imply conflicts of interest associated with less reliable and more expensive services for customers of private banks.

Empirical comparisons on the stability of government-/cooperative-owned versus private-owned banks reveal mixed results. In a review of older cross-country comparisons and country case studies, predominantly of developing countries, Taboada (2011: 5) concludes that "the bulk of the evidence on state-ownership of banks suggests that it is associated with poor bank performance". Nguyen et al. (2012) present mixed results for the period of 1997 to 2010. The government ownership of banks is associated with less stability in LMIC; the reverse effect holds true for HIC. This result indicates that national context matters regarding the performance of government-owned banks.

Turning to developed countries, Nocera et al. (2007) investigate a sample of large European banks and find that the stability of government-owned banks is lowest, followed by private-owned and cooperative-owned banks. In their sample of OECD countries, Hesse and Cihák (2007) find that cooperative banks are more stable than private banks. The authors conclude that the lower volatility of the returns of cooperative banks accounts for this effect. Ayadi et al. (2010) confirm this finding for Austria, Finland, France, Italy and the Netherlands. Only cooperative banks in Spain are less stable than their private peers. In Germany cooperative banks are less stable than savings banks but still more stable than private-owned banks. Overall, Ayadi et al. (2010: 145) conclude that while some indicators differ, "there are no consistent differences between cooperative banks and their commercial and savings bank peers in terms of profitability, cost-efficiency, and market power". Similarly, in their study of savings banks, Ayadi et al. (2009) find no significant overall consistent differences between savings and private-owned banks regarding stability, efficiency and earnings in Germany, Austria and Spain (period 1996 to 2005). Beck et al. (2009) analyse a bank-level panel database of Germany's private, savings and cooperative banks, excluding the big banks and the *Landesbanken*. They find that private-owned banks are less stable than government- and cooperative-owned banks.

With reference to the effects of ownership structure, a range of studies report that government-owned banks hamper economic development. La Porta et al. (2002) computed the assets share of the 10 largest government-owned banks for 92 developing and developed countries and found that a high initial percentage of government-owned banks is associated with slower economic growth and lower productivity growth (period 1970 to 1995). La Porta et al. (2002) conclude that government-owned banks tend to hamper efficient capital allocation and reduce efficiency pressure on the companies. According to Taboada's (2011) literature review, several studies confirm the findings of La Porta et al. (2002). Furthermore, a range of studies directly observed political capture; e.g. they show the effects of election years on the financial results of government-owned banks (Sapienza 2004; Micco et al. 2006 cited in Taboada 2011; Gropp and Saadi 2015).

Evidence in favour of dual-purpose banks mostly stresses the positive effects of regional savings and cooperative banks for regional development. Using a sample of German savings banks, Hakenes et al. (2009, 2014) show that both the lending activity and efficiency of savings banks are positively associated with regional economic growth. Furthermore, savings banks have a higher market share in economically lagging regions than private banks. This observation is seen as evidence of the supply duty of dual-purpose banks in peripheral regions. Ayadi et al. (2009) find a significant and positive association between the regional market share of savings banks and economic growth in Austria, Germany and Spain (period 1996 to 2005). With respect to cooperative banks, Ayadi et al. (2010) find similar results for Austria, Germany, Spain, Finland, France, Italy and the Netherlands. All in all, in their large study Ayadi et al. (2009, 2010) conclude that having both government-/cooperative-owned and private-owned banks is favourable for economic development.

However, it is important to note that Ayadi et al. (2009, 2010), Beck et al. (2009) and Hakenes et al. (2009) not only compare banking groups with varying ownership structures but also banking groups with varying geographical organisations. The German savings banks are not only public owned, they also operate in regionally bounded market areas which distinguishes them from most private-owned banks. Regionally bounded market areas also distinguish savings banks from public-owned *Landesbanken* and special-purpose banks. Section 2.1.2.4 discusses these geographical differences between banking groups and possible effects on economic development.

2.1.2.3 Traditional banking versus market-based banking

The strong increase in bank lending during the 2000s in most HIC fuelled doubts about the claim of homogenisation towards market-based finance put forward by the financialisation literature (Hardie et al. 2013). Table 2.2 shows that bank-based firm finance increased most strongly in France, the Netherlands and especially the

Table 2.2 Development of non-financial company funding from 2000–2007

	Lending	Securities	Equity
	Increase (%)	Increase (%)	Increase (%)
Belgium	20.7	25	32
Canada	26	38.5	27.4
France	45.6	18	21.5
Germany	5.2	123	17.9
Greece	63.1	325	29.6
Italy	62.8	190	−12.8
Japan	−28	2.5	21
Netherlands	45	6.3	3.5
Spain	42.3	−2.2	201.6
UK	74.9	40.3	N/A
US	51	59.6	24

Source: Hardie et al. 2013: 7

UK. Here lending increased by 74.9% between 2000 and 2007, while securities only increased by 40.3%.

Motivated by this observation, Hardie et al. (2013: 1) sharply criticise the traditional classification of bank-based and market-based financial systems:

> We argue that this dichotomized understanding of financial systems has contributed to the widespread intellectual incapacity to grasp the nature of changes to national financial systems and to explain, much less predict, the differential impact of the recent financial crisis on advanced industrialized economies.

According to the authors, a profound change has occurred in banking business practices since the late 1990s as banks' business has become more and more capital market controlled (i.e. financialised), enabling the excessive extension of lending observed (Hardie and Howarth 2013a). This development renders the traditional classification in bank-based and market-based financial systems insubstantial and rather connotes an alternative classification of 'traditional banking' versus 'market-based banking' plus market-based corporate financing, i.e. bonds and equity (Hardie et al. 2013: 17). In traditional banking, "banks make their own decision regarding whether to lend, and the amount, maturity, and interest rate of any loan"; in market-based banking, "it is the market that determines both banks' capacity to lend and even the particular decision to lend" (Hardie and Howarth 2013a: 23–24). The authors identify four developments which have caused the increasing dependency of banks on capital markets:

- On the assets side of banks' balance sheets, mark-to-market accounting directly links banks' balance sheets to market price movements, which causes changes in banks' evaluations of assets. The profitability of a loan which remains on the balance sheet at its original value depends on the creditworthiness of the borrower. In contrast, being marked to market, loan value depends on the market price, which tends to be euphoric in good times and pessimistic in crisis times (Brunnermeier et al. 2009).

• Shadow banking and securitisation also increase the connections of banks to capital markets on the assets side. Banks established single-purpose companies to buy assets from their balance sheets and issue securities for the refinancing of the companies. In good times the difference between assets' interest and the cost of borrowing yields profits, allowing banks to free balance sheets and extend lending. However, in crisis times the refinancing of single-purpose companies vanishes, and banks must support their single-purpose companies while they also face difficulties of refinancing.

• On banks' liability side, refinancing on capital markets (e.g. bonds) rather than through private deposits increases banks' dependency on capital markets.

• Furthermore, the equity base of public-listed banks depends on capital markets. As banks need to fulfil the capital requirements of the bank regulations, equity shortage restricts the banks' capacity to lend.

Table 2.3 contrasts traditional banking with market-based banking. For Hardie and Howarth (2013a), banking is market based when either market-based assets are financed by non-market-based liabilities (e.g. commercial banks investing deposits in government bonds); or non-market-based assets are financed by market-based liabilities (e.g. Spanish savings banks underwriting mortgage loans refinanced at money markets); or if both assets and liabilities are market based (e.g. German *Landesbanken* that invest in US subprime mortgage securities and refinance this investments with bonds).

Table 2.3 Traditional versus market-based banking

	Institutions	Loans	Funding/ Liabilities of Loans Retained	Credit Risk of Loans Retained	Accounting of Loans Retained
Traditional banking	Commercial banks/ savings banks	Retained on balance sheet	Customer deposits	Not hedged	At cost
Market-based banking	Commercial banks/ parallel banks (including investment banks)	Sold, in loan market, via securitisation or to shadow banks (originate to distribute)	Wholesale market (interbank, bonds, etc.)	Hedged via credit default swap	Mark to market

Source: Hardie and Howarth 2013a: 25 (modified)

Empirically, the authors estimate the degree of banks' market-based liabilities with the indicator "customers' loans minus customers' deposits divided by total bank deposits" (Hardie and Howarth 2013a: 41). Banks' market-based assets are estimated with the ratio of loans to total bank assets. Eleven HIC have been ranked according to these indicators (Figure 2.3). Both the asset and liability sides of banks in the UK and the Netherlands are market based. Banks' liabilities tend to be market based in Italy and Spain, and banks' assets are market based in Belgium and Germany.[1]

Despite this rough classification of countries' banking systems, the market-based banking classification helps understanding of the effects of the financial crisis. Countries scoring high in market-based assets were hit first by the financial crisis because of write-downs on these assets. Countries scoring high in market-based liabilities faced funding difficulties later in the crisis (Hardie and Howarth 2013a). The classification is less conclusive for corporate financing, however. Firm finance in Germany and Belgium performed well during the crisis despite their high market-based banking activities. Hardie and Howarth (2013b: 103) explain the German paradox partly by referring to the existence of "hundreds of domestically focused smaller savings and cooperative banks" which, the scholars assume, conduct traditional banking. Taken together, these small savings and cooperative banks constitute the market leader for enterprise finance in Germany (Gärtner and Flögel 2014). Hence, neglecting these small banks limits the validity of the empirical market-based banking classification. Indeed, neglecting small

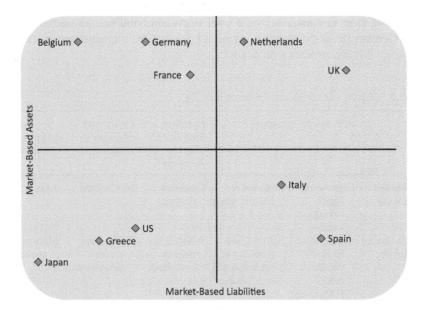

Figure 2.3 Market-based assets and liabilities on bank balance sheets (2007)

Source: Hardie and Howarth 2013a: 41 (reprint by permission of Oxford University Press)

banks is a common restriction of many cross-country comparisons, which often only analyse the balance sheets of the largest banks for reasons of feasibility (Burgstaller 2012).

2.1.2.4 Decentralised versus centralised banking

As early as 1995, Klagge argued for a classification of banking systems into decentralised and centralised systems. She proposed distinguishing banking systems by their degree of integration – whether regional banking markets are segregated or not – and the degree of centralisation of banks' headquarters. Klagge (1995) indicates that a decentralised but integrated banking system tends to be the best system for regional economic development because it keeps banking expertise and commitment for the region at the regional level and boosts banking competition. In his historical cross-country comparison, Verdier (2002) shows that regional governments patronise decentralised banks (like in Germany), whereas centralised states like the UK tend to support centralised banks. Klagge and Martin (2005) also analysed the spatial concentration of stock exchanges and venture capital firms and showed that Germany is more decentralised than the UK. Gärtner (2011) revisited Klagge's (1995) initial approach and proposed two characteristics to identify decentralised and centralised banks: the geographical market orientation and the place of decision making (Gärtner and Flögel 2013, 2014).

Concerning the geographical market orientation, banks show a regional or supraregional market orientation (Figure 2.4), which has the capability to alter the allocation of capital across space. As controversially debated in polarisation and post–Keynesian theories, regionally bounded banking markets may reduce capital drains from the periphery to the core regions which stimulates more balanced regional development (Chick and Dow 1988; Dow and Rodríguez-Fuentes 1997; Klagge and Martin 2005; Gärtner 2008). If banks have a regional market orientation, most assets and liabilities are regional; thus, these banks maintain regional savings-investment cycles and tend to slow capital drains. In the following discussion banks with regional market orientations are called *regional banks. Regional* refers to a market area that corresponds to ca. NUTS 3 regions (small regions like *Landkreise*, or districts) or smaller, because at this geographical reach it is still possible to visit all customers by car in about one hour (Gärtner and Flögel 2014). Of course, not all balance sheet positions of regional banks must be regional, as every bank needs liquid assets and liabilities to manage liquidity. Therefore, regional banks must only serve regional demand first and should not strategically pursue supraregional business (Gärtner and Flögel 2014). In contrast to this, a supraregional market orientation refers to banks whose assets and/or liabilities are not primarily regional. For example, international banks like Deutsche Bank of course also grant credits to regional firms. Yet, Deutsche Bank searches for investment opportunities internationally and thus facilitates capital flows across regions. Banks with supraregional market orientations are called *supraregional banks* in the text that follows.

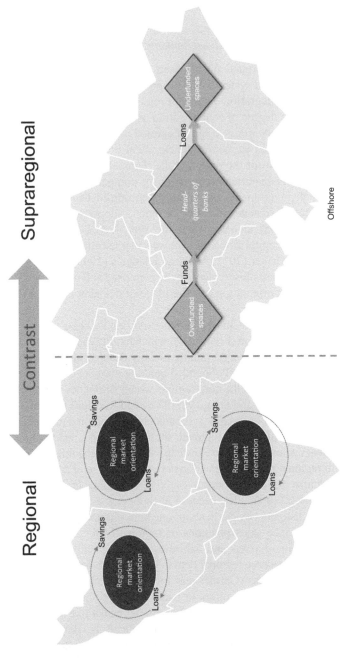

Figure 2.4 Geographical market orientation: regional versus supraregional banks

Source: Gärtner and Flögel 2014: 7

The second characteristic – the place of decision making – distinguishes banks that decide at a short distance to their customers from banks that decide at a long distance (Gärtner and Flögel 2014; Flögel and Gärtner 2018). Collecting information and driving investment decisions from this information is one key function of banking systems that influences economic development (Section 2.1.1). As recent advantages in the research field of distance and small firm finance indicate, short distance to customers increases the quality of information (Stein 2002; Pollard 2003; Berger et al. 2005; Alessandrini et al. 2009b), indicating distance's relevancy for the quality of credit decisions.

These two characteristics do not render one another redundant, because on the one hand bank regulation and the standardisation of decision-making processes (especially rating and scoring systems) tend to centralise the credit decision making of regional banks. For example, if a regional bank decides about loans only based on credit agencies' rating scores, this bank does not conduct credit decisions at a short distance to their customers (see top-left corner of Figure 2.5). On the other hand, supraregional banks can delegate decision-making power to the regional scale, e.g. if they delegate authority to the employees of an

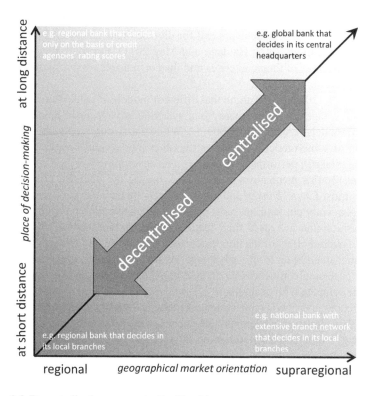

Figure 2.5 Decentralised versus centralised banking

Source: Gärtner and Flögel 2014: 14 (modified)

extensive branch network (see bottom-right corner of Figure 2.5). Thus, following Gärtner and Flögel's (2014) classification, decentralised banks are regional banks that also decide at a short distance to their customers (bottom-left corner of Figure 2.5). Centralised banks in contrast are supraregional banks that decide at a long distance from their customers (top-right corner of Figure 2.5). The sum of all decentralised and centralised banks determines the degree of centralisation of banking systems. Relatively decentralised banking systems are characterised by a high number and market share of decentralised banks. In contrast, centralised banks are the main lender in centralised banking systems (Gärtner and Flögel 2014: 13).

2.1.3   Diversity in banking: decentralised versus centralised banking

The financial crisis of 2008 demonstrated that, despite a proliferation of risk management and the international harmonisation of bank regulation, the stability of financial systems was insufficient. Even worse, the acceleration and global spread of the crisis in relation to the relatively low initial losses which caused the crisis indicates that the overall resilience of the developed financial systems was problematic at best (Hellwig 2008; Brunnermeier et al. 2009; Haldane and May 2011). Because of the self-reinforcing tendencies of homogeny and highly connected financial systems, several scholars call for diverse financial systems (Ayadi et al. 2009, 2010; Schmidt 2009; Haldane and May 2011). Diversity tends to reduce the contagiousness of financial crises and thus increase the stability of the overall financial system.

Ayadi et al. (2009, 2010) argue that different models of banks have advantages and disadvantages, whereas there "is a systemic advantage in having a mixed system of models" (Ayadi et al. 2009: ii). While disastrous events can damage the operation of some models, as long as the other models still operate the banking system in total still performs its functions. The development in Germany indicates that precisely this mechanism was at work during the financial crisis of 2008. Whereas most *Landesbanken* and a range of private banks experienced problems and consequently cut lending, most savings and cooperative banks operated in a stable fashion and increased their lending activities (Gärtner and Flögel 2015). Thus, the overall effect of the financial crisis on credit supply to the economy was less strong. In addition to this advantage, Ayadi et al. (2009) argue that diversity also increases innovativeness as diverse banking models develop varying solutions that compete with each other.

Differences in the ownership structures increase diversity in banking (Ayadi at al. 2009, 2010). However, in Germany the financial crisis affected some private-owned banks (e.g. Commerzbank) and some government-owned banks (e.g. West-LB, IKB) likewise. Accordingly, the *Landesbanken* and the large banks significantly reduced credit to non-financial firms in 2008–2009, whereas savings and cooperative banks increase lending in the same time period (see Figure 1.1, p. 3). Thus, not only differences in the ownership structure may cause diversity in banking, but also other structural aspects.

To detect diversity, Hardie and Howarth (2013a) propose the classification of traditional banking versus market-based banking. This classification is conclusive for Germany because it differentiates between savings and cooperative banks on the one hand and private and government-owned banks on the other hand (Hardie and Howarth 2013b). The former group of banks remained in the traditional banking mode and were consequently hardly affected by the global financial crisis of 2008, which explains their ability to increase lending in the crisis. The latter group of banks moved to the market-based banking mode, experienced heavy losses during the financial turmoil and consequently cut credits (Hardie and Howarth 2013b). However, a profound objection must be made to this conclusive argumentation. Applying the market-based banking concept to investigate diversity tends to be tautological. The same developments which reduce diversity in banking are also employed to distinguish between traditional banking and market-based banking. Of course, it is important to understand the profound changes in the banking industry which cause homogenisation. However, structural variables which direct banks to engage in diverse business practices also need to be identified.

The geographical classification has the capability to be one structural variable that causes the diverse banking practices of decentralised and centralised banks. And, in fact, most of the reviewed studies in Section 2.1.2.2 in favour of dual-purpose banks not only contrast government-/cooperative-owned banks to private-owned banks, but also regional savings and cooperative banks to supraregional private banks.

Three empirical findings support the hypothesis that decentralised banks in fact differ to centralised banks in firm financing. Firstly, the varying geographical organisation of the German banking groups accurately explains the observed differences in business finance during the financial crisis; e.g. regional savings and cooperative banks increased lending whereas supraregional private banks but also *Landesbanken* and other public banks cut down lending. Secondly, recent empirical findings prove for Germany that regional banks are in fact capable of balancing the allocation of capital (hindering capital drains from the periphery to the centres) and thus tend to improve firm finance in peripheral regions (Gärtner 2008; Conrad 2008; Christians 2010). The literature has long questioned regional banks' capacity to improve finance in the periphery because of self-reinforcing downward spirals in peripheral regions (Myrdal 1959). Thirdly, recent theoretical and empirical advantages indicate that geographical distance still matters in SME lending (Stein 2002; Alessandrini et al. 2009a), which further supports the hypothesis that decentralised banks differ to centralised banks in firm financing. Banks at a short distance are more likely to lend to informationally opaque SMEs and thus reduce their financial constraints (Agarwal and Hauswald 2007; Alessandrini et al. 2009a; Behr et al. 2013). However, because of ICT advantages − especially the obligatory use of rating systems by all banks − the assumption that regional banks 'naturally' decide credits at a shorter distance to SMEs than supraregional banks needs to be critically examined. The book in hand conducts this critical examination in the following chapters.

2.2 The geography of firm financing

In the discussion on the geography of firm finance – starting in the early 1990s – concern about uneven regional access to capital was triggered by two spatial developments of commercial banks. The first cause of concern was the concentration of banks caused by mergers and acquisitions (M&A) leading to a decrease of small and regional banks (Berger et al. 1999; for the USA, Berger et al. 1998). The second was the restructuring of bank branch networks that led mainly to a closing of branches in the periphery and in less affluent districts (Klagge 1995; Leyshon and Pollard 2000). The liberalisation of bank regulation, e.g. the easing of regional principles, increasing banking competition (also caused by liberalisation) and consequent margin pressure caused these developments. ICT advantages, i.e. the standardisation of banking processes and product innovations in commercial banking (ATM, telephone and online banking), further boosted the restructuring of the banking sector. Overall banks' service creation became less bounded to place (Klagge 1995; Berger et al. 1999). In fact, a range of commercial banking services no longer need bank branches or face-to-face interaction. Consequently, direct banks such as ING-DiBa, Comdirekt etc. have successfully gained market shares without branches and further heighten competition for the affiliated banks.

Against this background, the question of why geography still matters in firm financing is not trivial. Firms can access banking services without a neighbouring bank branch either via ICT and/or via the personal mobility of bank employees and customers. Basically, the literature advances three arguments as to why geography still matters in bank-based firm financing: firstly, because competition differs between regional banking markets; secondly, due to the allocation of capital across space being uneven – as discussed in polarisation and post–Keynesian theories (Chick and Dow 1988; Dow and Rodríguez-Fuentes 1997; Gärtner 2009b); and, thirdly, because distance has an impact on information transmission. The location of banks thus tends to influence firms' access to finance. The classification of decentralised versus centralised banking takes these three arguments into consideration (Section 2.1.2.4). According to this spatial classification, regional market orientation and the short distance of credit decisions from the customers characterise decentralised banks. In contrast, centralised banks operate in supra-regional market areas and decide at a longer distance from their customers. Savings banks represent a fairly decentralised type of bank and big banks a rather centralised type, it is argued for Germany.

This section explains why these two characteristics matter in bank-based SME financing. It extensively discusses the second characteristic, i.e. the place of (credit) decision making, on which this empirical study mainly focuses. Section 2.2.1 starts with key banking theories that link bank lending behaviour and information usage. Section 2.2.2 deals with distance and its influence on the transmission of soft information and credit decisions. The impact of geographical distance on information transmission in differentiation to other dimensions of proximity is discussed in Section 2.2.3. Section 2.2.4 advances a preliminary systematisation and expounds on the limitations of the elaborated strand of theory.

2.2.1 Information asymmetry, credit rationing and relationship banking

In contrast to most market transactions, financial transactions are characterised by the fact that service and return service do not usually happen simultaneously (Hartmann-Wendels et al. 2010). Funds providers (savers) firstly deliver the money to the users of funds (borrowers), who pay back the money plus a price (e.g. interest) at a contractually appointed future time. As the future is uncertain, various factors influence the willingness and ability of borrowers to repay the funds. To reduce uncertainty, savers and borrowers collect information (see Section 2.2.3.1 for a definition of *information*) to better predict the likelihood of repayment in the future. Thus, information comes into play to cope with the uncertainty of future events. Furthermore, information distribution between savers and borrowers is typically asymmetric; i.e. borrowers know more about their repayment ability and willingness than savers (Levine 1997; Sachverständigenrat zur Begutachtung der gesamtwirtschaftlichen Entwicklung 2008; Klagge 2009; Beck et al. 2009; Hartmann-Wendels et al. 2010; Turner 2010).

Asymmetrical information matters because it can hinder financial transactions which are beneficial for both parties (Hartmann-Wendels et al. 2010). Asymmetrical information occurs ex ante, i.e. before contract signing; e.g. savers do not know which borrowers are most likely to repay the funds. Information asymmetry also happens in the interim, e.g. savers do not know what borrowers do with the funds, and ex post, e.g. in case of repayment delays the savers do not know whether the borrowers cannot repay or do not want to repay the funds (Hartmann-Wendels et al. 2010; Handke 2011). To conduct financial transactions under conditions of information asymmetry, contract partners have the possibility to arrange incentive-optimal contracts that enforce borrowers' repayment. Alternatively, the contract partners can reduce information asymmetries by screening (ex ante) and monitoring (interim and ex post) (Hartmann-Wendels et al. 2010; Handke 2011). As delegated monitors, banks cost-efficiently conduct screening and monitoring of borrowers on behalf of the savers (Diamond 1984) and thus are able to amplify financial transactions.

This section introduces key theories on financial intermediation by banks and indicates to what extent geographical aspects influence banks' screening and monitoring. Section 2.2.1.1 discusses the screening and monitoring of banks and indicates that the quality and efficiency of screening and monitoring influence capital accumulation and hence economic development. The Diamond (1984) model on banks as delegated monitors and the Stiglitz and Weiss (1981) model on credit rationing are used to explain why poor screening and monitoring tend to deteriorate credit supply. Section 2.2.1.2 discusses the relationship banking model which deduces why lower banking market competition improves firms' access to finance. As competition differs between regional banking markets, varying levels of competition explain differences in regional access to finance for firms. Furthermore, the section contrasts relationship banking and transaction-oriented banking.

2.2.1.1 The screening and monitoring of banks

It is costly for savers to screen (selection) and monitor borrowers. High screening and monitoring costs hinder beneficial financial transactions and thus slow investments, which hampers economic development (see Section 2.1.1). Diamond's (1984) model shows how banks and other financial intermediaries reduce intermediation costs as delegated monitors (Diamond 1984; Hartmann-Wendels et al. 2010). Banks intermediate between savers and borrowers, and in this way reduce the number of financial contracts (Figure 2.6). However, in this setting all savers must monitor their banks, which tends to be very expensive as banks have numerous contracts with a great number of borrowers. Diamond's (1984) model is deemed to be the first model which explains the usefulness of banks despite this monitoring problem of savers (Hartmann-Wendels et al. 2010).

To solve the problem that savers must monitor their banks, the Diamond model combines the delegated monitoring of borrowers by banks and incentive-optimal contracts between the banks and savers that are enforced by so-called non-pecuniary penalties (e.g. loss of reputation). Thus, a bank "need not to be monitored by [all savers] because it takes 'full responsibility' and bears all penalties for any short-fall of payments to [savers]" (Diamond 1984: 402). With a diversified credit portfolio banks can massively reduce the risk of payment shortfall which lowers the likelihood that banks have to bear non-pecuniary penalties.

The Diamond model characterises the business practices of real banks. Banks lend funds to many borrowers using debt contracts (e.g. loans) and collect deposits from many savers. Usually savers do not monitor their bank closely but simply expect certain interest payments on their deposits. As banks heavily reduce the likelihood of non-pecuniary penalties with diversification (by lending to numerous and diverse borrowers), the main cost factor of their intermediation remains

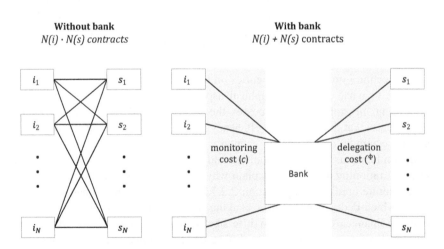

Figure 2.6 Contracts without and with banks

Source: author's figure following Hartmann-Wendels et al. (2010: 124)

the monitoring costs. In the Diamond model, the monitoring costs represent the effort to delete ex post information asymmetry. Yet, actual banks mitigate ex ante, interim and ex post information asymmetries. Furthermore, the quality of the screening and monitoring of different banks varies with respect to their techniques and experiences, and banks also must bear the cost of mistakes, i.e. the false estimation of project outputs. Understanding the screening and monitoring costs in this broader sense also accounts for the fact that banks cannot completely delete information asymmetry as the future outputs of projects remain uncertain.

Screening and monitoring mistakes increase the monitoring costs of banks and thus make financial intermediation more expensive, which is associated with a lower rate of capital investment and thus hampers economic development (Section 2.1.1). Furthermore, screening and monitoring faults reduce the efficiency of capital investment which also adversely affects economic development. Banks are prone to two basic types of errors in their screening and monitoring (Altman 1971, cited at Fletcher 1995: 37):

- Banks select and finance firms and projects that gain insufficient output or fail; i.e. they finance bad quality borrowers (type 2 error). For example, investors build apartments that stay vacant, firms purchase new machines but hardly use their capacities or companies develop products for which there is no demand. Banks thus waste capital, which consequently hampers economic development, and suffer losses from the loan default.
- Banks deny funding to firms or projects that would have gained sufficient output; i.e. they reject good quality borrowers (type 1 error). For example, funding gaps delay successful innovation, competitive companies cannot expand or successful firms even become insolvent because of liquidity shortages that their banks refuse to finance. This mistake of banks involves giving away the earnings of successful borrowers, which also hampers economic development, but does not cause losses from loan defaults.

Both types of error not only occur when banks screen but also when banks monitor firms. For example, if banks cut the credit lines of companies too late this gratuitously increases the losses at default. On the other hand, if banks cut credits too early this tends to cause the insolvency of sound firms.

Stiglitz and Weiss (1981) present a model which explains the rationality for (profit-maximising) banks to deliberately conduct the type 1 error and execute credit rationing to borrowers. Credit rationing occurs when banks refuse credit to a group of borrowers, although the borrowers offer to pay higher interest rates and good quality borrowers (borrowers with low default probabilities) are in the group (Hartmann-Wendels et al. 2010). In this respect, the model shows that an equilibrium credit market can exist where credit rationing is occurring; i.e., the interest rate does not balance the demand and supply of credits. Adverse selection and moral hazard explain this result. Banks face the risk that if they increase the interest rate, the number of risky projects increases. Less risky but also less profitable borrowers would offtake their credit demand (adverse selection), and existing borrowers have an incentive to increase the riskiness of their projects to gain higher earnings (moral hazard). As the profit of banks not only depends on interest earnings but also on the default rates (the riskiness of the projects), it tends to be rational for banks not to increase the interest rate in case of excessive demands but rather to refuse some loan applications. Thus, credit rationing can occur in equilibrium credit markets, and the likelihood of credit rationing increases with increasing information asymmetries (Stiglitz and Weiss 1981; Hartmann-Wendels et al. 2010).

2.2.1.2 Relationship versus transaction-oriented banking and market structure

Relationship banking, or *Hausbankbeziehungen*, refers to close bank relationships and is defined as a "long-term implicit contract between a bank and its debtor" (Elsas 2005: 34). Building on Stiglitz and Weiss' (1981) model, Petersen and Rajan (1995) developed a formal model which explains how relationship banking is capable of reducing credit rationing. The model starts with a two-period credit decision setting ($t = 0$ to $t = 1$ and $t = 1$ to $t = 2$), where at $t = 0$ information asymmetry between borrowers and a bank exists and at $t = 1$ information asymmetry is vanquished (Petersen and Rajan 1995; Hartmann-Wendels et al. 2010). Good and bad borrowers exist. Bad borrowers cannot repay (I) the credit (D) they have received in period one ($I_1 = 0$) and are out of business in $t = 1$ because the bank will not lend to these borrowers again for obvious reasons (see Figure 2.7). Good borrowers have the choice to invest in risk-free but less profitable projects in $t = 0$ which gain y_1^s in $t = 1$ or to invest in riskier and more profitable projects which gain the uncertain (p) output py_1^r in $t = 1$. If the riskier project fails ($py_1^r = 0$), the good quality borrowers will also not be able to pay their credits (D_0^r). They will consequently not get an additional credit from their bank, similarly to the bad borrowers. If borrowers can repay D_0^r, their bank is willing to lend another credit D_1^r, which gains the safe output y_2^r. Equally, borrowers who have selected the safe project in $t = 0$, and therefore can repay D_0^s, also receive another loan D_1^s and gain the safe output y_2^s.

Petersen and Rajan (1995) specify four model assumptions:

1   The safe projects have positive net value ($y_2^s + y_1^s - D_0^s - D_1^s > 0$).
2   The risky projects have negative net value ($p(y_1^r + y_2^r - D_1^r) - D_0^r < 0$).
3   Return of the second project is equal, regardless of whether borrowers choose the safe or risky project in $t = 0$ ($y_2^r = y_2^s > D_1^r = D_1^s$).
4   The returns in $t = 1$ are insufficient to finance the new projects in $t = 1$; hence, borrowers always need new credits in $t = 1$.

The bank has no information about the quality of borrowers at $t = 0$ (due to information asymmetry) but knows the fraction (θ) of borrowers which are good. Hence, the bank has to add a risk premium (r) to D_0, where the amount of capital which has to be paid back is $I_1 = D_0(1 + r)$ and r must be higher if θ is lower.

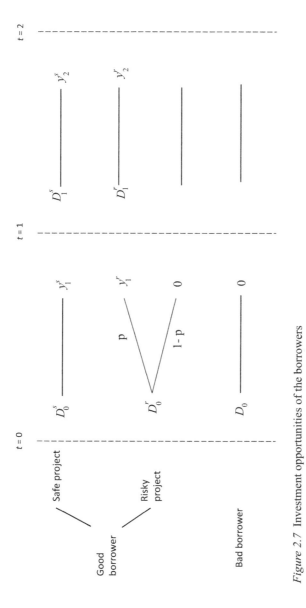

Figure 2.7 Investment opportunities of the borrowers

Source: from Hartmann-Wendels et al. 2010: 166 (translated and modified)

At $t = 1$, the bank is able to exactly differentiate between good and bad borrowers and does not need to charge r to compensate possible losses anymore. However, because of moral hazard effects, which the Stiglitz and Weiss (1981) model explains (see above), a higher r leads to lower θ because more good borrowers select the risky project to gain sufficient earnings. Hence, as the Stiglitz and Weiss (1981) model shows, it is rational for banks to stop handing out credits to groups of borrowers of certain θ (i.e. to conduct credit rationing) instead of increasing r.

However, in the two-period model setting, banks have an alternative solution to credit rationing as it is possible to compensate initial losses from lending in $t = 0$ by extracting extra return in $t = 1$ (I_2). The capacity of banks to do so depends on their market power (M). If a bank is the only supplier of credits (M is high), it can charge borrowers a high premium ($I_2 > D_1$) in $t = 1$, regardless of the fact that D_1 is riskless as no information asymmetries exist. However, if banking competition is high (M is low), banks are hardly able to charge a premium at all, because the riskless borrowers will easily get a credit (D_1) from another bank. In this setting, banks' ability to compensate initial losses intertemporally does not exist and thus they need to charge cost-covering I_1.

The Petersen and Rajan (1995) model adds the following formal solution (Hartmann-Wendels et al. 2010: 169): $$\upsilon(M) = \frac{D_0^r (1-p)}{M\left(y_1^s - p y_1^r\right) + (M-1)\left(D_1^s - y_1^s\right)(1-p)}.$$

Thus, as its most important result, the model predicts a lower fraction of good quality projects (θ) if the market power (M) of a bank increases (Hartmann-Wendel et al. 2010). In other words, the model predicts that if a bank has high market power, overall riskier groups of borrowers will gain credit offers; i.e. banks reduce credit rationing.

Certain empirical findings support this prediction of the relationship banking model while others reject it. Banking market structure often varies within national states. Competition tends to be higher in the urban centres and lower in the rural periphery (for Germany, see Fischer and Pfeil 2004; Fischer 2005; Gärtner 2008). Most studies show that lower competition is associated with higher interest rates (see the review in Degryse et al. 2009). In contrast to this, Petersen and Rajan (1995) confirm the prediction of their model with a study of US SMEs. They report better conditions and better access to finance for young firms in less competitive regional banking markets. Zarutskie (2006) reports similar effects with up-to-date data from the USA. For Germany, Fischer and Pfeil (2004; Fischer 2005) find that lower market competition fosters access to finance but causes higher interest rates. In contrast, Cetorelli (2002) and Agarwal and Hauswald (2007) report hampering effects of market concentration for regional economic development.

These mixed results may not be surprising because, in contrast to Petersen and Rajan's (1995) model, the market structure conduct performance (SCP) hypothesis predicts a positive causality between banking market competition and firm financing (Fischer and Pfeil 2004). In cases of a concentrated banking market, banks take advantages from oligopoly market power and charge higher interest rates or offer poor services to customers, for example. Thus, the conflicting effects from relationship banking and SCP overlap and tend to cause a non-linear causality between competition and firm finance. Mudd's (2013) study reports mixed effects which supports the notion that the causality between market structure and firm finance is non-linear. In banking markets where banks execute very high market power, a reduction of market power supports the access of small firms to credits, and in banking markets with moderate market power, increasing competition worsens the access of firms to credits. Handke's (2011) qualitative evidence also shows that some competition supports relationship banking because firms can only signalise their commitment to their *Hausbanken* if additional banks compete for these firms. However, Elsas' (2005) results for Germany conflict with Mudd (2013) and Handke (2011), indicating that other aspects also tend to affect the correlation between competition and relationship banking.

In this respect, Hartmann-Wendel et al. (2010) highlight that the M, or market power, of the Petersen and Rajan (1995) model need not only represent banking market competition but can also be the result of the information advantages banks have at $t = 1$. Because competing banks have not acquired this information about borrowers, they are in a worse position to offer competitive interest rates, as they have to charge a higher risk premium. For example, if a firm wishes to change its bank, the new bank does not know whether dissatisfaction with the old bank triggered the change or whether the old bank has declined the firm's credit requests due to poor borrower quality. However, in order that banks can gain informational advantages over their competitors from relationship banking, they must be able to use the information they gain in existing relationships. A range of scholars argue that small and regional banks, which decide on credits at a short distance to firms, tend to make better use of the proprietary information from relationship banking (Berger at al. 2005; Uchida et al. 2008; Mudd 2013). Therefore, relationship banking is frequently associated with small and regional banks and transaction-oriented banking with large banks.

In contrast to relationship banking, in transaction-oriented banking banks and firms interact rather impersonally and with a short-term orientation (Udell 2008; Handke 2011). Yet, the existing literature provides no exact delimitation between relationship banking and transaction-oriented banking. In fact, Udell (2008) and Berger and Udell (2006) claim that different types of transaction-oriented banking (lending) exist. Thus, relationship banking and transaction-oriented banking are two ideal types of banking techniques at opposite ends of a continuum, rather than techniques banks apply in a pure manner. Handke (2011) reports that most German commercial banks claim that they strive to be the *Hausbank* for their SME customers. Accordingly, attempting to identify relationship banking in actual borrower–bank relationships causes difficulties (Elsas 2005; Handke 2011). Three basic criteria indicate relationship banking between borrowers and banks (Boot 2000; Elsas 2005; Udell 2008; Handke 2011: 95ff):

1   A long-term orientation characterises relationship banking; i.e. borrower–bank relationships consist of multiple and repeated business transactions over time. This allows for the intertemporal equalisation of returns for banks and

may reduce credit rationing of (riskier) borrowers, as the Peterson and Rajan (1995) model predicts.

2   Information gathering over time enables banks (and borrowers) to gain much and different (i.e. proprietary, soft[2]) information in multiple transactions. The *Hausbanken* typically provide their customers with a whole range of financial services, e.g. payment transactions, overdrafts, loans, insurances. Banks and borrowers are able to reuse this information in their multiple transactions, allowing the initial high costs of information gathering to pay off.

3   The exclusivity of the relationships characterises relationship banking as well; i.e. customers purchase most financial services at their *Hausbank*.

In contrast to this, banks that conduct transaction-oriented banking focus on single transactions, rather than long-term relationships, and only collect some (hard) information for credit underwriting (Udell 2008). Whereas banks use a case-based evaluation for their borrowers in relationship banking, transaction-oriented banks conduct class-based evaluations; i.e. the risk of borrowers is evaluated against the average risk of their class. An expensive evaluation of the individual firms is not necessary (Handke 2011). Borrowers shop for the best price on competitive bank markets, and banks target as many borrowers as possible (with standardised products and competitive terms) to achieve economies of scale. An intertemporal equalisation of returns is not intended/possible (Udell 2008, 2009).

Udell (2008: 96) lists asset-based lending, factoring, leasing, small business credit scoring, equipment lending and real estate-based lending as transaction-oriented banking techniques. Most of these banking techniques have in common that they use (different types of) collaterals for credit underwriting; thus, collaterals are critical for transaction-oriented banking (Udell 2008). Interestingly, collaterals matter in relationship banking, too, as Handke (2011) shows. Firms use collaterals to voluntarily connect themselves to their *Hausbank* and to signal their commitment.

The advantages of relationship banking emerge in the interdependencies of its criteria (Handke 2011). Over the course of the relationship, synergies for borrowers and banks arise which reinforce the relationship through mutual advantages. Handke (2011) identifies three related advantages of relationship banking:

1   The knowledge advantage develops because banks get to know the borrowers well in multiple transactions over the course of their relationship. This reduces asymmetric information, and banks are able to evaluate borrowers' risk more credibly, which, in turn, enhances fairer pricing and/or enables riskier borrowers to continue to receive credits due to decreased adverse selection and moral hazard issues.

2   From this knowledge – i.e. advantages and mutual learning in close and long-standing bank relationships – trustful relationships tend to emerge. Trustful relationships improve flexibility for borrowers and banks (Handke 2011). For example, credit contracts do not have to consider every eventuality, because if circumstances change banks and customers are able to renegotiate contracts in

trustful relationships. Furthermore, banks have an initiative to develop tailor-made solutions for their customers' financial needs in close relationships.

3 Finally, due to the two aforementioned advantages, banks implicitly offer a liquidity insurance to borrowers in close relationships; i.e. they stand by their borrowers in bad times when firms are most urgently in need of liquidity. Handke (2011: 124) termed this the umbrella function of *Hausbanken*.

Basically, the literature highlights two disadvantages of relationship banking, namely the hold-up problem and the soft-budget constraint problem (Boot 2000). The hold-up problem tends to arise in close relationships if borrowers are "'locked in,' or informationally captured by the bank" (Boot 2000: 17). Because of the superior information of banks and the exclusivity of the relationships, they are able to hold up firms, i.e. offer unfavourable terms. The hold-up arises in the contrary direction with the soft-budget constraint problem. A bank which has loaned (a lot of) money to borrowers is more likely to "extend further credit in the hope of recovering its previous loan" (Boot 2000: 16). This fosters borrowers' adverse incentives. In the literature, solutions for both problems are discussed (Boot 2000; Handke 2011). Geography tends to matter for relationship banking as close and trusting relationships benefit from face-to-face interactions, especially in an early phase of the relationship (Torre and Rallet 2005; Bathelt and Henn 2014). Therefore, relationship banking is often associated with short geographical distance between banks and borrowers, whereas this tends to be unimportant for transaction-oriented banking (e.g. Berger et al. 2005; Uchida et al. 2008). The next section discusses the connection between distance, information and lending.

2.2.2 Distance, soft information and credit decisions

A relatively new strand of research argues that the spatial organisation of banks influences their credit decision making. According to one key argument, small and/or regional banks are superior in soft information processing and therefore superior lenders to informationally opaque SMEs (Berger et al. 2005; Alessandrini et al. 2009b; Alessandrini et al. 2009a; Behr et al. 2013). A range of scholars consider SMEs to be less transparent (informationally opaque) than larger companies as they are usually not publicly listed and do not issue bonds (Berger et al. 2005; Deakins et al. 2010; Handke 2011). Therefore, no trading record of SMEs' shares and bonds exist, and they do not have to publish extensive information frequently (e.g. quarterly reports). Furthermore, the annual financial statements of small firms tend to provide less extensive and reliable information; e.g. less reputed auditors conduct the auditing. Furthermore, soft information, like the character of the managing partners of the firms and the local context, matter for the risk evaluation of SMEs (Handke 2011).

The following sections discuss why distance has to be seen as crucial in lending to informationally opaque SMEs. Section 2.2.2.1 explains the Stein (2002) model, which is the key theory on distance and information processing. Actually, the Stein (2002) model does not directly discuss distance but focuses on decentralised (small) versus hierarchical (large) organisations; therefore, studies that contrast small and large banks are reviewed. Section 2.2.2.2 adapts the Stein (2002) model to distance and Section 2.2.2.3 reviews empirical studies of distance in lending.

2.2.2.1 Decentralisation versus hierarchy: the Stein model

The Stein (2002) model represents the main theoretical foundation of recent studies on the geography of banking, information processing and firm financing (Alessandrini et al. 2009a). Remarkably, Stein's model does not discuss the geographical organisation of banks directly but rather explains the influence of the organisational design of banks (and other organisations) on information collection and capital allocation. Nevertheless, Stein (2002) sees the practical relevance of his model in the massive consolidation of the banking industry and the observation that large banks tend to cut back credits to SMEs. In the literature this observation was explained with the diffuse notion that large banks possess disadvantages in handling informationally opaque SMEs (e.g. Berger et al. 1999). Stein transfers this diffuse notion to a formal model.

Stein differentiates between two models of decision making: decentralisation and hierarchy. The basic trade-off of these two decision-making models relates to efficient capital allocation and actors' efforts. According to the model, banks distribute capital more efficiently between different units under hierarchical circumstances. However, hierarchy offsets actors' efforts to collect information for the decision-making process if the actors cannot transmit their information up the hierarchy.

In the decentralised capital allocation model, two units (U_1 and U_2) are independent from one another and each have two units of capital. The units' division managers allocate this capital between two projects (Figure 2.8). U_1 and U_2 can be understood as two one-man banks, for example, where the division managers/customer advisors execute full decision-making power to allocate the capital between their two corporate customers. Each project is either a good (g) or a bad (b) project with the likelihood of 50% ($p(g) = 0.5$). Hence, each division manager has two g projects with $p = 0.25$, one good and one bad project with $p = 0.5$ and two b projects with $p = 0.25$. Applying Stein's (2002) model assumptions, the gains of investment are shown in the following numerical example:

- The investment of 2 units of capital in a g project leads to a profit of 0.8 ($g(2) = 0.8$).
- The investment of 1 unit of capital in a g project leads to a profit of 0.5 ($g(1) = 0.5$).
- The investment of 1 unit of capital in a b project leads to a profit of 0.0 ($b(1) = 0.0$).
- The investment of 2 units of capital in a b project leads to a profit of –0.9 ($b(2) = -0.9$).

Each division manager is able to screen his two projects by means of effort (e), which allows the division managers to be informed, i.e. observe the state of both

Decentralization

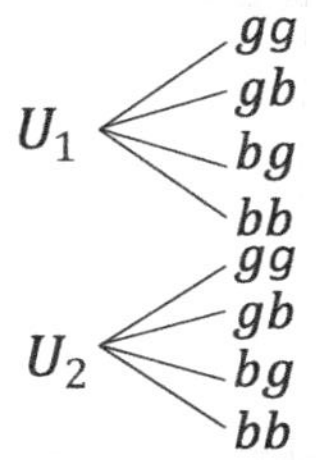

Expected return (p(g) = 0,5)	p	Division manager is informed	uninformed	Gain of being informed
gg	0.25	1.6	1.6	1.6
gb	0.5	1.6	1	
bb	0.25	0	0	0
expected return:		1.2	0.9	0.3

Hierarchy

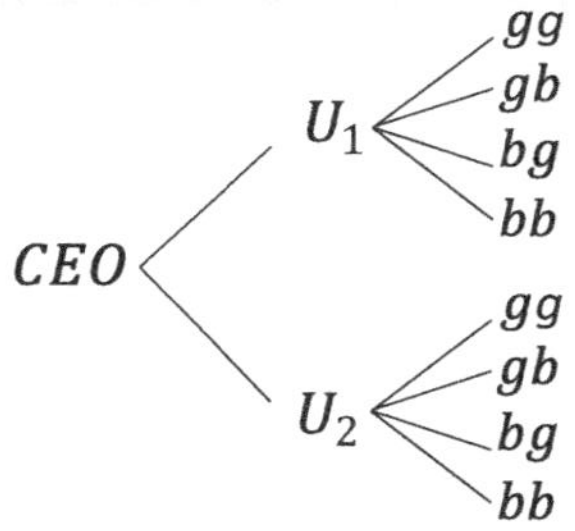

U_1	U_2	p	informed	uninformed
q = 0,6; CEO informed				
gg	gg	0.038	1.6	1.6
gg	gb	0.075	1.6	1.6
gg	bb	0.038	1.6	1.6
bg	gg	0.075	1.6	1.6
bg	gb	0.150	1.6	1
bg	bb	0.075	0.8	0.5
bb	gg	0.038	1.6	1.6
bb	gb	0.075	0.8	0.5
bb	bb	0.038	0	0
(1-q)=0,4; CEO uninformed				
gg		0.1	1.6	1.6
gb		0.2	1.6	1
bb		0.1	0	0
expected return:		1.26	1.005	0.255

Figure 2.8 Gain of being informed in decentralisation versus hierarchy

Source: author's figure

projects, with a probability of $p(e)$. In this context, the function $p(e)$ is increasing, concave and between 0 and 1. If the screening is successful, then the division managers will invest both units of capital in the g project, if they have one g and one b project. Otherwise, they will distribute their capital equally between the two projects. If the division managers remain uninformed, they will in any case distribute their capital equally between the two projects, as $b(2) - g(2) < 0$. Thus, the gain of being informed is 0.3 in this numerical example.

In the hierarchy model, in addition to the division managers, a CEO allocates the 4 capital units between the two divisions; i.e. every division manager gets between 0 and 4 units. The model assumes that the division managers cannot transmit information about the state of their projects to the CEO because of the 'softness' of the information. Furthermore, Stein (2002: 1899) assumes that the CEO is never fully informed about the stage of the projects of her division managers, but "only gets coarse information about the aggregate prospect of each division". If the CEO is informed, she knows whether one or both units have two good projects or not (star unit). Like the division managers, depending on her effort (e), the CEO is informed on the units with a likelihood of $q(e)$. If informed, the CEO distributes all 4 capital units to the star unit if one exists. Otherwise, she distributes the capital equally, considering the above-listed returns on investment and capital allocation equals the decentralisation model (each division receives 2 capital units).

As in the hierarchy model, a division manager has a probability to receive 0 capital units; this has an impact on his gain of being informed. Assuming $q = 0.6$, the gain of being informed is 0.255 in the numerical example under hierarchical circumstances and 0.3 for decentralisation. Furthermore, overall the hierarchy model yields higher expected returns, in the informed and uninformed stages, than the decentralisation model, because the CEO is capable of allocating all capital units to the star unit. However, the gain of being informed remains lower for the individual division managers (0.255 to 0.3) because they are at risk of having no capital allocated at all, which implies a complete waste of the research effort.[3] Furthermore, the average return in the uninformed hierarchy setting is lower than in the informed decentralisation setting (1.005 and 1.2). Therefore, whether the capital allocation of the decentralisation or hierarchy model gains higher expected returns depends on the effect of hierarchy on the effort of the division managers.

Stein (2002) specifies the following utility function of the division managers: $U = (y + I) - \gamma e$. The utility (U) of division managers depends on their gain on investments (y) plus the capital units their divisions receive (l_k), minus the effort (e) and a degree of effort aversion (γ).[4] By combining this utility function with the gain of being informed[3] in the decentralisation versus hierarchy model, Stein (2002) shows that decentralisation always leads to more research effort[5] by the division managers. Depending on the numeric specification of the variables, this can also lead to higher expected returns. However, these model findings only hold true under the assumption that division managers cannot transmit their information to the CEO. Otherwise, the hierarchical levels (CEO and division managers) share information and combine their research efforts (Stein 2002).

Building on this basic version of the Stein model, the consideration of different types of information produces enlightening conclusions. Stein (2002) defines two types of information, i.e. *soft* and *hard information*: "[S]oft information cannot be directly verified by anyone other than the agent who produces it" (1982), therefore its transmission within a hierarchical organisation or across distance (via ICT) causes difficulties. If, for example, a division manager evaluates that the manager of one of his two projects (firms) is honest, he can report this to his CEO. However, the CEO cannot verify this information easily ex ante, but must repeat the research effort of her division manager and herself conduct an extensive face-to-face interview with the director, for example. For obvious reasons, the CEO cannot expend this effort for every project under her supervision as her division managers do. In contrast to this, the transmission of *hard information* within a hierarchical organisation and across distances is subject to no restrictions. Actors unambiguously verify hard information such as financial statements, payment history or account information.

From the basic model and these two types of information, Stein (2002) discusses other model specifications that produce insightful results. If information is hard, Stein's (2002: 1904) model deduces that capital allocation in a hierarchy model always outperforms decentralisation. The outperformance occurs because the CEO's capital allocation yields gains without offsetting the effort of the division managers, as they are able to transmit their hard information to the CEO to influence her allocation decisions. This model specification explains why large banks face difficulties in SME lending where soft information is important, but have no disadvantage in lending to less informationally opaque large firms. In another model specification, Stein (2002: 1911) allows the hardness of information to be endogenous; i.e. the division managers decide whether to invest effort (e) to produce soft or hard information. If soft information gathering is more promising (p of being informed is higher for soft information gathering than for hard information gathering), a hierarchical setting causes too much hard information production, as only hard information influences the CEO's capital allocation decisions. Hence, hierarchy tends to cause excessive bureaucracy, and division managers spend a lot of time writing reports rather than collecting soft information about their projects (Stein 2002). This argument also explains why small banks are better in SME lending.

A range of empirical studies confirm Stein's (2002) model predictions, which is not surprising because the model was designed to explain the empirical findings. So studies often find that large banks allocate less assets to SME loans than small banks (Berger et al. 2004; see also Stein's 2002 review). Other studies from the USA, Italy and Belgium show that when large banks acquire small banks, they cut back small firm lending after the merger (Berger et al. 1998, 2004; Alessandrini et al. 2010). In this context, banks also remove good quality loans from their consolidated portfolios (Stein 2002). According to a range of studies, smaller banks have closer relationships to small firms and produce more soft information, which tends to reduce firms' financial constraints (Cole et al. 2004; Berger at al., 2005; Uchida et al. 2008, 2012; Behr et al. 2013). Utilising survey data of US firms from the 1990s, Berger et al. (2005) show that large banks are less likely to conduct relationship banking, are geographically more distant to and communicate in more impersonal ways with their SME clients than small banks. Furthermore, firms borrowing from large banks face stronger financial constraints than firms borrowing from small banks. In another study, Berger et al. (2004) compute the market share of small banks in 49 countries using bankscope data from 1993 to 2000 and show that a higher market share of small banks is associated with better economic performance. Mudd (2013) confirms the results in a similar study.

Overall, the empirical studies support Stein's (2002) model predictions. However, the empirical designs are not able to show whether the size of banks (alone) counts, or if differences in the geographical organisation of small and large banks also matters, as small banks are normally also decentralised banks, while large banks tend to be centralised. For example, the cited study of Berger et al. (2005) also finds that small banks have shorter distances to their clients than large banks, indicating the relevancy of distance in SME lending.

2.2.2.2 Distance, information transmitting and firm financing: why does it matter?

Distance has an influence on SME financing because banks face difficulties in transmitting (soft) information across distance (Klagge and Martin 2005; Agarwal and Hauswald 2007; DeYoung et al. 2008; Alessandrini et al. 2009a, 2010; Mason 2010; Canales and Nanda 2012). Disentangling bank size and distance in lending is unusual because the two aspects tend to go hand in hand. Therefore, unsurprisingly, a range of econometric studies mingle both aspects of the organisation of banks (e.g. Berger et al. 2004, 2005). However, bank size and distance are not the same. On the one hand, large banks have the opportunity to operate at a short distance to their customers with extensive branch networks, local decision-making power and mobility of staff. On the other hand, small banks are able to centralise credit-granting processes, e.g. by heavily relying on rating scores for credit decisions, and thus can offset the use of soft information in lending decisions.

When distance increases, soft information transmission becomes more and more difficult, resulting in the basic connection between distance and information. Several scholars argue that a simple metric understanding of distance insufficiently explains information transmission (Uzzi and Lancaster 2003; Boschma 2005; Klagge and Martin 2005; Alessandrini et al. 2009b, 2010). Rather, other dimensions of proximity vitally influence soft information transmission between actors. In this investigation, *distance* in its most general form is defined as the difficulty to transmit soft information between actors. Actors at short distances tend to reliably transmit soft information between one another, whereas actors at long distances face difficulties in reliably transmitting soft information. Section 2.2.3 discusses how distance hampers information transmission and defines geographical distance and other dimensions of proximity. For the time being, this most general definition of distance suffices to relate distance to the Stein model.

According to Stein's basic model, employees cannot transmit soft information at all. Therefore, the soft information of employees only influences credit decisions if the employees possess decision-making power. Allowing soft information to 'travel' between actors – at which the difficulty of transmitting soft information increases with the distance between sender and receiver – opens up Stein's (2002) model to distance. Applying this modification to Stein's model for bank-based SME lending implies that distance matters between two-actor pairs (Alessandrini et al. 2009b): firstly, between SME customers (projects in Stein's model) and their customer advisors (division managers in Stein's model) and, secondly, between customer advisors and supervisors (CEOs in Stein's model). Following the nomenclature of Alessandrini et al. (2009b), distance between SME customers and customer advisors is called the *operational distance* and the distance between customer advisors and supervisors is called the *functional distance*. Regarding operational distance, customer advisors gain soft information more easily in cases of shorter operational distance to borrowers; i.e., short operational distance (d^o) increases the likelihood (p) that the effort (e) of a customer advisor's screening will be successful (see Figure 2.9).

Allowing short functional distances to ease the transmission of soft information up the hierarchy implies that the impact of hierarchy on the efforts of customer advisors becomes distance dependent (Alessandrini et al. 2009b). Thus, the effort (e) of customer advisors to collect soft information increases if the functional distance to their supervisor decreases because it becomes easier to pass soft information up the hierarchy to influence supervisors' decisions. In addition, by receiving soft information from the customer advisors, supervisors' information bases are enhanced through short functional distance; i.e. supervisors are able to consider hard and soft information. Short functional distance (d^f) increases the likelihood (q) that the supervisors' screening efforts (e^s) will be successful. Overall, whereas short operational distance eases customer advisors' ability to access soft information, short functional distance is associated with enhanced bank-internal use of soft information, which encourages local staff to actually collect soft information.

2.2.2.3 Distance and firm financing: empirical studies

Several studies investigate the impact of distance between customers and banks (operational distance) and within the banks (functional distance). Using firm-level survey data from 1993, Peterson and Rajan (2002) report for the USA that operational distance has increased since the 1970s. Advances in ICT explain this development; firms increasingly communicate with their banks on an impersonal level. Interestingly, Peterson and Rajan (2002) report that banking market consolidation (i.e. reduction of branches) does not cause this increase of operational distance. Degryse and Ongena (2005) report a similar but less strong development for Belgium. Using newer survey data (from 2003), Brevoort et al. (2010) support Peterson and Rajan's (2002) findings. They report that the median operational distance increased by just 1 mile between 1993 and 2003 in the USA and that about 88% of firms' banks are located at a distance of less than 30 miles. A range

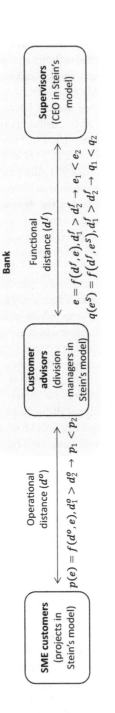

Figure 2.9 The impact of distance on credit decisions in the Stein model

Source: author's figure

of studies show that despite ICT advances the number of bank branches has not decreased in HIC, but inconsistent trends exist (Klagge 1995; Alessandrini et al. 2009b), and a newer ECB (2013) study reports a clear reduction in bank branches after the financial crisis of 2008.

Scholars have long been discussing the impact of operational distance on firm financing and have come to contradictory conclusions (e.g. Peterson and Rajan 2002; Alessandrini et al. 2009b). According to the theoretical consideration outlined in the previous section, shorter operational distance should reduce information asymmetry between firm customers and banks. Yet, the outcome of this effect is ambiguous because market-power and information-cost effects tend to overlap (Alessandrini et al. 2009b: 180–181). "At the market level, the literature [. . .] suggests that a large number of banks and branches per inhabitants reduce information asymmetries and transaction costs, positively affecting the credit availability to local firms and their performance" (Alessandrini et al. 2009b: 181). DeYoung et al.'s (2008) study uses loan contract data and indicates that longer operational distance increases information asymmetry, which is capable of causing loan default. However, measuring the effect of distance on lending is ambiguous, because if information asymmetry increases banks have the option to conduct credit rationing rather than accepting higher default rates.

Numerous studies report that firms at longer distances from banks pay lower interest rates (Peterson and Rajan 2002; Agarwal and Hauswald 2007; Bharath et al. 2007 for the USA; Degryse and Ongena 2005 for Belgium; Casolar and Mistrulli 2007 for Italy [cited in Degryse et al. 2009]; Mallett and Sen 2001 for Canada [cited in Degryse et al. 2009]). One explanation of these results is transportation costs (Degryse et al. 2009); i.e. banks price the lower transportation costs of short distance customers into their interest rates (assuming that customers have to visit their banks personally). Another explanation is banks' screening practices; i.e. banks only lend to relatively informationally transparent and less risky customers at a longer distance because they have less soft information about these clients. In return, they charge these less risky customers lower interest rates than riskier customers in the vicinity (Agarwal and Hauswald 2007).

Agarwal and Hauswald's (2007) study reports evidence for the bank-screening interpretation (second interpretation). The authors analyse a credit application dataset (loan-level data) of a large US bank that contains 26,000 small firm credit applications dating from 2002 and 2003. The bank organises its credit-granting process as follows: The customer advisors conduct a face-to-face interview with each small firm before they execute an internal rating system which creates a lending recommendation. Customer advisors are authorised to overrule this recommendation, yet supervisors closely monitor overruling, and customer advisors carry the responsibility for the performance of their credit portfolios. In this setting, Agarwal and Hauswald (2007) show that there is a higher probability of the bank offering a loan to customers who are located at a shorter distance to one of its branches. However, the interest rate is inferior to that offered to more distant firms. Furthermore, the bank less often rejects the credit applications of firms at a longer distance to one of the competitors' branches, but again offers worse terms than those offered in response to credit applications from firms located at shorter distances to the competitors. Based on these findings, Agarwal and Hauswald (2007) conclude that distance reduces the amount and quality of soft information available to the customer advisors. Furthermore, customer advisors utilise their soft informational advantages for spatial competition; i.e. they offer inferior interest rates to less transparent shorter distance firms. In addition, as the customer advisors conduct face-to-face interviews with every firm that applies for credit, the informational advantage is built on soft local information rather than soft information from face-to-face interactions.

Behr et al. (2013) report similar findings for the German savings banks. They use the rating dataset of the DSGV from 1995 to 2007 that contains 68,646 SMEs for their analysis. The scholars show that an increase in the loan share of the savings banks is associated with a higher investment of the firms relative to their capital stock. Furthermore, the investment of firms tends to be less cash-flow sensitive if savings banks have high credit shares (an increase in the loan share of private banks does not show such an effect). This effect is especially strong for firms which typically face higher credit constraints. Interestingly, the study identifies soft information as the channel responsible for this effect as it shows that only the subsample where the qualitative rating (which considers soft information) alters the total rating score displays the positive influence on the investment of firms described above. Furthermore, the authors prove that savings banks neither underperform nor take more risks than their private bank peers. Hence, Behr et al. (2013) conclude that regional savings banks reduce the financial constraints of SMEs by credibly using soft information in the credit-granting process. This does not deteriorate the stability of savings banks.

The study of Behr et al. (2013) shows the positive impact of savings banks on firm finance and indicates that savings banks' handling of soft information tends to cause the positive effect. However, the study is not able to identify whether the small size of the savings banks or short distances promote savings banks' capacity to handle soft information. Furthermore, the study does not observe whether operational distance, i.e. the extensive branch networks of savings banks, or functional distance, i.e. their decentralised headquarters, influence savings banks' advantage in soft information handling.

In this regard, Uchida et al. (2012) found that operational distance has no impact on the scope of soft information that banks' customer advisors receive about their SME clients in Japan. Similarly, Handke's (2011) qualitative analysis of bank-based SME financing in Germany indicates that operational distance is less important as *Hausbankbeziehungen* also develop over a long operational distance. According to Handke (2011), decision-making authority and the assertiveness of the customer advisors within their banks tend to be more important for the development of *Hausbankbeziehungen* than operational distance. This finding indicates the relevance of functional distance for lending to SMEs.

A body of literature shows that foreign banks are inferior in small firm lending in comparison to their domestic peers, and that they allocate fewer resources to SME finance (see for a review Alessandrini et al. 2010). Scholars explain this phenomenon with longer functional distance between regional subsidies and foreign headquarters (Alessandrini et al. 2010).

Alessandrini et al. (2009a, 2009b, 2010) explicitly compare functional distance and bank size as explanatory variables for SMEs' access to finance and innovation behaviour. They compute the functional distance of the bank branches to their decision-making headquarters for all Italian regions and show that firms located in regions with shorter functional distance conduct more innovations than those in regions with longer functional distance. The scholars calculate functional distance (as metric distance) as well as cultural distance (measured in voting differences) and show that both variables influence the innovativeness of firms. Alessandrini et al. (2009a, 2010) explain this result according to Stein's model. Banks need soft information to evaluate the innovations of SMEs, which they can communicate more easily to their headquarters in short functional distance regions; hence, SMEs gain finance for innovative projects more easily in these regions. In contrast, bank size does not have an equally strong association with firms' innovativeness. Alessandrini et al. (2009a) conclude that size and hierarchical levels, and especially functional distance, of banks have a relevant impact on their soft information processing and small firm financing. While the study controls for reverse causality and omits variable problems, doubt about the validity of the conclusion nevertheless remains because of the strong economic disparities of Italy. Thus, the short functional distance regions tend to be the affluent and competitive north Italian regions, whereas long functional distance regions predominantly belong to the less affluent south of Italy. Accordingly, regional differences in functional distance need not be the only cause of the varying innovativeness of firms.

Notwithstanding the doubt cast on the validity of Alessandrini et al.'s (2009a, 2010) study, a range of studies report results consistent with their conclusion. Zhao and Jones-Evans (2017) apply Alessandrini et al.'s (2009a) approach for the UK and prove functional distance to be associated with higher financial constraints of SMEs. Remarkably, operational distance does not show this association. On the bank level, Mistrulli and Casolaro (2008, cited in Alessandrini et al. 2010) find that Italian banks with longer functional distances lend to more informationally transparent and less risky customers. Similar results are also reported from Spain (Jiménez et al. 2009; Delgado et al. 2007, cited in Alessandrini et al. 2010). Other studies also directly compare the effects of functional distance and bank size (Mian 2006; Liberti and Mian 2009). Taking loan-level data into consideration, Mian (2006) shows for Pakistan that domestic banks are most active in relationship banking and lending to opaque firms, followed by Asian banks and branches of non-Asian foreign banks. In this context, bank size shows no association with relationship banking.

Utilising a unique credit folder dataset of 424 firms (sales > $50 million) of a large Argentinian bank in 1998, Liberti and Main (2009) observe the use of soft versus hard information in the credit decision process. More precisely, they trace the information use on different hierarchical levels and at different distances. The bank has a credit rating at which – besides financial ratios (hard information) – soft information is also included; i.e. local customer advisors must evaluate several aspects of the firms, such as management quality, and codify the information with a questionnaire. Based on this codified hard and soft information, actors at different hierarchical levels of the bank and at different locations decide about the credit proposals. Controlling for endogeneity, Liberti and Mian (2009) show that the locally collected soft information loses its relevance the higher up it travels in the hierarchy of the bank. Furthermore, the soft information of more experienced customer advisors loses less importance than the soft information of less senior customer advisors when it travels up the hierarchy and across functional distance (Liberti and Main 2009).

Remarkably, Liberti and Main (2009) report that functional distance rather than hierarchical levels causes differences in supervisors' appreciation of soft information. If the customer advisors (who produce and codify the soft information) and the supervisors in charge of credit decision are located in the same bank branch, then supervisors tend to be more likely to rely on soft information than supervisors (at the same hierarchal level) who are not co-located. Therefore, this study indicates that hierarchical levels probably do not per se discourage the use of soft information, but rather it is the effect of the functional distance between the agents of the credit decision process. Thus, in accordance with the assumption of the modified Stein (2002) model (Section 2.2.2), short functional distance tends to support the reliable transmission of soft information up the hierarchy to the supervisors. The following section now turns to the question of why shorter distance is able to ease soft information transmission.

2.2.3 Transmitting information across distance

So far, this book has defined distance by its effect on information transmission. This section discusses why shorter distance tends to ease the transmission of (soft) information. In the extensive research field of territorial innovation models, scholars have long emphasised that the co-location of actors eases knowledge sharing which boosts innovations and competitiveness (e.g. Maskell and Malmberg 1999; Rehfeld 1999; Butzin and Widmaier 2016, overview in Butzin 2013). However, current research challenges the relevance of co-location in light of ICT advantages and increased mobility and points out that co-location is neither necessary nor sufficient to facilitate knowledge exchange (Boschma 2005; Torre and Rallet 2005; Torre 2008; Bathelt and Henn 2014; Grabher and Ibert 2014). Also concerning distance and firm finance, the insufficiency of metric distances between actors' locations as an explanation for impeded information transmission is indicated (Uzzi and Lancaster 2003; Lo 2003; Klagge and Martin 2005; Alessandrini et al. 2010). This section tackles the issue of the transmission of information across distance firstly by defining data, information and knowledge, as studies on firm financing use all three terms (Section 2.2.3.1). Following this, Section 2.2.3.2 discusses non-metric aspects which are able to ease the transmission of (soft) information, and Section 2.2.3.3 turns to metric aspects that enhance information transmission.

2.2.3.1 Data, information, knowledge

Scholars use the terms *data*, *information* and *knowledge* to analyse the use and transmission of knowledge (e.g. Boschma 2005; Torre 2008; Zademach and Rimkus 2009). All three terms also are applied in research on banking (e.g. Vopel 1999; Stein 2002; Lo 2003; Horsch and Schulte 2010; Zademach 2014). As Figure 2.10 illustrates, for each of these terms, scholars specify a binary classification according to the transmissibility of data, information and knowledge. For example, actors can easily transmit hard information, whereas the transmission of soft information is constrained (see for the following discussion Gärtner and Flögel 2017).

Willke (1998) defines data as codified observations that are saved in numbers, words, tones, pictures and videos (Willke 1998, cited in Lo 2003: 31). Data has no meaning in its own right but builds the basis for the production of information (Bellinger et al. 2004). A range of publications within the applied banking literature classify data or facts binarily in quantitative and qualitative data (Theis 2009; Horsch and Schulte 2010). Only data from the financial statements of firms

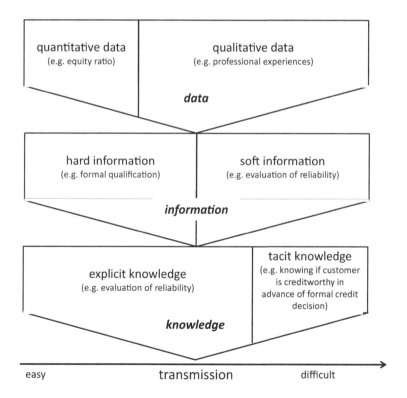

Figure 2.10 Data, information, knowledge

Source: Gärtner and Flögel 2017: 32 (translated and modified)

count as quantitative data and are input to the quantitative rating module of banks (Sparkassen Rating and Risikosysteme GmbH 2010). Laws strictly regulate the creation of these data (e.g. the *Handelsgesetzbuch*, the German commercial law and accounting standard, which is used also for taxation). Auditors, such as tax advisors or financial auditors, co-create and approve the reliability of the financial statements. In contrast to this, Horsch and Schulte (2010) call all other inputs to the rating process qualitative data. Thus, qualitative data comprise both fairly subjective estimations such as market outlooks and management reliability and rather objective facts like the formal qualification of the management and payment transactions. Qualitative data do not always exist in numerical form. Therefore, bank employees transform qualitative data into numerical symbols – using forms and questionnaires – to consider this data in rating systems.

"Information is data that has been given meaning by way of relational connection" (Bellinger et al. 2004: 1). Actors filter information out of data with their system of sensual perception and integrate the information into a systematic context that gives it meaning (Lo 2003: 32). Hence, information is a subset of all data that activates actors who interpret this information on the basis of their knowledge (Hamburg and Widmaier 2004). Accordingly, different actors gain varying information from the same data (Schmidt 2012). As discussed above, Stein (2002) advances a binary classification of hard and soft information. The transmission of hard information between actors across distance is straightforward because third parties possess the capability to verify hard information easily. Verification of soft information by actors other than those who produce it is difficult, which hampers distant transmission of this information. For example, the formal qualification of the management exemplifies hard information in the firm evaluation processes, as banks can easily verify this information with the help of certificates etc. An example for soft information is the customer advisors' evaluation of the management reliability of firms, as this evaluation has been developed in numerous interactions in long-standing business relationships.

Knowledge emerges when actors relate information to awareness, experiences, goals and beliefs which consequently guide their action (Ibert 2007; Schmidt 2012). Actors need knowledge to identify and use information, with the latter being able to change the knowledge of actors. At the same time, which data actors identify as information and which data thus influence their actions depends on actors' knowledge. Studies of the knowledge economy often use Polanyi's (1966) well-known binary classification of tacit and explicit knowledge (Vopel 1999; Lo 2003). Tacit, or implicit, knowledge implies that humans know more and can do more than they are able to express explicitly (Lo 2003; Hamburg and Widmaier 2004). Thus, tacit knowledge refers to actors' individual capacity to act (e.g. know-how) as well as to organisational practices. In this context, actors can only to some degree codify the knowledge they use for their actions, consequently bounding tacit knowledge to its users who transmit it predominantly in personal interactions (e.g. learning at vocational training). In contrast to implicit knowledge, the codification of explicit knowledge (e.g. in user manuals, patents) tends to be unproblematic.

Regarding credit decisions made by banks, the reliable evaluation of a firm's management by the bank employees exemplifies explicit knowledge. The employees are able to recall all their experiences with the management of the firm, experience gained in the course of long-standing business relationships, and then use this experience to justify their evaluation. An example of tacit knowledge is bank employees' instant estimation of a firm's overall creditworthiness, i.e. the question of whether a credit application will be accepted by the banks or not, before conducting the detailed evaluation. In this estimation, the bank employees have to anticipate customers' statements and documents, the rating results, supervisors' and credit officers' votes etc. Nevertheless, experienced bankers are able to conduct this estimation reliably and usually know in advance which credit applications the bank will accept and which will fail (see Section 4.2.4.1).

Against this background the relation between data, information and knowledge can be described as follows (see Figure 2.10, p. 53). Hard information often consists of quantitative data and represents an important element of explicit knowledge. Vice versa, actors filter soft information from qualitative data and integrate it into their tacit knowledge. However, as indicated above, the binary classifications specify varying boundaries. Thus, the transmission of qualitative data is much easier than the transmission of soft information, with tacit knowledge being the most difficult to transmit between actors. Only a very small part of all data, namely financial statement data, actually belong to the class of quantitative data. All data which third parties can relatively easily verify are classified as hard information. With respect to explicit knowledge, the boundary of the binary classification moves further to the right of Figure 2.10 in the context of banking. This is because explicit knowledge consists of all the information bank employees are able to express and codify. Only non-expressible knowledge of the bank employees belongs to the class of tacit knowledge.

2.2.3.2 Non-metric aspects of information transmission

Per definition, the specific feature of regional banks is short geographical distance between customers and employees in metric terms; i.e. operational and especially functional distances tend to be shorter than those of large banks. However, in the debate on the geography of knowledge exchange, it is now well-recognised that addressing mere geographical proximity between actors provides an unsatisfactory explanation of the enhanced processes of knowledge exchange (Torre and Rallet 2005; Boschma 2005; Torre 2008; Bathelt and Henn 2014). In this light Boschma (2005: 62) argues: "geographical proximity per se is neither a necessary nor a sufficient condition for learning [and knowledge exchange] to take place: at most, it facilitates interactive learning most likely by strengthening the other dimensions of proximity". Accordingly, the short geographical distance between customers and employees of regional banks is not sufficient to explain their enhanced capacities to process soft information in credit decisions. Therefore, this empirical investigation analyses metric and non-metric aspects of distance between the actors involved in credit decisions and their interplay. In the following, Boschma's (2005) proximity dimension classification is discussed before attention turns to a brief review of empirical banking studies about these non-metric dimensions of proximity.

Boschma (2005) distinguishes between cognitive, organisational, social and institutional proximity as four non-metric dimensions of enhanced information exchange between actors, along with geographical proximity. Furthermore, he points out that all five forms of proximity tend to reinforce each other (Boschma 2005). The institutional proximity dimension is not discussed further because it refers to the macro-institutional context which does not vary in the empirical investigation in hand (the German economic and financial system). For the sake of clarity, the term *proximity* is avoided for the three remaining non-metric dimensions of proximity, as other terms describe the dimension under consideration more accurately. In the following, cognitive affinity, organisational embeddedness and social embeddedness are defined:

- *Cognitive affinity* describes the similarity of actors' knowledge basis. The more the knowledge of two actors overlap, the higher their cognitive affinity. Cognitive affinity eases the communication between actors and increases the likelihood that different actors interpret information in the same way. Cognitive affinity tends to be high between bank employees because they undertake similar professional training and work in the same sector. In contrast, the cognitive affinity between bankers and their SME customers is often considered to be lower and can hinder information transmission, especially in small firm finance where managing owners tend to lack business knowledge and bankers understand little about the technical aspects of firms' business.
- *Organisational embeddedness* "is defined as the extent to which relations are shared in an organisational arrangement, either within or between organisations" (Boschma 2005: 65). Organisational embeddedness has a power and control dimension; e.g. managers possess the power to order information sharing between actors and sanction misbehaviour in a hierarchical organisation. Two employees of the same bank are strongly organisationally embedded, for instance, especially if they work in the same department. Organisational embeddedness between banks and their SME customers tends to be weaker. Nevertheless, in accordance with relationship banking, (debt) contracts and mutual dependencies organisationally embed these relationships, too.
- *Social embeddedness* refers to close ties or relations between actors (Granovetter 1985). "Relations between actors are socially embedded when they involve trust based on friendship, kinship and experience" (Boschma 2005: 66). For the study in hand, the relation between two actors is defined as socially embedded if the persons know each other personally, frequently communicate and interact with each other and have gained experience with one another. Studies on banking acknowledge that socially embedded, trust-based relationships ease the sharing of sensitive knowledge (e.g. Panzer-Krause 2011). Besides personal aspects, affections and antipathies etc., the

organisational design of the cooperation between actors impacts the development of social embeddedness (see Section 4.2.3.1).

If cognitive affinity, social embeddedness and organisational embeddedness are high, then actors easily transmit and verify soft information in social interactions. With low proximities, actors face difficulties to exchange soft information. In this context, the proximity dimensions tend to reinforce as well as substitute each other, and geographical proximity is often seen as an auxiliary proximity of the other proximities (Boschma 2005; Mattes 2012). A range of empirical studies apply Boschma's (2005) dimensions to analyse knowledge and information exchange between actors (Ponds et al. 2007). Accordingly, Boschma's (2005) proximity dimensions represent an appropriate conceptual basis to specify actors' capacity to transmit and verify soft information in banking.

However, the proximity debate is criticised for overstating the role of proximity for knowledge and information exchange. In this spirit, Grabher and Ibert (2014) show that individuals exchange knowledge in virtual communities where neither geographical nor social embeddedness exists between the community members. Grabher and Ibert (2014) conclude that, varying with context, distance between actors is even an asset and enhances knowledge exchange. Yet, the context of their study – virtual communities like the 'IKEA fans forum' – has very few similarities with the banking industry where bank secrecy prohibits the public spread of customers' private information.

The proximity debate is further criticised for conflating cause and effect. Rutten (2016: 16) points out the relevancy of social interaction for knowledge and information exchange and criticizes that "proximities are outcomes of rather than inputs for social interaction and that social dynamics rather than proximities reduce uncertainty and resolve coordination problems". Rutten's (2016) critique is relevant to the empirical study in hand, as the study focuses on the social interaction of individuals (e.g. customer advisors, supervisors, SMEs) and their capacity to transmit soft information. Yet, Rutten (2016) overgeneralises, as becomes evident by considering organisational embeddedness. Here the collaboration of individual employees results from the rules of the organisation (e.g. management decisions) and represents a given fact for the employees which has the capacity to improve their ability to transmit soft information. In a similar way, the other proximity dimensions may have been the outcome of past social interactions (e.g. job training that increased cognitive affinity between two actors) but represent a given fact in the actual situation of knowledge and information exchange, i.e. in the credit-granting process. Therefore, while taking Rutton's (2016) critique into consideration and remaining open for bidirectional causalities, Boschma's (2005) proximity dimensions are appropriate to understand the capacity of actors to transfer soft information in situations where credit decisions are actually conducted.

Empirical studies indicate the relevance of social embeddedness in banking. Uzzi and Lancaster's (2003) study of customer advisors' relationships to medium-sized US firms shows that public and private knowledge is important in banks' evaluations of firms and loan pricing. Customer advisors gain private knowledge mainly through socially embedded relations with their customers. Hence, embedded ties (i.e. relationship banking) boost the ability of banks and firms to learn from each other (see also Handke 2011; Panzer-Krause 2011). From these findings, Uzzi and Lancaster (2003) deduce that social embeddedness is especially important if actors rely on diverse and contentious knowledge bases.

Vopel (1999) analysed the knowledge-intensive work of investment banks in Germany from a critical perspective using qualitative interviews. In conformity with Uzzi and Lancaster's (2003) findings, Vopel (1999) detects the relevance of social ties and personal networks in investment banking. However, he points to decreasing cognitive affinity among bankers because of extensive specialisation, short termism (project-based organisation) and high competition between the bank employees of the same investment bank. All these aspects lead to an erosion of socially embedded cooperation and deteriorate knowledge sharing within investment banks. Consequently, Vopel's (1999) results indicate the impact of banks' organisational design on knowledge and information exchange between bank employees.

In line with Uzzi and Lancaster (2003), Lo (2003) argues in her qualitative study of the M&A market in Germany that the ICT revolution has made public and codified information ubiquitous, so personal contacts and private information have gained importance. Private information allows actors to differentiate themselves from their competitors. Furthermore, Lo (2003) shows that actors are reluctant to codify information, because they fear leaking of the information once it is codified. Lo's (2003) study indicates that short geographical distance still matters as it facilitates socially embedded interactions. Being part of the M&A business, knowing customers and maintaining contacts requires co-location in the financial centre of Frankfurt. Socially embedded ties, in turn, relax impersonal communication over distance; e.g. business partners find it easier to call and have an open talk once they know each other from previous face-to-face meetings. So Lo's (2003) study identifies advantages that firms gain when they co-locate in financial centres (i.e. personal socially embedded interaction), which have been confirmed by a range of other studies about financial centres (e.g. König et al. 2007, Wójcik 2009; Schamp 2009; Hall and Appleyard 2009; Hall 2011).

2.2.3.3 Metric aspects of information transmission

Geographical distance is defined here as metric distance between actors or organisations in Euclidean terms. If actors interact at a short metric distance of up to a few metres, this is called a *face-to-face interaction*. If organisations locate at a short geographical distance, e.g. in the same city or region, this is called *co-location*. Basically, the literature discusses two metric aspects that explain why geographical distance eases information transmission. Firstly, face-to-face interactions are often considered to be very efficient to communicate (soft) information (Torre and Rallet 2005; Bathelt and Henn 2014). Secondly, scholars, especially in the research field of territorial innovation models, argue that co-location enables actors to gain specific access to local information (Maskell and

Malmberg 1999; Rehfeld 1999; Bathelt et al. 2004; Degryse et al. 2009; Rehfeld and Terstriep 2013).

Face-to-face interactions are an information-efficient means to communicate, especially when actors need to transfer divergent and complex knowledge and soft information, because actors send verbal and non-verbal data (cues) simultaneously and spontaneously (Short et al. 1976; Walter et al. 2005, cited in Bathelt and Henn 2014). This fosters the discussion of complex and conflicting knowledge according to Torre and Rallet (2005) who report that business partners often conduct personal meetings at the beginning of new projects to get to know each other and to equalise knowledge. Additional meetings take place in cases of conflicts to negotiate solutions. partners can take each other's (spontaneous) reactions into account while discussing possible solutions. Face-to-face interactions also facilitate the communication of soft information because actors' spontaneous verbal and non-verbal actions and reactions help to verify or falsify soft information. Thus, the directness of reaction restricts tactical manoeuvring, e.g. the making-up of 'stories', easing the verification of soft information.

Co-location matters regarding information transmission because it supports face-to-face interactions, i.e. interactions become less expensive and time-consuming, explaining why information asymmetries between actors increase with geographical distance. However, developments in ICT (e.g. social networks, video conferences) facilitate distance communication (Torre and Rallet 2005; Bathelt and Henn 2014), and advances in transportation make business travel less expensive and time-consuming. Accordingly, the effect of co-location on face-to-face interactions tends to diminish. Nevertheless, co-location also matters in gaining information for the following two reasons:

Firstly, co-location fosters observations of people and objects; i.e. actors only need to see the objects, documents or movements of people etc. to obtain information. For example, Terstriep (forthcoming) finds that firms participate in clusters to observe their competitors. Banks gain information via observation, too; e.g. bankers are more likely to note delays in customers' construction works if they work in the cities where the construction sites are located (Gärtner and Flögel 2017).

Secondly, to territorial innovation systems research, co-location still matters because it gives actors access to specific 'local buzz', which is difficult to grasp for actors located outside. Bathelt et al. (2004: 38) describe local buzz as consisting

> of specific information and continuous updates of this information, intended and unanticipated learning processes in organized and accidental meetings, the application of the same interpretative schemes and mutual understanding of new knowledge and technologies, as well as shared cultural traditions and habits within a particular technology field, which stimulate the establishment of conventions and other institutional arrangements. Actors continuously contribute to and benefit from the diffusion of information, gossip and news by just 'being there'.

Whereas the idea of local buzz is that co-located firms automatically receive information, Bathelt et al. (2004) nevertheless stress that only firms of the clusters receive the local buzz. Thus, besides co-location, social embeddedness, cognitive and cultural affinity, and commercial interactions boost the quality and intensity of local buzz as well. Via their interaction with numerous firms, private customers and public organisations, regional banks and regional branches of supraregional banks are able to become vital receivers (and senders) of local buzz, which banks that are located out of regions cannot access (Degryse et al. 2009). Yet, co-location alone tends to be insufficient to enhance capacities to interact and transmit soft information between banks and firms, as demonstrated by the example of Deutsche Bank and a small retailer co-located in the Westend-Süd district of Frankfurt. As Deutsche Bank only deals with large companies at its headquarters, it is unlikely to know much about retailers' businesses at its doorstep. Accordingly, co-location is a relevant but not sufficient ingredient to enhance knowledge exchange (Maskell and Malmberg 1999; Rehfeld 1999; Bathelt et al. 2004) and support the development of social embeddedness and cognitive affinity between actors.

Overall geographical distance and the other dimensions of proximity are able to reinforce each other and also substitute for each other to a certain degree. Accordingly, short geographical distance tends to be especially relevant in banking if other dimensions of proximity are low, e.g. if bankers and managing owners need a lot of personal interaction to understand each other's businesses. Vice versa, long geographical distance tends to be less problematic if other proximities are high. Considering these interdependencies, the empirical study in hand analyses functional and operational distance in banking by considering all relevant metric and non-metric dimensions of proximity as well as their interplay.

2.2.4 Systematisation and problematisation: regional versus large banks

Three geographical influence factors have been identified which explain why geography matters in bank-based firm financing: geographical market delimitation, regional market structure and geographical distance (see Figure 2.11). Regionally segregated banking markets tend to hinder capital flows from the periphery to the centres and low market competition and short geographical distance foster firms' access to finance because they influence the conduct of banks. Importantly, the three factors also affect each other; i.e. market delimitation changes regional banking market competition and geographical distance. Competition and (organisational and functional) distance influence banks' screening and monitoring of enterprises. Theoretical deductions and empirical findings indicate that low competition and short distance are associated with reduced information asymmetries between banks and firms, though contradicting results also exist. Therefore, non-geographical factors, especially the non-metric proximity dimensions, bank–customer relationships and bank size, need to be taken into consideration to understand banks' business lending.

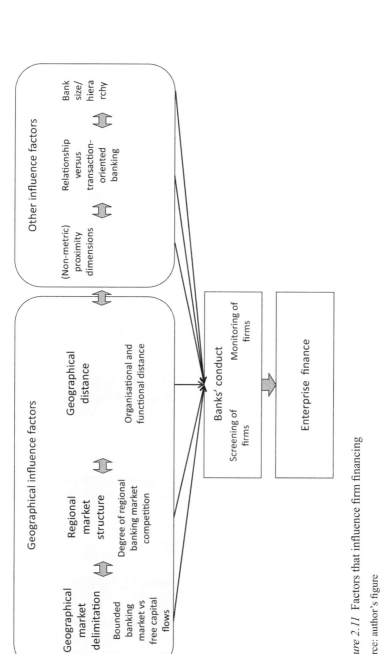

Figure 2.11 Factors that influence firm financing

Source: author's figure

Against this background, the differences in firm finance of regional versus large banks are hypothetically as follows: As decentralised institutes, regional banks lend at a shorter geographical distance (especially functional distance) to firms than centralised large banks and obtain reliable soft information about their firm clients, which reduces information asymmetries. As soft information especially pays out in lending to informationally opaque SMEs, decentralised banks are superior in lending to SMEs, reduce the financial constraints of small firms and thus gain market shares in the SME segment. Centralised large banks, on the other hand, obtain economies of scale and scope due to their larger size and develop superior sectorial competences (Kamp et al. 2007; Udell 2008). Centralised banks have advantages in achieving banking expertise – human resources and knowledge – because of their presence in leading financial centres (e.g. Alessandrini et al. 2009a; Schamp 2009; Gärtner and Flögel 2017). Therefore, they pursue lending to large corporations which demand advanced sectorial knowledge and banking expertise.

The hypothetical differences in firm finance of regional versus large banks outlined above neglect the developments of the banking sector, however. The facilitated standardisation and rationalisation of credit-granting and monitoring processes (through ICT advancements) and changes in bank regulation profoundly impact the way banks conduct credit decisions. Banks' internal rating systems tend to be an especially important instrument that standardises credit decisions by predicting the probability that borrowers will default. At present, rating systems are indispensable in modern banking (Leyshon and Thrift 1999; Alessandrini et al. 2009b; Pieper 2005; Riese 2006; Udell 2009; Berger et al. 2011). Since 2004, bank regulation in Germany has actually required the application of rating systems and the clear organisational segregation of the front office and back office in lending to SMEs (BaFin 2012a: BTO 1.4). All German savings banks as well as all German cooperative banks have developed their rating systems together within their associations (Sparkassen Rating and Risikosysteme GmbH 2010); accordingly, they apply the same centralised systems. Bank regulation and centralised rating systems contradict the notion that regional banks always decide on credits at a shorter distance to their clients than large banks. Rather, complex geographies of credit decision making have developed in modern banking which this empirical comparison of regional and large banks explores.

2.3 Placing the rating systems as non-human actors in credit decisions

Section 2.2 has reviewed a range of theories on the relevance of geography in bank-based firm financing. Although these theories conclusively explain the relationships between distance and credit decision making, they neglect the credit-granting practices of modern banks, especially the use of rating systems for the assessment of firms' default risk. This section discusses the conceptual question of how rating systems and other standardised screening and monitoring techniques can be included in the analysis of banks' credit-granting processes. To this end, this discussion applies theories from the humanities and social sciences, especially from the interdisciplinary research field of the social studies of finance (SSoF). However, their application causes a metatheoretical contradiction as economic theories and theories from the SSoF rely on contradicting metatheoretical foundations.

Section 2.3.1 presents the metatheoretical basis for the combined use of theories from economics and SSoF. It argues that combining theories from both research traditions does not cause a metatheoretical contradiction from the new realist ontology's point of view. Section 2.3.2 introduces actor-network theory (ANT), explains its concept of non-human actors and critically transfers this concept to rating systems. It argues that ANT's claim of generalised symmetry (i.e. analysing human and non-human actors equally) contradicts new realist ontology. Therefore, alternative theories are needed to approach 'the behaviour' of rating systems. Section 2.3.3 thus discusses the specific characteristics of rating systems for credit decisions with insights from SSoF and summarises key empirical findings regarding their use in the credit-granting processes of banks.

2.3.1 The new realist ontology: metatheoretical foundation for economic and social studies of finance theories[6]

SSoF emphasise the constructiveness of markets (Callon 1998; MacKenzie 2006; Bernd and Böckler 2009) as well as the agency of non-human actors (Callon 1998; Callon et al. 2008). Empirical studies influenced by SSoF advance the understanding of failures in modern finance and help to explain the financial crisis of 2008 (Engelen et al. 2010; MacKenzie 2011; Berndt 2011; Christophers 2013). Especially MacKenzie (2006, 2011) analyses rating practices and their effects on economic results and develops a systematic theory on how economic models such as rating formulas influence the economy. MacKenzie (2006: 12) claims: "[economics is] an active force transforming its environment, not a camera passively recording it". Apparently, this quote stands in contrast to the economic theories discussed in Section 2.2, as it accuses economic theories of constituting rather than describing the economy. Thus, it becomes vital to consider whether the combination of economic theories with putatively opposing theories from the SSoF causes contradictions on a metatheoretical level or rather advances understanding of banks' lending practices to SMEs.

From a metatheoretical point of view the putative contradiction emerges because economic theories are grounded in a realistic understanding of sciences; i.e. economics should research how the economy works and describe this in models and theories. Approaches in SSoF assume more anti-realistic positions; i.e. there is no independent real economy out there to be discovered, but rather humans (and scientists) constitute economies (Egner 2010; Mattissek et al. 2012; Steiner 2014a). In this context, theories of SSoF popular in financial geography – ANT (Jöns 2006) and the theory on the performativity of economics (Berndt 2011; Ouma 2012; Christophers 2013) – are called *post-dualist theories* (Steiner 2014a), as they consider non-human objects in the construction of reality.

To address this putative metatheoretical contradiction, the book utilises the new realist ontology. Put forward by the German philosopher Gabriel (2013, 2015), the new realist ontology represents one direction in the new and evolving research field on rethinking realism (e.g. Boghossian 2006; Bryant et al. 2011; Brassier 2011; Ferraris 2014). Not without self-confidence, Gabriel (2013) claims that the new realist ontology overcomes postmodern (anti-realistic) nihilism without falling back on a naïve realism. To accomplish this, Gabriel (2015) outlines a tolerant ontology and justifies epistemological pluralism but introduces the concept of fields of sense (FoS). Within FoS, one is in principle able to identify true facts. As will be shown in the following, the new realist ontology is capable of conforming to the realist and rather anti-realist theories used in this study.

Ontology is the "systematic investigation into the meaning of 'existence'" (Gabriel 2015: 187), thus addressing the question of what in principle exists. Ontology relates to epistemology, i.e. "the systematic investigation into the meaning of 'knowledge'" (Gabriel 2015: 318), thus addressing the question of how humans can truthfully know what exists. Whereas some metatheories merge ontology and epistemology and either privilege physical things or human thoughts, the new realist ontology admits the existence of both without privileging one or the other ontologically (Gabriel 2014). Hence, the new realist ontology is able to conform with both realistic and anti-realistic theories, as will be discussed in the following. Section 2.3.1.1 introduces the new realist ontology. Section 2.3.1.2 critically appraises the new realist ontology and outlines two criteria a theory must meet to conform with the new realist ontology. The following sections (2.3.2, 2.3.3) introduce the theories used in this study to conceptualise the rating systems as non-human actors involved in credit decisions and relate them to the new realist ontology.

2.3.1.1 The new realist ontology

The following discussion of new realism focuses on the new realist ontology elaborated by the German philosopher Markus Gabriel (2013, 2014, 2015). According to Gabriel (2013), postmodern radical constructivism (global anti-realism) assumes that there are no objective facts; rather, all facts are constructed by (scientific) discourses and research methods. Hence, humans cannot recognise the world; everything they recognise is manmade and represents just one perspective among others. Following Gabriel (2013), the opposite of this radical constructivist perspective are metaphysic worldviews that explain everything with a single (material) theory (old realism). At present, the popularity of metaphysic perspectives is increasing (Gabriel 2014). One interpretation of neuroscience which claims that all types of awareness, e.g. feelings, thoughts and dreams, are just states of the brain exemplifies a metaphysic worldview. Accordingly, the world differs from its appearance to humans and just consists of materiality and its physical and chemical states (Gabriel 2014). The notion that humankind remains very unimportant in the endless universe represents another example of material metaphysics.

In contrast to these two perspectives, Gabriel (2013) posits the new realist ontology by using one example. Consider three people observing the mountain Vesuvius from two positions on Earth (p1, p2 and p3). In this scenario, (material) metaphysics argues that only Vesuvius exists. Radical constructivists tend to argue for the existence of three objects: p1's Vesuvius, p2's Vesuvius and p3's Vesuvius. According to this worldview it might be possible that Vesuvius exists independently of the observations of p1, p2 and p3; however, one cannot be sure about this (Egner 2010). For Gabriel (2013), it is most reasonable to assume the existence of four objects here: Vesuvius and the three perspectives on Vesuvius (p1, p2 and p3). This four-objects perspective exemplifies the position of the new realist ontology.

Following Gabriel (2013), this four-objects perspective represents the most promising one as the other two perspectives make unjustified simplifications: "metaphysical (old) realism is exclusively interested in the world without spectators, whereas constructivism is exclusively interested in the world of the spectators" (Gabriel 2015: 11). Consequently, as both assumptions contradict human experience, the four-objects perspective tends to be most convincing (Gabriel 2013). As a matter of fact, p1 has a specific perspective on Vesuvius which may stimulate emotions, ideas and thinking. It differs from the p2 perspective and especially from the p3 perspective at the Vesuvius from another location on Earth. Yet, it is also a fact that all people who are able to see will perceive a thing (a massive thing identified as a volcanic mountain by geologists and named Vesuvius in our time), if they take the p1 position and if weather conditions remain constant. Accordingly, the new realist ontology sticks to the realist position that, in principle, humans have direct access to objects (e.g. things) with their senses, rather than being solely entangled in representations of objects (Ferraris 2014; Gabriel 2015). Thus, for example, the appearance of an object is a modally robust fact of the object and not only a human's representation of it (Gabriel 2015: 350). The numerous representations and perspectives of human beings on this object also exist as further objects.

To date, the new realist ontology has rejected privileging either the world of things or the world of thoughts, a perspective a range of scholars have called for (Murdoch 1997; Jöns 2006; Steiner 2014b). Furthermore, the approach admits that humans have the ability to sense material things similarly, a position empirical research builds upon (stating this is not to deny delusions and false conclusions: to err is human). However, as the new realist ontology adds more objects (the universe of things) to the countless perspectives of human beings, one actually ends up with more objects than with radical constructivism. Unfortunately, so far this argumentation fails to identify true statements; i.e. if all perspectives on Vesuvius contradict each other, which of these perspectives is true? To handle this problem, Gabriel (2015) introduces the concept of FoS. Everything that exists does so in a certain FoS. In this context it is sufficient for something to generally exist to appear in any one of the many FoS (Gabriel 2015, 65). Hence, the question is always not whether something exists, e.g. whether something is true or not, but in which FoS something exists, i.e. in which FoS something is true (Gabriel 2013).

"The fields of sense characterise what exactly it is for something to appear in them" (Gabriel 2015: 44). So each FoS appoints the property or sense by which it individuates an object, i.e. the property by which an object is identified as distinguished from other objects. Furthermore, FoS themselves only exist because they appear as objects in other FoS. Thus, their senses that individuate the objects appear as objects in other FoS. In doing so, these individuating senses are not proper properties[7] of the objects in the FoS. For example, consider a FoS encompassing circular and square objects. Shape defines the individuating sense of the objects in this FoS. However, shape itself is not a proper property of the objects in this FoS because all objects are shaped; thus they cannot be distinguished by the property shape. Yet, shape counts as an object in the FoS of the characteristics of (physical) things, along with colour, size, weight etc. Note, however, that the characteristics of (physical) things are not the only FoS where shape, colour, size and weight appear as objects; e.g. they also appear as objects in this piece of work.

Gabriel's FoS ontology highlights that "there is no possible rule singling out all fields of sense. In other words, fields of sense are really individuated without recourse to an overall principle of individuation" (2015: 243). Some FoS are individuated by human fields of vision, others by discursive practices, by physical relationships, by disciplinary boundaries or by artistic work etc. This leads directly to the final notion of new realist ontology, the 'no-world claim'. To Gabriel (2013, 2015) there is no FoS of all FoS; i.e. the all-encompassing world does not exist. "There is no field of sense that is ontologically absolutely privileged" (Gabriel 2015: 298). This statement is basically explained by the fact that this all-encompassing FoS would be outside of itself and hence contradict the all-encompassing claim. "Another way of putting this is to assert that there is no such thing as the meaning of it all and that this is the reason why there is no such as it all" (Gabriel 2015: 194).

With the help of FoS, the claim to explain all that is put forward by (material) metaphysic worldviews is unmasked as a confusion of different FoS. Taking the universe's metaphysics as an example, the universe belonging to the FoS of physics is simply not everything; e.g. Goethe's Faust or savings banks also exist. Indeed, Faust and savings banks can be located in the universe (i.e. on planet Earth which belongs to the solar system that is part of the Milky Way, etc.) and thus in the FoS of physics. However, this does not help to interpret Faust or to understand banks' lending practices. Similarly, Faust or the 'handbook of corporate credit business' (Ahnert et al. 2009) would not help to understand the universe.

Let us apply this new realist ontology to the topic of this book by considering the following statement: Geographical distance influences bank-based SME lending. Is this true or not? One easily asserts that this statement exists, at least as a written sentence in this book. The literature review in Section 2.2.2.3 also identified sentences with similar meaning in scientific papers (e.g. Berger et al. 2005; Alessandrini et al. 2009b), whereas other papers (e.g. Uchida et al. 2012) and theories (e.g. neoclassic) assert the opposite. Obviously, this can continue for a while. However, this empirical work aims to find out whether this sentence exists as a true statement about bank-lending practices to SMEs. Answering this question is difficult as, for instance, several (conflicting) theories state why distance may or may not matter in small firm lending (see Section 2.2.2). Hence, no single parameter exists that one is unambiguously able to sense. Gabriel (2015: 242) admits that "many fields [of sense] are hybrids, and what is mixed in them cannot be anticipated a priori. There is change and creativity. There are also different forms of temporality, change and alteration". Thus, to find out something about these 'hybrid fields' requires empirical research (Gabriel 2015: 246). Having said this, there cannot be one single epistemology for empirical research either, because of the lack of an overall principle for individuating FoS (no FoS of all FoS.) Rather Gabriel (2015: 329) endorses epistemological plurality, i.e. a plurality of knowledge.[8]

2.3.1.2 *Critical appraisal of the new realist ontology*

In its demand for plural knowledge, the new realist ontology equates to radical constructivist accounts, yet with the exception that the senses which individuate FoS are not only human constructs. For example, for an enquiry into the age of the Earth knowledge of the FoS of geology and related sciences takes precedence and not the Holy Bible. In this respect, Koch and MacDonald (2014) criticise a non-hermeneutic interpretation of the new realism and demonstrate that human (lexical) reference is necessary to distinctively individuate objects (e.g. FoS). Because of this, new realism must be hermeneutic and realistic while not denying the real existence of things and human ability to sense them (Koch and MacDonald 2014: 234). However, radical constructivists deny precisely this, arguing that humans necessarily gain all knowledge with their senses (including thinking). Accordingly, fundamental errors in our sensing, e.g. adulterant representations about objects, would prohibit sensing objects as they are (Egner 2010). Hence, absolute or objective knowledge about objects cannot exist, because human representation filters our senses.

Gabriel's response to radical constructivism is similar to the response of other realist philosophers (e.g. Boghossian 2006): The rejection of objective knowledge itself relies on one objective and true fact, the fact that humans in general fail to sense things as they are. The new realist ontology rules out this metaphysic claim:

> If knowledge cannot be unified by specifying any alleged universal and substantial structure holding knowledge as such together, there correspondingly is no position from which to undermine knowledge in one stroke. Epistemological pluralism, therefore is a bulwark against scepticism.
>
> (Gabriel 2015: 354)

Gabriel's response to radical constructivism tends nevertheless to be insufficient to finally settle this dispute due to the maintenance of the agnostic position: Humans cannot be sure of sensing things in a way that is at least partly true (e.g. Steiner 2014a). However, the new realist ontology takes a pragmatic position and assumes that humans have some sense of things independent of their representation of them, an assumption on which ANT also relies (see Section 2.3.2.1).

To sum up, the new realist ontology takes a tolerant position on what exists (basically everything) and advises epistemological plurality to gain knowledge of objects. To facilitate the realist notion of true facts, Gabriel (2013, 2015) introduces FoS: Something exists if it appears in a FoS. FoS themselves only exist because they appear in other FoS; the individuation of (and in) FoS is not only a construct of human cognition but is governed by plural senses. In this context, no overall rule exists to individuate FoS (no-world claim). Against this background, a theory must meet two criteria to conform with the new realist ontology. Firstly, the theory must not be grounded on radical constructivism, i.e. totally rejecting the human capacity to sense true facts. Secondly, the theory must also not be metaphysical, i.e. forwarding all-encompassing or all-explaining claims.

The strand of theory on distance and small firm finance discussed in Section 2.2.2 does not contradict these two criteria of the new realist ontology, which is hardly surprising as it represents a realist theory. It combines objects from the FoS of physics, i.e. the metric distance between actors on the surface of the Earth (geographical distance), and objects from human sociality, i.e. the way humans verify soft information for which face-to-face interactions are still relevant. In line with the first criteria of the new realist ontology, the theory is able to be a true or false description of its FoS (bank-based SME lending). Only empirical investigation can tell and the context most likely matters. Furthermore, neither does the theory strand on distance and SME lending encompass a metaphysic claim (second criteria); i.e. it clearly restricts its explanatory power. Even in terms of its FoS, the theory only demands moderate explanatory power, and leading supporters highlight a range of other facts which matter for bank-based lending to SMEs (Alessandrini et al. 2009b). Therefore, a combined application with other theories causes no difficulties.

Based on this argumentation, the new realist ontology is shown to be a suitable ontological foundation for this work, allowing the utilisation of theories from both research traditions: the realist economic theories and the rather anti-realist SSoF theories. Importantly in this regard, Gabriel (2015) insists on not confusing new realist ontology with metaphysical theories and their claim to explaining everything. Rather, new realist ontology denies that a theory of everything exists and restricts its explanatory power to its FoS (ontology). Accordingly, new realist ontology demands plural theoretical work and empirical research. The following section discusses theories that help to conceptualise rating systems as non-human actors in the credit-granting processes of banks and critically analyses whether these theories conform to the new realist ontology.

2.3.2 Actor-network theory and non-human actors

ANT claims to be a radically different sociology (Latour 2005). As will be shown in the following, this heroic claim in fact contradicts the new realist ontology. Nevertheless, ANT offers a convincing conceptualisation of the power of non-human actors which is promising for understanding the agency of rating systems. Section 2.3.2.1 introduces and Section 2.3.2.2 critically appraises ANT and outlines a modified concept of non-human actors which accords with the new realist ontology.

2.3.2.1 Actor-network theory

ANT was developed by Latour, Callon and Law on the basis of the constructivist science and technology studies of the 1980s (Murdoch 2006; Kneer 2009a). Science and technology studies investigate labs and other research sites and reveal the social constitution of scientific knowledge; e.g. tactics, negotiation and hierarchies make up the knowledge production in labs rather than rational methods. While not denying this observation, ANT argues that this social constructivist perspective neglects the relevance of technology and nature, i.e. non-human entities, in science. Building on this, ANT conceives an ontology consisting of actor-networks in which non-human actors also act (Kneer 2009b). Human geographers use ANT from time to time, especially because it crosses the human-nature border of the discipline (e.g. Murdoch 1997, 2006; Burgess et al. 2000; Jöns 2003, 2007). Hence, Steiner (2014b) classifies ANT as a post-dualist theory.

In conformity to relational economic geography (Bathelt and Glückler 2003; Yeung 2005), ANT states that the capacity to act is not an inherent attribute of well-defined human actors, such as the CEO, the customer advisor etc., but rather depends on relations between the actors. Actors are only able to act in a network of several human and non-human entities (Jöns 2003; Kneer 2009a). In their professional and mundane practices, humans engage in variegated negotiation processes, i.e. relation building processes, with other humans and also non-human entities to establish a network which enables them to act. A stabilised and working network becomes visible to other actors as an integral whole; i.e. it appears to others as a black box with the inherent capacity to act and intermesh with further networks (see Figure 2.12).

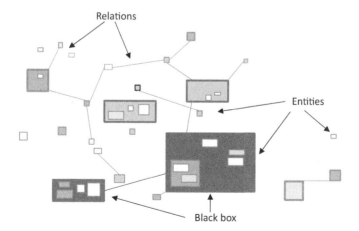

Figure 2.12 Actor-networks and black boxes

Source: Jöns 2003: 113 (translated and modified)

Jöns (2003) illustrates this process of negotiation, often termed 'translation' in ANT (Callon 1999), for the expansion of foreign banks in Hungary. She shows that not only the managers of banks and their strategies have affected the market expansion of foreign banks, but the availability of appropriate branches, technical infrastructure, cognitions about the regions, connectivity, distance to Budapest, trained bank employees and fitting branch managers etc. have also profoundly shaped the development of networks of foreign banks.

Building on the extended understanding of actors, for ANT "an actor is what is *made* to act by many others" (Latour 2005: 46). Therefore, ANT claims that all human and non-human entities are capable of becoming actors in certain network constellations. Importantly in this regard, ANT does not require intentionality of entities as a prerequisite to them becoming actors, thus rendering the actor concept reasonable. Callon's ([1987]1999) study of the scallops and fishermen of St. Brieuc Bay convincingly demonstrates what ANT is striving to achieve with its unusual understanding of actors.

In the study, Callon ([1987]1999) describes an actor-network in which scientists from France observed a scallop-breeding technique in Japan that uses specific devices, and wanted to apply this method in St. Brieuc Bay. A pilot study showed that some of the domestic scallops bred in these devices, and a scallop fishing stop was negotiated with the local fishermen. Henceforth, the scientists negotiated on behalf of the scallops and ascribed their function: 'Scallops want to breed in the devices'. Likewise, scientists negotiated and ascribed the function of the fishermen: 'Fishermen want to stop fishing so that the scallop population can grow in the devices and fishermen will fish more scallops in the future'. With this ascription, the fishermen and also the non-human scallops gained the power to act. In fact, in the second breeding period the scallops rejected their assigned function and did not breed in the devices again. The scientists tried to explain this, but as a consequence of the failure and due to rising scallop prices, the fishermen also rejected their function and started fishing. The actor-network of the scientists was broken.

ANT understands networks differently from the common use of the term in social network analysis etc. ANT networks represent a basic theoretical term referring to an association of entities (Kneer 2009a). All actors only act in actor-networks; e.g. a banker and his business suit already form an actor-network, as without appropriate clothing the banker cannot serve customers. So actor-networks capture the different relations, connections and ascriptions of heterogenic entities and develop through negotiation/translation. Actor-networks seemingly equate to the new realist ontology's concept of FoS. Yet, FoS tends to represent a more basic term as, for example, artwork and human fields of vision also represent FoS but are not seen as actor-networks in ANT. Hence, all actor-networks also tend to count as FoS but not all FoS count as actor-networks.

ANT is in fact not a theory but rather a methodology and ontology (Kneer 2009a, 2009b), as it demands researchers to follow and describe the actors and their actor-networks, rather than impose other (social) theories on them. To Latour (2005), humans have theories of the world, and therefore social science's task cannot be to impose on them yet another theory of the world. Hence, for ANT persuasive empirical research must exactly describes all the links and processes of the actor-network under study. If the researcher fully describes the actor-network, she also explains it. ANT demands empirical research to follow three principles (Kneer 2009a: 20–21):

1 Extended neutrality: No primary fixation of identities (actors) and positions.
2 Free association: No fixation of entities; non-humans are also capable of becoming important actors.
3 Generalised symmetry: Natural, social and technical processes should be described with the same uniform language; i.e. researchers shall not explain the behaviour of non-human actors with different theories to those they use for human actors.

As to ANT, everything consists of actor-networks; space is constituted by actor-networks as well (Murdoch 2006). Spatial configurations, e.g. centre and periphery, are made by connecting entities at different sites into the actor-networks through the process of negotiation/translation:

> [The] length of network determines scale – some networks remain tied to what we would normally see as local areas, other extends in a 'global' configuration. The networks stabilize spatial relations using a range of resources, assembled in ways that allow the flow of knowledge, materials, personnel and so forth up and down the network from the centre outwards.
>
> (Murdoch 2006: 72).

Building and keeping actor-networks across sites allows acting at a distance (Latour 1987, cited in Murdoch 2006). Latour's (1987) example of Pasteur's discovery of anthrax and the development of vaccination and implementation of it on French farms illustrates how Pasteur's lab became the centre and the farms the periphery at which Pasteur acted at a distance (Murdoch 2006). In a similar way centralised banks manage to assemble and extend actor-networks which tie local branches to the headquarters.

2.3.2.2 *Critical appraisal of actor-network theory: things, dynamic hybrids, thoughts*

A range of scholars criticise ANT (for an overview see Kneer 2009a, 2009b), which is hardly surprising considering its heroic claim to be a radically different sociology. This section discusses four key objections toward ANT and the handling of this critique which motivates ANT's restrictive use for this investigation.

ANT receives polemic criticism for its unusual assumption that things act intentionally and have a soul (Kneer 2009b). The previous section has already clarified that vitality and intentionality are not necessary for non-human actors to shape actor-networks because of ascriptions by humans. Scholars also criticise ANT for its explanatory ambition and accuse ANT of being a metaphysic theory (Murdoch 1997; Kneer 2009b). Kneer (2009b) argues that ANT wants to find out how and by which entities reality itself is really constituted. This claim to be a holistic theory capable of explaining everything is metaphysic. Furthermore, in ANT's attempt to identify the all-embracing order of the world it only uses social scientific methods and conducts secondary analysis of reality descriptions from the natural sciences with the methods of social sciences. Thus, from the perspective of the new realist ontology, ANT rejects the notion of multiplicity FoS and epistemological plurality but rather demands the application of qualitative social scientific methods in line with its generalised symmetry principle.

From the viewpoint of the new realist ontology, the metaphysic critique cannot be rejected. Rather it appears that Latour's (2005) 'new sociology' goes far beyond the object. What does ANT lose if it restricts its research interest to the realm of the social, e.g. to the question of how (parts of) society are constituted? This does not deny the importance of non-human entities for the constitution of social organisations and processes. It only implies excluding the question of why non-humans act as they act and leaves this question to the natural sciences (in conformity with the FoS concept of the new realist ontology). The study in hand applies such a restricted understanding of ANT and therefore does not describe the computer networks of banks in the empirical discussion, for instance.

Another critique of ANT is its negligence of mental entities such as thoughts, memory, feelings etc. (Jöns 2003). In this regard Kneer 2009b criticises the postulate of symmetry between human and non-human actors, as intuitively humans tend to be more active in actor-network creation. Jöns (2003, 2006) proposes a simple and persuasive modification to ANT on the basis of her empirical study of banking in Hungary. Succinctly expressed, she suggests modifying ANT's dualism of humans and non-humans to a trinity by including immaterial entities (Figure 2.13). Furthermore, the symmetric principle of ANT is changed, because humans have an asymmetric capacity as they translate between material and immaterial entities. They read signs (e.g. letters on a paper) and translate them into thoughts, or they produce things according to their thoughts (e.g. form physical things following their imaginations). Because animals and machines also have the capability to read signs and also act accordingly (e.g. computers), Jöns (2003) names all actors with the ability to translate between material and mental entities *dynamic hybrids*. For Jöns (2003), humans are the most complex dynamic hybrids in the known world; at present, animals, robots and computers only possess the capacity to conduct less complex translations between material and immaterial entities.

One final criticism of ANT relates to its methodological programme (Jöns 2003; Kneer 2009b). The demand for extended neutrality tends to be unrealistic (Kneer 2009b), because it would imply that ANT researchers are capable of observing actor-networks from a neutral and privileged observer position. A range of scholars have rejected the ability of researchers to gain this privileged observer position (Rose 1997). ANT's demand that all links of an actor-network should be followed amplifies this problem (Jöns 2003), as time, budget and cognitive constraints frustrate this empirical approach in a typical research project (Murdoch

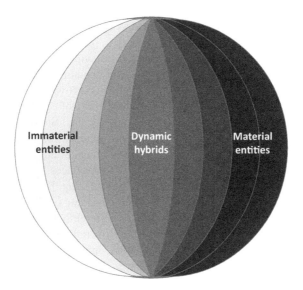

Figure 2.13 Trinity of actors

Source: Jöns 2006: 573. Acknowledgement of the permission to use copyright material by Taylor & Francis Ltd, www.tandfonline.com from Jöns, H. (2006) Dynamic hybrids and the geographies of technoscience: discussing conceptual resources beyond the human/non-human binary. In: *Social & Cultural Geography*, 7 (4), pp. 559–580.

1997). The difficult feasibility of ANT's empirical approach, together with the rejection of any theory-based assumptions, gives rise to the danger of reporting random observations and drawing poor conclusions from empirical snippets. Murdoch (1997: 744) proposes "first-order approximations" for research projects, "that is, shorthand descriptions of the most significant relations and actions within the networks". In this context, beside mundane experiences, the empirical results of previous studies and theories guide research to identify "the most significant relations and actions" (Murdoch 1997: 744).

To sum up, to conceptualise bank credit-granting processes this study sticks to ANT and sees all organisations as actor-networks, consisting of associations between human and non-human which also give non-humans the capacity to act. Therefore, banks' lending divisions are actor-networks, which facilitate lending decisions and the monitoring of credits, and in which rating systems and other non-human actors can act because humans ascribe power to them. Depending on the length and connections of the actor-networks, banks conduct lending at different distances to their SME clients. However, in line with the new realist ontology and modifying ANT, this study rejects the postulate of generalised symmetry, but uses the asymmetric actor concept of Jöns (2003, 2006). In this light banks' rating systems differ from other things (e.g. the desk in an office) because – like human actors – they translate between material and immaterial entities.

2.3.3 Understanding rating systems[6]

The previous section has indicated the process by which rating systems become actors in banks' credit-granting actor-networks in general. However, as the section has also rejected ANT's claim of generalised symmetry on the basis of the new realist ontology, one still needs a theory that explains the actual 'behaviour' or effects of rating systems in banks' lending actor-networks. The SSoF, especially MacKenzie's (2006) theory on the performativity of economic theories and models, represent a promising conceptual basis for this. Similarly to ANT, the heterogeneous research tradition of SSoF refers to science and technology studies and analyses the financial market and its actors, practices and techniques (Clark and Thrift 2005; Kalthoff 2009). Section 2.3.3.1 introduces MacKenzie's theory on the performativity of economics and discusses whether this rather constructivist theory accords with the new realist ontology. Building on this, Section 2.3.3.2 discusses in which way rating systems behave differently to human actors. Section 2.3.3.3 lists pros and cons of rating systems in credit decision processes, and Section 2.3.3.4 reviews studies that analyse the implementation and effects of rating systems in bank-based corporate finance.

2.3.3.1 The theory on the performativity of economic models

MacKenzie (2006: 12) claims that economics constitutes rather than researches the economy. MacKenzie and Millo's (2003) study of the Chicago mercantile exchange, option pricing and the Black-Scholes option price model evidently justifies this claim. The Black-Scholes model calculates option prices in relation to the underlying stock prices. The economists Black, Scholes and Merton deducted the model on the basis of (unrealistic) assumptions. MacKenzie and Millo's (2003) study shows that initially the option price model was not particularly good at predicting the actual prices at the option markets; however, its usage by market practitioners in arbitrage changed the prices in the way the model had predicted. MacKenzie (2006) names such a development 'Barnesian' performativity. With the (option) market crash of 1987 the conformity of actual and model prices was eventually destroyed, as market practitioners stopped using simple model results for trading. Consequently, the 'Barnesian' performativity of the Black-Scholes models ended (MacKenzie 2006).

For MacKenzie (2006: 19), 'Barnesian' performativity only makes up one subset of his classification concerning how economics becomes incorporated into the economy (see Figure 2.14). All aspects of economics that not only academic economists but also practitioners of the economy (e.g. managers, supervisors) perform are called 'generic' performative. If this application has any effect on economic processes, i.e. if it makes a difference, then MacKenzie (2006: 18) names this 'effective' performativity. 'Barnesian' performativity differs from 'effective' performativity because it does not have any effect but the "processes are being altered in ways that bear on their conformity to the aspect of economics in question" (MacKenzie 2006: 18–19). As the term indicates, counterperformativity accounts

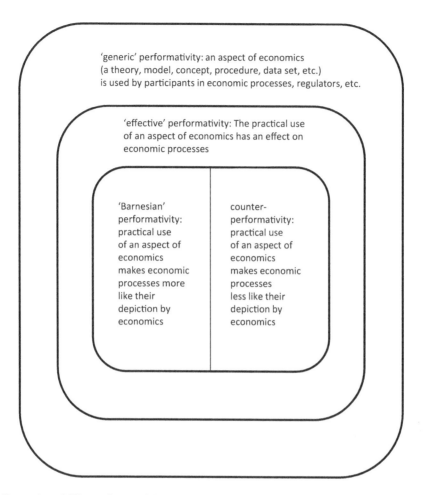

Figure 2.14 Different forms of the performativity of economics
Source: MacKenzie 2006: 17

for the conversion of 'Barnesian' performativity and means "that the effect of the practical use of a theory or model may be to alter economic processes so that they conform less well to the theory or model" (MacKenzie 2006: 19). 'Barnesian' performativity and counterperformativity count as strong meanings of performativity, as they alter economic results in the way (or contrary to the way) that the theories/models depict because of the model depiction (MacKenzie 2006: 24).

Rating models are prone to performative effects (Róna-Tas and Hiß 2008; Poon 2007) as banks and other financial actors rely heavily on rating models to predict the probability of default (PD), e.g. the likelihood that a firm fails to fulfil its liabilities within the following year. With their prediction of PD, rating models are capable of causing strong performative effects if they systematically over- or underestimate the actual default probability of firms. If a rating model calculates a poor rating score (PD) for a firm, then the bank of the firm in question tends to restrict lending as it expects a high likelihood of firm default. This, in turn, causes a liquidity shortage for the firm, and hence can cause a failure to pay liabilities (e.g. interest and principals). If the firm only fails because of the poor rating score and the following reduction of credits, the rating score causes 'Barnesian' performativity.

Figure 2.15 illustrates this for firms in crisis. With a strengthening of the crisis the probability of actual firm default increases (lower curve in Figure 2.15). The bank's rating model detects the firm's crisis; i.e. the rating score decreases as the crisis increases. If the model's rating score overestimates the firm's crisis, i.e. the firm's PD, and the bank acts accordingly and cuts the credit lines more radically than it would have done if aware of the actual default likelihood; this can actually cause the firm's failure to fulfil its liabilities (upper curve in Figure 2.15). The difference between the upper and lower curves make up the effect of 'Barnesian' performativity.

Counterperformativity arises, for example, if the rating model is so important for credit decisions that users manipulate the inputs of the model to gain a better rating score without reducing the true PD of firms. In this case, the bank grants loans that would not have been granted if the bank had known the actual risk of firm default (Figure 2.16). Thus, the predictive power of the rating models becomes undermined; i.e. the rating model underestimates the risk precisely because it is used in actual economic processes, as else model users would have had no incentive to manipulate the model inputs. Empirical studies document counterperformativity in the US subprime mortgage crisis. Here consumers manipulated their so-called FICO score (the main consumer credit risk model in the USA) and obtained credits which downgraded the predictive power of the FICO model (Róna-Tas and Hiß 2008; Rajan et al. 2010).

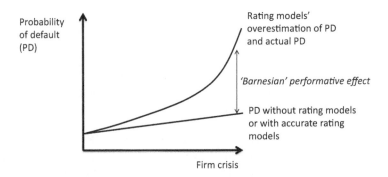

Figure 2.15 Rating models and 'Barnesian' performativity

Source: author's figure

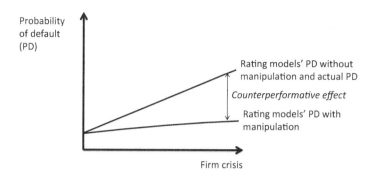

Figure 2.16 Rating models and counterperformativity

Source: author's figure

Turning to the new realist ontology, does the theory of the performativity of economics conform or rather conflict with this ontology? As explained above, the theory states that theories/models are capable of influencing actual market results with their depictions; e.g. 'Barnesian' performativity alters the actual market results in the way the model has depicted (upper curve in Figure 2.15). This, in turn, implies the existence of a possible market result independent of the model depiction (lower curve in Figure 2.15), as else there cannot be a 'Barnesian' performative effect (see also Svetlova 2012).[9] Hence, MacKenzie's theory on the performativity of economics requires the existence of both possible market results independent of the model and the model's depiction of market results that causes strong performativity. This requirement precisely conforms with the ontological claim of the new realist ontology. In fact, on the one hand, radical constructivist positions appear insufficient because they fail to capture the true existence of possible market results without model intervention, i.e. the market results as an effect of actual economic processes minus the model's performative effect (lower curve in Figure 2.15). On the other hand, material metaphysic worldviews are likewise insufficient because they tend to deny the existence of human perspectives on the world (i.e. theories/models) that are capable of causing 'Barnesian' performativity. Thus, for example, they deny that economic models not only describe economic processes but also manage to alter them.

In this context, MacKenzie (2006: 21ff) acknowledges the profound empirical difficulties that the comparison between 'actual market results', 'possible market results without model usage', and the 'model's prediction of market results' causes:

> It is therefore tempting to set the issue aside, and to abandon the strongest meanings of performativity (Barnesian performativity and counterperformativity). However, to do that would involve also abandoning a central

question: Has finance theory helped to create the world it posited – for example, a world that has been altered to conform better to the theory's initially unrealistic assumptions?

(MacKenzie 2006: 24)

In this regard Svetlova (2012) argues that strong performativity only rarely occurs and its occurrence depends on the institutional integration of the model into business practices (see also MacKenzie 2011). This argument does not oppose MacKenzie's performativity theory as the theory only claims that economic models can (not must) become strongly performative in the economy. Thus, MacKenzie's theory on the performativity of economics advances only moderate claims on its FoS (the use of economic models in the economy) and therefore also conforms with the second criteria of the new realist ontology. Whether an economic theory becomes strongly performative or not is an empirical question, and certainly not an easy one.

2.3.3.2 Why rating systems differ from human actors

Rating systems and credit scoring[10] have been a topic in geography for some time now (Leyshon and Thrift 1999; Leyshon and Pollard 2000; Pieper 2005; Gärtner and Flögel 2013; Zademach 2014), because they transform the geography of knowledge generation in banking. Leyshon and Thrift (1999: 434) state:

> The most significant development [. . .] has been the now routine use of credit-scoring systems, which are designed to overcome the chronic problems of information asymmetries in the industry and to distinguish 'good' from 'bad' customers 'at-a-distance'. The use of credit-scoring systems [. . .] represents a major transformation in the knowledge base of the industry.

Referring to ANT, Leyshon and Thrift (1999: 441) further argue that the 'obligatory passage point' to gain access to credits has changed from the face-to-face interview with the customer advisors of banks to the rating systems. In opposition to this view one could state that rating systems and other calculative assessment techniques standardise and accelerate (credit) decisions. Yet, this decision would otherwise have been conducted in similar way manually; i.e. rating systems just replace the manual work of bank clerks. Thus, in either way the management of the banks conduct the credit decision by setting the lending standards and policies. Against this background, four aspects are discussed which tend to explain why the use of computer-based rating systems differs from traditional (manual) risk analysis.

Firstly, rating systems prearrange credit decisions in a powerful way (Poon 2007); users have very limited possibilities to influence the results of the rating. Thus, rating systems are distant actors in the credit decision processes. The algorithms of the rating systems – implemented in the rating software programmes – define what data are input to the ratings, i.e. what information matter to evaluate the firms and how these data are assessed, weighted and consolidated. In this context, rating software tends to 'freeze' and hide decisions:

> Software is [. . .] "frozen organisational discourse" because the "arguments, decisions, uncertainties and processual nature of decision-making are hidden away inside a piece of technology or in a complex representation. Thus values, opinions, and rhetoric are frozen into codes, electronic thresholds and computer applications".
>
> (Bowker and Star 1994: 187, cited in Leyshon and Thrift 1999: 441)

Therefore, bankers' interactions with rating systems differ strikingly from interactions with humans. In traditional credit evaluation processes the customer advisors write reports, stress and downplay different aspects and negotiate the credit decisions with their supervisors. Evaluating a firm with a rating system suppresses such individual negotiations and hinders flexible case-based assessments.

If banks only consider the rating scores for credit decisions and rating systems do not permit the input of soft information, then banks conduct credit decisions almost totally remote from the local customer advisors and clients. Local staff poorly execute the collection of predetermined information and have hardly any decision-making power. Therefore, rating systems enable acting to take effect at a distance and reduces the local decision-making authority of bank employees (Leyshon and Thrift 1999). However, in the SME segment of ordinary banks, rating systems do not totally determine credit decisions (Kalthoff 2003; Svetlova 2012) and also permit the input of soft information and individual adjustments of the rating scores to a certain degree (Theis 2009; Sparkassen Rating and Risikosysteme GmbH 2010). Therefore, the usage of rating systems per se does not inevitably cause distant credit decisions but only has the tendency to centralise lending. It is important to note that rating systems also centralise the credit decisions of regional independent banks. All regional German savings and cooperative banks use the centrally developed and maintained rating systems of their financial groups (Theis 2009; Sparkassen Rating and Risikosysteme GmbH 2010). Therefore, neither the customer advisors nor the CEOs of these regional independent banks possess the power to change the algorithms of the rating systems they use. In this way rating systems tend to lengthen the functional distance of the credit decisions of regional banks despite their regional independence.

Secondly, rating systems not only centralise credit decisions, they also extend the information base of local credit decisions to the whole bank (Leyshon and Thrift 1999) or banking group in the case of the German savings and cooperative banks. This happens because banks' rating algorithms are developed empirically (Hartmann-Wendels et al. 2010). Banks use their customer databases to determine – with multivariate statistical methods like discrimination analysis – what data count in the rating process and how it is weighted (see Box 4.6, p. 183). In this way the memory of rating systems by far exceeds the memory of any humans involved in lending processes. Whereas bank employees assess customers on the basis of past experiences, rating systems assess customers against all customers of the banks of the same customer class. Therefore, the use of rating systems extends the information base of local credit decisions to the whole bank. However, this extension remains restricted to class-based evaluation only because of the technical limits to quantitative analysis.

Thirdly, the technical limitation of rating systems to quantitative analysis restricts information input to codified information and numerical data. This does not mean that soft information is ruled out (Altman et al. 2010; Liberti and Mian 2009; Hartmann-Wendels et al. 2010). With questionnaires, e.g. Likert scales, bank employees feed rating systems with soft information. Complex knowledge and information with uncertain effects, i.e. information where the impact on the PD is uncertain, can hardly be considered in rating algorithms at all. Despite these difficulties, rating systems are in principle capable of transmitting soft information across distance by considering codified soft information from customer advisors' evaluation in their algorithms. However, as soft information is per definition not easily verifiable by actors other than the actors who have created it, hardening soft information remains prone to manipulation, which tends to limit its consideration in rating systems.

Fourthly, several empirical studies highlight that rating systems and other standardised assessment techniques are popular in finance because they (conjecturally) objectify and legitimise decisions (Vopel 1999; Lo 2003; Kalthoff 2003; Mackenzie and Millo 2003; Hall 2006). Hence, bank employees have an incentive to delegate the responsibility for credit decisions, and thus also for wrong credit decisions, to the rating systems. In this way rating systems possess the tendency to become 'effective' performative even if banks do not allocate decision-making power to the rating scores at all, e.g. not define a rating score cutoff limit.

2.3.3.3 Pros and cons of rating systems for credit decisions

Banks' screening and monitoring of customers is costly. Processing costs and costs for faulty credit decisions arise (type 2 error). The application of rating systems for screening and monitoring has several advantages and disadvantages (Table 2.4). Cost-efficiency and speed represent the two main advantages of rating systems. Furthermore, the execution of rating systems requires less-skilled staff than manual customer evaluations. As the previous section explains, rating systems enable remote credit decisions, as the setting of the rating algorithms and the specification of cutoff limits appoint credit decisions. For example, if management wants to reduce the default rate in the loan book, then they just increase score-based cutoff limits (tighten the minimum rating score at which lending is allowed). Remote credit decisions also effectively hamper prejudice and cronyism. In this regard, access to finance for diverse social groups (social groups other than the white middle-class male bankers) eases with the introduction of private credit scoring (Leyshon and Thrift 1999). Considering these pros of rating systems, especially cost-efficiency, speed and remote control, it is not surprising that rating systems have become standard in the modern banking industry (Riese 2006).

Table 2.4 Pros and cons of rating systems

Pros	Cons
• Cost-efficiency and speed • Easy credit decision, less-skilled staff needed • Enables remote credit decisions; i.e. bank's management is able to set credit granting • Uses extended information base of banks • Objective credit decisions free of prejudice and cronyism	• Poor credit decisions because of missing variables • Risk of endogeneity ('Barnesian' performativity) • Risk of reactivity, i.e. gaming the system (counterperformativity) • Unobserved errors and their acceleration, e.g. underestimated correlation • Causing aligned action

Source: author's composition following Róna-Tas and Hiß 2008; Leyshon and Thrift 1999; Hellwig 2008; MacKenzie 2006

The disadvantages of rating systems are partly explained with reference to the performativity of economic models. Rating systems define what data are relevant for the evaluation of firms. Soft information and difficult-to-codify knowledge can hardly be respected in quantitative ratings; hence, the likelihood of poor credit decisions due to missing variables increases. Scholars have well documented this problem for the US subprime mortgage crisis where banks only considered very few variables in the securitisation of mortgages (e.g. FICO score), which led to a degradation of debtor quality (Róna-Tas and Hiß 2008; Rajan et al. 2010).

Related to this is the problem of counterperformativity, i.e. the manipulation of rating execution. Róna-Tas and Hiß (2008) give an illustrative description of how consumers manipulate the FICO score. Similarly, Berg et al. (2013) show for the private customer segment of a large German bank (analysing their rating database) that customer advisors manipulate the input of soft information to achieve rating scores above the cutoff limit of this bank; i.e. customer advisors "use multiple trails to move loans over the cut-off" (Berg et al. 2013: 1). This susceptibility to manipulation is shown to be a critical aspect of rating systems in general as the more power banks dedicate to rating scores the more worthwhile it is to manipulate the rating results (Svetlova 2012; Carruthers 2013). In a similar vein, if banks allocate very high decision-making power to the rating scores, the rating systems also have the tendency to become 'Barnesian' performative, as explained in Section 2.3.3.1.

Finally, on a more general level, the financial crisis has demonstrated how financial models guided action on financial markets – where ratings play a key role – causing aligned action with disastrous effects on the system's overall stability (Arnoldi 2009; Brunnermeier et al. 2009; Stiglitz 2010; Haldane and May 2011; Lockwood 2015). This effect is especially pronounced if unobserved errors steal into the algorithms/models, so that the actors of the financial markets systematically ill-evaluate risk. One such error which provoked the financial crisis was the systematic underestimation of PD correlation between different classes of assets (Hellwig 2008; MacKenzie 2011), i.e. the overestimation of the risk reduction effects of diversification. Considering these unfavourable effects of financial models in the financial crisis, it is interesting to note that models in fact became even more important after the crisis in an attempt to prevent a new crisis (Köhler and Bastian 22.09.2011).

2.3.3.4 Banks' use of rating systems and other models: empirical studies

This section reviews key studies of banks' implementation of rating systems and other quantitative models in organisational practice and discusses the extent to which rating systems determine corporate credit decisions. A range of studies show that banks use rating systems in SME finance (Berger et al. 2011; Behr et al. 2013). However, these studies cannot answer the extent to which rating systems determine banks' decisions. Some predominantly qualitative studies analyse this question for different segments of modern banking.

Using ethnography, Kalthoff (2003) discusses the use of quantitative models in banking. He studied the Eastern European expansion of Western European banks from the perspective of SSoF. Kalthoff (2003, 2005) conducted extensive and repeated participant observation at branches of a large bank from 1997 to 2001 where he observed the work of the corporate customer department (back office) in Warsaw (Poland). He reports that the corporate customer rating system did not have great influence on the actual credit decisions; i.e. credit decisions were conducted before the bankers executed the rating process. However, the rating scores document the credit risks and influence the terms of credits. Furthermore, Kalthoff (2003: 276ff) identified two important rules about how bank employees from different departments and hierarchical levels negotiate credit decisions. Firstly, the bank employees do not doubt the results of standardised analysis methods like balance sheet analysis but assume that the results are correct. Secondly, every employee involved in the credit decision has the right to communicate different opinions (and document them in the credit applications). However, the enforcement of arguments tends to be governed by hierarchy; i.e. at the end of the day the supervisors decide.

Svetlova (2012) presents an ethnographic study of two portfolio management departments of banks based in Frankfurt and Zurich and examines their use of discounted cash-flow (DCF) models. She shows that models do not determine decisions, "instead, [decisions] are the results of the enrichment of the model by 'other things, i.e. other significant factors that cannot be captured by the model" (Svetlova 2012: 430). Consequently, the 'culture' of model use also influences the likelihood that models become 'Barnesian' performative. Svetlova (2012: 423) calls for more research on the use of models in decision making: "Both poles of the spectrum – where models dominate and where human judgements prevail – should be investigated in more details".

Deakins et al. (2010) analyse the SME credit decision processes of banks in Scotland. They deduced five cases of credit applications by real firms and asked the customer advisors of different banks in qualitative interviews how their banks would decide these cases. Deakins et al. (2010) report that the customer advisors have discretion in credit decision making, so the sector as well as the geographical location influence credit decisions; i.e. operational distance negatively impacts the likelihood of gaining a credit. Furthermore, according to their findings customer advisors devote more effort to granting additional credits to existing customers rather than to new customers. In this context, customer advisors possess the highest discretion for medium-sized loans because banks decide small credits (ca. £50,000) using standardised credit scorings which limits advisors' influence. At the other end, the supervisors at the headquarters decide on large credits; hence, customer advisors also have limited means to influence such lending.

Hall (2006) describes the shift to quantitative models in corporate finance as a reaction to the uncertainty induced in London's banking market by the burst of the dot.com bubble: "London's corporate finance community constructed a rhetoric around the numbers and formulae that lie at the heart of quantitative financial narratives that valued them as more objective, accountable and accurate than words" (15). The shift to quantitative models, like DCF, reduced but did not totally substitute the qualitative evaluation of large corporate customers. Accordingly, face-to-face meetings of analysts with the management of the corporations have become less frequent.

Hesse et al. (2012) conducted a standardised survey of the organisational design of key credit-monitoring aspects of German savings banks. The study indicates relevant differences in the process organisation of the savings banks. The handling of critical customers differs, some savings banks redirect clients with non-performing loans to the restructuring and workout team early on, others keep such clients in the portfolio of their ordinary customer advisors. Using econometrical methods, the study finds that savings banks which use the latter organisation make less allowance for losses, thus keeping customers with their ordinary customer advisors tends to reduce losses. Hesse et al. (2012) suggest that this result can be explained by customer advisors' soft information which is used for a successful restructuring process. Furthermore, lower disclosure limits – i.e. if customers with relatively small credit volumes have to disclose financial statements – reduce non-performing loans. Interestingly, differences in the arrangements of banks' standardised early warning systems have no impact on bad debt.

In their survey and qualitative case studies, Breisig et al. (2010) highlight the impact of the controlling and incentive systems of banks on customer advisors' behaviour and document that German savings and cooperative banks also use standardised performance measurement systems. These systems reduce customer advisors' freedom of action as banks not only control for sales success but also for the activities of their customer advisors, e.g. the number of customer contacts.

In summary, Section 2.3.3 has conceptualised rating systems as actors in banks' credit-granting processes which differ from human actors because they are distant actors that extend the information base beyond the reach of human memory and restrict information to codifiable numerical data. The discussion of rating systems' pros and cons indicates a range of reasons for the use of rating systems in banking. However, various disadvantages potentially arise depending on the integration of rating systems for credit screening and monitoring. In this context, the susceptibility of rating systems to performative effects depends on the decision-making power banks delegate to the rating scores. The reviewed empirical studies demonstrate the importance of rating systems and other quantitative methods for modern banks and indicate that differences in their usage exist. Therefore, any comparison of banks' lending practices must consider the context, i.e. explicate the market segment, time, national and regional context, to avoid comparing apples with oranges.

2.4 Spot the differences: approaching distance in bank-based SME lending

Chapter 2 has argued that distance impacts banks' lending to SMEs, as long distance hinders the consideration of soft information for risk analysis and credit decisions. Because regional banks tend to decide at shorter organisational and functional distances than large banks, they are considered to be superior in financing enterprises, especially when lending to informationally opaque SMEs. However, several (geographical) studies highlight that short geographical distance is neither necessary nor sufficient to ease information transmission. Furthermore, bank regulation, ICT advantages and especially the extensive use of centralised rating systems seem to undermine this argumentation. Therefore, Section 2.3 conceptually approaches rating systems as one actor of banks' credit-granting processes. This actor differs from human actors (asymmetric actor concept), but is nevertheless capable of influencing the credit-granting process. Against this background this study specifies distance of (credit) decision making with two variables:

V1: The percentage of decision-making power of all actors involved in the credit-granting process. This variable indicates the actors to whom the relevant (soft) information of the SME must be transmitted. In this context, decision-making power is not an inherent attribute of actors, but banks' actor-networks relationally assign credit-granting power.

V2: The distance between all actors. This variable indicates the difficulty of soft information transmission and depends on non-metric aspects of proximity and geographical distance between actors.

The sum of V1 multiplied by V2 computes the total distance of credit decision to firms:

$$Total\ distance = \sum_{n}^{1} p_n \cdot d_n$$

p_n = percentage of actor (n)'s decision-making power (V1)
d_n = distance of actor (n) to SME customer (V2)

For example, if the customer advisor has full decision-making power ($p_1 = 100\%$) the distance between him and his SME customer determines the distance of the credit decision (Figure 2.17, no. 1). If his supervisor has full decision-making power ($p_2 = 100\%$), the distance between the customer advisor and the customer plus the distance between the customer advisor and the supervisor determines the distance of the credit decision (Figure 2.17, no. 2). If the customer advisor and the supervisor share decision-making power (e.g. $p_1 = p_2 = 50\%$), then decision-making power weights distance to both actors (Figure 2.17, no. 3).

Finally rating systems need to be placed as actors in this conceptualisation. Approaching V1 (p) is straightforward, because – like human actors – rating systems gain their decision-making power in relational assignments. Rating scores are able to determine credit decisions, e.g. if the lending policy of a bank proscribes credit granting to customers that have poor rating scores (hard cutoff limit). Banks can also ascribe little power to the rating scores, e.g. if a bank only uses the rating scores as orientation for the credit terms.

Approaching V2 (d) needs more conceptual work, because obviously geographical distance and non-metric aspects of proximity to the servers of the rating systems do not ease (soft) information transmission. Nevertheless, in the previous discussion on rating systems (Section 2.3.3) several aspects have been identified which indicate how bank employees manage to influence the rating scores. This study approaches the 'quasi-distance' between human actors and rating systems as the influenceability of rating scores by human inputs. Bank employees manage to influence rating scores in the credit-granting process in three ways:

- Firstly, humans influence the rating score with their input of soft information. The more the rating systems permit the input of soft information and the higher the weighting of this soft information, the stronger the influence of human judgments on the rating scores. For example, if customer advisors' judgments of CEO reliability accounts for 50% of the rating score, they can significantly manipulate the rating scores and use their soft information to influence lending decisions.
- Secondly, human actors are able to influence the rating algorithms by determining the weighting of the data. As will be shown in the empirical chapter, rating systems for SMEs permit the adapting of variable weighting, within limits, to indicate the relevancy of certain variables to firms' specifics. With these adaptations, bank employees manipulate the 'knowledge' of the rating systems comprised in the algorithms.
- Thirdly, as will be shown in the empirical chapter, rating systems for SMEs usually permit the manual changing of the rating scores within limits. In this way bank employees also directly influence rating results.

In the following chapter, the total distance of banks' credit decisions to SMEs is analysed by taking human actors and rating systems into consideration.

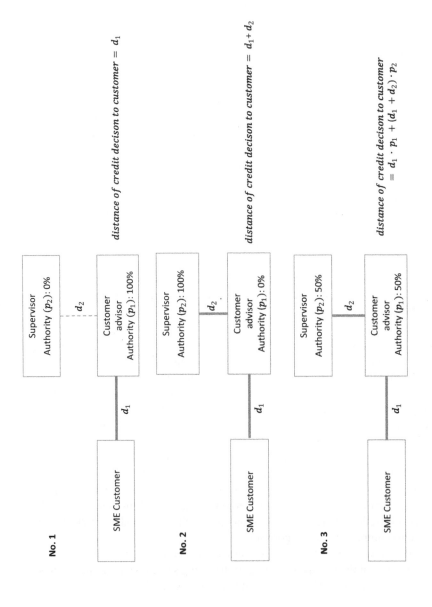

Figure 2.17 Total distance of the credit decision to the customer

Source: author's figure

Notes

1 The USA is not well represented with the indicators used by Hardie and Howarth (2013a) because the indicators do not capture parallel banking outside the commercial banking sector. This, however, accounts for a high share of lending.

2 For a definition and further explanation of hard and soft information see Section 2.2.2.1.

3 Gain of being informed with decentralisation $= 2 \cdot \Delta_2^d = (\frac{g(2) - g(1)}{2}) \cdot 2 >$ gain of being informed with hierarchy $= \Delta_4^h = \frac{(1-q)(g(2) - g(1))}{2} + 3\frac{q(g(2) - g(1))}{8}$ (see Stein 2002).

4 This function implies that division managers want to build 'empires' and try to receive as much capital for their units as possible (independent of the investment opportunities of their divisions). Once received, division managers prefer to invest the capital as profitably as possible.

5 Because $2 \cdot \Delta_2^d > \Delta_4^h$ and $p'(e) = \gamma/\Delta$ it follows $e_4^h < 2 \cdot e_2^d$ as p is increasing and concave, which means the additional likelihood of being informed decreases with every additional increase of effort (e). In other words, the division manager in a hierarchy would select a lower level of effort so that the cost of being informed (γe) does not outstrip the lower gains of being informed (Δ).

6 Parts of this section are published in Flögel (2015). De Gruyter *Zeitschrift für Wirtschaftsgeographie*, Walter De Gruyter GmbH Berlin Boston, 2015. Copyright and all rights reserved. Material from this publication has been used with the permission of Walter De Gruyter GmbH.

7 A proper property is a property where reference to this property puts one in a position to distinguish one object in a domain from another (Gabriel 2015: 43).

8 Importantly, the new realist ontology does not deny that empirical findings about some FoS can be false. However, "fallibility alone does not generalise to any form of scepticism or radical doubt. It just means that there are all sorts of conditions of failure" (Gabriel 2015: 321).

9 Svetlova (2012: 419) interprets MacKenzie's performativity theory in this way: "The application of financial models not only informs and influences professional practices (generic and effective performativity) but also shapes markets by creating (or increasing) a fit between the real (market) world and the model world (Barnesian performativity)".

10 Banks' credit scoring differs from banks' rating systems for firms in that scoring is normally highly automated and banks conduct scoring on demand for new credit decisions. In contrast to this, banks execute firm ratings annually for credit-monitoring purposes.

3 The German banking system

Methods and case descriptions

3.1 Methodology

This section explains and justifies the empirical approach applied to compare the credit-granting processes of regional and large banks. Section 3.1.1 describes ethnography and justifies its selection as a methodology. Section 3.1.2 presents the key methods applied, interviews and participant observation. Section 3.1.3 explains the nomenclature of the empirical data. Based on the empirical data, Section 3.1.4 discusses personality, i.e. the way in which the researcher influences the results of the study, and outlines the data analysis process and the data representation.

3.1.1 Ethnography

Ethnography is understood as the "recording and analysis of a culture or society, resulting in a written account of a people, place or institution" (Coleman and Simpson 2016). Most closely associated with participant observation and in-depth engagement with specific communities (Hart 2009), the methodology of ethnology is not restricted to observations (Müller 2012). Rather ethnography demands an opportunity-driven use of methods (Breidenstein et al. 2013). Müller (2012: 179) compares ethnographers to 'sniffer dogs' or discreet detectives interested in all kinds of details. Breidenstein et al. (2013) specify four characteristics of ethnography (see Figure 3.1):

- Firstly, the research object of ethnography is social practices in the sphere of public lived sociality. Neither people's individual biographies nor demography, i.e. the study of larger societies, are suitable for ethnographical inquiries. Ethnography tends to consider everything at once – the language, underlining academic and popular discourse; cognitive schemata; situated practices; institutions and material culture – that is present in the situation of social interaction under study.
- Secondly, ethnography is field research. The researcher should be present at the sites where the social interactions take place and should even involve herself or himself in the social interactions on these sites to discover and feel the structures and conditions there.
- Thirdly, ethnography advises an opportunity-driven use of methods. The circumstances in the research field influence the methods ethnographers apply

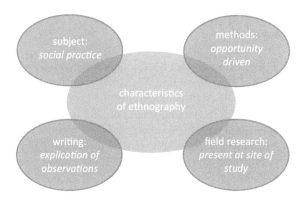

Figure 3.1 Characteristics of ethnography
Source: Breidenstein et al. 2013: 32 (translated and modified)

and what kind of data they collect. Writing ethnographies usually involves a combination of different types of data.

• Fourthly, the writing practices characterise ethnography. Ethnographers transfer observations of social situations that have not been explicated before into written text. Therefore, they produce new and variegating knowledge; i.e. they create a new representation of their research objects.

Ethnography is increasingly used in economics and economic geography (see Box 3.1). In contrast to 'classical' anthropological and sociological studies, ethnographies in geography tend to investigate specific phenomena rather than social groups. Geographers analyse the assembling of markets (Cook et al. 2004; Ouma 2015) or the application of models in real estate markets (Ouma and Bläser 2015) and conduct multi-site analyses to follow the phenomena (Cook et al. 2004; Hart 2009). The study in hand also applied ethnography in this phenomenon-oriented way and conducted multi-site ethnography because banks' credit-granting processes happen at several sites.

ANT indicates the selection of ethnography as the methodology for this empirical comparison. The study aims to analyse and compare banks' actor-networks, which conduct the credit-granting processes. To ANT, the relations and ascriptions of actors constitute action, and researchers best understand action from within the actor-network. Thus, being as close as possible to all relevant actors and their positions in the actor-network is indispensable to understanding how actors are "made to act by many others" (Latour 2005: 46). This position exactly meets the key methodological justification of ethnography:

Basically the co-presence of the observer with the action is suggested because of two assumptions: the assumption that sociality mainly happens in *situations* and the assumption that participants in the situation have privileged access to the social relevancies *of a situation*.

(Breidenstein et al. 2013: 41 [translated])

Box 3.1   Ethnography in economics and economic geography

The ethnographical tradition goes back to anthropological studies on less well-known tribes (e.g. Malinowski 1979 [1922]), further developed in the Chicago school, as well as to ethnographies of everyday life (e.g. Goffman (1969 [1959], cited in Breidenstein et al. 2013). Whereas these studies were less concerned with the modern economy, a range of sociologists and anthropologists conducted ethnographies of contemporary capitalism (Miller 2004 [1998]) and firms (Kalthoff 2003; for an overview see Fendo 2009). Currently ethnography is becoming increasingly popular in economics (Fendo 2009) and (cultural) economic geography (Cook et al. 2004; Franz 2010; Ouma 2010, 2012; Brinks 2012; Bruns and Henn 2013). Several new textbooks (Crang and Cook 2007; Breidenstein et al. 2013) and a special issue (Müller 2012) also document the increasing popularity of ethnography.

Therefore, ethnography is suitable to analyse the practices and processes of banks' lending. Furthermore, the application of ethnography in the context of the empirical study is advisable for reasons of feasibility. Banking tends to be a sensitive topic; i.e. banks' risk assessment and credit decision-making methods are commercially sensitive (Deakins et al. 2010), and bank secrecy prohibits the spread of information about banks' clients. Accordingly, gaining access to relevant actors (e.g. the customer advisors, supervisors, credit officers) was a key empirical challenge where the method opportunism of ethnography gives sufficient flexibility in the selection of methods.

3.1.2 Methods: interviews and participant observations

Doing ethnography usually implies using different data collection methods. Interviews and participant observations represent the key methods of this study. The empirical investigation started with problem-centred interviews in order to advance understanding of the banking sector and to gain access to the communities. Using the snowball sampling principle, interviews were conducted from April 2013 to February 2014. The investigation approached bank employees involved in every credit-granting stage and actors from organisations related to banking (banking education, banking supervision, banking consulting, banking associations). In line with ANT, the intention to follow the credit-granting processes guided the selection of interview partners; i.e. the interviewees were asked for contacts to actors they cooperate with in lending. To gain many varying perspectives, interviews were conducted with employees from different hierarchical levels, including 'ordinary' bank employees without managerial or other exposed functions.

The Appendix gives an overview of the interviews and other empirical data gained in the empirical investigation. For every problem-centred interview the interview guideline was altered because interview partners had different backgrounds and expertise. Furthermore, as understanding of the banking sector increased as the project advanced, some questions became redundant and were altered. Nevertheless, three basic elements – initial questions about the work/function of the interviewee, expert-specific questions and two final questions about relevant differences between savings and large banks and personal job satisfaction – formed the (unchanged) structure of every interview.

In total, 40 interviews have been conducted. Alongside 23 purposeful interviews (conducted for the sake of this project only), an additional 17 opportunity-driven interviews were held, partly in interviewing pairs with colleagues in the context of another research project (Gärtner and Flögel 2017). In these cases, interview guidelines respected the research questions of both projects. Furthermore, there were certain opportunities for ad hoc interviews, for instance at a practitioner conference. Spontaneity prevented the application of interview guidelines in these cases. The Appendix does not report on the ad hoc interviews conducted during participant observations because the observation protocols document their results. Two interviews took place as small focus group discussions with three and four interviewees. The average interview lasted 58 minutes, the shortest interviews took about 20 minutes and the longest lasted almost 2 hours. All but 3 of the 23 purposefully conducted interviews were taped and transcribed. Protocols document the 17 opportunity interviews. Three of the interviews were conducted via the telephone; the other 37 were held face-to-face. Most interviews took place in meeting rooms of the interviewees' organisations. The interview language was always German.

The research process of participant observation involves gaining access, getting an observer position, collecting data and exiting the field (Breidenstein et al. 2013). Applications were made for student internships at savings and large banks in order to gain access. One application was successful in a savings bank (savings bank 1), where a two-month full-time internship was conducted as a trainee from 5 November 2013 to 10 January 2014. In the following, the observer position and data collecting approach are described.

Even a relatively small savings bank comprises a range of departments and working groups, of which only a few are involved in lending to SMEs. Therefore, obtaining a fitting observer position which provided access to the relevant information was central, and multi-site observation advisable. Accordingly, the applications asked for an internship in the department where the SME customer advisors work and in addition politely suggested work in other departments, too (e.g. back offices, supervisor offices, bank controlling). Savings bank 1 openly responded to the request and enabled observation to be carried out in different working groups of the back-office department for 2 weeks, followed by a 1-month stay in an SME customer advisor team and a 13-day internship in the bank controlling department. Finding an observer position that allowed data collection proved to be unproblematic in two departments (customer advisor team and back-office department) because the human resources officer explained the research background and requested the colleagues to show and explain their work. Adjustments in the observer position were also possible; e.g. an office change allowed observation of the busiest room of the customer advisor team. Observations in the controlling department were more restricted due to a lack of communication about the research aim of the internship. The experience in the controlling department underlined the suitability of the observer positions in the other two departments studied.

Collecting and recording data is the purpose of participant observation and a sensitive issue (Girtler 2001; Mattissek et al. 2012). On the one hand, tape recording or taking notes tends to disturb the observed social situation or is forbidden. On the other hand, writing down observations afterwards always results in data losses. As banking secrecy precludes open recording, the participant observation applied the hidden recording approach of Girtler (2001). During working hours, activities focused on limited note-taking as far as the situation allowed. Just after finishing time (while commuting), all relevant observations of the day were recorded. The evening included the compilation of the daily protocols at the computer, under consideration of all handwritten notes of the day. The very early protocols consisted of key words, but formulating paragraphs proved easier and quickly superseded this approach. The scope of the daily protocols varies from ca. 200 to 1,300 words, and there are a total of 41 daily protocols.

As research questions were of a broad nature, a large proportion of the observations in the customer advisor and back-office teams of savings bank 1 were relevant. At the beginning of the internship, records included as many observations as possible because of uncertainty about which aspects could become relevant for the analysis. As knowledge evolved during observation, the focus shifted to specific aspects and open questions. Beside the observations themselves, the actors participating, the setting (e.g. where it took place) and the source of the observation were noted. In line with Girtler (2001), the daily protocols also report any striking tactics, motives or emotions of the actors. During the period of observation at savings bank 1 the research utilised six main data sources:

- Internal interactions and communications between bank employees as well as banker–customer interactions was a main data source. From time to time the bank employees explained their interactions or answered questions about them afterwards.
- The bank employees explained several processes and tasks while they conducted their routine work. In this context they allowed observation, the asking of questions and, where applicable, accepted help with their work.
- The bank employees gave ad hoc interviews, asked about the aim of the participant observation and answered questions regarding their work. Ad hoc

interviews with the team leaders were especially typical in the initial days in a new working group.
- The chats of the bankers, e.g. during the breakfast break, provided another data source if the topics of the conversations related to the job.
- A range of internal documents, e.g. official instructions, reports and process manuals, supplied very relevant data for understanding the credit-granting process.
- As mentioned above, the daily protocols also report the context, like the office furniture, outline of the offices and premises etc.

Smaller participant observations supplemented the participant observation at savings bank 1. Attendance at the undergraduate lecture series 'Banking and finance 1: financial risk management' by Prof. Paul and Dr. Schulte (CEO of a savings bank) at Ruhr University Bochum aided preparation for the interviews, as did attendance of an undergraduate introductory lecture at a prestigious German (financial) business school, following an interview. In addition, the *Kontaktseminar Wirtschaft* of the *Studienstiftung des deutschen Volkes* (i.e. the German National Academic Foundation) proved valuable. The *Kontaktseminar Wirtschaft* offers *Studienstiftung* fellows contacts to major employers through fictive job interviews. Two of these fictive job interviews with banking business consultancies provided contacts leading to four problem-centred interviews. Though these smaller participant observations are by-products, they nevertheless provided data worthy of consideration in the empirical analysis.

3.1.3 Nomenclature of the empirical data

This section explains the nomenclature of the empirical data. The Appendix lists all not publicly available qualitative empirical data used in this investigation and displays the key characteristics of these data. Beside the transcripts and protocols from the qualitative methods, the Appendix also comprises unpublished documents from the organisations under study. The Appendix does not list publicly available data, such as published documents, practitioner textbooks, internet sources etc., as they are quoted in the literature list. In exceptional cases, published documents of the organisations under study are not referenced in the literature list but listed in the Appendix in order to protect the anonymity of the organisations in question.

Table 3.1 explains the nomenclature of the qualitative empirical data. Cases refer to the banks studied. In this category, *SK* stands for savings banks (German: *Sparkasse*), *GB* for large banks (German: *Großbank*) and *Geno* for cooperative banks (German: *Genossenschaftsbank*). All data unrelated to a specific bank case are labelled with *O* for 'other'. For example, transcripts of interviews with business consultancies and banking associations belong to this group.

Department/Organisation indicates the department of the bank if the data relates to a bank. *BS* stands for bank controlling (German: *Bankensteuerung*), *M* stands for market or customer advisor department, and *MF* stands for back office

Table 3.1 Nomenclature of the empirical data

	Cases	Department/Organisation	Type of Data	Date	Number
Example:	SK1	BS	PP	02.01.14	
	Savings bank 1	Bank Controlling	Participant observation protocol		
Possible characteristics	SK1 Savings bank 1	M Market (e.g. customer advisor)	IT Interview transcript	Date of data collection	2 Equal labelling by chance
	SK2 Savings bank 2	MF Back Offices (risk analyst, administration market etc.)	IP Interview protocol		I First interview with the interview partner
	SK3 Savings bank 3		PP Participant observation protocol		II Second interview with the interview partner
	SK4 Savings bank 4	BS Bank Controlling (e.g. accounting, risk management, controlling)	D Document		
	GB1 Big bank 1				
	GB2 Big bank 2				
	GB3 Big bank 3	OB Other bank department			
	GB4 Big bank 4	BC Business consulting			
	Geno1 Cooperative bank 1	E Education (e.g. business school)			
	GenoZ cooperative central bank	SGV Savings banks organisation (e.g. association, academy)			
	O Other organisation (non-bank)	O Other			

Example: SK1 BSPP02.01.14

Source: author's compilation

(German: *Marktfolge*). *O* is used for all the other departments, e.g. the human resources department. If the data does not relate to any of the bank cases, then the type of organisation is stated. Other organisations are business consultancies (*BC*), educational institutes related to banking (*E*), savings banks organisations including savings banks academies (*SGV*) and others (*O*). The type of data indicates if the data is an interview transcript (*IT*), an interview protocol (*IP*), a protocol of a participant observation (*PP*), or a document (*D*). The date (dd.mm.yy) specifies when the data was collected/created, e.g. the date of interview.

In 12 cases the nomenclature states a number (2, I, II) behind the date. The number 2 indicates that by chance two empirical data have the same name, and was added to distinguish the data sources. Data from the same department/ organisation labelled with I and II indicates that a second interview was conducted with the same interview partner.

3.1.4 Reflexion on positionality and data analysis

The debate about the 'crisis of ethnographic representation' criticises traditional anthropological ethnographies (Clifford and Marcus 1986). Ethnographers do not describe social situations in an innocent way, but ascribe culture, beliefs and practices to the communities they study (Clifford and Marcus 1986; Breidenstein et al. 2013). Furthermore, traditional ethnographical accounts tend to be rich in othering or notification strategies; i.e. they make the observed community exotic or similar to their own community (Breidenstein et.al. 2013).[1] In this regard, from a constructivist perspective Mattissek et al. (2012) point out that research results never describe the observed situations in an objective way, but are always subjective and selective: "Consequently research results are techniques of specific constructions. The observation is influenced by the aims and beliefs of the observer" (154).

As Section 2.3.1 outlined, in conformity with the new realist ontology this work takes an optimistic perspective on humans' epistemological capacities. To pointedly recall the argumentation: New realist scholars accuse the constructivism to make one unexplained and (in the end) not justifiable assumption itself – the assumption that humans cannot sense facts/objects as they are. Whereas many examples for human delusions exist, in our everyday experiences this assumption tends to be artificial because people are able to agree on facts most of the time (Gabriel 2013; Ferraris 2014). Transferring this argumentation to participant observation implies the expectation that another researcher who is equipped with the same research questions and theoretical considerations would gain similar results if she repeats the participant observation and uses the same analysis methods. Whereas this study does not claim objectivity for the empirical results, it aims to gain inter-subjectivity, i.e. objectivity in its specific FoS. Accordingly, the ambition of the ethnography in hand is to represent the 'job reality' in the studied banks in a way that the employees feel represented accurately. Furthermore, other researchers should be able to retrace the results of this empirical work. To this end, the following section outlines the researcher's position in the research project

(Section 3.1.4.1), and Section 3.1.4.2 explicates the qualitative data analysis process and explains the presentation of results.

3.1.4.1 Researcher's positionality

Reflexion of the researcher's positionality is intended to avoid the 'god-trick', i.e. to avoid pretending that the researcher is able to see "everything from nowhere" (Rose 1997: 308; McDowell 1992). So outlining positionality aims to make a researcher's position in the research project – and influence on the results – known rather than invisible (Vira and James 2011; Mattissek et al. 2012). However, Rose (1997) also points out the difficulties of objectively and unambiguously understanding one's positionality in research, i.e. understanding one's power, motivations, blind spots and influences on the research process and results. The difficulty arises because – as ANT expresses it – neither agency nor identity of the researcher are fixed as inherent attributes but rather, like other actors, the researcher is entangled in numerous actor-networks that induce action.

Notwithstanding the difficulty of understanding positionality, it is imperative to make the researcher's position explicit to situate the production of ethnography (Vira and James 2011). So 'I need to introduce myself into this ethnographical study'. Born in the German Democratic Republic in 1985, a critical attitude toward real existing socialism and planned economies tends to influence my research interest in market economies. Beside human geography, I studied economics and political sciences. At the research department Special Capital (at the Institute for Work and Technology) where this study was compiled, a main research topic is regional savings banks. Accordingly, previous projects on savings banks have shaped the empirical approach used to compare regional and large banks. Social and financial connections with banks should also be mentioned. The Spatial Capital department received research grants for two projects from the Academic Sponsorship of the Savings Banks Financial Group. Contacts to the Academic Sponsorship helped to gain access to the savings banks. Owing to the PhD scholarship from the *Studienstiftung des deutschen Volkes*, this research project was conducted independently of any banking grant and was also less entangled in academia and work at the research department.

The observer position at savings banks 1 proved suitable to trace the credit-granting processes and allowed access to the mundane work of the bank. My presence in the working groups caused very limited irritation to the bank employees observed, despite the uncovered approach of the participant observation; i.e. all working groups were aware of the purpose of the internship. The support of the human resources department and the confidentiality agreement (see Box 3.2) explain the suitable observer position. Furthermore, the presence of observers is familiar for the bank employees as *Auszubildende*, or trainees, regularly work in the teams for a limited time. Savings bank 1 hires ca. four trainees who work in almost all working groups of the bank during their three-year training (SK1MFPP08.11.2013). Thus, explaining their work is a familiar activity for the bank employees observed.

Box 3.2 Banking secrecy

Bank secrecy is not specified in one specific law but regulated by several laws and contracts, such as the employment contract agreements between the banks and their employees. The tariff agreement of the savings banks regulates bank secrecy for all German savings banks. Its legal basis is the German federal data protection act (BDSG) and the data protection acts of the *Bundesländer*, or federal states (SK1DDatenschutz). Three types of data are governed by these secrecy regulations; the order ranks their importance:

1. Private and financial customer data (enacted by the § 5 BDSG, § 3 TVöD-S)
2. Data about the bank employees
3. Data related to the bank (e.g. risk and return figures, strategies, reports)

The data are to be protected against access by:

- Criminals
- Curious persons (e.g. neighbours, friends, family, ex-partner, etc.)
- Competitors of the bank

Accessing customer or employee data is only permitted if the conduct of the professional task demands this and bank secrecy also applies after the termination of employment at the bank (Figure 3.2).

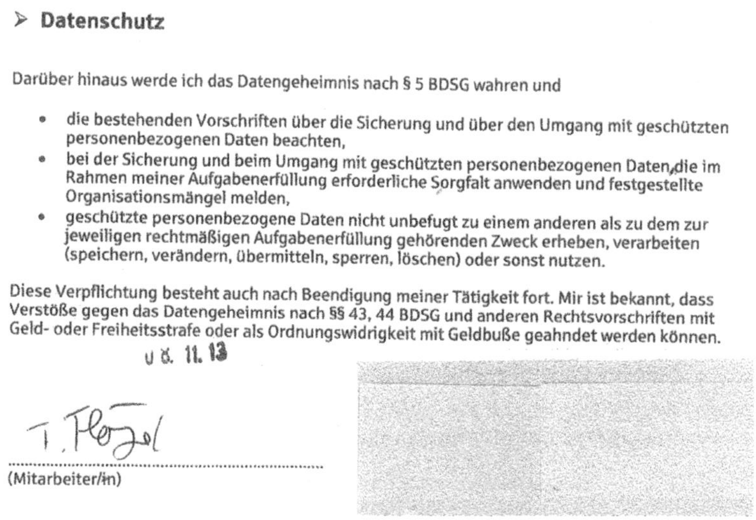

➢ **Datenschutz**

Darüber hinaus werde ich das Datengeheimnis nach § 5 BDSG wahren und

- die bestehenden Vorschriften über die Sicherung und über den Umgang mit geschützten personenbezogenen Daten beachten,
- bei der Sicherung und beim Umgang mit geschützten personenbezogenen Daten, die im Rahmen meiner Aufgabenerfüllung erforderliche Sorgfalt anwenden und festgestellte Organisationsmängel melden,
- geschützte personenbezogene Daten nicht unbefugt zu einem anderen als zu dem zur jeweiligen rechtmäßigen Aufgabenerfüllung gehörenden Zweck erheben, verarbeiten (speichern, verändern, übermitteln, sperren, löschen) oder sonst nutzen.

Diese Verpflichtung besteht auch nach Beendigung meiner Tätigkeit fort. Mir ist bekannt, dass Verstöße gegen das Datengeheimnis nach §§ 43, 44 BDSG und anderen Rechtsvorschriften mit Geld- oder Freiheitsstrafe oder als Ordnungswidrigkeit mit Geldbuße geahndet werden können.

(Mitarbeiter/in)

Figure 3.2 Signed assurance on data protection

Source: SK1DDatenschutz

Notwithstanding the suitable observer position, the bank employees were aware of the observation, as one occasion illustrates: The employees of the customer advisor working group and I visited a neighbouring working group, where a team assistant was celebrating her 25th anniversary at savings bank 1. Circa 15 colleagues were chatting, drinking and eating in the team assistant's office when a banker from a neighbouring working group approached me about the observation. The daily protocol records the situation as follows: "I am addressed by one colleague who asks me what I will write about this [anniversary] get-together in my scientific work. I respond that I will report that the cake is good" (SK1MPP29.11.13). Also, at the end of a stay in one team, the team leader issued a reminder of the confidentiality of information received (SK1MPP16.12.13). However, bank employees' awareness of the participant observation had a limited influence on the processes and situations observed for two reasons. Firstly, because of the high workload of the observed teams, bank employees had no time to change their routine behaviour. And secondly, the confidentiality agreement gave the bank employees little reason to hide anything. Accordingly, the reliability of the observations gained tends to be high.

In contrast to the situation with participant observation, most interview partners carefully select the information they reveal. The interviews were not conducted under the confidentiality of bank secrecy and a tape recorder was present, which tends to explain the caution. At one interview appointment the interviewee asked whether the interview was internal (whether I am an employee of the Savings Banks Financial Group) or external (OITSGV30.05.2013). Assuring anonymity eased but did not overcome the reluctance to speak openly. Despite the general reservations of the interview partners about speaking openly, the tendency of interviewees to reveal needed information on the rules and processes of their organisation differed considerably. To illustrate, the following transcripts of two interviews with customer advisors on the question of credit-granting authority demonstrate the range of detailed information gained in the interviews.

Interview example for an unprecise answer:

F.F.:   What is your credit-granting authority, about?
Answer: I don't know if I [laugh] if I can tell you hm, but they are quite extensive.
F.F.:   Maybe you just tell me roughly, I just want to understand it approximately. I will not analyse it in any detail, it is just for my understanding.
Answer: Yes we can do quite a lot in our own competency, the thing is also that you cannot give an absolute number.

(SK3MIT24.09.2013)

Interview example for a detailed answer:

What I am allowed to do is up to [PD 2.1%], that's a green traffic light, which means I can do the credit alone, and then between [PD 2.1%] and, well I need to check, ca. [PD 3.6%], I get a yellow traffic light, that is the responsibility of the [central back office department in a big German city].

(GB1MIT11.02.14)

Beside personal factors of the interview partners (e.g. age, position, standing in the organisation), their inclination to speak openly tends also to be influenced by the researcher. Alongside my 'daily performance', the time of interview, i.e. before or after the internship, influenced the outcome of the interviews. The internship at savings bank 1 provided knowledge on the challenges and annoyances of bank employees' daily work. Using this knowledge in interviews tended to increase the inclination of bank employees to speak openly. In fact, one customer advisor noted in the interview how his statement contradicted the official position of his bank:

> [When a customer is dissatisfied with the service of the private customer seg-ment], then it is not the [private customer segment of the big bank] but [the big bank] in total that had created the problems. And this also feeds back to the corporate customer segment. This holds true the other way around too. We as the bank, official statement, you have to cut this out of the interview somehow [laugh]. No officially we want to have the customer in total, but I always have to keep in mind that problems can occur if he is everywhere.
>
> (Source of transcript veiled to protect interviewee)

Overall the challenge of the interview method was clearly to mitigate bank secrecy. This was not at all a restriction in the participant observation. Therefore, interview statements tend to be rather general or correspond to the official representation of the banks. Nevertheless, it was possible to gain insights into the routine work and organisational practices of the interviewed banks.

3.1.4.2 *Analysing and presenting the qualitative data*

The analysis of the qualitative data consisted of three steps: a preliminary analysis conducted right after the interviews and participant observations, a second analy-sis before the writing of the empirical chapter (Chapter 4) and a third topic-based analysis during the writing phases. MaxQDA (release 11.0.5), a qualitative data analysis software program, supported the organising and analysing of the qualita-tive data. The whole analysis was conducted in the German language. The author translated all the interview and protocol excerpts presented in this book.

The first analytical step aimed to secure the information gained and achieve an overview of all information to identify possible knowledge gaps. In this step the protocols and interview transcripts were coded deductively. The second ana-lytical step screened the data on the basis of the theoretical foundation focusing on distance and information transmission. Thus, the analysis deductively speci-fied codes for information and knowledge as well as functional and operational distance. Furthermore, the screening involved inspection of the transcripts and protocols on the meta-level for hints on positionality, official representations, misleading statements etc. The final step saw the topic-related analysis of the empirical data during the writing-up phases.

Restricted access caused an asymmetry in the qualitative data gained for the comparison of regional and large banks. Despite numerous attempts, none of the large banks approached allowed the participant observation. Accordingly, the scope, level of detail and reliability of data are lower for the large banks. Two aspects ease this limitation. Firstly, the combination of data from different methods constitutes a usual practice of ethnography (Breidenstein et al. 2013). Secondly, six informative interviews with bank employees from *big bank 1* provided detailed information for the comparison. The fact that two interviews with big bank 1 took place after the internship (GB1M11.02.14 and GB1M13.02.2014) tends to explain the scope of information gained. In fact, one interview partner commented on the scope of information concerning big bank 1's credit-granting process as follows: "exactly Mr Flögel, you are well informed" (GB1MIT13.02.14). Nevertheless, the comparison between regional and large banks remains limited because of the data asymmetry.

The data obstacle was mitigated as follows. The study makes the limitation explicit, allowing consideration of the limitation in the interpretation of the results. Furthermore, the comparison focuses on the two bank cases where the most detailed and reliable information was gained: savings bank 1, where the participant observation took place, and big bank 1. Data from the additional bank cases (see Section 3.3) are only used for further illustration and to assess the generalisability of results. However, as the scope and details of information about savings bank 1 exceed that of big bank 1 and all the other banks under study, results from savings bank 1 are discussed in detail, disregarding the comparison. This helps to understand the general practices of banks' credit-granting processes and explore the geography of information transmission.

Even without this data asymmetry, the generalisability of the results of this study is moderate because of its qualitative research design, with a 'sample' of two banks in-depth studied and eight additional bank cases. Accordingly, representativeness of results in the conventional sense is impossible; rather this empirical comparison aims to explore 'exemplary' cases that stand for ordinary regional and large banks. To deduce a moderate conclusion from the empirical data and to claim validity beyond the particular case under study, the generalisability of findings is discussed in the representation of empirical data. To this end, the study uses the results from the other eight regional and large banks studied – which vary in depth, focus and scope – for the assessment of generalisability. Furthermore, Section 3.3 outlines the context of the bank cases studied to explicate the business environment of the analysed banks. In addition, the qualitative results are triangulated with secondary statistics on the German banking system, banking groups as well as quantitative data from the annual financial statements and risk reports of the in-depth contrasted banks.

Research ethics form a sensitive issue in the presentation of data, as the study uses data from informants who did not overall voluntarily participate in this research project. In contrast to the interviews, a range of people involved in the participant observation did not explicitly approve their participation or even know that they were part of a study. To be clear, the participant observation at savings bank 1 did not take place undercover but with the permission of the human resources department and the head of the departments under study. Nevertheless, the bank employees observed did not explicitly express their approval, and savings bank 1 introduced me to the customers as an 'ordinary' student trainee without further explanation. Also, the results of the interviews raise researcher ethics issues, because bank secrecy protects a range of topics covered during the interviews. As the interviews aimed to get as detailed information as possible and interview partners were assured of anonymity, the data from the interviews must also be handled with caution. Against this background several requirements for anonymisation must be met. Outsiders should not be able to identify persons, organisations or departments that take part in this study. As insiders will be able to deduce the identity of individuals, no participant of this study – neither interview partners nor observed people – shall face personal disadvantages from their participation in this study and the representation of empirical results must protect the privacy of the participants. Furthermore, the responsibility of this study also extends to the organisations (banks) that made this research possible; hence, representation of results should not cause damage to particular organisations. Finally, as self-protection, the representation at savings bank 1 must conform to the data protection agreement (see Box 3.2).

To fulfil these requirements, this study exercises the following writing strategy. Names of persons and organisations are altered, of course, and this book only reports personal and biographical information if necessary and in a limited way to protect privacy. Information that obviously reveals the organisations is altered or blanked in order to make sure that outsiders cannot identify persons and organisations. Square brackets ([]) indicate alterations. In a few cases the source of information is veiled to protect individual persons. Furthermore, the representation of results respects the data protection agreement. This implies, firstly, that customer-related information is systematically altered, e.g. with respect to firms' size, sector and financial information, so that even insiders are unable to identify individual firms unambiguously. Secondly, this representation randomly alters information about savings bank 1, like figures, limits, strategies, etc., as banking secrecy also protects this information (see Box 3.2). Altering does not affect the general conclusion; i.e. ratios and key meanings remain unchanged. To avoid double standards, this altering strategy is also applied for big bank 1.

3.2 The German banking system

This section introduces the German banking system and compares the regional and supraregional banking groups to uncover signs of continuity and change in Germany's bank-based financial system. Section 3.2.1 gives a basic overview of the structure of the German banking system, and Section 3.2.2 introduces German bank regulation. Section 3.2.3 traces the development of enterprise finance and compares regional and supraregional banks, and Section 3.2.4 discusses the structural development of the contrasted banking groups. Overall Section 3.2 indicates that signs of continuity tend to be stronger for regional than for supraregional banking groups, although the need to adapt to cost pressure similarly affects both.

3.2.1 The structure of the German banking system

As a special feature, three banking pillars – the private-owned commercial banks, the public-owned savings banks, *Landesbanken* and special-purpose banks and the cooperative banks – constitute Germany's banking system (Hackethal et al. 2006; Gärtner 2008; Klagge 2009). As universal banks, financial institutes from all three pillars compete with one another for customers in almost all market segments. Except for the special-purpose banks, the banking pillars are subject to the same bank regulations (Hackethal et al. 2006). The banking pillars matter because bank regulation only allows M&A within the pillars, protecting the tripartite structure. Furthermore, as Section 2.1.2.2 discussed, public and cooperative banks are dual bottomline institutes that have to fulfil other (social) goals beside making profits. Table 3.2 displays the key structural figures of the banking pillars and their banking groups.

The private banking pillar is the largest in terms of derivatives and deposits, and the second largest in terms of balance sheet total, loans to non-banks and capital, and the smallest in terms of number of banks and branches. The private banking pillar consists of the four big banks: Commerzbank (Frankfurt), Deutsche Bank (Frankfurt), Deutsche Postbank (Bonn) and UniCredit Bank (Munich) (Deutsche Bundesbank 2010). In this context, Deutsche Bank owns Deutsche Postbank, and UniCredit belongs to the Italian UniCredit banking group. The four big banks operate 73% of the private bank branches and account for 62% of balance sheet total. Surprisingly in this context, the 179 'regional banks and other commercial banks' hand out and collect a larger amount of money in terms of loans to non-banks and deposits. In this category, the Deutsche Bundesbank statistics summarise all other private commercial banks that report to the Bundesbank. Banks that mainly engage in private wealth management (e.g. Bankhaus Lampe), purchase financing (e.g. Volkswagen Bank) and regionally delimited commercial banks (e.g. NATIONAL-BANK) belong to the banking category of 'regional banks and other commercial banks'. NATIONAL-BANK operates in a similar fashion to savings banks; i.e. as a universal bank it only serves customers in the city of Essen and its surroundings. The 114 branches of foreign banks are especially active in collecting deposits relative to their loan volume (deposits exceed loans 2.3 times). The German branches of the Spanish universal bank Banco Santander or the US investment bank J.P. Morgan belong to this statistical category (Deutsche Bundesbank 2010).

The public banking pillar is the largest in terms of branches, balance sheet total, loans and capital. Public banks show average capital ratios. At 6.6% the cooperatively owned banks have the highest capital ratio, followed by the publicly owned banks (6.3%) and the privately owned banks (5.1%). The public banking pillar actually consists of two banking groups. Firstly, the *Sparkassen-Finanzgruppe*, or savings banks financial group (savings banks and *Landesbanken*), owned by the

Table 3.2 Key structural figures of the three German banking pillars in million euros (2013)

	Number of banks	Number of branches		Balance sheet total		Lending to non-banks		Derivative assets		Obligations to non-banks (deposits)		Capital	
	Total	Total	Ø	Total	Ø	Total	Ø	Total	Ø	Total	Ø	Total	Capital ratio
Private pillar	**297**	**10,440**		**2,766,999**		**837,846**	**2,821**			**1,184,425**	**3,988**	**142,130**	**5.1%**
Big banks	4	7,614	1,904	1,719,949	429,987	346,210	86,553	565,580	141,395	525,176	131,294	80,394	4.7%
Regional banks and other commercial banks	179	2,581	14	816,777	4,563	441,649	2,467	0	0	542,733	3,032	53,283	6.5%
Branches of foreign banks	114	245	2	230,273	2,020	49,987	438	0	0	116,516	1,022	8,453	3.7%
Public pillar	**447**	**13,212**	**30**	**3,165,618**	**7,082**	**1,443,582**	**3,229**	**167,978**	**376**	**1,177,306**	**2,634**	**200,982**	**6.3%**
Savings banks financial group	426	13,183	31	2,216,276	5,203	1,187,597	2,788	83,989	197	1,116,984	2,622	145,943	6.6%
Landesbanken	9*	443	49	1,092,582	121,398	444,369	49,374	83,936	9,326	301,962	33,551	61,673	5.6%
Savings banks	417	12,740	31	1,110,790	2,664	708,263	1,698	53	0.13	799,244	1,917	84,238	7.6%
Special-purpose banks	21	29	1	949,342	45,207	255,985	12,190	0	0	76,100	3,624	55,071	5.8%
Cooperative pillar	**1,083**	**12,635**	**12**	**1,034,232**	**955**	**497,234**	**459**	**0**	**0**	**596,834**	**551**	**68,589**	**6.6%**
Cooperative central banks	2	13	7	272,937	136,469	33,070	16,535	0	0	32,344	16,172	13,811	5.1%
Cooperative banks	1,081	12,622	12	761,706	705	461,633	427	0	0	559,574	518	54,755	7.2%
Sum	**1,827**	**36,287**	**20**	**6,966,849**	**3,813**	**2,778,662**	**1,521**	**167,978**	**92**	**2,958,565**	**1,619**	**411,701**	**5.9%**

Source: author's compilation based on Deutsche Bundesbank (2014b)

* Whereas nine *Landesbanken* reported to the *Deutsche Bundesbank* in 2013, only seven operate as 'ordinary' *Landesbanken*, because WestLB is in the process of liquidation and the federal state of Berlin has sold the *Landesbank Berlin* to the savings banks financial group.

Stadt- und Landkreise and *Bundesländer* (municipalities and districts and federal states, respectively). Secondly, *Förderbanken*, or special-purpose banks, owned either by the Federal Republic of Germany (KfW) or the federal states (e.g. NRW. Bank) (Klagge 2009; Deutsche Bundesbank 2010). In total, the 417 regionally delimited savings banks account for the majority of branches and have the highest lending to non-banks and deposits volumes. The seven *Landesbanken* carry out central bank functions for the savings banks financial group, serve large customers and are the financiers of their states. The *Landesbanken* and especially the 21 special-purpose banks report lower deposits in relation to their loan portfolios, which their special refinancing model explains. As part of the savings banks financial group, *Landesbanken* receive funds from savings banks. The solvency of the public-owned special-purpose banks is secured by government guarantees; e.g. the KfW refinances its loans by bonds at terms close to those of German government bonds.

The special-purpose banks represent a speciality of bank-based corporate finance in Germany (Klagge 2009). They do not directly interact with firm customers, as the low number of branches already indicates. Rather they offer loans, guarantees and mezzanine and equity capital to firms via the firms' *Hausbank*. The federal government and state governments sponsor subsidies for specific funding instruments of their special-purpose banks to promote political and social goals (e.g. loans for SMEs, loans for job creation in East Germany or equity capital for start-ups). The private, public or cooperative *Hausbanks* generate the contacts to customers, conduct the screening and monitoring and keep the default risk. For this intermediation service they receive commissions from the special-purpose banks and keep a share of customers' interest payments (OOIT01.03.13). Remarkably, until 2013 KfW – the third largest single bank in Germany – was not supervised within the 'ordinary' bank regulation framework headed by the Federal Ministry of Finance, but by the Federal Ministry of Economics (OOIT01.03.13) and still has a special status.

The cooperative banking pillar is the largest in terms of the number of banks and has the smallest banks on average. More than 50% of all German banks have cooperative owners. The cooperative banking group consists of 1,081 cooperative banks of which most are regionally delimited, small universal banks. Although smaller in size, these banks are equivalent to savings banks in term of products and customers and tend to be their biggest regional competitors. A range of cooperative banks execute no regional delimitation but conduct sector-specific market segmentation, e.g. the Deutsche Apotheker- und Ärztebank for medical professions, the private-customer-only Sparda-Bank West and the GLS-Bank for ecologically sustainable investments (Zademach 2015). Since its merger with WGZ in 2016, the DZ Bank conducts central bank functions for all cooperative banks and serves large customers.

As Section 2.1.2.4 indicates, the spatial classification of decentralised and centralised banking requires a division of banks across these three pillars according to their regional market orientation. Figure 3.3 displays the banking pillars and the regional orientation of the banks. Regional and supraregional banks

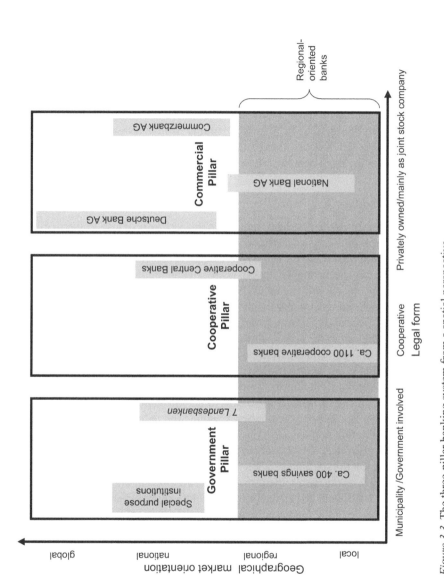

Figure 3.3 The three-pillar banking system from a spatial perspective

Source: Gärtner and Flögel 2014: 6

belong to all three banking pillars (see Gärtner 2011; Gärtner and Flögel 2014). All 417 regional savings banks conduct regional market delimitations, mainly at the municipal level (NUTS 3), as the regional principle specifies. Savings banks legislation codifies the regional principle. The principle obliges savings banks to place branches only within the territory of their authority (the responsible munici-palities) and to lend to institutions, companies and private individuals in that ter-ritory first. The principle's aim is to keep regional savings in the region to fulfil regional demands for credits, with the intention of promoting regional develop-ment. Similarly, the majority of the cooperative banks apply similar regional mar-ket segregation on a voluntary basis (Bülbül et al. 2013). The regional principle restricts competition within the public and cooperative pillar (Breuer and Mark 2004; Gärtner and Flögel 2014). A limited number of private-owned banks also operate in regionally restricted market areas, e.g. NATIONAL-BANK. All other German banks of the three banking pillars have supraregional market orientations.

3.2.2 Bank regulation

Germany implemented its first bank regulation in 1931 in response to the world financial and economic crisis (Hartmann-Wendels et al. 2010). Bank regulation has the key aim of protecting the savings of bank customers. The central function of banks in the modern economy further justifies bank regulation (Pieper 2005). The *Gesetz über das Kreditwesen* (KWG), or German Banking Act, is the most important law governing bank regulation in Germany. A range of other laws, like the *Pfandbriefgesetz* and the *Sparkassengesetze* of the federal states, supplement the KWG. In addition to the KWG, numerous *Verordnungen*, or regulations, gov-ern banking supervision and regulate the business conduct of banks.

The *Solvabilitätsverordnung* (SolvV), or solvency regulation, sets minimum capital requirements in relation to the risks of banks to ensure a risk adequate provision with capital. The greater the risk to which the bank is exposed, the more capital it must hold. Solvency regulation specifies the determination of capital requirement in relation to the underlying asset classes by means of risk weighting (SolvV, see also Box 4.1, p. 159) and is publicly debated under the heading Basel II and Basel III. On the one hand, experts argue that Basel II capital requirements have been too low, as the requirements were unable to prevent the global financial crisis (Hellwig 2010; Paul 2011). On the other hand, experts accuse Basel II capi-tal requirements – and the increased requirements of Basel III in reaction to the financial crisis – of hampering lending to SMEs, as these credits tend to involve high risks and accordingly high capital requirements (Everling and Langen 2013; Ruhkamp and Frühauf 2010).

The *Mindestanforderungen an das Risikomanagement* (MaRisk), or mini-mum requirements for risk management, represents a very relevant regulation for the day-to-day credit business because it specifies the organisation of the credit-granting process. MaRisk implements the so-called qualitative bank regu-lation of Basel II and came into power in 2005. MaRisk unifies the 'minimum requirements for the credit business' (Mak), 'minimum requirements for the

trading business' (MaH) and various aspects of compliance and revision regulations (Hartmann-Wendels et al. 2010). MaK was published in 2002 and came into
power in June 2004 (BaFin 2002). It regulates key aspects of the credit-granting
process, especially the separation of the *Markt* (front office), where the customer
advisors work and grant credits, and the *Marktfolge* (back office) that controls
credit risks. It further governs the obligatory use of risk classification systems,
i.e. rating systems (BaFin 2002), and therefore profoundly changed the credit-
granting practices of banks.

Two organisations, the *Deutsche Bundesbank*, or the German Federal Bank, and
the *Bundesanstalt für Finanzdienstleistungsaufsicht* (BaFin), or Federal Financial
Supervisory Authority, supervised banks in Germany at the time of the empirical enquiry.[2] At the so-called supervisory review process, every German bank is
annually classified according to its stability and systemic relevance by a quantitative rating and a qualitative report. The Deutsche Bundesbank collects the legally
enforced announcements (figures and reports) of the banks, analyses banks' audit
reports and creates first reports. Based on these reports, the BaFin conducts the
final assessment of the risks and adequacy of capital. Together the Deutsche Bundesbank and BaFin conduct audit meetings with the banks. Table 3.3 displays the
risk classification results of the supervision review process in 2014. BaFin can
enforce several regulatory measures such as the recall of CEOs, intervention or
the ordering of extraordinary supervisory board meetings in cases of norm violations and even possesses the power to cancel bank licenses (Hartmann-Wendels
et al. 2010). Through these regulatory measures, banking supervision executes
immense power over banks, not least owing to the ultimate power to shut down
banks by cancelling licenses (Paul 2011). New bank regulations tend to enforce
supervisory power, as they give a high degree of discretion to supervisors in the
interpretation of the rules (OBCIP05.02.14).

The efforts to harmonise international regulatory standards have triggered
bank regulation since the 1980s. In light of the global integration of banking,
harmonisation of national bank regulation has become necessary to prevent
regulation arbitrage, i.e. to avoid banks locating their business in places with
low regulatory standards (French et al. 2009; Paul 2011). The Basel committee
on banking supervision – the forum of national banking supervisory authorities

Table 3.3 Risk classification of German banks (2014)

Banks		Quality of banks				
		A High	*B Medium high*	*C Medium*	*D Low*	*Sum*
System relevancy	High	0.2%	0.7%	1.3%	0.2%	2.5%
	Medium	4.1%	4.9%	1.6%	0.6%	11.2%
	Low	38.1%	37.5%	9.3%	1.4%	86.3%
	Sum	42.4%	37.5%	9.3%	1.4%	100%

Source: BaFin 2014: 105

located at the Bank for International Settlements in Basel – develops guidelines that inform national bank regulations and ought to be transformed into national laws. In the European Union (EU) the Basel recommendations are mitigated at the EU level before the member states implement them into national laws. The following list highlights key changes of the international bank regulations (see Paul 2011):

- A 1988 recommendation now called Basel I outlined a set of minimum capital requirements for banks, focusing on a rough risk-weighting of assets. Assets of banks were grouped into five categories according to their default risk with risk weights of 0% (lowest risk class, e.g. government bonds) to 100% (highest risk class, e.g. corporate credits). Banks were required to hold 8% capital of their risk-weighted assets. Basel I triggered the homogenisation of EU bank regulation and was implemented with the capital adequacy regulation (CAR 1) in 1993.
- Basel II reshaped bank regulation decidedly. It consists of three pillars: firstly, quantitative minimum capital requirements; secondly, minimum organisational standards and qualitative supervision of banks; and, thirdly, measures to increase market transparency. With respect to capital requirements it specifies a more advanced approach to risk-weighting than Basel I. Now three types of risk determine the minimum capital requirements: *default risks*, i.e. the risk that a contract partner cannot fulfil the contractually agreed payments/obligations; *market risk*, i.e. the risk of losses from the value fluctuation of banks' publicly traded assets; and *operational risks*, i.e. "the risk of loss resulting from inadequate or failed internal processes, people and systems or from external events" (Bank for international settlements 2006: 144, Hartmann-Wendels et al. 2010). Pillar 2 of Basel II sets guidelines for the basic organisation of the supervisory review process (drafted above). Pillar 3 aims at giving potential investors (and savers) information about the actual risks of the credit institutes with the intention of letting market forces lower the risk preferences of banks. A key element of pillar 3 is the annual disclosure reports all banks must publish giving detailed information about the capital and risk structure. The EU mitigated Basel II with the capital requirement directive (CRD) which Germany implemented in the SolvV, set into force in 1 January 2007. Furthermore, the MaRisk published in 2005 implements the qualitative bank regulation into German law.
- Basel III does not replace Basel II requirements but supplements Basel II with the intention of overcoming the shortfalls of bank regulation in the context of the global financial crisis. It proposed an increase in the amount and quality of capital that banks have to hold; e.g. banks are obligated to hold a minimum of 4.5% Tier 1 capital[3] (plus a 1.5% capital conservation buffer) in relation to their risk-weighted assets. Furthermore, Basel III introduced the observation of the leverage ratio, i.e. the relation of capital to total non-risk-weighted assets, with the intention of specifying a maximum leverage ratio in 2017 (Höpfner 2014). In reaction to the liquidity shortages

of many banks in the financial crisis (Shin 2009; Brunnermeier et al. 2009; Marshall et al. 2011), Basel III specifies liquidity risk regulation and monitoring. *Liquidity risk* in banking emerges when the duration of assets (e.g. loans) exceeds the duration of the liabilities refinancing these assets. With CRD 4, Basel III recommendations came into power in the EU in 2014. At the time of the empirical enquiry (April 2013 to February 2014), the CRD 4 regulation had not yet been implemented in Germany, and hence did not affect the day-to-day business of banks directly. Nevertheless, Basel III regulations were an issue; e.g. savings bank 1 employed a temporary project team of four experts for the implementation of the new regulation, indicating the expenditure new banking regulation causes, especially for small banks.

3.2.3 The development of enterprise financing in Germany

Enterprises can finance investment and working capital internally by withholding earnings or externally by attracting capital from external organisations or persons. External capital is available as equity capital or debt (Klagge 2009, see Figure 3.4). Firms that want to attract new external capital have the alternatives of issuing new shares (equity capital) or bonds (debt) at stock exchanges or 'over the counter' that are sold and bought by investors on a regular basis. Firms can also attract equity capital from private investors, such as private equity firms, relatives or banks and debt from banks and other creditors. These claims are usually not publicly traded, and investors stick to their investment for the contractually agreed time period. Equity capital investments give the investors control rights over the firms and count as subordinate claims to debt. Hence these investments tend to be riskier; i.e. investors face losses first, but also participate in the possible gains of the firms. Debt investors (e.g. a loan-granting bank or a private bond buyer) possess no control rights, but only have the right to the contractually agreed payments and only bear the default risk. A range of mezzanine financial instruments exist for firm finance that combine different aspects of equity and debt and are subordinated to debt finance. Banks (especially special-purpose banks) and other investors offer mezzanine finance for SMEs and start-ups in Germany (Flögel and Gärtner 2011).

	Equity capital	Debt
Public traded	Shares	Bonds
Non-public traded	Private equity (e.g. business angels, venture capital firms)	Credits (e.g. banks, suppliers, pawnbrokers)

Figure 3.4 External instruments of firm financing

Source: Klagge 2009: 4 (translated)

The dispute about whether Germany's bank-based financial system is undergoing profound changes or whether continuity dominates is far from settled (see Section 2.1.2.1), and new developments like the low-interest phase and Basel III tend to cause changes in banking. Considering the available data, bank-based finance dominates external funding of German non-financial firms[4] but lost market share until the financial crisis of 2008 (Figure 3.5). At 79%, credits were the main source of external funding for non-financial firms in 2013. In January 2013 banks granted credits of €1,185 bn, an increase of 4.4% in comparison to 1999. Nevertheless, the market share of credits in relation to market-based finance decreased by 11% between 1999 and 2007. The growth of bonds mainly explains this development. In 1999 bonds only accounted for 0.3% of all external funds, growing to 6.6% in 2013. At 11.9%, shares are the main source of market-based finance for German non-financial firms. From 2002 to 2013 the nominal share value increased by €12.5 bn, indicating its limited relevancy as a source of new external funding since the burst of the dot.com bubble. At €36.6 bn, the nominal value of the portfolio of private equity firms is the smallest external funding source. Its value strongly increased in the early 2000s and has remained constant since 2010. With the financial crisis of 2008, the relative decline in bank-based finance tends overall to have stopped, indicating the persistence of bank-based firm finance in Germany.

As outlined in Chapter 1, when comparing lending by banking type, the simultaneous market share gains of the regional banking groups, i.e. savings and cooperative banks, characterise the development of bank-based firm finance in the period of 1999 to 2015 (Figure 3.6). Savings and cooperative banks are grouped as regional banks, as they mainly operate in regional market areas (see Section 2.1.2.4 for the definitions of regional and supraregional banks). Big banks, branches of foreign banks, *Landesbanken*, cooperative central banks and special-purpose banks are grouped as supraregional banks owing to their national or international market reach. Since 1999, regional banks have increased their credit volume from €398 bn to €544 bn in 2015. The increase in market share was accelerated by a decrease in lending by supraregional banks from €497 bn in 1999 to €415 bn in 2015. Initially triggered by a strong decline in big banks' market share up to 2004 with the financial crisis, *Landesbanken* in particular have reduced their credit volumes since 2008, accelerating the market share decrease of supraregional banks.

Market share gains of regional banks are explained to a large degree by gains in the service sector, whereas with a market share of 49.4% supraregional banks continue to be the most important lenders in the manufacturing sector (Table 3.4). The strong and constant engagement of supraregional banks in manufacturing compared to all other sectors tends to be explained by the fact that manufacturing companies, on average, need larger credits, and banks are able to secure these credits with physical collaterals like machinery. With a market share decline of 13.7%, supraregional banks lost most in the service sector. Big banks have reduced their credit engagement in services constantly; *Landesbanken* have followed this

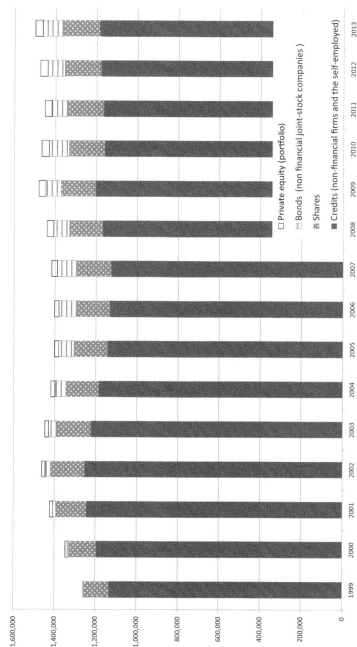

Figure 3.5 External funding of German non-financial firms in bn euros

Nominal share value of all German joint-stock companies, including banks and other financial institutes; bonds before 2008 of all non-monetary financial institutions, including insurances and other financial institutes; statistical break in the private equity statistics in 2008.

Source: author's compilation based on Deutsche Bundesbank 2015 and BVK 2014

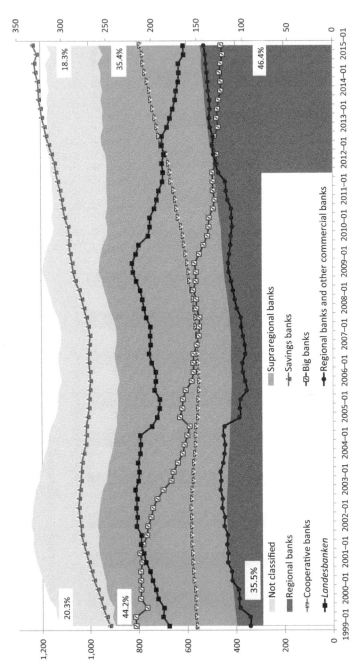

Figure 3.6 Credits to non-financial firms and the self-employed by regional and supraregional banks and selected categories of banks in bn euros

Source: author's composition based on Deutsche Bundesbank 2015

Table 3.4 Market shares of regional and supraregional banks by selected sectors

		All sectors	Manufacturing sector	Service sector	Trading sector	Agriculture and forestry sector
Credit volume bn	**2013**	€1178.33	€130.2	€649.1	€124.9	€46.2
Development of credit volume	**1999–2013**	3.9%	−20.0%	3.7%	−28.1%	52.4%
Regional banks' market share	**1999**	37.6%	40.1%	29.3%	44.2%	73.3%
	2013	45.1%	41.5%	44.9%	51.5%	75.5%
Supraregional banks' market share	**1999**	42.5%	48.7%	45.4%	39.0%	16.6%
	2013	35.6%	49.4%	31.7%	30.9%	12.7%

Source: author's composition based on Deutsche Bundesbank 2015

trend since the financial crisis (Deutsche Bundesbank 2015). As the service sector is the largest credit market, the decline in their market share accounts for the overall market share decline of supraregional banks to a sizable degree.

Figure 3.7 displays the development of equity capital and bank debts of German non-financial firms. The Deutsche Bundesbank compiles this data from the consolidated balance sheets of firms' annual financial statements (Deutsche Bundesbank 2014a). The figure shows an increase of firms' equity capital, i.e. internal financing, as the proportion of equity capital to total assets almost double from 16.3% in 1997 to 27.9% in 2012 for all non-financial firms. SMEs even exceed this increase, as their equity share quadruplicated in the period (from 6% to 24.1%). In line with the equity capital increase, the proportion of bank debts to total assets decreased by 9.1% for all non-financial firms (12% for SMEs). With 24.7%, bank debts remain a far more important source of funding for SMEs than for non-financial firms overall. The nominal volumes of bank debts and equity capital show that an increase in equity capital volumes rather than a decrease in bank debts has caused the relative decline of bank debts. Thus, since 2008 bank debts have only declined by €19 bn (€18 bn for SMEs), whereas equity value has increased by €213.8 bn (€80.4 bn for SMEs) in the same period (Deutsche Bundesbank 2014c). Therefore, the relative decline in bank debts is the result of the asset value increase of non-financial firms rather than banks' credit cut back.

To sum up, despite an increase in market-based finance until the financial crisis in 2008, at 79% credits overall dominate the external funding of firms in Germany. In the context of bank-based firm finance, the market share gain of regional banks at the expense of supraregional banks is striking. In 2013 supraregional banks only exceeded the credit-granting of regional banks in the manufacturing sector. External funding lost importance for German firms in the period of 1997 to 2012. Asset value increases of non-financial firms rather than reduced lending predominantly account for this development. Why firms have preferred to retain funds (increase equity capital) instead of paying out gains cannot be answered from the statistics.

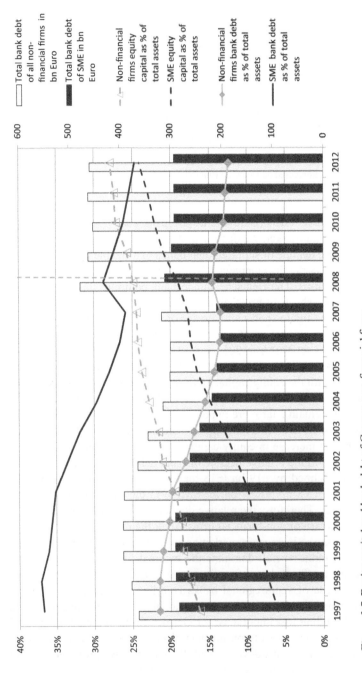

Figure 3.7 Equity capital and bank debt of German non-financial firms

* Projection of the consolidated financial statements of firms. Break in the statistical series between 2007 and 2008. Only *Kapitalgesellschaften* (e.g. AG, GmbH) considered.

Source: author's composition based on Deutsche Bundesbank 2014c: Statistische Sonderveröffentlichung 5

3.2.4 The structural development of the German banking system

The previous section indicates that banks continue to dominate enterprise finance in Germany. This section looks at the actual structural development of the German banking system. In light of market-based banking, Section 3.2.4.1 investigates the key assets and liabilities of German banks and finds no distinct indications of a trend towards market-based banking. Section 3.2.4.2 turns to the spatial development of the banking groups and reports, on the one hand, indicators for a spatial concentration of regional and supraregional banks, but also outlines, on the other hand, the persistence of the decentralised distribution of regional banking groups' employees. Section 3.2.4.3 traces trends and developments in the (credit-granting) processes of banks against the background of cost pressure in the banking sector. It shows that the so-called 'industrialisation' of banks tends to affect regional and supraregional banks.

3.2.4.1 Market-based banking and key assets and liabilities of the banking groups

Banks' financialisation motivates the classification of market-based and traditional banking (Section 2.1.2.3). Concerning firm financing this classification is relevant because market-based banking influences banks' lending decisions. According to Hardie and Howarth (2013a), business lending by market-based banks, i.e. banks where the capital market directly or indirectly influences the key liabilities and assets, does not significantly differ to direct financing of firms from capital markets. In the following the key liabilities and assets of regional and supraregional banks are examined with regard to market-based banking.

Banks' key liabilities, i.e. sources of banks' refinancing, indicate no systematic shift towards market-based banking in Germany (Figure 3.8). The value of non-bank deposits over all German banks increased by 64% to €3,374 bn between 1999 and 2014 (Deutsche Bundesbank 2015). A low decrease in debt securities can be observed in the same period (Deutsche Bundesbank 2015). As Table 3.2 (p. 103) shows, no funding gap existed in Germany as non-bank deposits exceeded loans in 2014.

The market-based refinancing of supraregional banks tops this of regional banks (Figure 3.8). Debt securities in relation to the non-bank deposits of supraregional banks exceeded the 100% threshold from 2004 to 2008 and stood at 89.6% in 2014, indicating its high but diminishing importance for supraregional banks' refinancing. In contrast to this, debt securities in relation to the non-bank deposits of regional banks did not pass the 10% threshold in the entire time period and decreased strongly from 2008 to 1.7% in 2014. Thus, market-based refinancing proves almost unimportant for regional banks, whereas it remains a key refinancing basis for supraregional banks. Having said that, the comparison needs to be contextualised because the bulk of supraregional banks' debt securities are issued as *Pfandbriefe* (German covered bonds) by the central institutes of the regional banking groups (i.e. the *Landesbanken* and cooperative central banks)

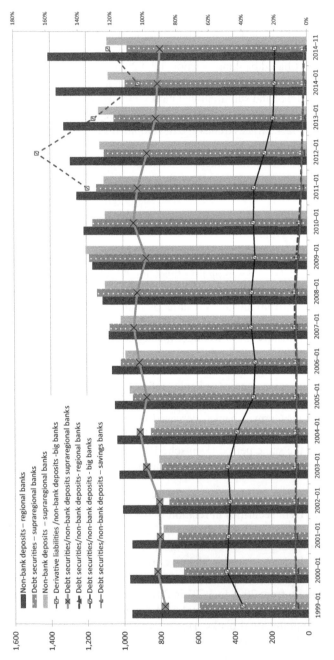

Figure 3.8 Important sources of banks' refinancing in bn euros

Deutsche Bundesbank statistics only report derivative liabilities since 2011.

Source: author's composition based on Deutsche Bundesbank 2015

and mortgage banks. Consequently, the securities are traded within the banking groups, rather than on active security markets (Hardie and Howarth 2013b). In this line, big banks' debt securities have decreased in relation to non-bank deposits since 2002 and accounted for only 19.5% in 2014. Nevertheless, big banks use other sources of market-based refinancing, especially derivative liabilities that accounted for 121.2% of big banks' non-bank deposits in 2014. Since being reported in 2010 derivative liabilities have shown a volatile development in relation to non-bank deposits, so the volumes always exceed non-bank deposits, indicating the importance of derivative liabilities for the four big banks.

Turning to the assets side, besides loans, German banks invest in market-based assets, i.e. bonds, shares and derivatives. In total the volumes of German banks' bonds and shares grew by 52% between 1999 and 2014, from €908 bn to €1,380 bn, showing a peak in 2009 with €1,609 bn. In the same period banks' lending (to non-banks) increased by 19%, from €2,641 bn to €3,153 bn (Figure 3.9). In addition to bonds and shares, the €839 bn in derivative assets are an important market-based asset and in the five years of reporting a volatile and inconsistent trend becomes visible. Overall, the percentage of market-based assets grew in the period from 1999 to 2008; its steady growth tends to have stopped since 2009.

The comparison of regional and supraregional banking groups shows that up to 2005 the percentage of bonds and shares in regional banks' portfolios exceeded that of supraregional banks (Figure 3.10). This is a surprising finding, considering the conceptual notion that regional banks mainly invest within their regions. Regional banks' bonds and shares accounted for 40.9% of lending to non-banks in 1999 and only moderately declined to 39.4% in 2014. An increase in lending (+ €366 bn) rather than a decrease in market-based assets (+ €132 bn) explains this development. In the same period, supraregional banks' bonds and shares in relation to lending to non-banks increased by 21.9% to 55.7% in 2014. An increase in bonds and shares by €224,9 bn and a decline in lending by €255.8 bn, especially since the financial crisis, explain this relative growth of supraregional banks' market-based assets, indicating that supraregional banks have in fact shifted to market-based banking on their assets side. The great importance of derivative assets in supraregional banks' portfolios further supports this conclusion. Among regional banks only savings banks report derivative assets of €60 million only in November 2014. In contrast, supraregional banks report derivative assets of €834,5 bn of which €692 bn belong to the balance sheets of big banks, followed by the *Landesbanken* and cooperative central banks (Deutsche Bundesbank 2015).

To sum up, no distinct development toward market-based banking, neither for regional nor for supraregional banks, can be detected. Whereas market-based refinancing tends to be unimportant for regional banks, as debt securities only account for 1.7% of non-bank deposits, market-based liabilities remain a key refinancing basis for supraregional banks. Concerning the assets side of banks, surprisingly, regional banks reported a higher proportion of market-based assets relative to lending to non-banks than supraregional banks up to 2005. The situation changed because supraregional banks increased market-based assets whereas

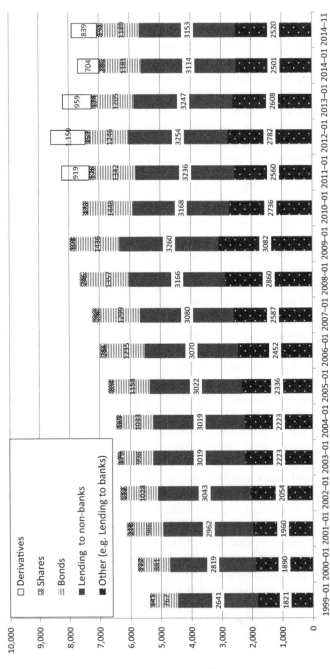

Figure 3.9 Key assets of German banks in bn euros

Deutsche Bundesbank statistics only report derivatives since 2011.

Source: author's composition based on Deutsche Bundesbank 2015

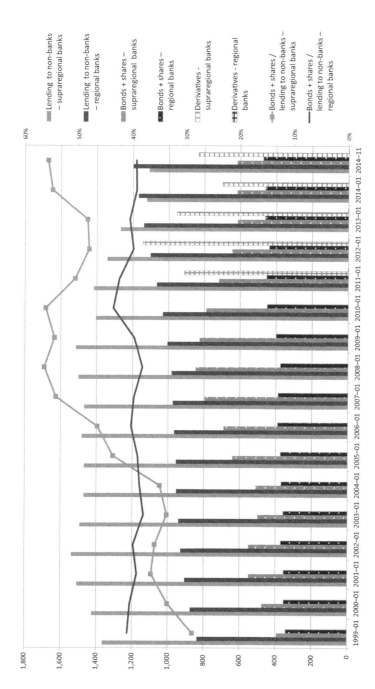

Figure 3.10 Key assets of regional and supraregional banks in bn euros

Source: author's composition based on Deutsche Bundesbank 2015

regional banks increased lending to non-banks, suggesting that regional banks actually focused more on traditional banking in 2014 than in 2005.

3.2.4.2   The spatial development of the banking groups

This section turns to the (changing) geography of the German banking system and especially looks for trends of spatial concentration. Overall the number of banks has sharply decreased since German reunification in 1990, by 62% from almost 4,703 to 1,807 banks in 2014 (Figure 3.11). Whereas the intensity of concentration was especially strong up to 2005, with an average annual decrease of ca. 1.5%, bank concentration continues. Looking at the banking groups shows that regional banks account for the bulk of this development. The number of cooperative banks (−70% since 1990), and to a lesser extent savings banks (−46% since 1990), has decreased sharply due to mergers within these two banking groups (Deutsche Bundesbank 2012). In contrast to this, the number of supraregional banks has increased by 39% since 1990 which is largely explained by an increase in the number of branches of foreign banks (+88%) (Deutsche Bundesbank 2015). The number of big banks has fallen from five to four in the period because of the acquisition of Dresdner Bank by Commerzbank.

Figure 3.12 displays the development of bank branches since 2005 and indicates the shrinking of the branch network. Supraregional and regional banks account for this development. From 2005 to 2014, the former have closed 33.7% of their branches and the latter 12.9%. The savings banks operated most bank branches in 2014 (11,957; −14.3% since 2005), closely followed by the cooperative banks (11,269; −11.4% since 2005) and big banks (7,443; −34% since 2005). Therefore, operational distance is tending to increase for regional and supraregional banks alike in Germany.

Map 3.1 shows the distribution of banks' central offices (headquarters). The central offices of regional savings and cooperative banks are rather equally distributed across Germany. Especially the distribution of savings banks' headquarters reproduces the distribution of municipalities' headquarters, as the municipalities carry their savings banks and the regional principle restricts savings banks from doing business outside their municipalities. In contrast, private banks predominantly locate their central offices in the regional financial centres. While a couple of exceptions to these location patterns exist, e.g. the *Bankhaus J. Faisst* is located in the peripheral town of Wolfach in Baden-Württemberg, it is striking that especially East Germany (except Berlin) does not have a single headquarters of a private bank (Gärtner 2013). As discussed in Section 2.2.2.2, the uneven distribution of banks' headquarters is able to influence regional economic development due to its impact on functional distance and hence firm finance.

The spatial distribution of bank employees gives approximate information about the geographical concentration of banks' value creation. Gärtner and Flögel (2013) use the *spatial concentration index* (SCI) as a proxy indicator to designate decentralised and centralised banking groups (Gärtner 2011). Figure 3.13 displays the SCI of selected banking groups on the basis of data from 2008.[5] SCI expresses

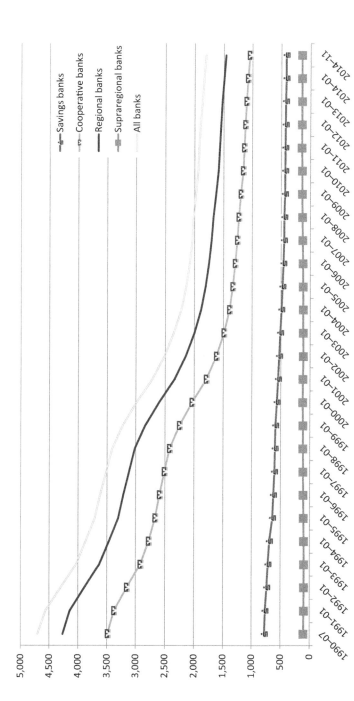

Figure 3.11 Number of banks

Source: author's composition based on Deutsche Bundesbank 2015

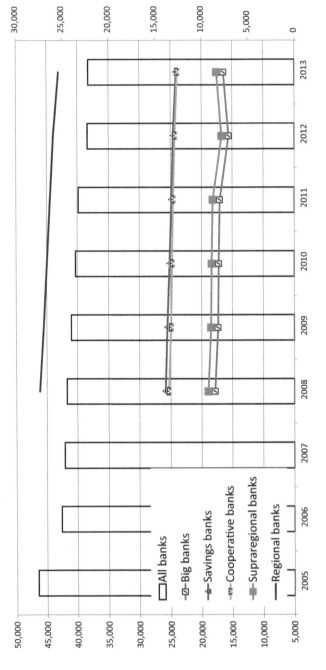

Figure 3.12 Number of bank branches

* Central offices + branches

Source: author's composition based on Deutsche Bundesbank 2015

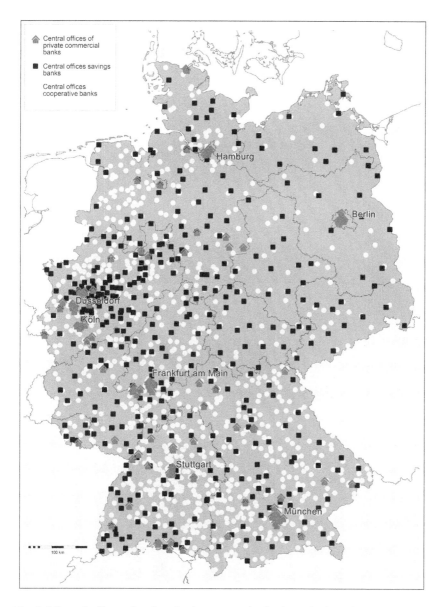

Legend text within image:
- Central offices of private commercial banks
- Central offices savings banks
- Central offices cooperative banks

Map 3.1 Central offices of savings banks, cooperative banks and private banks

Source: Gärtner and Flögel 2015: 35 (translated and modified)

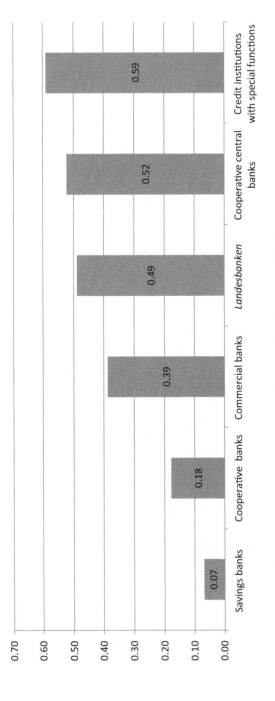

Figure 3.13 Geographical concentration of employees of selected banking groups (2008)

Source: Gärtner and Flögel 2014: 5

the spatial concentration of bank employees in relation to the spatial distribution of employees from all sectors at the NUTS 3 level. The indicator shows values from 0 to 1 on an interval scale; i.e. higher values indicate increased spatial concentration but permit comparison of ratios of differences. Savings banks have the lowest SCI, consistent with the observation above that savings banks' central offices are equally distributed across Germany. The SCI of cooperative banks is the second lowest, confirming the decentralised structure of this regional banking group. The second range in comparison to savings banks tends to reflect the underrepresentation of cooperative banks in East Germany (Gärtner and Flögel 2014). Due to employment data delimitation, the SCI was only calculated for all commercial banks; i.e. the group comprises the big banks and the other commercial banks, including the limited number of private-owned regional banks. Its spatial concentration exceeds that of savings and cooperative banks. *Landesbanken*, cooperative central banks and special-purpose banks show high SCI values, consistent with their supraregional market orientation. Overall, the SCI analysis confirms the heuristic classification of German banking groups into regional and supraregional banks conducted in Section 3.2.1.

Turning to a dynamic perspective, Figure 3.14 reports the SCI for all banks in Germany from 2000 to 2013. Between 2000 and 2007, the SCI moderately increased from 0.172 to 0.185; i.e. German banks tended to concentrate their employees in this period. Since 2007 there has been a slight decrease in SCI, indicating a decentralisation of bank employees. Data of banking group employees are only available from 1999 to 2008. In this period the SCI of commercial banks increased from 0.305 to 0.387, whereas the SCIs of the regional savings and cooperative banks decreased; i.e. employees of both regional banking groups were less centralised in 2008 than in 1999. Thus, a spatial concentration of Germany's bank employees cannot be detected overall; regional banks demonstrate a tendency to decentralise while commercial banks tend to centralise employees.

To sum up, banking sector concentration in Germany has increased. M&A within the regional banking groups mainly triggers a diminishing of the number of banks. Whereas the M&A of regional banks tend to affect banking competition in a limited way because of regional market delimitation, functional distance in terms of branches to headquarters distance grows. The decline in the number of bank branches of all banking groups indicates an increase in operational distance. In contrast to these spatial concentration trends, the spatial distribution of bank employees shows no overall trend toward spatial concentration, but rather designates differences between regional and supraregional banking groups. The former have tended to further decentralise and the latter to further centralise their employees, indicating the persistence of differences between these banking groups in terms of spatial organisation.

3.2.4.3 Profit pressure, 'industrialisation' and standardisation

A range of scholars see the cost pressure in banks' core business, the credit business, as the key driver for changes of the German banking system (Deeg 2001;

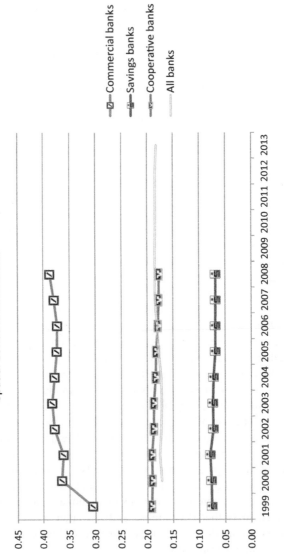

Figure 3.14 Development of the spatial concentration of bank employees

Source: author's calculation based on Bundesanstalt für Arbeit (2014)

Breuer and Mark 2004; Sokolovsky and Löschenkohl 2005; Riese 2006). In this context, Betsch (2005) and others argue that the specific German three-pillar banking system causes especially high competition and low profit opportunities for banks; this may be efficient for the German economy but causes difficulties for the banks (Sachverständigenrat zur Begutachtung der gesamtwirtschaftlichen Entwicklung 2004). Competition is heightened, because new competitors (e.g. direct banks, foreign banks) enter banking markets that were traditionally geographically delineated and because non-bank competitors offer bank products, e.g. retailers offering loans. An increase in discerning customers, who are well-informed about products and prices via the internet, further boosts banking competition (Piper 2005; Betsch 2005; Riese 2006). While cost pressure grows, cutting back banks' expenditures remains difficult because banks have to cope with the tightened bank regulations, not only with respect to capital requirements, but also with respect to process standards, compliance, risk management and reporting (Section 3.2.2). The following discussion of the key earning and cost components of regional and supraregional banks indicates productivity gains in banking which tend to be achieved by the so-called 'industrialisation' of banks.

KEY COST AND INCOME COMPONENTS

Figure 3.15 demonstrates that the relative interest surplus (interest surplus/balance sheet total) of German banking groups has declined since 1990 and dropped to less than 1% in 2012. In 2013 the relative interest surplus improved by 0.02 percent points to 1.01%. A decrease in the interest costs of banks because of the current low-interest phase stimulated by the expansive monetary policy of the ECB, rather than higher interest earnings, tends to explain the interest surplus raise in 2013.

The share of the main income components differs between regional and supraregional banks; nevertheless, interest surplus is the most important income component for both regional and supraregional banks (Figure 3.16). At almost 80% the interest surplus was more important for regional banks than for supraregional banks (65%) in 2013. At 22%, commission surplus was the only other relevant income position of regional banks. Supraregional banks, and especially the four big banks, gained a relatively higher surplus with trading (11%) and commissions (27%) than regional banks. The differences in earning tend to reflect the deviating business activities of the banking groups. The growth in the commission surplus of regional (+32%) and supraregional banks (+31%) outperformed interest surplus growth (regional banks +13%; supraregional banks +16%) between 1999 and 2013 (Deutsche Bundesbank 2015: GuV statistics). Nevertheless, interested surplus, i.e. credit business, remains the most important income component of all banking groups.

In contrast to the decreasing interest surplus, Figure 3.17 does not support the claim that banking business in general is becoming less profitable in Germany. Though the impact of the financial crisis is visible, profit before revaluation does not overall decline between 1999 and 2013 for regional and supraregional banks.

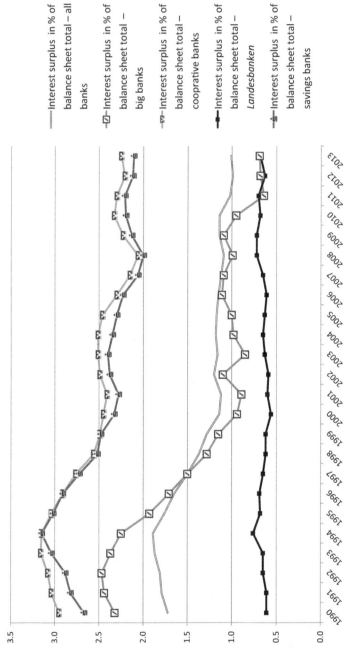

Figure 3.15 Interest surplus of selected German banking groups

Source: author's composition based on Deutsche Bundesbank 2015

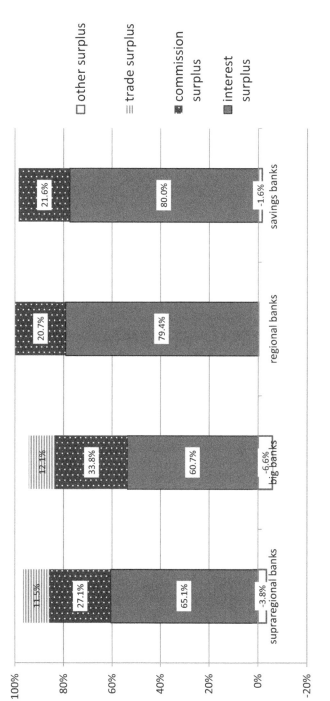

Figure 3.16 Income components of selected banking groups (2013)

Source: author's composition based on Deutsche Bundesbank 2015: GuV statistics

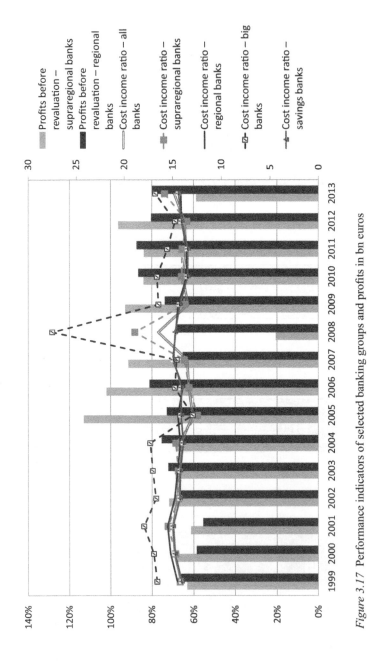

Figure 3.17 Performance indicators of selected banking groups and profits in bn euros

Source: Author's composition based on Deutsche Bundesbank 2015: GuV statistics

As the relatively constant cost income ratio (CIR) of on average 65% indicates, increases in earnings tend to compensate for cost increases. The comparison of regional and supraregional banks in terms of profits reveals that profits of all supraregional banks slightly exceed regional banks' profits but were more volatile between 1999 and 2013 (Deutsche Bundesbank 2015: GuV statistics). Profits of supraregional banks dropped to €4.4 bn during the financial crisis in 2008 due to losses of €17.7 bn in trading, quickly recovered in 2009, but remained below the value of 1999 in 2013. Regional banks' surplus reached its lowest point in 2001 (ca. €11.9 bn). During the financial crisis in 2008, the surplus dropped by 20% (compared to 2007) to ca. €14 bn and amplified up to 2011. Concerning the CIR (cost/earning) comparison, on average, the CIR of regional and supraregional banks is similar. Interestingly in this context, big banks' CIR underperforms, indicating that big banks spend more money per earning than regional and all other supraregional banks. Overall, Figure 3.17 shows that the CIR of all German banks has not deteriorated since 1999. This indicates that German banks must have increased their productivity, i.e. granted more credits at given cost, as the relative interest surplus has diminished since 1990.

'INDUSTRIALISATION' OF BANKS

As indicated above, given that despite a decreasing relative interest surplus banks' nominal profits remain constant, banks must have increased their productivity. Banking 'industrialisation' tends to explain productivity gains. Banking experts see the 'industrialisation' of banks as a solution to cope with cost pressure in the banking sector (Sokolovsky and Löschenkohl 2005; Riese 2006). As the term 'industrialisation' indicates, the concept's main assumption is that banks manage to reduce costs with economies of scale and the standardisation and automation of processes. Hence, banks should specialise, separate and centralise processes (e.g. all back offices function in one credit 'factory') and focus on core competences and products, reducing the depth of their production (outsourcing of non-core competences). To increase surplus, banks also are advised to introduce the centralised management of risks, costs and selling (Jeck and Bufka 2004; Sokolovsky and Löschenkohl 2005; Riese 2006). Business consultants trigger the 'industrialisation' of banks and, for example, redesign back-office processes (Deckers and Goeken 2010). Riese (2006: 53 ff.) identifies the following 'industrialisation' trends in the private and firm customers' segment of German banks:

- A reduction in the overall number of bank products and the customising of the remaining products by changing a handful of parameters. Furthermore, banks promote the financial products of other providers instead of producing the products themselves.
- Banks increasingly push their customer advisors to sales, especially sales of fee-earning products (e.g. insurances). Freed from administrative work (e.g. documentation, financial statement analysis), customer advisors are obliged to concentrate on customer contacts and sales. Customer segmentation, i.e. focusing on potential and highly profitable customers in contrast to offering

similar services to all customers, and customer relationship management (CRM) further supports the sales orientation of banks. CRM helps to increase cross-selling and fee-earning business, as CRM computer programs identify sales opportunities and 'fitting' products for customers. The arrangement of banks' incentive systems represents a further important instrument to boost sales. Although the push of customer advisors toward sales is criticised (Breisig et al. 2010), it nevertheless represents a key development trend of 'industrialised' banking (Deckers and Goeken 2010).

- Banks' back offices offer cost-cutting potential by realising economies of scope with standardisation, automation and centralisation, leading to lower per unit costs and higher processing speed. In this context, banks strive for straight-through processes that totally substitute human involvement, which especially automates payment transactions but also reduces human involvement in credit administration. For example, banks' ICT can automatically create credit contracts from the customer database and credit parameters, thus avoiding double inputs of data. This 'industrialisation' of back-office work tends to reduce flexibility in the arrangement of credits as straight-through processes complicate deviations from the standards.

- One key trend of the 'industrialisation' of banks is the standardization of credit decisions, i.e. credit scorings and customer ratings. This trend motivated the study in hand because it undercuts the assumption that modern regional banks 'naturally' conduct credit decisions at shorter distances to firms than large banks. A range of private customer loans are approved by straight-through processes like commercial credits that use an instant credit scoring based on credit agency information. As discussed in Section 2.3.3, at present, computer-based firm ratings are standard in the banking sector; however, they are not straight-through processes but involve the inputs and judgments of human actors. In this context, Riese (2006: 91) indicates an opposing trend to 'industrialisation', the reintroduction of human judgments in savings banks' credit-approval processes for SMEs.

- 'Industrialisation' also influences banks' management and controlling. Banks have turned to the active management of risks and performances based on quantitative data and figures such as value at risk. Just as an engineer controls the factory from the dashboard, extensive controlling aims to enable top managers to control banks' risks and returns. In this way they are able to identify business opportunities, create diversified portfolios and adjust the risk-return according to bank owners' demands (Horsch and Schulte 2010).

- Finally, Riese (2006) sees the concentration processes in the German banking sector and the reduction of bank branches as an indication of banking 'industrialisation'. As reported in Section 3.2.4.2, the concentration process continues, indicating that banks' 'industrialisation' proceeds.

With the disenchantment of Citibank,[6] "a trend-setting success story" (Riese 2006: 58 [translated]), the term 'industrialisation' has lost popularity. Nevertheless, Deckers and Goeken (2010) see further potential for the 'industrialisation' of

German banks, suggesting the process has passed the point of no return. Concerning the comparison of regional and supraregional banks, it is important to note that the literature does not restrict banking 'industrialisation' to large banks and the private customer segment, but also explicitly addresses savings and cooperative banks and lending to SMEs (Schäfer 2004; Niestrath 2006; Wemhöner and Grunwald 2008; Theis 2009; Hilse et al. 2010). Hence, the empirical comparison must analyse the extent to which the aforementioned 'industrialisation' trends influence the credit-granting of regional and supraregional banks.

To sum up, Section 3.2.4 reveals signs of both change and continuity in the German bank-based financial system. While the section indicates the persistence of traditional banking, signs of changes in the context of the spatial and business organisation of banks, i.e. banks' 'industrialisation', are evident. Signs of continuity tend to be stronger for regional than supraregional banking groups, i.e. increased traditional banking in terms of assets and liabilities and a decentralisation of employees; however, the trend of cutting costs through banking 'industrialisation' affects regional and supraregional banks alike. Therefore, whether regional banks really differ from supraregional banks in their credit-granting processes remains an open question which needs to be investigated through an in-depth comparison.

3.3 Selection and description of bank cases

This section explains the selection of cases and introduces the bank cases under study to explicate the context in which the analysed banks operate. Bank case selection was guided by the aim to compare banks that differ in terms of geographical market orientation (regional versus supraregional banks) in order to identify differences in the processes of granting credit to SMEs. Nonetheless, the bank cases must compete in the same SME segment to avoid 'comparing apples and oranges'. Thus, the goal of the case selection was to contrast banks with maximum differences in their geographical market orientation but which are simultaneously competing for the same SME customers.

As outlined in the previous section, owing to their regional market orientation, savings and cooperative banks represent the two regional banking groups in Germany. Of these, the savings banks finance group was selected for study for feasibility reasons, i.e. reliable contacts to the savings banks from previous research projects. The regional principle restricts the market reach of savings banks to the region, i.e. the municipal level, and they are the largest banking group in terms of credits to non-financial firms and the self-employed. In total, four savings banks were investigated, of which savings bank 1 represents the in-depth case study where two months of full-time participant observation allowed detailed insights into the bank's credit-granting processes.

The study in hand focuses on the group of big banks as the supraregional bank case. Big banks directly compete with savings banks for SME customers (GB1MIT13.02.14, GB1MIT11.02.14) and conduct business in supraregional market areas; i.e. they have Germany-wide and, with the exception of Deutsche

Postbank, international market areas. The other groups of supraregional banks are less suitable for the comparison because *Landesbanken*, cooperative central banks and special-purpose banks and branches of foreign banks compete with savings banks in limited ways. As members of the savings banks financial group, *Landesbanken* are obligated to cooperate with the savings banks. In a similar way, special-purpose banks collaborate with the savings banks in the (subsidised) SME credit business (see Section 3.2.1). The central institutes of the cooperative banks compete with the savings banks via their associated regional cooperative banks.

As shown in Section 3.2.3, big banks lost market shares in the corporate credit segment from 1999 to 2015. Nevertheless, they granted credits of €123.3 bn to non-financial firms and the self-employed in 2015 and were the second most important financier in the manufacturing sector, indicating their continuing relevance for firm finance. In this context, interview partners pointed out that big banks were revisiting the smaller-scale SME credit business at the time of the empirical enquiry (2013–2014) because it had proved itself to be stable and profitable since the financial crisis and the current low interest rate environment (GB1MIT25.09.13II, OBCIT07.02.14II, GB1MIT13.02.14). Hence, the selection of savings and big banks allows the comparison of banking groups that in fact compete directly for the same SMEs but differ in terms of geographical market orientation, which suggests differences in the spatial organisation of their credit decision processes.

The selection of actual bank cases within the banking groups was governed by accessibility. The challenge of gaining access not only related to the fact that experts rejected interview requests but also to the difficulty of getting into contact with appropriate experts, e.g. customer advisors and credit officers in the relevant SME segment. Not a single interview was agreed upon without prior contact. Connections to the DSGV and the Association of German Banks (private banks) mitigated the challenge, and after initial interviews the snowball sampling method generated 23 informative expert interviews. The interviews were used to inquire about the possibility of undertaking participant observation at the banks. A range of interview partners provided contacts and information about how to apply to their banks. Savings bank 1 approved the application for a two-month full-time student internship after a job interview. Applications for internships to the big banks were not successful, thus the results from savings bank 1 are compared with the interview findings. Big bank 1 was selected as the in-depth contrast case to savings bank 1, because this bank revealed most information and the interviewed branch operates in the same region as savings bank 1, allowing a comparison of credit granting in similar regional contexts.

The following section outlines the key features of the savings banks financial group and introduces savings bank 1 and the other regional bank cases in order to provide information about the respective context (Section 3.3.1). The section indicates the relevance of the savings banks financial group for the business of regional savings banks. Section 3.3.2 describes basic aspects of the group of big banks and introduces big bank 1, identifying a higher spatial division of labour than in savings banks. Furthermore, the section introduces the three additional supraregional banking cases.

3.3.1 Savings banks and other regional banks

The savings banks are the regional banking case study for the empirical comparison. Beside participant observation, overall 13 interviews with four different savings banks and 5 interviews with other experts associated with the savings banks financial group were conducted (Appendix).

The savings banks financial group consists of ca. 600 organisations that employ ca. 346,000 people (Simpson 2013). Among the 417 regional savings banks and a range of other banks, firms and associations also belong to the savings banks financial group (see Table 3.5). The financial group differs from a group of companies or a holding company like Deutsche Bank, because the decentralised savings banks and their local authorities own and control the central institutes. Therefore, in contrast to a corporate group, the CEOs of savings banks' central institutes are not allowed to decide top-down, but have to achieve consensus for joint action bottom-up (Breuer and Mark 2004). In this way the savings banks financial group represents a *Verbundsgruppe*, i.e. an association of independent firms by law and ownership, a common form of commercial organisation in Germany, especially in retailing (Flögel et al. 2013).

Organisations of the savings banks financial group operate at three geographical scales. At the regional scale (ca. NUTS 3 level), the 417 savings banks are controlled by their respective local authorities (i.e. municipalities: cities, towns

Table 3.5 Structure of the savings banks financial group

Scale \ Section	Owner	Credit institutes	Associations
Nation		DekaBank Deutsche Leasing	DSGV A range of associated institutes, associations and firms, e.g.: – Sparkassen Rating and Risikosysteme GmbH – University of the savings banks financial group – Academic Sponsorship of the savings banks financial group e.V.
District (about NUTS 1–2)	States	7 *Landesbanken* 10 Public building societies 11 insurances	12 (regional) savings banks associations: – 11 savings banks academies – A range of associated firms
Region (about NUTS 3)	Municipalities	417 savings banks	

Source: Gärtner and Flögel 2017: 115 (translated and modified)

and counties) and operate as universal banks in their region. The 12 savings banks associations operate at the district scale. The savings banks and municipalities on the territories of the savings banks associations control the associations. These savings banks associations own 10 public building societies and 11 public insurance companies and, together with the states, seven *Landesbanken*. The 12 savings banks associations control the DSGV and the DekaBank. Both organisations operate for the whole savings banks financial group at the national scale (see Box 3.3).

Box 3.3   The savings banks financial group

The local authorities are responsible for their respective savings banks but do not own them as they have no proprietary rights over the 'institutions under public law' and legislation prohibits the sale of savings banks. The administrative councils, i.e. supervisory boards, control their savings banks, and the head of the local authority, i.e. the mayor or county commissioner, leads the administrative councils. The councils consist of regional politicians, savings banks' customers and employees of the savings banks, in accordance with employees' right of co-determination. The administrative councils set key guidelines (e.g. the *Sparkassensatzung*, or articles of the savings bank) and appoint the CEO. German banking supervision treats savings banks like all other banks; therefore, every institute frequently has to report to the Deutsche Bundesbank. Unlike private banks and *Landesbanken* that employ private auditing firms, the regional savings banks associations have auditing departments (so-called *Prüfungsstellen*) that conduct the auditing of the savings banks.

The 12 regional savings banks associations are governed by general assemblies that consist of representatives from the savings banks and local authorities. The operative management of the regional savings banks associations is conducted by the presidential board that also makes personnel and strategic decisions. Regional savings banks associations have numerous functions. They represent the interests of their members vis-à-vis the state policy, *Landesbanken* and the national organisations of the savings banks financial group; they organise the *Stützungsfonds*, or deposit guarantee funds, of the regional savings banks that protect customers' deposits and provide a range of services for their member savings banks. With these auditing, guaranteeing and service functions, regional savings banks associations become key agents that supervise the robustness of their member banks, an important task as all member savings banks guarantee for one another via the *Stützungsfonds*.

The corresponding states and the regional savings banks associations control the seven *Landesbanken*. In principle, they operate as central institutes for the savings banks; i.e. they manage payment transactions, equalise liquidity and support savings banks' customers in international business and with special products. Furthermore, *Landesbanken* have the functions of state banks and development banks for their states, yet a large number of states have established separate development banks. As universal banks *Landesbanken* also conduct business on their own, which became a focus of public debate in the financial crisis of 2008 when all but one of the *Landsbanken* suffered heavy losses in this business.

Regional savings banks associations and the *Landesbanken* control the DSGV which lobbies for the savings banks financial group on the national and international scales. The association has offices in Berlin, Bonn and Brussels, and its president is the publicly recognised representative of the financial group. Different departments, e.g. the marketing strategies department, the economics department, and affiliated companies, e.g. the *Sparkassen Rating and Risikosystem GmbH*, belong to the DSGV and create knowledge and services for the whole savings banks financial group. The *Finanz Informatik GmbH & Co. KG*, the central IT service provider, also operates at the national scale, but is directly owned by the regional savings banks associations and the *Landesbanken*.

Sources: Ach and Heinrich 2007; Simpson 2013; Gärtner and Flögel 2017; OSG-VIT04.03.13, DSGV 2014

A range of principles govern the business strategies of and cooperation within the savings banks financial group (for an overview of all principles see Theis 2009). The *öffentlicher Auftrag*, or public mandate, justifies the whole existence of the public savings banks and is specified in the savings bank laws of the states and the articles of every savings bank (Brämer et al. 2010). Savings banks were founded as publicly supported self-help organisations in the eighteenth and nineteenth centuries with the purpose of facilitating the savings of the poor and financing small local firms. The public mandate still governs savings banks' business (OSGVIT04.03.13) and obliges savings banks to supply financial services to all groups of society, meet the regional credit demands and promote economic development. Education for financial literacy, i.e. 'saving mentality', and the support of civic engagement are additional obligations of the savings banks financial group (Brämer et al. 2010). According to one interview partner of the DSGV, the public mandate remains an important pillar of the corporate culture of the savings banks financial group, as does the group's long history (OITSGV04.03.2013). Nevertheless, as independent banks, every savings bank also develops its own corporate culture, particularly shaped by its CEO.

The horizontal (regional principle) and vertical (subsidiarity principle) division of labour characterises cooperation within the savings bank financial group (Gärtner and Flögel 2017). Specified in saving banks laws (e.g., § 3 of the

Sparkassengesetz Nordrhein-Westfalen, 18 November 2008), the regional principle basically stipulates that a savings bank may only conduct business in the region of the municipality concerned. Savings banks tend to interpret the regional principle flexibly with respect to lending, so they are able to lend beyond the so-called *Ausleihbezirk*, or lending district. The *Ausleihbezirk* is specified in the article of every savings bank and establishes the geographical area where credit granting is allowed. Nonetheless, the regional principle bans the active promotion and operation of branches outside the municipality concerned. Accordingly, the regional principle reduces competition between the savings banks.

In contrast to the regional principle, the subsidiarity principle is not specified by law but represents a general guideline of cooperation within the financial group (Gärtner 2008; Gärtner and Flögel 2017). The subsidiarity principle implies that the higher scale should conduct business which the lower scale cannot do efficiently, e.g. lending to large corporations. Also in line with the subsidiarity principle, the savings banks financial group creates a range of services for savings banks at the district or national scale, e.g. finance ICT and rating systems. In this way, savings banks are able to realise economies of scale within the financial group and at the same time preserve regional independence (Schmidt et al. 2014). Nevertheless, delegation of functions to a higher scale implies a reduction of regional independence, thus the impact of the savings banks financial group on the processes of credit granting is considered in the empirical analysis.

3.3.1.1 Savings bank 1

Savings bank 1 was selected for the in-depth case study of the regional banks. A two-month internship in different departments from November 2013 to January 2014 and four (group) interviews provided conclusive empirical data about the bank. Savings bank 1 is one of the larger German savings banks; it is above the 2013 median values in terms of balance sheet total, deposits, lending and branches (see Table 3.2, p. 103, for the mean values of banking groups' key assets and liabilities). In terms of the arithmetic mean, savings bank 1 reports an above average balance sheet total and deposits and mean values concerning lending and branches. It operates in an urban market area with a weak economic structure. No changes in the market area of this savings bank have occurred in the last 80 years (e.g. no bank mergers), implying a high level of business continuity. Its employees perceive the organisation and strategies of savings bank 1 as traditional and public-mandate oriented (SK1MPP03.12.13). For 2013, savings bank 1 reported a successful business year with retained earnings of ca. €2.5 million.

Savings bank 1 consists of departments and subordinated working groups. The CEO and the second *Vorstand*, or managing director, are each in charge of designated departments (Figure 3.18). On the second tier, the department heads supervise the working groups. The team leaders of the working groups are involved in everyday business; working groups consist of ca. 5 to 20 employees. In line with MaRisk bank regulation, like all other banks, savings bank 1 distinguishes between market (or front-office) departments (corporate customers and trading)

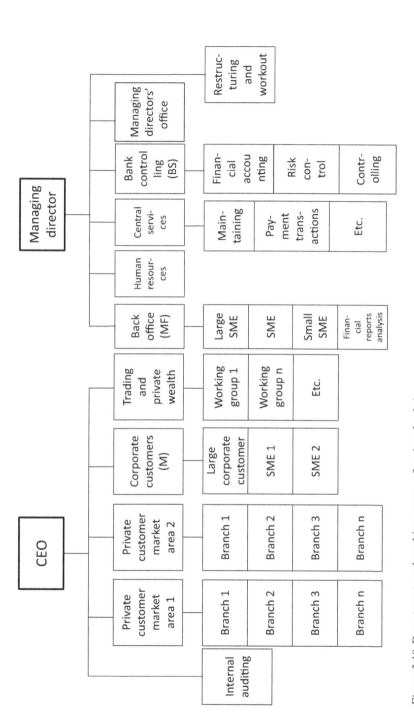

Figure 3.18 Departments and working groups of savings bank 1

Source: author's figure

and back-office departments up to CEO level (BaFin 2012a: BTO 1.1 and BTO 2.1). The corporate customer department (market) and the back-office department deal with SME customers directly; the restructuring and workout team gets involved in cases of imminent insolvency. Small corporate customers, with total business credits volume of less than €100,000, are served in the ca. 30 branches of the savings bank by the private customer advisors. Two other departments deal with SME customers indirectly. The bank controlling department conducts the risk reporting, limit setting and (standard) condition determination for all credits and the internal credit auditing regularly checks a random sample of credit approval processes ex post.

Participant observation as a student trainee was conducted in the corporate customers department (*M*), the back office for corporate customers (*MF*) and the bank controlling department (*BS*). The corporate customers department consists of three working groups: one for large corporate customers located at savings bank 1's headquarters and two for SMEs, one at the headquarters and one at a major branch. The internship took place in the SME working group of the major branch. The working group serves SMEs with a total amount of business credits ranging from above €100,000 up to ca. €5 million. However, these thresholds are permeable; e.g. the working group also serves one large *borrower unit*[7] with total credits of over €20 million.

The back-office department for corporate customers consists of four working groups (all of which were observed) and is located at savings bank 1's headquarters. One working group is responsible for small firm customers, one for SMEs, one for large corporate customers and one team conducts the balance sheet analysis. Three working groups, i.e. financial accounting, risk control and controlling, and the temporary project team for Basel III/CRD 4 implementation form the controlling department. The internship predominantly took place in the accounting working group, where workload was high due to the year-end accounting at the time of observation. In addition, default risk management was observed. Overall participant observation took place in all working groups that directly deal with SMEs, and also involved observation of the controlling of default risk.

3.3.1.2   Other regional bank cases

With savings bank 2, one group interview (SK2OIP18.03.13) and four individual interviews were conducted: one with the head of the trading department (SK2OIP13.03.13), one with the head of the *Vorstand* office (SK2OIP13.03.132), one with the head of the market department (SK2MIP13.03.13) and one with the head of the private customers and small firm department (SK2MIP13.03.132). Savings bank 2 is the smallest bank of the four savings banks cases, with a balance sheet total and lending below the arithmetic mean of all savings banks. It serves a rural market area with a below-average per capita GDP. In the last three decades, savings bank 2 has been involved in two mergers, and a restructuring programme was taking place at the time of interviewing in spring 2013.

At savings bank 3, two interviews with customer advisors, one in charge of SMEs (SK3MIT24.09.13) and one in charge of large SMEs (SK3MIT18.08.13), were carried out in autumn 2013. Although smaller than savings bank 1, savings bank 3 is still one of the larger German savings banks in terms of the median values of balance sheet total and lending and operates in a rural but not peripheral market area in a prosperous region of Germany. Savings bank 3 reported a successful business year in 2013. Two interviews were conducted with savings bank 4 in the autumn of 2013: one interview with a customer advisor for SMEs (SK4MIT25.10.13) and one with a customer advisor for large SMEs (SK4MIT25.09.13). Savings bank 4 is one of the large savings banks; its balance sheet total and lending are clearly above average in terms of mean and median values. The municipality responsible for savings bank 4 is a major German city, and savings bank 4's extensive *Ausleihbezirk* comprises not only the major city but also the neighbouring municipalities. Savings bank 4 reported a successful business year in 2013.

Within the cooperative banking pillar two interviews with employees of one cooperative central institute (cooperative central bank) and two interviews with the CEO of a small regional cooperative bank (cooperative bank 1) were carried out. Cooperative bank 1 is the smallest of all the banks investigated and operates in the same rural market area as savings bank 2.

3.3.2 *The group of big banks and other supraregional banks*

The group of big banks are the supraregional bank case study of this empirical comparison. In contrast to the savings banks financial group, no association between the four German big banks exists, and the four only represent a statistical aggregated type of bank by Deutsche Bundesbank. Accordingly, big banks compete with one another unrestrictedly, and no association exclusively represents the big banks. The association of German banks and its 11 regional subassociations conduct lobbying and manage the deposit protection fund for all 447 private banks in Germany (Bundesverband deutscher Banken e.V. 2014).

The two largest German big banks, Deutsche Bank and Commerzbank, were founded as merchant banks in the nineteenth century. In the course of their development, Deutsche Bank and Commerzbank acquired a range of (regional) banks and other financial companies, e.g. Commerzbank controlled ca. 300 firms in 2013 (Commerzbank 2013a), and became large and internationally active universal banks. It was only after World War II that private customers and SME business emerged as a relevant business segment for the big banks (OSGVIT04.03.13, GB2OIP11.03.13, Historische Gesellschaft der Deutschen Bank e.V. 2009). At present, all four big banks operate as universal banks and consider corporate lending as a relevant business segment. For example, Commerzbank's so-called *Mittelstandsbank*, i.e. its corporate banking division, was its most profitable segment in 2013 with an earnings before interest and taxes of €1.1 bn, a remarkable result considering the fact that Commerzbank overall only earned €0.7 bn in 2013 (Commerzbank 2013b). The example illustrates that SMEs are in fact a relevant business segment for big banks at present. In contrast to the savings banks that were founded with the aim of providing finance for small firms, the big banks entered the SME business more than 100 years later.

Overall, 11 interviews with four different German and international large private banks as well as one interview with a representative of the association of German banks (private banks) were conducted (Appendix). Of these, big bank 1 represents the in-depth supraregional bank case study for the comparison with savings bank 1. Six interviews provided extensive information about the bank, especially about one of its SME customer branches. Three interviews were conducted with customer advisors from this branch (GB1MIT11.02.14, GB1MIT25.06.13I, GB1MIT25.09.13II). Furthermore, one interview was carried out with a former regional SME-segment market area manager (GB1MIT13.02.14), one interview with a manager of a sectorial-specialised risk analysis department (GB1M-FIP05.11.12) and one interview with a trainee from big bank 1 (GB1MIP11.09.13). Big bank 1 is one of the four German big banks and operates branches countrywide and abroad.

In particular, the study focuses on the SME customer branch of big bank 1 and compares it with the observed SME customer team of savings bank 1. The two units are located in the same region and directly compete for the same SMEs; i.e. at savings bank 1 one firm was observed which also had a loan from big bank 1 (SK1MPP28.11.13). Big bank 1's SME customer branch under study has 10 employees and, similar to savings bank 1, the big bank segregates SMEs according to their size. This segregation is not static but takes customer demands into consideration (GB1MIT25.06.13I). Customers with a turnover of ca. €2 million to €10 million form the small SME segment of big bank 1, and customers with a turnover of above €10 million to ca. €200 million comprise the segment of medium-sized SMEs. Another division of big bank 1 is in charge of large corporations. For the purpose of readability, SME size classes are similarly named in the following discussion, independent of banks' internal nomenclatures:

- *Small SME*: revenue < €500,000; total business credits of borrower unit < €100,000
- *Medium SME*: revenue €500,000 to €10 million; total business credits of borrower unit €100,000 to €5 million
- *Large SME*: revenue €10 million to €200 million; total business credit of borrower unit more than €5 million

The organisational design of big bank 1's departments is more complex than that of savings bank 1 owing to its size. Table 3.6 gives an overview of all departments that directly deal with SME customers or their files routinely and their geographical reach. The bank organises the SME customer business at three geographical scales; at the regional/municipal scale the customer advisors are the direct contact persons for SMEs. Big bank 1 subdivides back-office functions in administrative work that is conducted at the district scale, and several risk analysis departments and other subdivided work processes that are conducted at the national scale.

Table 3.6 Overview of big bank 1's departments that directly deal with SME customers and their spatial scale

Spatial Scale	Departments
Nation	• Sectorial-specialised risk analysis departments (ca. 10 specialised back-office departments for large SMEs)
	• Risk analysis department for medium SMEs
	• Financial reports analysis and rating department
	• Collaterals department
	• Payment transactions department
	• Law department
	• Internal credit auditing department
District (about NUTS 2)	• Product specialists (payment transaction, foreign business, risk management)
	• Administrative back offices
	• Regional market area management
Region/municipality (about NUTS 3)	• SME customer branches (customer advisors)

Source author's table, following interview GB1MFIP05.11.1, GB1MIT11.02.14, GB1MIT25.06.13I, GB1MIT25.09.13II, GB1MIT13.02.14

Overall, Table 3.6 indicates the substantial (geographical) division of labour in big bank 1, which will be explored in Chapter 4.

Interviews with three other large banks were carried out. While the scope of information remains lower than that gained through the inquiry at big bank 1, due to the limited number of interviews per bank, the findings nevertheless help to assess the generalisability of results. At big bank 2, two interviews were conducted, one with an employee in a leading position in the SME segment and the other with the historian of the bank. The second interview primarily focused on the historical development and corporate culture of big banks in general (GB2OIP11.03.13). As one of the four German big banks, big bank 2 runs a nationwide branch network and also has international subsidiaries. At big bank 3, a large foreign bank with market presence in Germany, two interviews took place with one interview partner who worked in the SME segment. With big bank 4 – a subsidiary of a large foreign bank focusing on large corporation and private wealth management in Germany – one interview about risk management and bank controlling was carried out.

Notes

1 Concern about ethnographical representation also relates to the fact that a range of ethnographers write in a powerful way about less powerful communities (Breidenstein et al. 2013; see also literature review in Rose 1997). Therefore, what ethnographers write about these communities forms the perception of them in the scientific community and wider society. The ethnographical study in hand analyses the banking sector, an industry with an active lobby (Admati and Hellwig 2014). Hence, the concern to ill-represent the 'powerless' tends to be less striking for this study.

2 The single supervisory mechanism (SSM) shifts supervisory responsibility partly to the ECB by establishing a division of labour between national and ECB banking supervision (Pukropski et al. 2015). Especially big banks tend to be affected by the new regulation as ECB directly supervises these 'significant' institutes. 'Insignificant' banks, e.g. banks whose assets do not exceed €30 bn, stay under the supervision of the national organisations. As SSM came into power in November 2014, it was irrelevant at the time of empirical enquiry (April 2013 to February 2014). Consequently, this section introduces the 'old' bank supervision which was in power at the time of enquiry.

3 Tier 1 capital, i.e. the core capital of a bank, consists predominantly of common stock and retained earnings. Tier 1 capital has the highest loss-absorbing capacity (Paul 2011).

4 Non-financial firms include firms and the self-employed from all sectors except banks, insurances and other financial firms.

5 Because of rearrangement in the labour market statistics, a comparison of regional and supraregional banking groups has been precluded since 2009.

6 The customer advisory and cross-selling practices of Citibank were criticised for their hidden costs in overdraft contract (Czycholl 2008) and high losses in Lehman Brothers investments (Ludwig 2009). Consequently, Citibank was renamed Targobank and sold in 2010.

7 A borrower unit consists of all customers of the bank that are connected economically or by law; e.g. a company, its subsidiaries and its partners form one borrower unit. Bank regulation requires the creation of borrower units to identify cluster risks, and borrower units represent the principal unit by which banks specify the limits and conduct credit decisions.

4 SME credit decision making of savings versus big banks

4.1 The informational basis of credit decisions

Banks collect numerous types of information and data and aggregate these in reports and rating systems for new credit applications (screening) and to monitor existing credit engagements. This section lists key informational sources banks use in credit appraisal and describes basic calculation techniques. Section 4.1.1 lists information banks rely on in the SME segment and discusses the 'softness' of this information. Section 4.1.2 explains three basic calculation techniques – annual financial statement analysis, cash flow analysis and blank credit calculation – and outlines the data-collecting processes of the analysed banks. Overall, the section indicates the discretion enjoyed by bank employees in the basic calculations, even though the calculations are based on hard information.

4.1.1 Soft and hard information

As discussed in Section 2.2.2, the study in hand utilises the distinction between soft and hard information to analyse the geography of credit decision making. Actors are able to transmit hard information easily across distance, whereas third persons face difficulties to verify soft information. Thus, the transmission of soft information becomes more difficult when distance between sender and receiver increases. This is not to deny that banks also codify and transmit soft information across distance. However, soft information cannot be directly verified by distant actors who have not been involved in its production. The empirical results show that the 'hardness' or reliability of hard information varies considerably in banking practices, qualifying the dichotomy between soft and hard information. *'Rather' hard information* allows direct verification by third parties in principle but verification is constrained in the actual situation of appraisal. In contrast, soft information can only be verified ex post, if at all, by distant actors not involved in its production.

In practice, the two banks studied in-depth evaluate two different aspects of a credit application. Firstly, banks assess the creditworthiness of the customer, i.e. the firm, its managers and owners, in order to decide if the bank wants to conduct business with this customer in general (Section 4.1.1.1). Secondly, banks evaluate the creditworthiness of projects in order to decide whether to approve the new credit the customer has applied for and its specific terms and conditions (Section 4.1.1.2). The rating systems for SMEs of the savings banks and big bank 1 analyse aspects of customers' creditworthiness only; the decision on projects tends to be downstream to the decision on customers.

4.1.1.1 Creditworthiness of customers

Hard information, especially *annual financial statements*, builds the basis of the firm evaluation. Banks request firms' annual financial statements (or tax declarations in case of self-employed people) of at least the last three years. In existing customer relationships the statements are usually available due to the annual disclosure. As annual financial statements inform banks about the economic conditions of the firms, this information remains indispensable for credit decisions and is required by bank regulation (§ 18 KWG). Banks use the annual financial statements in the financial rating (Section 4.2.2.1) for the annual financial statement analysis (Section 4.1.2.1) and for cash flow calculations (Section 4.1.2.2). Available cash flow, a high equity share and, very importantly, a positive or at least not a negative trend in the financial figures lead to a positive assessment of firms' creditworthiness (GB1MIT11.02.14, SK1MFPP05.11.13). Annual financial statements count as hard information as tax advisors or auditors approve their reliability and balance sheet fraud is a criminal offence.

The dated nature of annual financial statements lessens their informational content for banks (Horsch and Schulte 2010, GB1MIT25.06.13I, SK3MIT18.08.13), because firms disclose financial statements in the middle of the following year at the earliest. Small SMEs, especially, tend to delay reporting to the end of the following year in order to delay taxation (SK1MFPP08.11.13). Therefore, banks usually rely on more up-to-date data to assess the economic conditions of firms for new credit applications (SK1MPP25.11.13, GB1MIT25.09.13II). These data are, on the one hand, the *Betriebswirtschaftliche Auswertung* (BWA), or business assessments, and on the other hand, account information (balances, trends, revenues, etc.).

The booking system of firms and firms' tax advisors compile the BWAs that enable banks to calculate financial ratios like cash flow, which are comparable to the financial statement analyses but up-to-date. The reliability of the BWAs is lower than the annual financial statements, because important bookings may be absent, e.g. relevant annual expenses, thus distorting the informational content of the financial ratios. Furthermore, the observation that firms accidentally booked their BWAs incorrectly, which was only discovered because of serious errors (SK1MPP28.11.13), indicates the diminished reliability of BWAs, qualifying them as 'rather' hard information. BWAs' reliability can be increased by so-called plausibility checks by tax advisors (SK1MPP16.12.13).

Account information tends to be the most reliable and timely information available to the banks. The rating and risk monitoring systems of the savings banks and big bank 1 utilise account information. Bank employees perceive customers with very good financial statements but literally no money on their business and private accounts suspiciously (SK1MFPP14.11.13). However, account balances tell only half the story, i.e. they represent incomplete information, when customers also keep accounts with other banks. Accordingly, informational content is particularly diminished if a customer keeps his current accounts with another bank and is amplified in exclusive *Hausbank* relationships, e.g. if all firm and private accounts are kept at the bank in question. To mitigate the problem of incomplete information, banks access external sources to gain information on the economic conditions of the customers.

Bank inquiries and credit agency reports, e.g. from Creditreform and Schufa, represent the two common external sources for gaining customer information. Bank inquiries are requests by a bank for information about a customer's account history at another bank, implemented in a standardised questionnaire where the informing bank 'ticks off' basic information like "the economic conditions of the customer are sound or regular" (SK1MPP04.12.13). Whereas big bank 1 obtains credit agency reports for every SME annually, savings bank 1 requests bank inquiries and reports for new customers or non-main-bank customers only. Negative information from bank inquiries and agency reports tends to cause the rejection of new customers; positive information does not guarantee approval. The reluctance of banks to rely on external information is related to the inability to verify the information directly in the situation of credit decisions. Bank inquiries in particular involve asymmetric incentives as the informing bank has an incentive to report positive information on its customers with financial difficulties in order not to discourage other banks. In this context, information retaining was observed twice. In one case, savings bank 1 withheld a profitability warning concerning a firm and backdated the bank inquiry to a date where the information was still unknown (SK1MPP20.11.13). In the other case, savings bank 1 received a bank inquiry which turned out to be wrong ex post (SK1MPP19.11.13). Both observations indicate the diminished reliability of bank inquiries, suggesting them to be 'rather' hard information.

The qualitative evaluation of customers comprises the assessment of the private living circumstances, the personal characteristics and the management characteristics of managing owners/managers, as well as an assessment of the firm's characteristics and sector. Banks need these assessments to gain an extensive picture of firms' riskiness and the qualitative modules of savings banks' and big bank 1's SME rating systems request qualitative evaluations, too. Bank employees utilise diverse sources of information for the assessments, comprising private sources like personal communication and experience with the customers, account information, BWAs, etc., and public sources such as certificates, local rumours and newspapers. Typically, bank employees combine soft with hard information in order to increase the reliability of assessments. In this context, information is also used to cross-check, i.e. verify, (soft) information.

The following illustrates cross-checking in the context of the assessment of management characteristics. Soft information from the declaration of the manager and the impression of the bank employees builds the basis of the assessment together with 'rather' hard information on the formal qualifications and work experience of the manager (OSGVIT01.03.13, GB1MFIP05.11.12, GB1MIT25.09.13II, SK3MIT18.08.13). The initial assessment conducted on this basis is then validated in the course of the business relationship. If, for example, the manager repeatedly predicts business developments correctly (in terms of sales and profitability etc.), then a positive initial assessment of the management will be consolidated; if not, the initial assessment will worsen. In this way, the reliability of banks' qualitative assessments tends to increase over time in existing business relationships.

Finally, customers provide unrequested warnings to their banks to inform the bank about problematic upcoming events like liquidity shortages or a strong diminution of sales and thus demonstrate their trustworthiness to the bank. In fact, banks expect an open information policy from their customers and assess customers who try to hide problems negatively (GB1MIT11.02.14). Especially, larger SMEs tend to provide their banks with forecasts, i.e. liquidity plans and sales and profitability forecasts, regularly. The reliability of the forecast is lower than that of the annual financial statements and BWAs, as it is only verifiable ex post (SK1MPP10.12.13, Geno2MIT23.0214II). Nevertheless, banks have to use the forecasts to calculate cash flow and financial ratios for start-ups for which no financial statements exist, for distressed firms if current cash flows do not justify the extension or maintenance of credits and for new projects that have a strong influence on cash flow.

4.1.1.2 Creditworthiness of projects

If customers want new credits or changes to the existing contracts, they forward their demands to the banks – either in written form (e.g. e-mail) or verbally via telephone or face-to-face meetings – which is relevant (hard information) for credit decisions. How much credit do customers want (size), for which period (duration), what for (e.g. investment loan, mortgage, overdraft line), how much equity capital do they invest, what collaterals do they offer etc.? All this influences the cash flow needed to repay the credits as well as the riskiness of lending. Nevertheless, this information is subordinated to the general decision about whether banks want to conduct business with these customers (GB1MFIP05.11.12), although interconnections exist. On the one hand, the creditworthiness of customers influences the credit terms via the rating scores. On the other hand, as exemplified later (Section 4.3.1), in cases of customers with critical creditworthiness the terms and conditions, e.g. collaterals and equity capital, of the credit become crucial for a positive lending decision.

Not every credit decision involves a project evaluation, thus prolongation of existing credits and minor increases in credit lines only involve the evaluation of the customers. Projects are business start-ups; investment in machines, cars and other mobile assets; investments in research and development; property purchases etc. Banks evaluate projects on the basis of the project descriptions, which usually comprise target figures, i.e. sales and profitability plans, liquidity plans. The scale of the project descriptions depends on the complexity of the projects:

> The more complex the investment gets the more he [the customer] has to deliver to us. If he wants to open e.g. a totally new branch of production, then he has to explain the market opportunities for that etc., also target figures, documents concerning which customers he wants to do it with, who he will sell to, how he wants to get into the market. Hence, we set the standards higher depending on the importance.
>
> (Geno2MIT23.02.14II)

For investment in large projects, banks request that the expected returns of projects cover principals and interest payments (SK3MIT18.08.13). Minor projects, like the leasing of a car, must be covered by the regular cash flows of the firms; hence, banks do not need to forecast for minor projects. The plan figures taken alone are soft information; therefore, banks try to gain proof of the soundness of the forecasts, e.g. rental contracts, purchase contracts, tax advisors' or business consultancies' plausibility checks. Figure 4.1 presents the information note that savings bank 1 sends to new customers that ask for start-up finance. Savings bank 1 seeks to 'harden', or cross-check, the soft plan figures by requesting tax advisors' expertise and alternative financial information (Schufa report, tax declaration notice, assets statements etc.).

If possible, savings bank 1 uses the assets of the financed projects as collateral. The physical assets evaluation is conducted on the basis of the *exposés* that contain object descriptions, key figures, purchase prices and photos of the objects: "If I finance a customer's machine, then he gives me the exposé. Thus bankers like to have pictures [laugh], so that you know what you are financing" (SK3MIT24.09.13). Whereas banks tend to hesitate to use mobile assets as collateral for non-leasing/factoring credits, because of their uncertain recoverability (Section 4.1.2.3), real estate tends to be the most important collateral in credit business. Savings banks, especially, use charges on the land not only for mortgages but as robust collateral for all kinds of risky loans (Handke 2011, GB1MIT11.02.14).

The success of firms in prior projects importantly influences banks' willingness to lend for new projects again. Banks keep records of former business interactions in the customer files. Beside official documents like contracts, correspondence and reports, these files also contain internal information, e.g. notes and minutes from customer talks, memos, internal work instructions etc. Experienced bankers tend to know this information on customers as they actively witnessed the situations in person (SK1MPP20.11.13, SK1MPP09.12.13). In this way, consistent with the relationship banking theory (Section 2.2.1.2), customers gain bank internal reputations in the course of business relationships.

Overview of documents to be submitted:
- Business idea/concept (with explanations of the sector, business location, competitors, staffing, offers, advertising, etc.)
- Investment plan (without VAT)
- Determination of liquidity requirements (liquidity plan on a monthly basis for two years)
- Profitability forecast for three years with an explanation of how the figures were calculated (created by a tax advisor or business consultant)
- In case of takeovers: draft of the purchase agreement, annual financial statements of the last three years, as well as preliminary results of the current year
- In case of start-up companies: company contract drafts
- Commercial lending draft
- Detailed, seamless curriculum vitae (with monthly data)
- Photocopy of identity card (front and back)
- Complete assets statements, including evidence (e.g. photocopies of bank books, insurance certificates, balance of building savings accounts, deposit statements, photocopies of the land register excerpts, loan contracts, balance confirmations, surrender values, leasing contracts, etc.) for married persons with legal matrimonial property schemes, records of the assets of the wife as well as common assets
- Proof of equity contribution of at least 15%
- Collateralisation proposals
- Last income tax assessment together with explanation and appendix (in case of prior self-employment in addition the financial statements for the past three years and an explanation of why the previous self-employment was abandoned)
- Schufa report
- Permission for the collection of bank enquiries
- Statement of private expenditure (form enclosed)

Figure 4.1 Overview of the documents needed for business start-up loans

Source: SK1DInfos für Gründer (translated)

4.1.2 Data-collecting processes and basic calculation techniques of banks

Banks execute routine data-collecting processes and conduct basic calculations to evaluate the riskiness of lending to firms. The following sections explain these processes and describe how savings bank 1 organises them. As data availability allows, the sections further discuss the process organisation at big bank 1 and the other banking cases and identify differences. Section 4.1.2.1 describes the process of annual financial statement analysis, one of the most important sources of hard information banks rely on. Section 4.1.2.2 explains the calculations and judgments bank employees conduct to determine a customer's future ability to cover interest and principal payments, which is the single most important criterion of credit decisions. Section 4.1.2.3 turns to collaterals and their appraisal.

4.1.2.1 Annual financial statement analysis

Bank regulations require the annual financial disclosure, which causes a considerable amount of work for the back offices of banks. Section 18 KWG states that banks may only grant credits of more than €750,000 if they are aware of borrowers' economic conditions, especially the annual financial statements. This implies that banks have to make sure that firms disclose their annual financial statements until their overall credit volumes are below €750,000. Two interview partners reported that 10 to 15 years ago it was a delicate affair to ask firms for their financial statements, as managers did not like to open the books. Nowadays almost all firms are used to this routine and post the financial statements when they have been compiled (GB2MIP27.11.12, GB1MIT25.09.13II). Savings bank 1 as well as big bank 1 voluntarily exceed the § 18 KWG requests and ask for the annual financial statements of their corporate customers with a credit volume above ca. €250,000[1] (SK1MFPP07.11.13, SK1MFPP18.11.13, GB1MIT25.09.13II).

Banks collect the annual financial statements of their corporate customers in extensive databases. These databases are important sources of information which banks use to develop and maintain the rating systems (Section 4.2.2.1) and – via the ICT-based financial statement analysis – compare individual firms with sector averages from the databases. As the savings bank financial group has the highest market share in corporate lending, it collects the highest number of clients' financial statements of all the banks and banking groups in Germany, especially for SMEs (OSGVIT01.03.13, GB3MIT29.05.13I). This extensive financial statements database represents a notable competitive advantage for the regional savings banks, indicating the importance of the savings banks financial group for the business success of individual savings banks.

At savings bank 1 a specific financial statement analysis working group of the back-office department conducts the disclosure process (SK1MFPP07.11.13, SK1MFPP12.11.13). An automatic reminder mechanism, integrated into the savings bank's ICT system, requests the annual financial statements; i.e. the centralised Finanz Informatik GmbH & Co. KG automatically mails the first reminder letter in the middle of the following year and the second reminder in autumn. At the same time that the second letter is posted the customer advisors responsible receive tasks via the ICT system to remind the overdue firms. Savings bank 1 tries to process all statements by the end of the following year. Missing statements from firms that must disclose according to § 18 KWG have to be reported to the supervisors (up to the CEO). The financial statement analysis working group of savings bank 1 enters and processes the annual financial statements and applies a priority group system. The team has to process the financial statements of new credit applications instantly; the annual disclosure statements from customers with credits above €750,000 should be processed within four weeks, and those from customers with credits of over €250,000 within six weeks (SK1MFPP07.11.13). Three credit officers enter the financial statements in a web-based system. A second officer cross-checks all entered statements, in accordance with the 'four eyes' principle.

The *Deutscher Sparkassenverlag*, or savings banks publishing house, develops and maintains the so-called EBIL ICT system (Meyer 2000; Middelberg and Plegge 2010) that collects the financial statements of all customers of the savings banks financial group and feeds their large financial statement database. EBIL automatically creates an EBIL report that includes key financial ratios, a three-year trends analysis and a comparison of the firm with its size class sectorial average (at WZ 2008 five-digit level) (SK1MFPP 07.11.13, see Figure 4.2). Savings bank 1 uses the financial statement reports for internal risk monitoring, and selected customers receive the reports as an advisory service.

As participant observation showed, entering the annual financial statements involves discretion despite the hardness of information and the fact that guidelines and handbooks standardise the input of financial data (Meyer 2000; Riebell 2006). The classification of a limited number of balance sheet positions is open to discretion. For example, does the loan of a managing owner to his firm count as equity capital or debt? Are neutral incomes of a firm a one-time earning or regular income? Savings bank 1 decides these unclear positions on a case-by-case basis (SK1MFPP07.11.13). If discrete classifications decidedly alter financial ratios, credit officers and customer advisors are especially likely to discuss the classification in person.

At savings bank 1 the credit officers have to write qualitative assessments about the financial situation of firms with poor rating scores, which involves discretion. Credit officers assess firms on the basis of the actual and historical EBIL reports and the financial statements. Furthermore, they study the appendix of the financial statements (that comprises a management report and a statement from the tax advisors) in more detail than they do for customers with sound rating scores (SK1MFPP07.11.13). The final financial statement analyses are posted to the customer advisors in charge of the customers for the annual disclosure round at savings bank 1. The financial statement analysis consists of the firm's annual financial statement, the EBIL report and (if the rating score is poor) the verbal assessment of the statement from the credit officer. Customer advisors check and comment on this so-called circular, execute the rating, check the ability to cover future interest and principal payments (see next section) and send the circular to the credit officers in charge of these customers. The credit officers again check and comment and send the circular to the supervisors in charge. When all actors have checked and signed the circular, the disclosure and credit prolongation process is completed.

At big bank 1 a centralised department conducts the financial statement analyses; i.e. it scans the annual statements and puts them into the ICT system. Like

List 5	Metallverarbeitung Biegeknecht GmbH	Date: November 3, 2009
	Balance sheet as of December 31, 2008	Legal basis: German commercial code

Company key: 04032009/12600   Business key figures

	Company			Sector average*	
Key figures	Tax balance 12/31/06	Tax balance 12/31/07	Tax balance 12/31/08	from	to
Corporate earnings					
Returns on sales (%)	3.1	4.7	6.6	2.4	9.8
Cash-Flow-Rate (%)					
through profit or loss (before taxes)	12.2	11.3	15.6	4.6	12.5
Operational profitability (%)	4.0	5.2	5.0	3.1	9.5
Gross profit ratio (%)	59.5	58.2	59.9	46.0	64.2
Personnel costs ratio (%)	30.9	31.0	30.6	21.8	38.1
Depreciation ratio (%)	9.2	6.6	9.0	1.3	2.4
Ratio of depreciation on					
Fixed assets (%)	28.1	27.3	28.1	18.0	34.1
Interest ratio (%)	1.4	0.9	1.3	0.2	0.9
Rent ratio (%)	4.1	3.7	4.1	1.3	3.7
Return on capital (%)	8.4	13.2	15.2	8.6	36.3
Return per employee (TEUR)					
Gross profit per employee (TEUR)					
Assets and liabilities					
Total capital turnover (n-times)	1.9	2.4	1.9	1.9	4.8
Intensity of investments (%)	44.5	41.4	44.4	8.8	26.3
Period of receivables (in days)	48.9	41.2	48.4	25.8	53.7
Storage period (in days)	114.4	102.7	114.5	24.3	99.4
Investment ratio (%)	0.0	0.0	0.0	0.9	3.3
Financial situation					
Dynamic leverage factor (years)					
through profit or loss (before taxes)	3.5	2.6	3.1	1.5	5.1
Equity ratio (financially) (%)	19.6	30.3	5.7	12.6	42.3
Asset coverage (%)	70.1	98.1	38.9	98.1	235.7
Short-term liquidity (%)	81.3	91.9	59.9	11.4	44.2
Days payables outstanding (days)	33.6	20.2	33,6	27,4	72,0
Short-term indebtedness (%)	38.3	33.2	51.9	52.5	70.0
Self-financing ratio (%)				180.8	545.2

Figure 4.2 Key financial figures of the financial statement analysis

* The industry comparison is made with balance sheets from the size categories 50: 2,500,000 to 5,000,000 EURO, legal basis: all types repair of fabricated metal products, machinery and equipment / 17 balance sheets were considered; as of 08/2009 / final

Source: Middelberg and Plegge 2010: 56 (translated and modified)

savings bank 1, big bank 1 applies a priority system. Bankers are allowed to order a limited contingent of overnight analyses for very urgent cases. Normal processing takes about 6 to 20 days (GB1MIT11.02.14). The ICT analysis system tends to be comparable to that of the savings banks and also conducts deep sector comparisons (GB1MFIP05.11.12, Meyer 2000).

Bank reports on the financial statement analysis comprise a number of financial figures and ratios. The EBIL report of the savings banks includes figures related to the corporate earnings, assets and liabilities and the financial situation (Theis 2009; Sparkassen Rating und Risikosysteme GmbH 2010; Middelberg and Plegge 2010; Figure 4.2). Selected figures gain special importance as the rating systems use them. Big bank 1 uses seven figures for its financial rating (GB1MIT11.02.14, see Section 4.2.2.1). According to Middelberg and Plegge (2010) the saving banks' rating systems use 14 figures that are listed and defined in Table 4.1. Banks also use the financial figures for their risk assessment; e.g. observations at savings bank 1 indicated that bank employees especially study the capital and cash-flow situation of firms and its development (SK1MFPP 06.11.13).

Table 4.1 Financial figures of the savings banks financial rating

Name	Calculation	Unit and direction*
Corporate earnings		
Cash-flow-rate 1	Extended cash flow/short-term debt * 100	% ↑
Cash-flow-rate 2	(Operating revenues + depreciation of fixed assets)/(debt – liquid assets) * 100	% ↑
Dynamic operating revenues	Operating revenues/short-term debt * 100	% ↑
Return on investment (ROI)	Extended cash flow/balance sheet total * 100	% ↑
Interest ratio	Interest payments/total cost * 100	% ↓
Rent ratio	Rental payments/overall performance * 100	% ↓
Gross profit ratio	Gross profit/overall performance * 100	% ↑
Assets and liabilities		
Storage period	Stocks * 360/material costs	Days ↓
Storage ratio	Stocks/overall performance * 100	% ↓
Financial situation		
Equity Ratio (financially)	Equity capital/balance sheet total * 100	% ↑
Liquidity ratio	Liquid assets/balance sheet total * 100	% ↑
Days payable outstanding	(Payable trade outstanding + acceptance)/material costs * 360	Days ↑
Capital commitment	(Short-term bank debt + short-term payable trade outstanding + short-term other debt)/overall performance * 100	% ↓
Debt structure	(Payable trade outstanding + acceptance + bank debt)/debt * 100	% ↓

* ↑ higher values indicate economically sound firms; ↓ lower values indicate economically sound firms.

Source: author's summary following Middelberg and Plegge 2010; Ahnert et al. 2009

4.1.2.2 *Cash flow and future ability to cover interest and principal payments*

Cash flow analysis tends to be the most important aspect of banks' evaluation of firms because it indicates the capacity of firms to pay back debt and interest. Banks calculate the so-called customers' future ability to cover the interest and principal payments, i.e. customers' ability to serve debts, by subtracting the debt service (the amount of interest and principal payable) from the debt service limit (available income) deduced from past financial records (Meyer 2000). Although cash flow analysis builds on hard information, i.e. annual financial statements and BWAs, its execution involves discretion, as the observation at savings bank 1 revealed.

At savings bank 1 the customer advisors are in charge of calculating customers' future ability to cover interest and principal payments; credit officers review the calculation. The bank employees conduct the analysis 'by hand'; i.e. they fill in a PDF form with the required financial items (see Figure 4.3) which automatically adds up the debt service and the debt service limit (SK1MFPP05.11.13). Though the savings bank's ICT system can also determine customers' ability to cover interest and principal payments automatically, the observed bank employees prefer to conduct the analysis 'by hand', because they perceive the ICT-based calculations as complex and inappropriate for specific cases. For example, in an evaluation of a mortgage application, the ICT system included an expiring loan so the automatic calculation suggested the client was unable to serve the debt, yet the officer in charge deemed the expiring loan to be irrelevant as it was almost repaid (SK1MFPP05.11.13). This example indicates that bank employees prefer manual calculation to enable individual judgments.

In particular, individual judgments and discretion are pivotal for the calculating of the debt service limit. Beside the classification of balance sheet positions, the determination of customers' living expenditures requires decisive discretion and influences position 19 ("personal drawings") of the calculation in Figure 4.3. Savings bank 1 considers the private affairs of the customers in its calculations even for relatively large capital enterprises. In one case, aware of the 'thinness' of the walls between owners' business and private accounts, the bank considered an owner's private affairs even though the *GmbH*, or PLC, had a revenue of ca. €3 million (SK1MPP25.11.13). Although orientation values for determining customers' living expenditures exist (considering basic information like the number of family members), the bank employees use the orientation values only if no specific information is available. If the customer advisors also keep the customers' private accounts, they are well aware of customers' private spending (SK1MPP19.11.13, SK1MPP25.11.13) and consider this information for debt service limit calculations instead of the orientation values. Overall, savings bank 1 tends to calculate customers' ability to serve debt prudently, especially for unknown customers. Notwithstanding the fact that cash flow analysis builds on hard information, it still involves the exercising of discretion. This discretion, in turn, grants customer advisors and credit officers a decisive influence on credit

C. Debt service

Borrowed funds						Interest p.a. + Principal p.a. = Debt service p.a.	
						After completion of investment	After expiration of amortization
Creditor	Amount EUR	%	EUR	%	EUR	EUR	EUR

1. Loan
  1.1 Current loan(s)
  1.2 New loan(s)
2. Current account
  credit(s)
3. Other
(e.g. acceptance credit
  or personal loan)
4. Total							

D. Debt service limit

	Last statement 19 . . .		Planning period*	
	EUR	%	EUR	%
1. Revenue (net)		100		100
2. − cost of goods				
3. = gross profit				
4. − other ordinary income				
5. = operating revenues				
6. − personnel costs				
7. − other ordinary expenses (without interest and depreciation)				
8. = extended cash flow				
9. − interest				
10. = available cash flow				
11. − depreciation of fixed assets				
12. = operating revenues				
13. + extraordinary income/÷ extraordinary expenses				
14. = net profit				
15. Extended cash flow (transfer of line 8)				
16. + other income and deposits				
17. Subtotal				
18. − income and wealth tax				
19. − special expenses and other personal drawings				
20. − expected input of equity for replacement investment				
21. − other				
22. Debt service limit in the planning period				
23. The debt service limit is in the planning period through the capital service of exhausted with a share of:	EUR %		EUR %	

Figure 4.3 Savings bank's form to calculate customer's future ability to cover interest and principal payments

* Planning period = the first 12 months after completion

Source: Ahnert et al. 2009: 298 (translated and modified)

decisions because a given future ability to serve debt tends to be the single most important precondition for positive credit decisions.

Similar to savings bank 1, the customer advisors of big bank 1 conduct the assessments of the future ability to cover interest and principal payments (GB1MIT25.09.13II, GB1MFIP05.11.12). Yet, in contrast to the regional bank, the SME customer advisors have no direct access to information about customers' private affairs, as the private customer division of big bank 1 holds the private accounts of firms' managing owners (GB1MIT11.02.14). Therefore, even if the customers have their private accounts at big bank 1, the SME customer advisors tend to be less familiar with the private living conditions of their customers. In principle, SME customer advisors are able to contact their colleagues from the private customer division of big bank 1, although the interview partners did not emphasise this cooperation. Rather, information exchange tends to be restricted to basic information like the level of private credits (GB1MIT11.02.14, GB1MIT25.09.13II). In fact, one interviewed SME customer advisor was in favour of a strict division between private and corporate affairs. He indicated that his corporate business relationships had already been compromised because clients were dissatisfied with the advisory service of the private division (GB1MIT11.02.14). Limited information about customers' private affairs tends to be irrelevant for SMEs of the large size class which depend less on single owners. Nonetheless, observation at savings bank 1 indicated the relevance of private affairs when determining actual debt service limit for SMEs of the medium size class due to the 'thinness' of the walls between owners' business and private accounts.

The interview partners from the other banks studied confirm the relevance of the cash flow analysis (Geno2MIT23.02.14II, SK3MIT 24.09.13, SK3MIT18.08.13, SK4MIT25.09.13, SK4MIT25.10.13, GB3MIT29.05.13I). One customer advisor in charge of SMEs at savings bank 3 emphasised the aspect of proportionality in the evaluation of customers' ability to serve debts:

> Well, customers' ability to cover interest and principal is very important and if a small plumbing firm came up with the idea to hire ten people and to finance ten cars without having the orders, then you would advise him not to do it now but to increase capacities step by step.
>
> (SK3MIT24.09.13)

Surprisingly, cooperative bank 1 uses Riebell's (2006) manual for the financial statements and cash flow analyses, the manual brought out by the publishing house of the competing savings banks (Geno2MIT23.02.14II). In line with the use of the same manual, the market CEO of cooperative bank 1 emphasised the similarities of their cash flow analysis to that of the competing regional savings banks. He also indicated the case-related discretion of the cash flow analysis:

> There is discretion, correct. But basically the aim is to find out the operating revenues, the classical, original earnings from the operating business.

Interest and amortisation is added and that is the extended cash flow. And the extended cash flow is compared to the amount of interest and principal the customer has to pay, hence the whole thing is very schematic, but between us and the savings banks it is identical.

(Geno2MIT23.02.14II)

To sum up, customers' future ability to cover interest and principal payments represents a precondition for positive credit decisions for regional and big banks alike. Although its determination uses hard information, customer advisors and credit officers of savings bank 1 possess discretion which grants them a decisive influence on lending decisions. Furthermore, if possible, savings bank 1 routinely considers the private affairs (e.g. private spending) of the managing owners in detail, whereas big bank 1's strict division between the private and business customer segments tends to restrict such detailed consideration. The actual private spending of managing owners especially has the potential to alter savings bank 1's assessment of firms' ability to serve debt, indicating the relevance of managing owners' private affairs in SME lending.

4.1.2.3 Collaterals and blank credits

The appraisal of collaterals is subordinated to the evaluation of customers' future ability to serve debt, because if customers cannot pay back debt, then additional credits cause over-indebtedness. Following Ahnert et al. (2009), collaterals serve two functions: firstly, they reduce loss giving default (LGD), and secondly, they increase the repayment incentive. In banking practice, the latter aspect gains importance when customers deliberately, i.e. regardless of their solvency, delay repayments (SK1MPP10.12.13). Empirical data indicates that savings bank 1 and big bank 1 demand private collateral from the managing owners of medium-sized SMEs, which is uncommon for large SMEs (GB1MIT11.02.14, SK1MPP03.12.13).

Banks classify the different kinds of collaterals according to their recoverability (Ahnert et al. 2009). A guarantee of the managing owners that is not backed by assets counts as soft collateral and banks use it to increase the 'moral' repayment obligations (GB1MIT11.02.14, Geno2MIT23.02.14II). Banks are able to determine recoverability values for securities (e.g. upon accounts receivable trade), pledges (e.g. upon stocks) and chattel mortgages (e.g. machine leasing). Nevertheless, savings bank 1 only considers cash, e.g. savings books, and real estate as hard collateral (SK1MPP27.11.13). As Box 4.1 explains, the focus on real estate tends to be explained by the different regulatory methods savings banks use to determine minimum equity capital requirements in comparison to large banks. Collateralisation with real estate is one of the very few options for savings banks to reduce regulatory capital requirements, whereas large banks' minimum equity capital decidedly depends on clients' rating scores.

Box 4.1   The SolvV regulation: minimum capital requirements, rating and collaterals

SolvV defines two methods for how banks can determine the minimum equity capital they have to hold to secure default risks: firstly, the relatively simple credit risk standardized approach (KSA), which all but one German savings bank use (all savings banks in this study use the KSA approach); and secondly, the internal rating–based approach (IRA) that larger banks use (all supraregional banks in this study use the IRA). Implementing the IRA is more expensive but tends to calculate lower minimum equity capital requirements, as was intended by the Basel II regulation, to set incentives for banks to use the more sophisticated risk-controlling models and techniques required for IRA (Hombach and Schmidt 2011; Paul 2011).

The KSA defines four standardised risk weights to determine the amount of equity capital banks have to hold for their different asset classes relevant for the SME segment (see Figure 4.4; Paul 2011: 31): 100% for cooperate credits (> €1 million); 75% for retail credits, including SME credits (< €1 million); 50% for commercial real estate–backed credits; and 35% for residential real estate–backed credits. Risk weights are multiplied with the according assets class values and multiplied by 8% (the regulatory capital factor) to calculate the minimum equity capital that banks are required to hold. With KSA, the internal rating scores of firms do not influence capital requirements but rather real estate collateralization influences the asset classes and hence capital requirements. For example, if a business loan is backed by residential real estate, then the risk weight is only 35% instead of 100% (Hombach and Schmidt 2011; Paul 2011).

In contrast to the KSA, firms' internal rating scores significantly influence the minimum equity capital banks have to hold with the IRA, as the rating score specifies the PD (Figure 4.4). With the IRA, banks calculate the expected losses and unexpected losses for every asset class, with the PD and LGD specified from historical credit portfolio data (see Paul 2011). Equity capital need to secure the unexpected losses only because expected losses should be covered by the risk premium banks charge on credits (Paul 2011, OED08.07.13). Risk weights decidedly increase with the deterioration of the rating scores. They tend to be lower for credits to firms with good and normal rating scores and higher for firms with poor scores in comparison to the KSA. This rating score differentiation of capital requirements is intended to support risk-adjusted pricing (see Section 4.2.5.1) and to direct banks to invest in less risky firms (Middelberg and Plegge 2010). In principle, the IRA takes all kinds of collaterals into account, because collaterals influence the LGD. The IRA further considers credits that are collateralised with real estate in a specific retail asset class (Paul 2011).

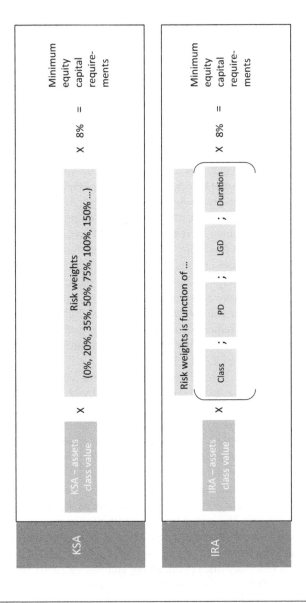

Figure 4.4 The KSA and IRA in comparison

Source: Hombach and Schmidt 2011: 76 (translated and modified)

The collateral value calculation of the charge on land is based on the values from the property valuation report of the surveyors. From these values, senior rights, specified in the land charge register, are subtracted (SK1MPP13.12.13) and the lending limit is multiplied to determine the collateral values at savings bank 1 (Ahnert et al. 2009: 365). Savings bank 1 subtracts the charge on the land collateral value from the overall amount of credits; the remaining credit volume is called *blank credits*. As will be examined later, the amount of blank credits represents an important risk indicator which influences the allocation of credit-granting authority at savings banks. In contrast, blank credit volume has no influence on the allocation of authority at big bank 1, as the bank considers only the total amount of credits regardless of collateralisation (see Section 4.2.4.2).

Banks define lending limits individually according to their risk and business strategies. Lending limits decidedly influence the inclination of savings banks to lend as they influence blank credit volumes. Savings banks designate higher limits to residential real estate, i.e. between ca. 50% to 80%, than to commercial real estate, in anticipation of the lower recoverability values for commercial real estate (Ahnert et al. 2009). Striking in this context, savings banks also tend to consider the regional economic situation when defining lending limits, in line with the tendency for economically weak regions to have less liquid real estate markets. Accordingly, savings bank 1 uses a limit of ca. 80% for residential real estate for its urban market area (SK1MFPP05.11.13), whereas the rurally located savings bank 2 applies a limit of ca. 50% (SK2MIP13.03.132). The department head interviewed justified the low lending limit of savings bank 2 with the uncertainty of sales prospects for residential real estate and ironically noted that they should actually advise customers building a house in the villages to insure for 'demolition' in case they want to move away (SK2MIP13.03.132).

Whereas the lower lending limits in economically less dynamic regions are rational from the point of view of risk appraisal, they tend to have an unfavourable effect in terms of balanced regional economic development as they result in the systematic constraint of lending in economically weak regions compared to economically strong regions. Therefore, as discussed in an interview with a financial business consultant (OBCIP23.10.13I), savings banks specifications of lending limits reinforce regional disparities in real estate price developments. Differences in lending limits tend also to impact on SMEs' access to finance because real estate is used as collateral to secure risky business credits (Section 4.3.1). This relation tends to amplify inferior access to finance for SMEs in economically weak regions and, in turn, potentially reinforces regional disparities.

4.2 The organisation of credit decisions at savings and big banks

Banks conduct credit decisions collaboratively and involve actors in different places at varying distances in the credit-decision processes. Thus, to compare the organisation of credit decisions to SMEs of regional and supraregional banks with a focus on distance, the complex geography of credit decision making must be traced. As deduced in Section 2.4, in order to identify total distance of banks' credit decisions to SMEs the percentage of decision-making power of every actor involved and distance between these actors must be specified. Section 4.2 determines these two variables on the basis of the empirical data and deduces the total distance of credit decision making of savings bank 1 and big bank 1.

The regular process of credit granting is organised as follows. SMEs send credit requests to their customer advisors, who create a credit application and execute the rating together with the back offices. Depending on the riskiness of credits and banks' internal rules, supervisors and back offices have to approve the credit applications. Figure 4.5 displays the principle kinds of actors that get involved in the credit-granting processes and differentiates their geographical location between regional and supraregional banks. In line with the conceptualisation in Section 2.3, the rating systems are included as separate actors involved in the lending processes.

The presentation of the empirical results in the next four sections is organised as follows. The first subsection of each section outlines the empirical results on the principal design/work of the actor under consideration, discusses the actor's distance to the customer advisors – the main interface of customer–bank interaction – for savings bank 1 and contrasts the findings with big bank 1. The following subsection compares the decision-making power of the actor from both banks. The first two subsections only consider banks' organisation of the credit-granting processes for SMEs of the medium size class (revenue €500,000 to €10 million; total credits of borrower unit €100,000 to €5 million). Striking differences to SMEs of the other size classes and to the eight other bank cases are outlined in the final subsection – to enable an assessment of the generalisability of findings – that also presents a systematisation of the qualitative findings regarding distance and decision-making power.

Section 4.2.1 discusses the customer advisor–customer relationships, i.e. operational distance. This section shows that savings banks and big bank 1 alike designate personal customer advisors for their SME customers at the regional scale and strive to achieve relationship banking rather than transaction-oriented banking. Section 4.2.2 discusses the customer advisors–rating systems relationships and shows that big bank 1 grants greater decision-making power to its rating systems than savings bank 1. Section 4.2.3 analyses the customer advisors–credit officers' relationships and reveals notable differences in the cooperation of these actors between the banks studied in-depth. In Section 4.2.4 the customer advisors–supervisors' interactions are outlined, indicating the frequent involvement of high-level supervisors in credit decisions to medium-sized SMEs at savings bank 1, something that is not scheduled in big bank 1. Section 4.2.5 presents other indirectly involved actors in the processes of credit decisions. Finally, Section 4.2.6 deduces and compares the total distance of savings bank 1's and big bank 1's credit decision making to SMEs. This section demonstrates that, for specific credit applications, big bank 1 in fact decides at a shorter distance to SMEs than savings bank 1. The high involvement of supervisors in the regional bank explains this unexpected finding; i.e. big bank 1 delegates decisive credit-granting authority to its

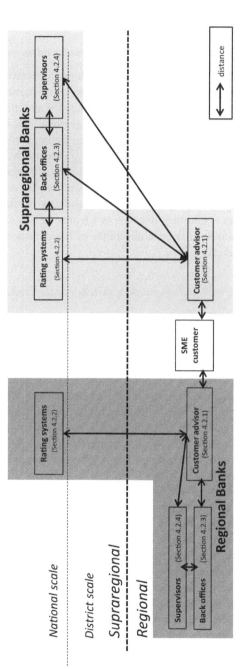

Figure 4.5 Approaching distance between SMEs and regional versus supraregional banks

Source: author's figure

branches. However, in cases where firms are rated medium or poor, savings bank 1 always decides on credit applications of medium-sized SMEs at a short distance.

4.2.1 The relationship between customers and customer advisors

Whereas close customer–customer advisor relationships characterise relationship banking, banks and customers interact at arm's length in the transaction-oriented banking model (Section 2.2.1.2). This section searches for structural differences in the customer advisor–customer relationships of regional and big banks; i.e. it contrasts their operational distances. The empirical findings indicate similarities in the general conduct of customer services; e.g. savings banks 1 and big bank 1 strive to achieve relationship banking. Nonetheless, differences exist concerning the execution of face-to-face meetings as well as the arrangements of bank branches, resulting in varying degrees of accessibility for the clients. Section 4.2.1.1 contrasts the operational distance of savings bank 1 and big bank 1, and Section 4.2.1.2 discusses the generalisability of the empirical observations and systemises the findings.

4.2.1.1 Communication with and operational distance to the customers

OPERATIONAL DISTANCE AT SAVINGS BANK 1

Savings bank 1's market area comprises the territory of the municipality responsible and a much larger *Ausleihbezirk*. The bulk of SME clients are located in the municipality, where two SME customer advisor working groups serve them. One working group is located at savings bank 1's headquarters on the main street of the major city and one SME team is located in the largest branch on the main street of the second largest town of the municipality. The two working groups split the market area, yet the border remains permeable; i.e. the bank directs new customers to a working group according to their locations, but existing customer relationships are not altered.

Savings bank 1's customer advisors working group of the second largest town was observed. It has six employees, the team leader Mrs Weber,[2] a team assistant and four customer advisors. In addition to her team-leading function, Mrs Weber is in charge of numerous customers and serves the larger clients of the team. Mrs Hennecke supervised the student internship of the one-month participant observation. As an experienced customer advisor she serves about 50 to 70 clients without a specific sector or product specialisation. Mrs Friese is specialised in start-ups and young companies as well as publicly subsidised loans, factoring and leasing. Mrs Weber has been working for the longest time in the working group; Mrs Hennecke and Mrs Friese joined the team ca. 10 years ago. They previously worked as customer advisors for SMEs in neighbouring savings banks (SK1MPP25.11.13). Mrs Kurz is the junior customer advisor with three years of work experience in the SME team (SK1MPP21.11.13). She serves fewer and smaller customers and executes less lending power than the other customer advisors. The fourth customer advisor does not serve SMEs. All four customer advisors have gained occupational qualifications at a savings banks academy besides their vocational training as *Bankkauffrau/-mann*, or bank clerk, but no academic degrees.

The customer advisors are in principle responsible for all financial and insurance demands of their corporate clients, including the private demands of the managing owners, and try to build long-term and extensive business relationships (SK1MPP03.12.13). They also offer products that are not derived from savings bank 1 itself, but from partner firms of the savings banks financial group, for which they get the support of product specialist (Box 4.2). In fact, savings bank 1 tries to increase commission fee earning (cross-selling) and offers a whole range of fee-earning products from its partner firms like leasing, factoring and insurances. Nevertheless, the credit business remains the main business and the key income source of the savings bank (see Section 4.2.5.3).

Box 4.2   Product specialists

The customer advisors of savings bank 1 and big bank 1 consult product specialists in a cause-related fashion if the SME wants to purchase specialised products. Product specialists participate in the counselling meetings together with the customer advisors and present the product offers, e.g. leasing, factoring, complex insurances, packaged retail investment products. Savings bank 1 has internal product specialists and external specialists from the savings banks financial group. For example, Deutsche Leasing has specialist teams at the district scale where each specialist is in charge of fixed savings banks (SK1MPP09.12.13). Savings bank 1 receives commissions for all the products Deutsche Leasing sells to its customers. The internal and external product specialists also advise the customer advisors, who tend to be less experienced with certain specialised products, and answer practical questions concerning how to complete forms, the calculation of conditions etc.

Big bank 1 uses product specialists in a similar way to serve medium-sized SMEs, though the customer advisors are not allowed to sell certain products, e.g. commodity derivatives, but have to include the specialist in charge. Large SMEs are always served by product specialists in addition to their 'ordinary' customer advisors. The big bank has specialist teams for payment transactions, foreign business, risk management and large credits (GB1MIT25.09.13II). Located on the district scale the product specialists directly interact with the large SME customers. This organisation implies that every product specialist has a specified customer base and the customers directly contact their specialist in charge (GB1MIT25.09.13II).

The communication between customers and customer advisors at savings bank 1 is frequent, familiar and ad hoc. Telephone calls are the most important means of communication, followed by ad hoc meetings, e-mail and mail, scheduled meetings at savings bank 1 and visits to customers' firms. Most face-to-face meetings take place at the bank branch, and customers frequently visit their advisors spontaneously without prior notification (SK1MPP13.12.13). Meetings are seldom held at the clients' sites. The fact that customer advisors must send a departure note to their supervisor at headquarters to notify them of firm visits indicates their rarity. An important indirect means of communication is account keeping, which provides customer advisors with up-to-date information about the firm and the private situation of their clients (see Box 4.3).

Box 4.3   Account keeping and payments transactions

A considerable amount of customer advisors' routine work deals with payments transactions and account keeping. Firms demand payment transaction–related services (e.g. bank transfers via remittance slips) and products (e.g. online banking software, cash and credit cards) to manage payments and liquidity. Although specialised back-office teams process payment transactions (e.g. scanning and processing remittance slips), customer advisors are nevertheless in charge of solving problems, have to explain changes in the products and negotiate new terms and conditions (GB1MIT11.02.14, SK1MPP27.11.13). The advisors tend to dislike this kind of work, as it comprises a lot of administrative tasks; e.g. the change to SEPA was an especially striking topic at the time of the empirical enquiry (GB1MIT11.02.14, SK1MPP03.12.13). The disposition of accounts lies in the responsibility of the clients, yet if they do not keep their accounts within limits the customer advisors have to decide whether to allow transactions, i.e. tolerate overdrafts, or not (GB1MIT11.02.14, SK1MPP19.11.13). Customer advisors normally approve overdrafts as their first task in the morning. Banks' ICT systems list all transactions that need to be approved. Like for all credit decisions, customer advisors have certain limits for the approval of overdrafts, and supervisors must approve larger and long-term overdrafts.

At savings bank 1, Mrs Hennecke approves ca. one to two transactions on a working day, and the number of overdrafts increases towards the end of the month as firms need to transfer wages (SK1MPP28.11.13). Mrs Hennecke accepts minor overdrafts of financially sound customers without talking to these customers when the overdrafts result from carelessness. Frequently overdrafts relate to unexpected short-term liquidity problems. In such cases clients normally call to explain their problem and outline a plan for repayment which customer advisors tend to accept from financially sound firms with moderate overdrafts. Nevertheless, such unauthorized overdrafts lead to a strong deterioration of firms' rating scores so that customer advisors expect managers to anticipate and communicate liquidity shortages in advance to enable an extension of the current account credit line ex ante. Financially distressed firms usually face liquidity shortages and the acceptance of overdrafts is a delicate and communication-intensive affair. On the one hand, acceptance or rejection is an instrument to enforce changes in firms' management (e.g. reduction of private spending). On the other hand, the rejection of important transactions may cause firms' insolvency (e.g. if firms cannot pay important suppliers) (SK1BSPP19.12.13). Overall the necessity of approving overdrafts ensures that savings bank 1's customer advisors are well-informed about the liquidity situation of firms and leads to very frequent contact with financially distressed firms.

Interviews with customer advisors of big bank 1 indicated similar practices in account keeping and payment transactions (GB1MIT25.09.13II, GB1MIT11.02.14). They also highlighted the higher flexibility of savings banks in the arrangement of terms. Thus, according to one team leader, savings banks offer free accounts to important customers and cross-subsidise this by higher interest rates (GB1MIT25.06.13I). Big bank 1 lacks this flexibility, because fee income from payments transactions and interest earnings from loans are booked in different segments of the bank.

Observation at savings bank 1 indicates that the means and style of communication depend on the occasion and on the length of the customer relationship. In general, advisors use the polite form of address but talk rather directly and in a familiar way with well-known clients. Communication with new customers tends to be more official and polite (SK1MPP03.12.13). Three typical occasions for communication and the style of communication were observed:

Minor interactions related to account keeping (see Box 4.3), document exchanges (e.g. signing a contract, handing in the annual financial statements) or exchanges of minor information. They are very frequent (on average more than 10 times a day for the total working group), and normally last only a few minutes. For example, one of Mrs Hennecke's clients called from his mobile phone and requested an account balance without knowing the number of the account; Mrs Hennecke managed to find out the number with the little information at hand and informed him of the balance instantly (SK1MPP28.11.13). On another occasion Mrs Hennecke called a customer as she did not understand the high level of booked revenue on the firm's BWA. After the call she was certain that the BWA was incorrect as the client could not explain the high revenue, i.e. "the client reckons that they have had a lot of work this year" (SK1MPP28.11.13), and in fact it turned out that orders had been booked twice. Beside telephone communication, customers also show up in the branch to hand in documents, payment slips etc. The location of the branch in the central business district encourages these short face-to-face interactions which are also used for small talk.

Extensive discussions and information exchanges relate to the initiation of new business, e.g. loan requests, site visits for property purchases or new production line openings; the negotiation of minor and uncritical contracts, e.g. the extension of overdrafts; major technical problems, e.g. problems with online banking; short-term liquidity problems; and the annual rating and advisory meetings. Customer advisors do not conduct this kind of communication ad hoc, but agree upon dates for telephone talks, face-to-face meetings or site visits.

Depending on the topic, the customers and savings bank 1 also forward information and documents to prepare these discussions in advance, and discussions take place in a friendly but efficient atmosphere. For example, Mrs Weber called for the assistance of an important customer because a range of minor loans had to be renewed and asked the customer to call back. When the managing owner returned the call, Mrs Weber started with small talk; i.e. she knew of a newborn baby in the family and offered her congratulations. Then she quickly named the new interest rates for the loan renewal and the customer agreed. Finally, Mrs Weber asked if she could do anything else, and the managing owner declined. The talk was friendly but quite brisk, which Mrs Weber explained was due to the long-standing customer relationship. They treat each other fairly (with give and take); minor credits are offered at fair prices without extensive negotiations and the customer receives some services for free in return. For large new loans the negotiations can become intensive, however (SK1MPP20.11.13). Another example is a firm that needed a minor temporary increase of its overdraft credit line and e-mailed this inquiry with an explanation of the demand and an up-to-date BWA to Mrs Weber. After browsing through the BWA, Mrs Weber conducted an extensive phone call with the managing owner where she addressed open questions and negotiated the terms of the overdraft credit (SK1MPP25.11.13).

Hard negotiations are held if customer advisors and customers disagree on relevant aspects of their business relationships. This relates to the terms of new loans, to the extensions of credits to distressed firms or to delays in payments and other major contract violations. Savings bank 1 conducts hard negotiations most of the time face to face in confidential surroundings like the meeting room. The customer advisors arrange the topics of the negotiations in advance and exchange arguments and documents in preparation of these meetings (e.g. via telephone or e-mail). More than two people frequently participate in these meetings; e.g. clients take their tax or business advisors to these meetings and customer advisors invite their supervisors. Hard negotiations tend to be emotional affairs. In one case Mrs Kurz negotiated with a client who had delayed interest payments and demanded a strong reduction in the monthly payments of interest and principal. Mrs Kurz wanted to keep on negotiating because she assumed that the client had extra income (e.g. illegal work) and was not trying hard to repay his debts. In the face-to-face negotiation, the customer and his business advisor accused Mrs Kurz of being unwilling to compromise and said she would ruin the family, i.e. "Christmas is coming and what shall the family live on?" (SK1MPP10.12.13). After the hard negotiation Mrs Kurz reported that she remained firm and did not give in to the client's demand. She also explained that she takes these kinds of customers *Nachhause* and thinks about them after finishing work (SK1MPP04.12.13). The observation not only exemplifies the emotional character of hard face-to-face negotiations but also indicates that there is a risk that such negotiations produce unwanted results from the customer advisors' point of view.

OPERATIONAL DISTANCE AT BIG BANK 1

Big bank 1 maintains a Germany-wide extensive branch network, in which not every branch hosts a customer advisor team. The team under study is located in the central business district of a town within the *Ausleihbezirk* of savings bank 1; thus, the interviewed employees of big bank 1 in fact directly compete for the same SMEs with the in-depth studied savings bank. The branch under study serves a market area of three municipalities and is in charge of firms belonging to the size classes of medium SME and large SME (GB1MIT25.06.13I). Therefore, taking the territory of the municipality responsible for savings bank 1 as a benchmark, operational distance in geographical terms is shorter in the savings bank than in big bank 1. This result holds especially true if one considers that savings bank 1 has located two customer advisor teams for medium-sized SMEs in its market area.

Mr Holz is the team leader of big bank 1's customer advisor team under study; he also serves some large SMEs on his own besides carrying out his team-leading functions. The team serves ca. 500 large and medium SME clients and has 10 employees (GB1MIT25.06.13I). The majority of Mr Holz's customer advisors have a graduate degree and 10 to 40 years of work experience at a bank. In the medium-sized SME class, customer advisors serve about 80 to 120 clients. Mr Maske is one of the customer advisors in charge of ca. 90 borrower units; he estimates that ca. 50% of his customers have big bank 1 as their main bank. Mr Maske studied extra-occupationally at a university of applied sciences besides his vocational training as a bank clerk. After study he started as a junior SME customer advisor in another branch of big bank 1 before he changed to the branch under study (GB1MIT11.02.14).

Big bank 1 seeks to be the *Hausbank* of SMEs and highlights the fact that they are able to satisfy the needs of ambitious firms for all kinds of financial and insurance services bank-internally (GB1MIT13.02.14, GB1MIT25.06.13I). Savings banks can only offer these kinds of products via the business partners of their financial group. Big bank 1 strives to achieve long-term relationships with its clients and minimise changes of customer advisors. However, due to job mobility the length of relationships between clients and advisors is on average shorter than that of the savings banks (GB1MIT25.06.13I). At the time of interview in 2013, Mr Holz and Mr Maske had only been at the branch for two and three years, respectively, but they have one colleague who has client relationships that have lasted more than 25 years. Mr Maske also saw advantages in occasional customer advisor changes. At the same time, he pointed out the knowledge advantages of long-term relationships:

> And after seven years I found out that seeing something new, new customers, is also positive. You see the customers with very different eyes when they are new, compared to customers you have served for seven years. Because it is the case that, as every banker will confirm, you often decide in favour of the customer. If you get to meet new customers, you don't do that.
>
> (GB1MIT11.02.14)

> It is like this, at some time when you, I mean at [city X] I served the customers for seven years, then I give the customer who I have known for seven or five years, then I do not look too closely at the annual financial statements, because – as the saying goes – he does his business, he knows how to do his business, and if any special events happened in the business year then I normally know that anyway as a corporate customer advisor in an intensive customer relationship. Hence, I can do 'blub' and pass it on, of course [pass on the annual financial statements to the analysis department without examining them closely].
>
> (GB1MIT11.02.14)

The two interview excerpts address two aspects of relationship banking. On the one hand, the reduction of information asymmetries in long-standing and intensive customer relationships are outlined. This also helps to reduce effort by reusing available knowledge. Here savings bank 1 tends to have advantages because of higher continuity in staffing. On the other hand, long-standing customer relationships involve the risk that customer advisors become uncritical about well-known customers, as Mr Maske pointed out. Here big bank 1's higher job mobility of employees guarantees frequent changes and potentially leads to a more critical monitoring of existing customers in comparison to savings bank 1.

The empirical investigation identifies relevant differences in the customer–customer advisor communication between big bank 1 and savings bank 1. Acording to Mr Holz, similar to savings bank 1 the telephone is the most important means of verbal communication at big bank 1, followed by face-to-face meetings (GB1MIT25.09.13II). However, in notable contrast to the savings bank, big bank 1's advisors mostly visit their clients rather than clients coming to the branch. The contrast in the micro-geographical design of the offices support the different face-to-face meeting patterns; whereas the SME team of savings bank 1 is very accessible for customer visits, the branch design of big bank 1 restricts access to the SME customer advisors (Box 4.4).

Box 4.4 The micro-geography of operational distance

The comparison of bank branches' micro-geography reveals notable differences between the accessibility of the customer advisors in savings bank 1 and big bank 1 (see Flögel and Zademach 2017). Figure 4.6 illustrates the micro-geography of the customer advisor offices of both branches studied. Savings bank 1's customer advisor team has four offices and shares the meeting room with other working groups of the branch. Mrs Weber occupies an individual office with a small table for meetings. The team assistant is placed in the office next door, Mrs Hennecke and Mrs Kurz share the neighbouring office and the last office is occupied by Mrs Friese and the other advisor. The doors between the offices are open most of the time.

Two constructional features cause the high accessibility of savings bank 1's offices. Firstly, all office doors to the second floor of the counter hall remain unlocked and customers can easily access the second floor via a large staircase in the middle of the counter hall. Therefore, aware of the accessibility, existing customers very frequently drop by unannounced. The only exception to this rule is Mrs Weber's office which customers can only access through the team assistant's office. Secondly, the offices open onto the busy main street and a large glass front allows a view into the offices from the street. Curtains make sure that no details can be observed but, nonetheless, any customer is able to see at a glance from the outside if her or his customer advisor is at her or his desk.

Similar to savings bank 1, the corporate customer advisor team of big bank 1 occupies the second floor of a branch where a team for private customers also works (Figure 4.6: right-hand side). The team leader Mr Holz is shielded from the other offices by his assistant's office. Striking differences in the accessibility became visible at the interview appointments. Visitors cannot access the advisor team without previous registration at the counter, as the door to the second floor is locked. Hence, visitors must register at the counter. Service staff here call the customer advisors and only direct visitors to the second floor if the advisors confirm the meeting. This constructional and organisational feature prevents clients from popping into advisors' offices without announcement. In fact, customer advisors even have the possibility to hide, as they only have to instruct service staff to pretend that they are out of the office. It was further noted that the service staff did not know the SME customer advisors by name, which underlines the rarity of customer visits at the advisor team of big bank 1. Overall, the observations indicate the influence of the micro-geography design of bank branches on accessibility for clients, an aspect not considered so far in the analysis of operational distance.

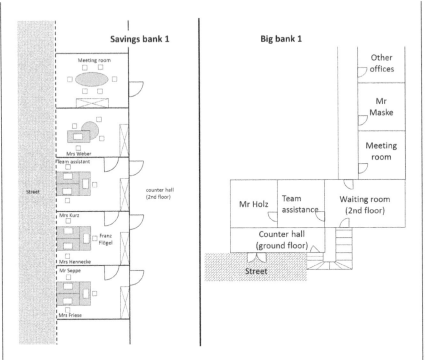

Figure 4.6 Outline of the offices of savings bank 1's and big bank 1's SME customer advisor teams under study

Source: author's illustration

Big bank 1 has specified that each SME customer is to be visited at least twice
a year; though Mr Holz pointed out that they meet managers in active customer
relationships more often anyway (GB1MIT11.02.14). Mr Holz estimated that ca.
5% of all meetings take place at big bank 1 only, all other meetings take place at
the sites of the clients (GB1MIT25.06.13I). Accordingly, Mr Holz conducts three
to four customer meetings a week (GB1MIT25.09). Big bank 1 sees the high
frequency of site visits as a service orientation and instrument to maintain close
customer relationships. The interview with the leading manager of big bank 1 suggested that, due to the strong competition for financially sound SMEs nowadays,
banks "cannot wait in their branches for customers to pop in" (GB1MIT13.02.14).
However, the frequency of site visits necessarily implies that the customer advisors of big bank 1 are less often at their desks than the advisors of savings bank
1. This absence tends to be a disadvantage for customers who are used to spontaneously contacting their advisors for minor interactions, as observed at savings
bank 1.

4.2.1.2 *Generalisation and systematisation: the relationship between customers and customer advisors*

Comparable to the two banks analysed in-depth, the other bank cases studied indicate that they also strive to achieve relationship banking with SMEs and offer personal services; i.e. SMEs have fixed customer advisors as contact partners. The other regional banks interviewed report similar operational distances to those of savings bank 1. Like savings bank 1, they serve small SMEs in all of their branches and medium SMEs and large SMEs in centralised teams. Savings bank 2, for example, reported that they serve their very large market areas with two SME customer advisor teams, one in its headquarters and the other in an important branch and a very small team in another important branch. The geographical distances between each of the three locations is ca. 30 kilometres (SK2MIP13.03.13). The exact definition of the customer size classes differs between the regional banks; e.g. savings bank 2 regards clients with €50,000 business credit as medium-sized SME customers, whereas savings bank 4 uses the same threshold of €100,000 as savings bank 1 (SK2OIP18.03.13, SK4MIT 25.10.13).

Differences have been observed in the operational distance of supraregional banks. Big bank 2 maintains an extensive branch network similar to big bank 1. The interview partner underlined the relevance of geographical proximity for serving SMEs, but he also pointed out that big bank 2 cannot maintain qualified advisors in all of its branches (GB2MIP27.11.12). Therefore, similar to big bank 1, big bank 2 locates its SME customer advisor teams in selected branches only. Accordingly, the density of the SME customer advisor teams of big bank 1 and 2 is lower than that of the regional savings banks, especially if one considers that savings banks in total operated 13,212 branches and the four big banks operated 7,614 branches in 2013 (see Section 3.2.1).

Big bank 3's service to SMEs differs from big banks 1 and 2, not only because the bank operates only a handful of branches in Germany, but also because it does not apply a regional subdivision to its market area:

F.F.: And you were in charge of which market area, the Ruhr?

Answer: That changed a little bit. I started with a customer base that stretched from Hamburg to Stuttgart, although furthest away there was not so much, in Hamburg two to three customers and in Stuttgart one, and the main business areas were the Köln-Bonn region, so yes for the freelancers. That was explained by the fact that we did not organise our work according to branches but that we cooperated with different agents who were present in these market areas.

(GB3MIT29.05.13I)

As the interview partner explained, big bank 3 gains contacts customers of the medium-size SME class via agents, i.e. regional business consultancies that support the start-ups of resident physicians and dentists. The customer advisors visit their geographically distant customers only once a year. Therefore, the example of big bank 3 shows that SMEs are also served at long operational distances in Germany, by gaining initial contact through specific networks of agents.

To sum up, Figure 4.7 systematises the empirical findings and highlights differences. This study confirmed that regional and big banks in Germany strive to conduct relationship banking with financially sound medium-sized SMEs and offer personal services to their customers; i.e. the SMEs have fixed customer advisors who serve all demands. Both banks studied in-depth operate at a short geographical distance to their SME customers. Savings bank 1 locates two customer advisor teams for customers of medium-sized SMEs in its regional market area (municipality); big bank 1 has one team in the same municipality that, in addition, serves two adjusted municipalities and large SMEs. Thus, the geographical distance to SMEs is shorter for savings bank 1 than for big bank 1, though both banks serve SMEs at the regional scale. Verbal communication between customers and advisors can be frequent depending on the occasion, and the telephone represents the most important means of communication, followed by face-to-face meetings at both banks.

Notable differences relate to the sites of face-to-face meetings, as at savings bank 1 meetings with customers usually take place at the bank branch (also for minor ineractions), whereas big bank 1's advisors visit the clients at their firms (for larger meetings). The micro-geographical design of the branches supports these differences in face-to-face communication. Unrestricted accessibility enables unannounced customer encounters at savings bank 1, whereas barriers prevent SMEs from dropping by without registration at big bank 1. These micro-geographical differences in the accessibility of bank branches have so far not been considered in the analysis of operational distance and potentially influence relationships between customers and banks.

4.2.2 Rating systems

> If the PC is offline, you can go for breakfast. Yes it is just like that, you need the current loan values, you need the current account balances.
>
> (SK3MIT24.09.13)

As the quote above indicates, modern banking depends heavily on connected ICT systems. Box 4.5 introduces the key ICT systems of the savings banks and big bank 1 and illustrates that rating systems are one among a range of ICT systems which banks apply. Nevertheless, rating systems differ from other ICT systems owing to their central position in lending; i.e. they evaluate multiple pieces of information and systematise them to a single rating score that guides lending decisions. Therefore, rating systems have been considered as non-human actors of banks' credit decision processes. As conceptualised in Section 2.4, comparable to human actors, functional distance to the rating systems depends on how much the bankers are able to influence rating scores with their soft information. Section 4.2.2.1 discusses the design of the rating systems and deduces functional

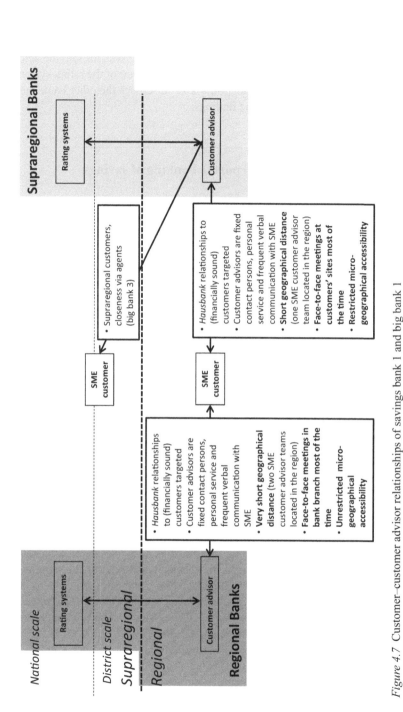

Figure 4.7 Customer–customer advisor relationships of savings bank 1 and big bank 1

Source: author's figure

distance, i.e. the degree to which soft information influences the rating score. As with human actors, the decision-making power of rating systems depends on the relational ascription of power, i.e. the integration of rating systems into the actor-networks of banks. Section 4.2.2.2 compares the integration of the rating systems at savings bank 1 and big bank 1. Section 4.2.2.3 discusses the other bank cases and size classes and systematises the findings.

Box 4.5   ICT systems in corporate banking of savings banks and big bank 1

The savings banks use one integrated banking ICT system, the browser-based One System Plus (OSPlus), developed and maintained by the Finanz Informatik GmbH & Co. KG. Containing numerous modules which allow adaptation to the business policies of each savings bank, OSPlus is used in a range of bank departments. For example, customer advisors calculate credits with OSPlus, credit officers conduct risk monitoring and the bank controlling department uses the system to compile the annual financial statements of the bank (SK1MPP29.11.13, SK1MFPP15.11.13, SK1BSPP17.12.13). OSPlus captures all employees, customers, credits, contracts and accounts of the savings banks and is also the booking system (SK1MFPP15.11.13). It is possible to conduct the whole credit-granting and monitoring process within OSPlus, from the creation of the credit proposal, to the compilation of the credit application and contracts and the pay-out of the credit, to the monitoring of the credit repayment and management of collaterals (SK1MFPP08.11.13). However, savings bank 1 does not use OSPlus for the whole process of lending to medium-sized SMEs but compiles credit applications and contracts 'by hand'. Beside OSPlus the savings banks use standard office programmes and certain specialised software systems that normally have interfaces with OSPlus; e.g. the SME rating systems is an individual software programme that exchanges information with OSPlus (SK1BSPP03.01.14). Participant observation at savings bank 1 further demonstrated the use of an intranet that contains all guidelines and hand-books, informs bankers about news and changes and records the current products and standard terms (SK1MPP25.11.13).

Notably, interview partners of the savings and big banks mentioned the competitiveness of savings banks' ICT systems in retail banking (GB1MIT11.02.14, GB1MIT25.09.13II, GB3MIT29.05.13I, OSGVIT01. 03.13). Big bank 1 applies various programmes and intranet applications to conduct the functions of OSPlus. Customer advisors frequently use at least six systems: a financial statements system, a task management system, a credit calculation system, a system that comprises information about credit history, a rating system and an accounts and booking system (GB1MIT11.02.14). Furthermore, comparable to savings bank 1, the intranet of big bank 1 informs bankers about news and changes and records the current standard terms of the bank (GB1MIT25.09.13II). The bankers see this fragmentation of programmes as a disadvantage because not all of the information needed is available at a glance (GB1MIT11.02.14). The frequent mergers and business strategy changes of large banks were given in explanation for their less competitive ICT systems because every change causes extensive adaptions of the ICT systems (OSGVIT01.03.13). Currently, large banks are investing heavily in their bank ICT.

4.2.2.1 The design of and functional distance to the rating systems

All savings banks apply the same rating systems that are developed and maintained by the Sparkassen Rating und Risikosysteme GmbH, a company of the DSGV located in Berlin. The savings banks decided to develop their rating systems conjointly, because large customer datasets are needed to gain valid ratings and economies of scale are high (OSGVIT30.05.13, OSGVD, Theis 2009; see Box 4.6, p. 183).The Sparkassen Rating and Risikosysteme GmbH offers a range of ratings and scoring systems for the different market segments (see Figure 4.8). Guidelines of the DSGV specify the selection and execution of the rating systems; within these guidelines the savings banks enact their own rules for the use of the systems. For SMEs, savings banks apply the so-called *StandardRating* for all 'ordinary' ratings of firms' default probability. The *Immobiliengeschäfts Rating*, or real estate business rating, not only rates the company but also evaluates the real estate investment and is provided for commercial real estate financing (Niestrath 2006, SK1MFPP11.11.13). Depending on the volume of credits, small SMEs are rated using the *KundenKompaktRating*, or minor customer rating. The minor customer rating does not require the annual financial statements disclosure which makes its application less time-consuming for savings banks and customers alike (SK1MFPP05.11.13).

Big bank 1 also applies different rating systems for its corporate clients. The bank rates SMEs with total credit volume of up to €5 million with a less extensive rating system and operates different ratings for larger corporations. A specific department develops and maintains the rating systems centrally (GB1MFIP05.11.12, GB1MIT11.02.14, GB1MIT25.06.13I). The following subsections compare savings banks' *StandardRating* with the less extensive rating for SMEs of big bank 1.

THE *STANDARDRATING* OF THE SAVINGS BANKS

The *StandardRating* classifies SME customers in 18 rating score classes. Rating score 1 represents the best rating class with a PD of 0.08%; rating scores 16, 17 and 18 designate different degrees of default (Figure 4.9). The *StandardRating*

Figure 4.8 Ratings and scorings of the savings banks

Source: Theis 2009: 89 (translated and altered)

Rating score	Probability of default (PD)
1	0.08%
2	0.12%
3	0.17%
4	0.30%
5	0.40%
6	0.60%
7	0.90%
8	1.30%
9	2.00%
10	3.00%
11	4.40%
12	6.70%
13	10.00%
14	15.00%
15	20.00%
16	Default
17	Default
18	Default

Figure 4.9 Rating scores and PD classes of the savings banks financial group

Source: translated from Sparkassen Rating and Risikosysteme GmbH 2010: 6

is a software program that consists of four modules (Figure 4.10). The finance rating builds the basis of the rating process. Ten to 14 financial figures of firms' annual financial statements – automatically imported from the EBIL system – are assessed with the financial rating score (see Table 4.1, p. 154). The qualitative rating module deduces a rating score on the basis of qualitative data. Both scores are summarised according to a specific weighting to create the so-called customer rating score, which represents the final rating if the following two modules do not contain additional information.

The third module screens for warning signals on the watch list of OSPlus (see Box 4.9, p. 200). Warning signals are short-term signals of a strong increase in firms' PD, e.g. overdrafts, delays in interest payments or fraud cases. They cause strong detrition of the rating scores (Theis 2009). In the final module the rating considers any cross-guarantees with other entities. If guarantees of entities with low PD exist, e.g. public bodies, the rating scores improve. If the firms guarantee for entities with high PD, e.g. other firms with poor rating scores, the rating scores decline (Theis 2009).

The qualitative rating module is based on hard and soft information. Bankers call the hard information of the qualitative rating module *hard qualitative facts*. This is, on the one hand, the account behaviour of the customers: Are firm and private accounts within the limits? Increasing or decreasing current account credit line usage? The *StandardRating* automatically takes this information from OSPlus. On the other hand, hard information in the qualitative rating module relates to 'rather' hard information, i.e. facts that the bankers have to input in answer to simple questions: Duration of the customer relationship in years? Is a successor appointed (yes/no)? Soft information (called *soft qualitative facts*) is

Figure 4.10 The structure of the *StandardRating*

Source: Sparkassen Rating and Risikosysteme GmbH 2010: 13 (translated)

also input into the qualitative rating module. The customer advisors assess different aspects of the firms by answering questions with Likert scales. In order to increase reliability, the *StandardRating* offers so-called guardrails that guide customer advisors' assessments (see Table 4.2 as an example).

Different versions of the *StandardRating* exist for the divergent types of SMEs (Figure 4.11). The savings banks apply special ratings for start-ups and freelancers, and corporate customers are rated with different *StandardRating* versions according to their net sales. The extent of the qualitative rating and the weighting of the data differ between the rating versions. For efficiency and reasons of appropriateness, the scope of the qualitative module increases with the size of the firms. For the *StandardRating* for commercial customers (for SMEs with revenue below €2.5 million), the customer advisors have to answer eight questions in addition to account behaviour and the financial rating (Theis 2009). These questions relate to the qualification of management, planning and timeliness of reporting. For the *StandardRating* of firm customers, customer advisors have to fill in a range of questions concerning planning and controlling, management, market and products and the value chains of the firm (Figure 4.12).

The *StandardRating* explicitly does not evaluate the sector of firms in order to avoid sector discrimination, e.g. a downgrading for all construction companies. In an interview the manager of the Sparkassen Rating and Risikosysteme GmbH indicated that the inclusion of firms' sectors was discussed in the initial development of the *StandardRating* but the savings banks decided against it because they argued that good firms can be creditworthy in every sector (OSGVIT30.05.13). Nevertheless, the *StandardRating* adapts the rating modules to include four basic sectors – trading, service, production and 'other sectors' – for feasibility reasons (e.g. storage management is not evaluated in the *StandardRating* for the service sector).

In the empirical development of the rating systems, the rating algorithm is specified; i.e. the developer specifies the variables considered in rating execution and

Table 4.2 Example of a rating question and guardrails to codify soft information

Question	Guardrail	
How do you assess the quality management of the firm?	Example for best assessment: • Holistic quality management is implemented and controlled centrally • Certificates available (e.g. following DIN EN ISO 9000ff.)	Example for poorest assessment: • No quality management • No certificates • Losses due to quality problems • Recalls of products

Source: Theis 2009: 98 (translated and modified)

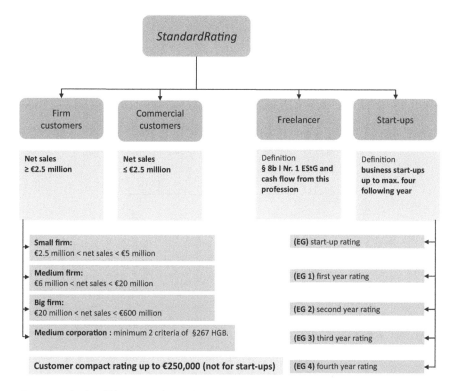

Figure 4.11 The different versions of the *StandardRating*

Source: Theis (2009): 93 (translated and altered)

their weighting (see Box 4.6). Banks keep their rating algorithms confidential, on the one hand, in order to prevent counterperformativity as customers could manipulate the rating scores if they knew the exact weighting of variables (Middelberg and Plegge 2010, Section 2.3.3.1). On the other hand, the rating algorithms are considered commercially sensitive and are hidden from competing banks (Theis 2009). Bank employees also do not know the precise weightings of every variable of the rating. Weightings differ between the different rating versions, size classes and sectors (OSGVIT30.05.13). Following Theis (2009: 100), the financial rating accounts for 50% of the overall commercial customer *StandardRating* basic score and the equity ratio represents the single most important financial ratio. Account behavior is weighted at 20% of the qualitative commercial customer rating score and the eight questions are weighted at 80% together. The *StandardRating* of firm customers tends to weight cash flow and return on investment higher in comparison to the algorithm for commercial customers. The exact weighting depends on firms' net sales.

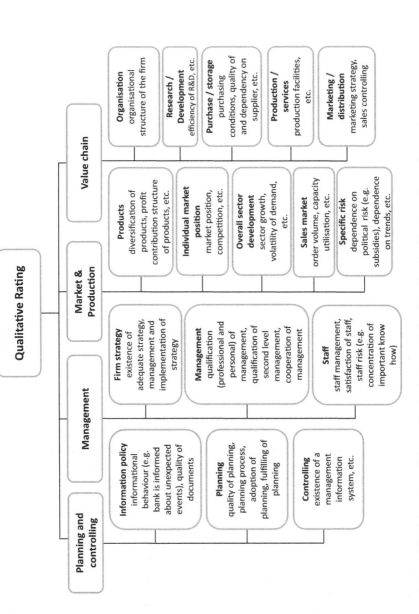

Figure 4.12 Subsections of the qualitative rating module of the *StandardRating* and sample questions

Source: from Theis 2009: 99, Sparkassen Rating and Risikosysteme GmbH 2006a, 2006b, 2006c, 2006d (translated and altered)

Box 4.6   Rating development and maintenance

As rating systems should predict customer probability of default (PD) within the next year, the aim of rating system development is to create an algorithm that allocates firms to PD classes. The savings banks financial group developed the *StandardRating* as the first of its rating systems in the late 1990s and rolled it out for application to all savings banks in 2002. The interviewed manager from the Sparkassen Rating and Risikosysteme GmbH pointed out that the development of the quantitative rating module was rather easy, because the EBIL dataset, with its long time series of financial statements, already existed (OSGVIT30.05.13). However, developing the qualitative rating module caused difficulties as the databases needed to be compiled:

> Ok hard figures are not everything, there is much more to consider at a firm, the whole series of so-called soft facts. There it was – of course – the task at the banks to go down to the credit files, really to go into the archives and look at the files and to check, what are the characteristics of firms that default and what was striking during the period before, what good and bad criteria were there [. . .] when later there was a default. Hence this was really difficult detailed work for the colleagues of the savings banks.
>
> (OSGVIT30.05.13)

Banks analyse the reliability of their rating algorithms annually. So-called back-tests review if as many customers have defaulted as the rating score had predicted. These tests assess the prediction power of every rating variable. At irregular intervals banks alter the algorithm according to the test results. The Sparkassen Rating and Risikosysteme GmbH also collects dummy variables – variables that are not considered in the current rating result – to assess their prediction power for future modifications of the algorithms (OSGVIT30.05.13).

This high rating maintenance effort on the part of banks is not entirely voluntary, although superior rating systems are an important competitive advantage. The application of rating systems with low validity either leads to an underestimate of firms' default risk, causing banks to take higher risks than intended, or to financially sound customers being rejected if the rating algorithm overestimates risk. Both aspects tend to influence the profitability of banks. BaFin allows banks to use IRA to calculate minimum capital requirements only if their rating systems fulfil detailed quality criteria, including the regular validity and back-tests analyses (Theis 2009). Therefore, BaFin accredits the rating systems of banks. Big bank 1 uses IRA, and its rating systems are accredited. Equally, the rating systems of the savings banks are BaFin accredited, though only one savings bank uses IRA. The Sparkassen Rating and Risikosysteme GmbH sees the BaFin accreditation as a quality certificate for its rating systems (OSGVIT30.05.13). The BaFin accreditation for IRA indicates that the rating systems of big bank 1 and savings banks produce similar rating results, since the rating scores are approved for use for the determination of banks' minimum equity capital.

Bank employees are able to influence the rating scores of the *StandardRating* with their soft information by answering the soft qualitative questions. As Theis (2009: 85) points out, savings banks explicitly aim to use the soft information advantage (due to geographical proximity and close/long-standing customer relationships) in the ratings to render their rating results superior to those of their competitors. However, the impact of soft information on the rating scores remains limited, as the weight of hard and 'rather' hard information in the qualitative rating module is decisive. This tends to be true for the commercial customer *StandardRating* in particular, where customer advisors have to answer eight questions mainly relating to 'rather' hard information. For larger SMEs the amount of soft information increases considerably; i.e. more than 40 questions are asked in the qualitative rating module.

Bankers are able to include soft information in the rating score using two other mechanisms. Firstly, they can influence the weighting of specific questions of the qualitative module in order to indicate the importance of the questions for the firms concerned (SK1MFPP11.11.13). Secondly, savings banks allow for the so-called overwriting of the rating score, i.e. its altering within limits. Overwriting is intended for firms where the financial statements inappropriately represent the actual financial situation, and must be justified in written form (SK1MFPP06.11.13). Participant observation indicated the reluctance of customer advisors to use overwriting rating scores (it was never observed) so as not to be responsible in case of firm default. Thus, instead of improving the rating score of inappropriately represented firms, customer advisors prefer to arrange special terms in order to offer appropriate credit terms (SK1MFPP06.11.13). This observation at savings bank 1 indicates that bank employees do not always exhaust the possibilities to influence rating results with additional information but rather take the information into account elsewhere.

THE SME RATING SYSTEM OF BIG BANK 1

Although the rating scores of the banking groups have different nomenclatures, they can be compared using the PD dedicated (Table 4.3). Big bank 1's rating scale classifies customers in numerous default classes (GB1D2 [disclosure report of big bank 1][3]). Big bank 1 applies a less extensive rating system consisting of six modules for SMEs with corporate credits of up to €5 million: (1) master data module with the basic information of the firm, (2) account behaviour module

Table 4.3 Nomenclature and PD classes of the rating systems of German banks

PD range	Commerzbank	Deutsche Bank	Hypo Vereinsbank	Kfw	Savings banks financial group	Postbank	Cooperative banks financial group
Up to 0.3%	1.0 to 2.4	iAAA to iBBB	1+ to 3−	BK1	1 to 3	pAAA to pBBB	0+ to 1d
0.3% to 0.7%	2.6 to 2.8	iBBB to iBBB	3− to 4−	BK2	3 to 6	pBBB to pBB+	1e to 2a
0.7% to 1.5%	3.0 to 3.4	iBB+ to iBB−	4− to 5−	BK2 to BK3	6 to 8	pBB+ to pBB	2b to 2c
1.5% to 3%	3.6 to 3.8	iBB− to iB+	5− to 6	BK4 to BK5	8 to 10	pBB to pB+	2d to 2e
3% to 8%	4.0 to 4.8	iB+ to iB	6 to 7	BK5 to BK6	10 to 12	pB+ to pB	3a to 3b
8% and higher	From 5.0	From iB−	> 7	BK6	12 to 18	From pB−	3c to 3e

Source: Initiative Finanzstandort Deutschland 2010 (translated and altered)

(overdrafts etc.), (3) financial rating module that comprises seven financial figures, (4) the qualitative rating module, (5) the external rating report of Creditreform or other credit bureaus and (6) a module that captures cross-guarantees with other entities (GB1MIT11.02.14, GB1MIT25.09.13II).

Similar to the savings banks' *StandardRating*, soft information is input into the qualitative rating module that includes 40 to 50 questions in five to six subcategories (GB1MIT11.02.14). The following list of subcategories and questions was noted from a soft fact sheet of big bank 1 (GB1D): market and market position (market share?, small or big player in its market?); owner and manager (trustworthiness?, how does he act?); planning (are planned figures met?); BWA (negative numbers in the BWA?, business development like decline in sales etc?). This incomplete list indicates similarities to the *StandardRating*, as a range of questions in the qualitative rating module actually ask for 'rather' hard and hard information. Mr Maske explained this for the BWA subcategory:

> The BWA, for example, is not inserted into the system according to its numbers, but is inserted by questions. Are there thus negative developments in the BWA, is business development declining, are sales declining, is profit declining, is the decline in profit larger than 50%? Facts are inserted there in this way.
>
> (GB1MIT11.02.14)

The weighting of the different variables of the rating algorithm depends on the size of the firms. For smaller SMEs, the financial figures are relatively more important than for larger firms (revenues above €10 million) where the qualitative rating becomes more important (GB1MIT25.06.13I). In general, big bank 1 emphasises the relevance of account behaviour (GB1MIT25.09.13II). Mr Holz estimates that, on average, over all firm size classes financial figures account for 20%, qualitative rating for 30% to 40% and account keeping for 10% to 15% of the rating score (GB1MIT25.06.13I, GB1MIT25.09.13II). As for the *StandardRating*, an overwriting of the rating score is possible in order to counter inappropriate representations of firms' financial situation by the financial statements. Customer advisors must justify rating score overwriting; changes are limited to two PD classes (up and down) and need to be approved by the back office (GB1D2). According to Mr Holz's estimation, his team overwrites less than 10% of all rating scores. Hence, the team studied in the big bank tend to use overwriting more often than savings bank 1.

To sum up, a range of facts indicate that the rating systems of savings bank 1 and big bank 1 tend to calculate similar results. Firstly, and most importantly, both rating systems are approved by the bank supervision for IRA, which indicates that the rating algorithms must determine comparable PD for similar firms in general. Secondly, both rating systems consist of the financial rating module and a rating module for qualitative data, in which customer account behavior represents an important input. Thirdly, soft information is input into both rating systems, although many questions of the qualitative rating actually ask for hard and 'rather' hard information. Fourthly, overwriting is possible in both rating systems. One difference is the obligatory use of external rating scores in the SME rating system of big bank 1, whereas the *StandardRating* of savings banks does not permit the input of external ratings. Furthermore, the financial figures tend to be more important in the *StandardRating*, whereas big bank 1's SME rating gives weight to the sector of firms (in the master data module). Overall, both rating systems are influenceable by soft information but, considering the relevance of hard and 'rather' hard information in the qualitative rating modules, soft information accounts for much less than 50% of the rating score.

4.2.2.2 *The integration of the rating systems in the credit-granting process*

This section firstly describes the execution of the ratings at savings bank 1 and big bank 1 before it compares the decision-making power of the rating systems.

RATING EXECUTION

The market and back-office departments cooperate in rating execution, which is integrated into banks' overall disclosure process for existing customer credits (Section 4.1.2.1). At savings bank 1 the customer advisors send the annual financial statements to the EBIL team after a first check. Following the data input, customer advisors execute the financial and qualitative rating and the two additional rating modules, if necessary. One credit officer reviews all rating modules and a second credit officer confirms the final rating score ('four eyes' principle). With this procedure, savings bank 1 appoints the official rating scores of firms which remain valid until the new rating and disclosure process is finished in the following year. This whole process can be executed within minutes for well-known clients if necessary. For example, in one case it took less than 10 minutes after the EBIL was created: Mrs Hennecke started the *StandardRating* software and transferred the financial figures from OSPlus into the programme with one mouse click. She then answered the eight questions of the commercial customer qualitative rating module in under a minute, as she had known this firm for a long time (the other two rating modules were not relevant). After these inputs were completed, Mrs Hennecke called Mr Flick, her credit officer in charge, who checked her work, and his colleague approved the rating within minutes (SK1MPP11.12.13).

Comparable to savings bank 1, the customer advisors of big bank 1 check and then forward the financial statements to the analysis team who enter the data into the ICT system of big bank 1 and start the rating process. Following this, the customer advisors complete the qualitative and the five other rating modules. However, in contrast to savings bank 1, credit officers do not review all executed ratings of big bank 1. Ratings of SMEs with overall credits of less than €1 million are only checked if the rating score is critical (medium and poor rating scores). Thus, the customer advisors appoint uncritical ratings themselves. Customers with critical ratings scores are always approved by the central back-office department of big bank 1. Furthermore, this back-office department checks and approves the ratings of all SMEs with total credit volumes of more than €1 million (GB1MIT11.02.14). Nevertheless, ca. 60% to 65% of all SME customers of big bank 1 remain below the €1 million limit (GB1MIT25.09.13II), and ca. 80% of these clients have a sound rating score (GB1MIT25.09.13II, GB1M-FIP05.11.12). Hence, this calculation indicates that the central back-office department of big bank 1 approves ca. 50% of all SME ratings, whereas all SME ratings are approved by the back officers of savings bank 1.

DECISION-MAKING POWER OF THE RATING SYSTEMS

Savings bank 1 defines four competence classes in relation to the rating score. The overall credit volume is not restricted by the rating score; i.e. customer advisors are always allowed to grant collateralised credits of up to €400,000. Yet, blank credit volume is limited in relation to the rating score of the SMEs (Table 4.4). Customer advisors can grant blank credits up to €200,000 if the firms have very sound rating scores (PD 0.08% to 0.4%), €100,000 for PD 0.6% to 3.0%, €50,000 for PD 3.6% to 6.7% and €25,000 to firms of the poorest rating score classes. In case of poor ratings (from score 10, PD 3%), customer advisors have to explain the unsound rating score and must produce a written statement to justify lending despite the rating result. Furthermore, the credit risk strategy of savings bank 1 points out that credits to customers with scores below rating score 10 shall only be granted with extra care. However, the score is no hard cutoff limit; high-level

Table 4.4 Rating score and credit competences of the customer advisors of savings bank 1 and big bank 1

Savings bank's score	PD (average)	Savings bank 1*	Big bank 1**
1–5	0.08%–0.4%	Overall: €400,000 Blank: €200,000	Overall and blank: €1 million
6–9	0.6%–2% 2.1%–3.0%	Overall: €400,000 Blank: €100,000	Overall and blank:
10–12	3.0%–3.6%	Overall: €400,000 Blank: €50,000 Extra care: written	€1 million Only with approval of the back office
	3.6%–6.7%	justification needed	New credits are rejected
From 13	From 10%	Overall: €400,000 Blank: €25,000 Extra care: written justification needed	In case of credit prolongation customers are transferred to the intensive care team

*If the credit is risk-relevant, then the back office conducts the second vote, which is not considered in the table.
**Limits respect the total credit volume of all corporate and private credits of the borrower unit.

Source: Author's composition from SK1D, Sparkassen Rating and Risikosysteme GmbH 2010, GB1MIT11.02.14, GB1MIT25.06.13I, GB1MIT25.09.13II, GB1D2.

supervisors are able to approve credits independently from the rating score. In fact, savings bank 1 does not use a hard cutoff limit with the explicit aim of keeping flexibility in its credit decisions (SK1BSPP10.01.14, SK1D). Also, the decision-making power of the back office is independent of the rating score at savings bank 1, in contrast to big bank 1.

Big bank 1 defines three limit classes in relation to the rating score and does not respect collaterals for the allocation of credit-granting authority (see Table 4.4). In class 1 (PD up to 2%), the customer advisors have the unlimited authority to grant credits of up to €1 million. In class 2 (PD 2.1% to 3.6%), the back office executes the final vote. Firms with a worse rating score than PD 3.6% are finally rejected and do not get new regular credits at all from big bank 1. In Mr Holz's estimation, ca. 80% of the rating scores of customers with a credit volume of less than €1 million are better than PD 2.1%. In ca. 16% of cases the back office gets involved, and 4% are rejected because of insufficient rating scores (GB1MIT25.06.13I).[4] Mr Maske explained this process:

> What I am allowed to do is up to [PD 2.1%], that's a green traffic light, which means I can do the credit alone, and then between [PD 2.1%] and, well I need to check, ca. [PD 3.6%], I get a yellow traffic light, that is the responsibility of the [central back-office department in a big German city]. And a red traffic light for a new customer means that the debate is over [and the credit rejected].
>
> (GB1MIT11.02.14)

An additional department, the intensive care unit, gets involved in so-called credit prolongation, the annual renewal of existing credits, if SMEs are rated with a score below PD 3.6%, as Mr Maske further explained:

> For existing customers, because we have to renew every credit annually, there is a separate department that looks at these customers, we call it the intensive care unit for credits. Different reasons are possible why the rating of a customer crashes, e.g. permanent usage of a current account line of credit can lead to a negative assessment of account behaviour, and because the account behaviour module is the strongest module in our rating system, it is possible that he automatically gets a red rating, although he is not too bad in terms of the financial figures. And then we have to talk about it, do we restructure the credits, do we conduct a refunding and then he may automatically get a better rating score.
>
> (GB1MIT11.02.14)

Mr Holz and Mr Maske stressed that the customer advisor and the rating system – "the machine" – conduct credit decisions of up to €1 million autonomously if the rating score is below PD 2.1% (GB1MIT11.02.14, GB1MIT25.06.13I, GB1MIT25.09.13II). The arrangement of the credits, e.g. in terms of collaterals and duration, does not impact the credit decision power of big bank 1's customer advisors (GB1MIT11.02.14). If a rating score is below 2.1%, advisors possess the power to grant a blank credit of up to €1 million to a new customer.

Aware of the high decision-making power of the customer advisors, Mr Holz and Mr Maske emphasised two approaches – random reviews of the internal auditing and experienced customer advisors – through which big bank 1 seeks to ensure conformity to the rules and responsible lending decisions. Mr Holz indicated that he has never experienced purposeful manipulations of the rating execution by one of his team members, despite different interpretations of facts and figures. The internal auditing of big bank 1 reviews a random sample of the credit decisions in order to ensure compliance to the rules:

> From time to time a random sample is taken that exactly checks this request and the revision annually looks at this sample and says I look at precisely those cases that are not reviewed in order to check whether the colleague has given correct answers.
>
> (GB1MIT25.09.13II)

Mr Maske and Mr Holz stressed that because of the lack of a second review, big bank 1 employs experienced customer advisors to serve the medium SME size class. In this context, Mr Maske pointed out the risk-sensitivity of customer advisors in loan underwriting:

> Let me put it like this, if a customer wants to have €900,000 and the system says I have a green light, then of course common sense kicks in and the little business man, the customer advisor then says okay we must talk about collateral and about the credit structure and if the customer says I want to have €900,000 blank and he has a critical rating, close to the cutoff limit, [. . .] that is of course impossible without collaterals. But in theory I could do it.
>
> (GB1MIT11.02.14)

The interview excerpt indicates the consideration of collaterals for credit underwriting although they are not respected in the allocation of credit competences. The excerpt further illustrates the extensive decision-making authority of customer advisors for firms with sound rating scores. In direct comparison, savings bank 1's customer advisors execute credit competences of 10% in terms of blank credit volume (€100,000 vs. €1 million, if the PD of the firm is between 0.6% and 2%) and rating execution is always reviewed by the back office. Considering the strict cutoff limit for SMEs with poor rating scores (PD 3.6% or less) and the second vote of the back office in cases with medium rating scores, the rating system is seen to possess profound decision-making power at big bank 1. In contrast, at savings bank 1 rating scores 'only' allocate credit-granting authority; hard rejections on the basis of the score are not applied.

In this context, the empirical data reveal differences in customer advisors' handling of the rating execution. Savings bank 1's employees tend to execute the rating after conducting the actual lending decision in order to save work in case of rejection (SK1MPP04.12.13). In contrast, at big bank 1 Mr Maske first executes the rating and then talks to the clients in order to know whether he has the entire decision-making authority (GB1MIT11.02.14). These different practices further indicate the relatively higher power of rating scores for credit decisions at big bank 1 than at savings bank 1.

In light of MacKenzie's (2006) theory on the performativity of economic theories and models (Section 2.3.3.1), the findings outlined above indicate differences in banks' susceptibility to performative effects. The way the rating is integrated into the credit decisions of big bank 1 tends to be more prone to strong performative effects compared to savings bank 1. The big bank dedicates substantial decision-making power to the rating result and only reviews a random sample of the executed ratings, whereas savings bank 1 reviews every rating executed. Accordingly, from a theoretical point of view, 'Barnesian' performative effects, i.e. potentially when firms' rating scores are below the cutoff limit, as well as counterperformative effects, i.e. if customer advisors and firms manipulate rating results in order to get the score above the cutoff limit, are more likely at big bank 1.

Having stated this, one must highlight that the empirical development of the rating algorithms overall minimises, but does not extinguish, the potential for strong performative effects. As one precondition for strong performativity, the rating results must deviate from the actual PD of firms. In contrast to algorithms deduced from economic theories, the empirical development and frequent adaption of the rating algorithms for SMEs according to the results of the back-tests enforce a similarity of predicted and actual PD. Back-tests do not extinguish strong performativity completely; if a 'Barnesian' performative effect already caused real firm defaults, a back-test cannot detect this. Back-tests are capable of detecting counterperformativity in so far as they reveal rating models' underestimation of PD. If banks alter their rating algorithms according to the counterperformative effect, rating executions without manipulation will lead to an overestimation of firms' actual PD (see Section 2.3.3.1). This overestimation of PD is, in turn, able to cause 'Barnesian' performative effects for firms that do not manipulate the rating execution, indicating the challenge of detecting and handling the (possible) strong performativity of rating systems.

Savings bank 1's integration of the rating system tends to be less prone to strong performativity. However, observation indicates that the introduction of rating systems nevertheless influenced the way savings banks conduct lending. The interview partner from the Sparkassen Rating and Risikosysteme GmbH illustrated the effect of the introduction of *StandardRating* on savings banks' lending decisions:

F.F.:   Is the statement true that at the end of the day the CEO can decide everything if he wants to?

Answer: Yes, I think so. But of course he needs more, more arguments and better arguments, because there are more guidelines and more, like I said concerning the topic of risk adjusted pricing; if the system calculates an interest rate, then not charging this interest rate has to be very well justified. This situation differs to the past where no interest rate was calculated at all. Therefore, I think it has become more difficult, because more things have to be documented, good arguments are needed as to why certain things are perhaps done and at which price and so on. So this is certainly a little bit more difficult but I think this is also right, to have really good reasons, and if it seems certain that this is a good deal then nobody says it is not allowed, but conducting the business has to be justified. And maybe that should have already been a requirement in the past.

(OSGVIT30.05.13)

The interview excerpt suggests, on the one hand, that rating results strengthen the risk awareness of decision-makers. On the other hand, similar to big bank 1, savings banks determine the standard interest rate for loans in line with the rating score of firms to provide for possible losses. Thus, rating scores tend to cause 'effective' performativity in the sense that they strengthen awareness of default risk and support pricing in line with the predicted default risk.

4.2.2.3   Generalisation and systematisation: rating systems

The way in which the rating systems are integrated into the process of credit granting to SMEs differs between the savings banks concerning customer advisors' credit-granting authority in relation to the rating scores (SK4MIT25.10.13). Here the comparison indicates relatively low lending authority at savings bank 1 compared to other savings banks. Mrs Hennecke and Mrs Friese pointed out that they used to execute twice as much authority with their old savings banks (SK1MPP25.11.13). Also in contrast to savings bank 1, other savings banks define cutoff limits, i.e. minimum rating scores, in their credit risk strategies (Theis 2009). Of the three other savings banks interviewed, the large savings bank 4 reported that they apply a rating score cutoff limit for blank credit volume of large SMEs (SK4MIT25.09.13). In interviews, customer advisors from savings banks 2 and 3, as well as the customer advisor for medium-sized SMEs of savings bank 4, did not mention the rating score as a relevant criterion for a positive credit decision. Rather, they stressed customers' future ability to cover interest and principal payments as important criteria for positive credit decisions (SK2MIP13.03.13, SK3MIT24.09.13, SK3MIT18.08.13, SK4MIT25.10.13). Overall the interviews with the other savings banks indicate similarities with savings bank 1 in so far as firms' rating scores 'only' allocate decision-making power but do not determine credit decisions for SMEs of the medium size class.

Big bank 1 applies a substantially different approach for the rating of SMEs of the large size class. A different rating system is applied which emphasises the long-term sector outlook and the firm's position within the sector (GB1MIT25.09.13II). Strikingly, in the large SME size class the customer advisors tend to emphasise the relevance of individual judgment rather than rating results, as Mr Holz pointed out:

Well, just considering the rating is the wrong approach in the end and if we find out that the customer is too badly rated, but in our view the credit is feasible, then we push the credit through all instances. Then we have to talk to the back office, they may see it in the same way. If they don't see it in the same way, then you go one level up and discuss the credit in this way again, and then you have to see that you get around it. That way the rating is actually only relevant for the price, rather than for the feasibility.

(GB1MIT25.09.13II)

The integration of rating results into the credit-granting process allows the use of individual judgment, as one of the ca. 10 sectorial specialised back-office departments always reviews the rating executions and exercises a second vote, independent of firms' rating scores. Thus, in contrast to proceedings in the medium SME size class, no credit application is rejected on the basis of the rating score alone at the big bank. This finding indicates the recognition of big bank 1 that rating results can be inappropriate for lending decisions in exceptional cases, but it nonetheless does not permit deviation from the rating score cutoff limit in the medium SME size class.

To sum up, Figure 4.13 illustrates the key findings of the rating systems comparison; differences between the observed regional and supraregional banks are highlighted. In direct comparison the savings banks' *StandardRating* and big bank 1's SME rating do not fundamentally differ; hard and soft information are input into the rating process and customer advisors possess the power to overwrite the rating score within limits. Differences relate to the obligatory input of an external rating into big bank 1's rating system, something which the *StandardRating* does not provide, for example. The differences do not lead to profoundly divergent rating results because bank regulations have approved the rating systems of both banks for IRA; hence, similar credit default risk evaluation is to be expected.

Striking differences have been detected in the integration of the rating systems in the lending processes, especially regarding their decision-making power. Whereas savings bank 1 defines no cutoff limit with the explicit aim of maintaining flexibility in credit decisions, big bank 1 defines a strict threshold. Medium-sized SMEs below this threshold, i.e. firms that have rating scores of PD 3.6% or worse, will not get a new ordinary credit at all at the big bank. For firms with sound rating scores (PD < 2.1%), the customer advisors of big bank 1 execute up to 10 times more decision-making power in terms of blank credit volume than is the case at savings bank 1. Furthermore, the back-office department of savings bank 1 always reviews the rating executions and therefore gets involved in every lending process to SMEs if a new rating score has to be appointed. Hence, customer advisors of savings bank 1 must interact with several actors for most credit decisions to SMEs, whereas the customer advisors and the rating systems conduct over 50% of all regular lending decisions alone at big bank 1.

It thus becomes clear how firms' rating scores decidedly influence credit decisions at big bank 1, whereas savings bank 1 'only' allocates decision-making power to the human actors in relation to the rating results. The high decision-making power and the less frequent reviews of the rating executions tend to make the rating system of big bank 1 more susceptible for strong performativity compared to savings bank 1. Nevertheless, the empirical findings indicate that rating

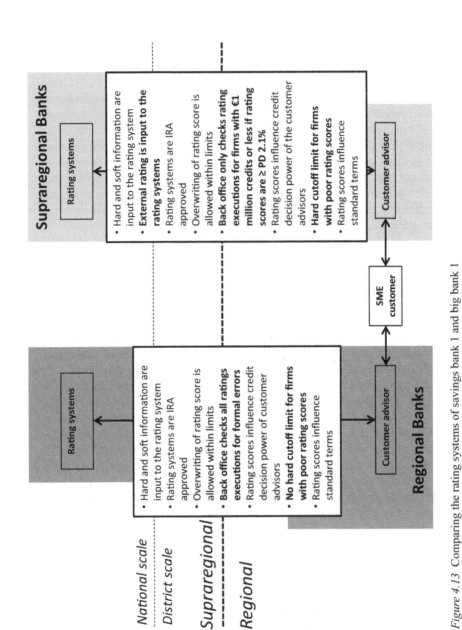

Figure 4.13 Comparing the rating systems of savings bank 1 and big bank 1

Source: author's figure

scores tend to raise the default risk awareness of savings banks' decision-makers, and hence cause 'effective' performativity. Therefore, the rating results have the potential to influence the credit decisions of savings bank 1, too.

4.2.3 Back offices

This work defines *back offices* as all units of a bank that are directly involved in the ordinary credit-granting and monitoring processes and are downstream from the customer advisors and their supervisors, comprising the back offices in the definition of MaRisk and the administrative back-office units. As this section shows, big bank 1 splits its back-office function and applies a higher (spatial) division of labour, whereas the back-office employees are less specialised at savings bank 1. The back offices influence credit decisions for two reasons. Firstly, bank regulation requires that a second department, i.e. the back office, independent of the market department, approves risk-relevant lending with a second vote (see Box 4.7). Secondly, back-office departments conduct numerous administrative tasks and reviewing jobs that influence the screening and monitoring of banks. The discussion of the organisation and jobs of the back-office departments in this section reveals profound differences between savings bank 1 and big bank 1 in terms of functional distance to the back offices (Section 4.2.3.1). Following this, the integration of the back-office departments in banks' credit-granting processes is discussed (Section 4.2.3.2). Finally, Section 4.2.3.3 generalises and systematises the findings.

Box 4.7   Second vote and risk-relevant lending

Bank regulation enforces a segregation of credit decisions in order to reduce risk with the intention of meeting the principal agent problem that potentially arises in lending due to conflicts of objectives (Breuer and Mark 2004; Hartmann-Wendels et al. 2010). Under the assumption that banks' customer advisors tend to have limited incentives to be risk sensitive, because of sales-oriented incentive systems and a bias in favour of the clients, a counterbalance agent should conduct an independent inspection of the credit application. Bank regulation respects this principal agency consideration in the MaRisk:

> The core principle for structuring credit business processes shall be the clear organisational segregation of the front office and back office up to and including management board level. [. . .] Depending on the nature, scale, complexity and riskiness of the exposure in question, a credit decision shall require two positive votes by the front office and back office.
>
> (BaFin 2012b: BTO 1.1)

For so-called non risk-relevant lending transactions, the second vote of the back office is not requested. Banks define criteria for non risk-relevant lending according to their risk profile, following MaRisk's coarse guidelines: "standardised retail business could normally count as non risk-relevant lending" (BaFin 2012b: BTO 1.1). The threshold for risk-relevant lending and the annual disclosure requirements (Section 4.1.2.1) are independent of each other, and banks define different criteria for sisclosure and risk-relevant lending (SK1MFIT02.09.13).

4.2.3.1 The work of and functional distance to the back offices

Division of labour between the market department and back offices is, on the one hand, intended to reduce risk (see Box 4.7). On the other hand, banks want to increase efficiency with specialisation (see 'industrialisation' of banking, Section 3.2.4.3). Customer advisors focus on sales and client contacts; the specialised back-office teams conduct the administrative work (SK4MIT25.09.13). Accordingly, the back-office work includes different jobs, which are exemplary listed in the following for savings bank 1:

- Administrative work mainly comprises management of existing credits and keeping the files. Savings bank 1 manages all new credits with OSPlus, credit officers entering and updating the data in the system. OSPlus conducts many jobs automatically (e.g. calculating the up-to-date loan amount); nevertheless, manual work is needed (e.g. checking the payout criteria before disbursing loan tranches). Furthermore, the credit officers maintain the basic customer files that comprise all original documents and contracts, and savings bank 1 stores the files in the basement archive of the headquarters (SK1MFPP15.11.13, SK1MPP16.12.13). Banks need original error-free documents in case of legal proceedings, a requirement for which the back office is responsible (SK1MFPP15.11.13).
- Credit officers are involved in the monitoring of existing credits and credit prolongations together with the customer advisors and supervisors (e.g. annual disclosure, risk monitoring via the watch list). They are especially in charge of the administrative work and have to ensure that the bank meets its contracts. OSPlus partly monitors collaterals and delay in payments automatically, yet manual work is required. For example, the back office has to manually inform special-purpose banks that guarantee firm loans about clients' delays in principal payments (SK1MPP10.12.13). The monitoring function also comprises assessment and reviewing tasks; e.g. the credit officers review the calculations of future ability to cover interest and principal payments produced by the customer advisors.
- Credit officers compile the credit applications and write the contracts. After the customer advisors have appointed new credits, the credit officers write the

credit application on the basis of customer advisors' information. These applications are then decided upon by the authorised actors (SK1MPP16.12.13). Following positive credit decisions, the credit officers create the loan contracts on the basis of the credit applications. Credit officers use PDF forms to compose the credit applications and contracts (SK1MPP19.11.13).

- Credit officers review the vast majority of credit-granting and prolongation processes for errors at savings bank 1. Customer advisors write and approve applications alone only for very small credits (e.g. minor temporary increase of an overdraft) (SK1MPP25.11.13). The reviewing job comprises, for example, inspecting whether credit-granting authority is met, reviewing the calculations and examining whether all necessary original documents are available.
- Finally, for risk-relevant lending the back office conducts the second vote, as ruled by MaRisk regulation. Here the back office has the right to reject credit applications or demand changes in the credit structure (e.g. volume, duration, collaterals) in case of risk concerns. This right of second vote differs from the reviewing jobs, where the credit officers are only allowed to demand changes if they detect formal errors (SK1MFIT02.09.13). At savings bank 1, the supervisors of the back office conduct the second vote; credit officers elaborate the second vote decisions for their supervisors.

This list of jobs indicates two aspects. On the one hand, the credit officers have decision-making power beyond the second vote (see Section 4.2.3.2). On the other hand, credit officers conduct many jobs in cooperation with the customer advisors, entailing frequent communication.

THE BACK-OFFICE WORKING GROUP OF SAVINGS BANK 1

One working group of savings bank 1's back-office department processes all medium-sized SMEs. The team is located at the headquarters and executes all back-office and service functions for the two SME customer advisor teams of savings bank 1, except the annual financial statement processing. Mr Mirow heads the working group with ca. 10 employees. These are the credit officers and assistants who conduct specialised jobs like the booking. Every customer advisor has a credit officer on the back-office team; one credit officer works with one customer advisor (SK1MFPP14.11.13). The office of Mr Flick and Mr Müller was observed, the credit officers in charge of Mrs Hennecke and Mrs Weber. Both officers have worked at their positions for over five years; Mr Müller, especially, is very experienced. At the time of the observation (November and December 2013), the workload of the back-office team was very high because of illness; hence, Mr Flick and Mr Müller had to conduct the work of other credit officers and were temporarily in charge of two customer advisors each.

With a geographical distance of ca. 20 minutes by car, functional distance to the customer advisors team in the branch studied hinders ad hoc meetings. Accordingly, customer advisors predominantly use the telephone for verbal communication with their credit officers. Different communication patterns were observed for the customer advisor team of the headquarters where the telephone also comes first, yet the customer advisors also go to their credit officers to deliver and discuss documents. Communication is further based on written documents, like work instructions, calculations and forms. The internal post team transmits physical documents between the departments and branches twice a day (in the morning and in the evening) (SK1MFPP18.11.13). The bank employees often communicate indirectly via ICT; e.g. credit officers approve customer advisors' rating execution with a simple button click in the rating software (SK1MPP11.12.13).

Customer advisors verbally communicate with their credit officers on a daily basis in an informal manner, addressing each other with the informal *du*. The frequency of communication depends on the occasion; on average, Mrs Hennecke and Mr Flick call each other more than once every working day. Similar communication frequencies have been observed for the other customer advisor–credit officer pairs. Most calls last a few minutes and are simply to clarify certain aspects or coordinate actions. For example, the customer advisors write short work instructions to order credit applications, with key information on the applications. As they do not specify all information in detail, the credit officers call to clarify. A range of occasions for communication between the back office and customer advisor team initiate a series of interactions with different communication means. Communication often relates to deviating/unclear calculations and interpretations as well as disagreements on action. The two examples in Box 4.8 illustrate the cooperation between customer advisors and credit officers.

Box 4.8   Examples of customer advisor–credit officer cooperation

On one occasion the future ability to cover interest and principal payments was calculated wrongly for one of Mrs Hennecke's clients who was monitored intensively. Mrs Friese conducted the calculation based on the plan figures and a BWA for Mrs Hennecke, who quickly browsed, signed and then posted this calculation to her credit officer Mr Flick. Mr Flick called the next day and explained why he thought the calculation was wrong and e-mailed his calculation. Mrs Hennecke checked this calculation and the BWA and compared it to her calculation, which contained two errors. With the new calculation the customer failed to demonstrate a future ability to cover interest and principal payments. Mrs Hennecke posted Mr Flick's correct calculation with her signature to the back office and called Mr Flick to inform him and discuss how to continue with this customer (SK1MPP16.12.13). As the customer failed to serve debt on the basis of the new calculation he needed to be discussed at the watch list meeting (SK1MPP16.12.13, SK1B-SPP 19.12.13, see Box 4.9).

On another occasion Mrs Hennecke wanted to offer a mortgage with very low equity contribution (by savings bank 1's standards) to attract a new customer. Because the credit was risk-relevant, the back office had the second vote, and Mrs Hennecke called her credit officer to explain the unusual terms. Mr Flick promised to ask Mr Mirow, the team leader in charge of the second vote, and call back. Mrs Hennecke called Mr Flick again a couple of hours later because the credit was urgent but Mr Flick talked in a strange way on the telephone. After five minutes Mr Flick called back and explained that he had been unable to talk openly because Mr Mirow was in his office and further outlined his support for the unusual terms because of the high collateral value of the property. However, Mr Mirow disliked the low equity contribution and did not promise to agree (SK1MPP10.12.13). Mrs Hennecke was visibly annoyed about this result as the daily protocol reports: "Mrs Hennecke is visibly grouchy and said if the savings banks don't want to earn money then that's just the way it is. The customer should go to the cooperative bank and there's no Christmas bonus" (SK1MPP09.12.13). Both examples indicate the informal and close cooperation between the customer advisor–credit officer pairs.

Although the examples in Box 4.8 illustrate smooth cooperation between customer advisors and credit officers, the observed cooperation was not without conflict. Different customer assessments caused disagreements and the need for negotiation (SK1MPP11.12.13, SK1MPP03.12.13). The different relationships to the customers presumably foster disagreements as credit officers usually have no contact to clients and also do not want personal contacts (SK1MPP11.12.13, SK1MFPP12.11.13). This higher distance, intended by bank regulations, tends to result in different access to soft information and a different assessment of customers. A former credit officer of savings bank 1 expressed this:

F.F.:   When it comes to evaluation, what does the back office do differently?
Answer: Well, I think, the back office doesn't know the clients personally from the talks, and so, I'd say, it interprets them differently. A person's creditworthiness is different, is interpreted differently, if, I have known you as a customer for 10 years from talks and cooperation than if I only know your files, and that is simply a different kind of evaluation that can play a role. The back office is traditionally more dispassionate, somewhat more number-oriented.

(SK1BSIT02.09.13)

A second temporary cause of conflict was the high workload of the back-office team. Credit applications and contracts were drawn up slowly (SK1MPP19.11.13). The back-office team tried to manage this problem and process urgent cases first.

Nevertheless, delays in the production of applications strained customer relationships, as problems in credit applications were detected very late, and the customer advisors started to doubt credit officers' efforts (SK1MFPP 11.11.13).

The high social embeddedness of the cooperation tends to explain why communication remained very smooth and solution oriented despite these current conflicts and different perceptions. The cooperation is socially embedded in so far as the credit officers and customer advisors have gained experience with each other and know what they can expect and also what they cannot expect from one another. The fixed pairwise and long-term character of cooperation encourages the mutual dependency of customer advisors and credit officers and strengthens social embeddedness. In addition, the fact that the two teams used to be one unit until 2004, and still celebrate their Christmas party together, reinforces social ties between the two departments.

These organisational causes of social embeddedness are not related to short geographical distance per se. In fact, due to the remote location of the customer advisor team under study, face-to-face interactions between the customer advisors and credit officers' pairs take place primarily when customer advisors have appointments in the headquarters. This happens, on the one hand, for infrequent specific occasions; e.g. during the period of observation, Mrs Weber met her credit officer Mr Müller twice in order to discuss a credit of €1.5 million at acute risk of default. On the other hand, the pairs meet quarterly after the so-called watch list meetings which take place in the headquarters. At these formal and high-level consultations the savings bank decides on the monitoring and treatment of credit engagements at substantial risk of default (see Box 4.9). The credit officers do not participate in the watch list meetings themselves, as only the back-office team leader Mr Mirow represents the perspective of the back office. Nevertheless, all customer advisors use the opportunity to meet their credit officers after the watch list meetings. At these informal get-togethers the customer advisors report about the results of the meeting and discuss their risky clients (SK1BSPP19.12.13).

Box 4.9   Intensive care and watch list

OSPlus automatically generates warning signals on the basis of customers' account behaviour, repayments, etc., and bank employees are able to specify warnings signals manually (SK1MFPP14.11.13). Based on the warning signals, savings bank 1 has specified criteria to identify risky customers that need to be monitored closely in the so-called watch list module of OSPlus. Depending on the blank credits, the rating score and the severity of the warning signals, clients are automatically appointed to the watch list and discussed quarterly at the watch list meetings. Participants in these high-level meetings include the CEO and all managing directors, the heads of the market and back-office departments, the team leaders of the back office, the restructuring and workout team, the internal revision teams and those customer advisors in charge of the clients concerned (SK1BSPP19.12.13). The handling of customers from the watch list is decided at the meetings. The system specifies three treatments: a customer transfer to the restructuring team; a classification to intensive care, implying close monitoring by the customer advisor team; or no changes in the client relationship. Furthermore, specific actions are agreed upon at the meetings, like high-level meetings with the client or a restructuring of debt (SK1BSPP19.12.13). In advance of the meetings the customer advisors and credit officers conduct a survey at OSPlus for risk-relevant borrower units, in which they propose how to treat their clients on the watch list (SK1MPP11.12.13).

Overall, observation suggests the role of face-to-face interactions for reinforcing socially embedded cooperation between the customer advisor–credit officer pairs tends to be subordinated to organisational embeddedness. The pairwise organisation of front- and back-office work causes daily interaction and reciprocal understanding between the pairs even though personal meetings are rare. Having stated this, business and social meetings (i.e. Christmas party, personal get-togethers) take place and potentially strengthen the social embeddedness.

THE MARKET ADMINISTRATION TEAM AND THE BACK-OFFICE
DEPARTMENT OF BIG BANK 1

Big bank 1 splits the administrative jobs and the risk analysis/second vote function into separate departments. A centralised back-office department conducts the second vote for risk-relevant credits at the national scale. The so-called market administration teams conduct the administrative and reviewing jobs at the district scale. Furthermore, central departments at the national scale conduct collaterals management, document scanning and storage, financial statement analysis and the input of the financial figures into the rating systems (GB1MIT25.09.13II).

The administration market team of big bank 1's SME branch under study is located at a geographical distance of ca. 30 minutes by car. Each SME customer has a designated administrative officer in charge. However, customer advisors and administrative officers do not cooperate pairwise, so that Mr Maske works with four administrative officers (GB1MIT11.02.14). The administrative officers execute fewer jobs than the credit officers at savings bank 1. They review new credits, compile contracts and create credit applications which they fill with basic information, e.g. client name, loan amount (GB1MIT25.09.13II). The customer advisors have to supplement the written credit justifications (GB1MIT11.02.14). According to Mr Maske, the market administration team is the department of big bank 1 with which he most frequently interacts. The following interview excerpt indicates the cooperative and solution-oriented nature of this interaction:

> I also have a colleague in [the market administration team] with whom I work together the most and he does the tests for me. So he enters, he simulates an entry [of a new loan] to see if everything works. I tell him how I want to do it and then he says, okay, it works, you can issue that contract. If the customer accepts the loan, the administrative officer can call up the simulation again and then basically releases it as a real loan.
>
> (GB1MIT11.02.14)

Administrative officers themselves have no face-to-face contact with clients, but are directly addressed by clients for contract-related topics like document posting or the ordering of certificates of bank guaranties (GB1MIT11.02.14). The interview partners at big bank 1 did not report face-to-face interactions with their administrative officers, even though the geographical distance is comparable to that of savings bank 1. The lack of pairwise cooperation indicates higher functional distance to the administrative officers than is the case in savings bank 1. Yet empirical data is vague on the cooperation, as the interviewed customer advisors hardly discussed the administrative officers, which tends to underline their minor role in the actual credit decisions.

Generally, big bank 1's employees most frequently communicate via e-mail due to the issue of people being out of the office, as Mr Holz explained:

> We do more and more by e-mail, that's just the way it is, [. . .] because we have the problem that people are out so much, you can hardly get in touch with them by phone. So I'd say, first by e-mail, then by phone, then personally.
>
> (GB1MIT25.09.13II)

The back-office department in charge of the second vote operates centrally at the national scale in a big German city at a distance of more than 200 kilometres from the customer advisor team observed. Almost all the credit applications of medium-sized SMEs that need a second vote are analysed and decided by this large team of credit officers who process credit applications randomly and hence are not familiar with the customers or the customer advisors (GB1MIT13.02.14). Mr Maske highlighted the disadvantage of this organisation:

> So my job is to convince the back office. And we in the [medium-sized SME class] find it a bit harder because we don't have a permanently assigned credit officer. In [a large German city] I have a whole team. You know many, but not all of them, and I don't know what this one or that one pays attention to. There are questions of wording, and one person likes this better and another that. So I have to try and phrase it so everyone will like it eventually. In the segment of [large SMEs], they have a fixed assigned credit officer.
>
> (GB1MIT11.02.14)

Furthermore, Mr Maske pointed out that big bank 1 does actually not desire intensive communication. Nevertheless, communication happens, and credit officers
usually cooperate and are compromise oriented:

F.F.:   When you don't agree with the back office, do you talk to each other on
            the phone or is that unwanted?

Maske: Of course, well, I'd say that in the [medium-sized SME class] it's not
            really appreciated but nevertheless we are all just human. So we talk on
            the phone or communicate via e-mail and try to find a compromise. In
            some situations, they remain unyielding and say no, but then we have
            the option of declaring a dissent although that's quite difficult in small-
            scale business. It means that we return to the table, have a third or fourth
            person check everything and then we try to find a compromise.

F.F.:   But such an escalation procedure is not provided for the small-scale
            segment?

Maske: Not really, but it still exists, even though it's not official.

F.F.:   I assume you would only do this if you thought a customer had been
            evaluated completely wrongly?

Maske: Well, usually before a credit officer even in small-scale business rejects
            something, he will call and say, listen, I've looked this over, I can't do it or
            I can only do it subject to certain conditions. That's usually the case, then
            I have the permission but I must fulfil certain conditions. Conditions can
            mean, provide collateral, find a guarantor or ensure that the equity ratio
            doesn't fall by arranging covenants. We rather do that, rejections are rare.

                                                                (GB1MIT11.02.14)

Considering the interview results quoted here, striking differences between big
bank 1 and savings bank 1 in terms of the organisational embeddedness of cooperation between customer advisors and credit officers become apparent. The large
credit officers team and the random processing of customer cases at big bank 1
hamper socially embedded cooperation. Accordingly, Mr Maske does not personally know all credit officers by name (GB1MIT11.02.14). Furthermore, no mutual
dependency exists in the cooperation because, in contrast to savings bank 1, the
credit officers are not involved in everyday customer business, which is the job
of the administrative officers of big bank 1. As Mr Maske suggests, low social
embeddedness in the cooperation with credit officers is intended by big bank 1
to ensure independent second votes in line with the intention of MaRisk. Nevertheless, from a theoretical point of view, the low organisational integration and
subsequent low social embeddedness of credit officers hinders the transmission of
soft information. The former market area head of big bank 1 who knows savings
banks from his current work as a business consultant also underlines the disadvantage of this low organisational embeddedness:

    In savings banks the one who executes the rating knows the case very
    well, normally as they also conduct the processing. That means he can ask

questions relatively quickly, he can clear up minor details with the market department, whereas in private banks, everything is rather incognito, so everyone has his own stuff to do and it gets difficult when the market department wants to resort to the back office. Well, when it's the other way around, you can see who made the request, but if the front office has subsequent deliveries or thinks I have to speak to the person who is working on this now, so he gets it right and why is this so, that is often done anonymously, that is definitely an important point.

(GB1MIT13.02.14)

As the interview excerpt further indicates, the organisational integration of the credit officers prevents an accumulation of knowledge for the second votes. Credit officers are neither familiar with the customer cases they decide on nor with the regional context, and they also do not know the customer advisors who have created the credit application. Therefore, they have to rely on the credit application and information provided to them from the customer advisors. In contrast to this, by working with the customer advisors in serving the clients on a daily basis, the credit officers of savings bank 1 have co-created most information themselves and thus accumulate customer and regional knowledge as well as experience with the customer advisors. In light of the finding that bank employees cross-check different sources of information to verify 'rather' hard and soft information (Section 4.1.1), the credit officers of big bank 1 must find it more difficult to verify this kind of information due to limited sources of information and lack of knowledge about the clients. It follows that influencing credit officers' credit decisions with 'rather' hard and soft information tends to be more difficult at big bank 1 than at savings bank 1.

4.2.3.2　*The integration of the back offices in the credit-granting process*

The credit-granting authority of the back office of savings bank 1 is restricted to risk-relevant lending. Savings bank 1 defines risk-relevant lending by two thresholds: total credit volume above €1.2 million or blank credit volume above €200,000 (SK1MFPP14.11.13). The back office executes the right to reject new credit applications and the prolongation of credits which exceed these thresholds (second vote). The head of the back-office department executes the second vote; if absent, the team leader Mr Mirow stands in (SK1MFPP14.11.13). In cases of a negative second vote the market department has the option to start a so-called escalation procedure at which the next level of decision-makers of the market and back-office departments decide on the credit application. However, according to the CEO, his savings bank 1 has never used this official proceeding because the bank employees agree upon critical credit decisions in advance (SK1OIP01.10.12). The credit officers prepare the credit application and second vote. It is important to note that less than 1% of all borrower units of savings bank 1 exceed the risk-relevant threshold (SK1D). This number is higher in SME lending but still remains below 50% of all borrower units because SME credits tend to be collateralised by real estate. Independent of the second vote the back office (i.e. the credit officers) influences credit granting by three jobs:

- The annual financial statement analysis and, in cases with poor rating scores, the verbal discussion of the statements; as discussed in Section 4.1.2.1, both of these involve limited discretion in the interpretation of financial figures.
- The approval of the rating execution. Here credit officers review and cross-check the qualitative rating module for plausibility. This restricts discretion in the interpretation of qualitative facts for the customer advisors. For example, the quality of management's planning can hardly be assessed as very good if the firm never meets its plan figures.
- The compilation of the credit application and the reviewing of calculations. This influence of credit officers not only relates to the detection of obvious errors in the calculation (see Box 4.9), but also to discretion in the interpretation of numbers, as explained for the cash flow calculation (Section 4.1.2.2). As sufficient cash flow to serve debts represents the single most important precondition for a positive credit decision, the credit officers' job of reviewing the calculation of a client's future ability to serve debts grants them a decisive influence on lending.

While the back office at savings bank 1 is not in a position to reject non risk-relevant credit applications, the three indirect means of influence listed above indicate a power to influence credit decisions. Credit officers can represent a credit application which is not completely safe so that it appears very risky. In this case the market department still possesses the right to grant the credit but the customer advisors must take responsibility for lending as the customer file documents the doubts of the back office. Therefore, customer advisors tend to discuss risky credit decisions in advance with the back-office department and the vast majority of credit decisions are conducted in consensus, also for non-risk credit business.

The credit-granting authority of big bank 1's back-office department depends on the rating score of the customers (see 4.2.2.2). Credits of €1 million and above are risk-relevant and credit officers always vote on them. Credits below €1 million with a critical rating score are also voted on by the credit officers. As discussed in Section 4.2.2.1, less than 50% of all SMEs at big bank 1 need a second vote. According to Mr Holz, the second vote is positive in ca. 66% of all cases; in 33% of cases the back-office demands additional requirements (e.g. additional collaterals) or rejects the credit applications (GB1MFIP05.11.12). Officially, the back-office vote represents the final decision in the medium SME size class as no escalation procedure is intended. Big bank 1 perceives an extensive credit-granting procedure as too costly for these – from the big bank's point of view – small credit engagements (GB1MIT25.06.13I). Nevertheless, Mr Holz and Mr Maske indicated that supervisors are able to arrange a new assessment of a credit application in exceptional cases (GB1MIT13.02.14, GB1MIT11.02.14). Furthermore,

Mr Maske highlighted the compromise-oriented nature of cooperation with the credit officers and pointed out that total rejections of credit applications are rare (GB1MIT11.02.14; see interview excerpts, p. 203). Notwithstanding this assurance of sound cooperation with the credit officers, it is revealing to compare the outlined findings with the organisation of big bank 1's back office for SMEs of the large size class outlined in the following section.

4.2.3.3 Generalisation and systematisation: back offices

Big bank 1 has designed the back offices of the large SME segment so as to support accumulation of customer and sector knowledge by the back officers and to reduce functional distance to clients and customer advisors. Credits of more than €5 million, as well as complex credits below this threshold, are reviewed by one of the ca. 10 sectorial specialised back-office departments at the national scale (GB1MFIP05.11.12). Each large SME client has a designated credit officer. The credit officers visit the customers together with the customer advisors and the other specialists of the bank (GB1MIT11.02.14, GB1MIT25.06.13I, GB1MIT25.09.13II). Accordingly, the credit officers and the other specialists are normally personally known to the customer advisors and customers:

Holz: Most of them, yes. We normally know the back office because we like taking them along to meet customers.

F.F.:   Because that is discussed beforehand.

Holz: Because they discuss current sector issues with us. Also, I usually know the colleagues from the specialist departments, and so do some of the other colleagues. The collateral department has met quite a few clients, there is frequent contact, yes, we usually introduce them so they know the working level.

(GB1MIT25.09.13II)

Face-to-face meetings help to foster personal connections, which support smooth cooperation. As Mr Holz pointed out, personal conections to the back officers increase the speed of credit decisions: "Depending on how well you know the colleagues from the back office, credit decisions can be done quickly in 2 to 3 weeks, or it can sometimes take weeks and months" (GB1MIT25.06.13I). Hence, the customer advisors try to meet credit officers regularly and discuss important decisions face-to-face:

F.F.:   I meant whether you know the colleagues, not the customers?

Holz: Yes, sure. We also try on a regular basis to meet with the back office. We have been to Frankfurt or Munich to discuss things there, because it's easier face-to-face than when we do it over the telephone. When we have important things to discuss, we regularly go there.

(GB1MIT25.09.13II)

Mr Holz and Mr Maske highlighted the advantage of the sectorial specialisation of the back office departments and further indicated the advantages of having assigned credit officers:

> About the topics that only concern soft facts, the back office can say little or nothing at all. That's why we often take colleagues along to meet clients. Because, say, I claim the CEO – as we also evaluate the quality of the management – is great, but I only know this one and no others in the sector, and then the back-office colleague comes and says, I know 10 others in the sector and he is a loser compared to them, that is of course information I can't have. I have a personal impression of him, we get along well, the figures appear to be quite good, business seems to be going well . . . these are [additional information from the back office] where we say, okay, I'll keep a close eye on that firm.
>
> (GB1MIT25.09.13II)

> For loans with foreign structures, I have a permanently assigned credit officer. They specialise in a sector, that means the colleague is perfectly familiar with the sectors. So I don't have to write anything about the sector, he knows better anyway. [. . .] And I'm always assigned the same person and can get used to working with him. Because there are colleagues who want a five-page [credit application] and there is one who prefers just half a page. That's the way it is.
>
> (GB1MIT11.02.14)

As the interviews demonstrate, big bank 1's design of the back office for large-size SMEs combines sectorial specialisation and short functional distance. Both interviewed customer advisors highlighted the advantages of this design in comparison to the random and impersonal interaction in the medium SME size class. Mr Maske acknowledged the informational advantages of the sector specialisation and highlighted the benefit of knowing the credit officers personally, as this helps him to adjust the credit applications to officers' preferences. Mr Holz stated that he actively builds personal relationships to his credit officers in order to achieve smooth cooperation and fast credit decisions for his clients. For him the combination of sector specialisation and soft information on firms comprises the informational advantage credit officers bring to the credit decision, supplementing his evaluation of clients.

Regardless of these advantages, big bank 1 considers the back-office organisation used for its large SME customers as too costly and inappropriate for medium-sized SMEs (GB1MIT25.09.13II). Considering the fact that the back-office departments are centralized at the national scale, back officers need to travel considerable distances to meet with firms, though travel costs are minimised by locating the back offices in the appropriate industrial cluster; e.g. the maritime economy back office is located in Hamburg (GB1MIT25.09.13II). This explains the slim and impersonal back-office organisation that is in place for medium-sized SMEs, as discussed in the previous section. It follows that big bank 1's long functional distance to the back officers for medium-sized SMEs is not only intended to control risk in line with MaRisk, but also aims to reduce costs, otherwise the bank would have implemented long functional distance in its large SME segment, too.

Turning to savings bank 1, in comparison with savings banks 3 and 4, the bank studied in-depth applies a lower division of back-office labour (SK4MIT25.09.13, SK3MIT18.08.13). For example, savings bank 3 has a credit administration team comparable to the market administration team of big bank 1. The financial statement analysis team of savings bank 3 also checks the rating execution and a separate credit officer team conducts the risk analysis and second vote (SK3MIT18.08.13). This higher specialisation is notable considering the fact that savings bank 3 is smaller than savings bank 1 in terms of lending. The interview partner of the Sparkassen Rating and Risikosysteme GmbH confirmed that savings banks apply varying organisational designs for the rating execution in the back office (OSGVIT30.05.13). Overall, all savings banks' customer advisors interviewed reported smooth cooperation and easy communication with the back offices (SK3MIT24.09.13, SK3MIT18.08.13, SK4MIT25.09.13, SK4MIT25.10.13), as savings banks are "houses with short ways" (SK3MIT24.09.13) and back-office colleagues are always known personally.

Figure 4.14 systematises the key findings from the comparison of the back offices; differences are highlighted indicating striking differences in the organization of back offices at savings bank 1 and big bank 1 for SMEs of the medium size class. Functional distance to the customer advisors is short and division of labour is low at savings bank 1. The credit officer team conducts all back-office jobs except the financial disclosure and cooperates pairwise with the customer advisors. In contrast, functional distance is long and division of labour is high at big bank 1. The market administration team conducts administrative tasks for assigned customers; no pairwise cooperation with the customer advisors is applied. At the national scale, the back-office department conducts the second vote and processes the numerous credit applications of big bank 1 randomly. This difference in the division of labour leads to an accumulation of customer knowledge by the credit officers of savings bank 1, whereas credit officers of big bank 1 cannot accumulate knowledge from prior assessments.

Participant observation in savings bank 1 revealed the close social embeddedness of cooperation between customer advisors and credit officers, caused by the organizational embeddedness, i.e. pairwise cooperation, daily job-related interactions and mutual dependency. As geographical distance between the back office and the customer advisor team in the major branch studied precludes ad hoc face-to-face interaction, personal meetings are rare. Thus the role of face-to-face interactions for reinforcing socially embedded cooperation between the customer advisors and credit offices pairs tends to be subordinated to organisational embeddedness. In contrast to savings bank 1, the back-office design of big bank 1 restricts socially embedded cooperation, and face-to-face interaction between customer advisors and credit officers does not take place. In fact, big bank 1

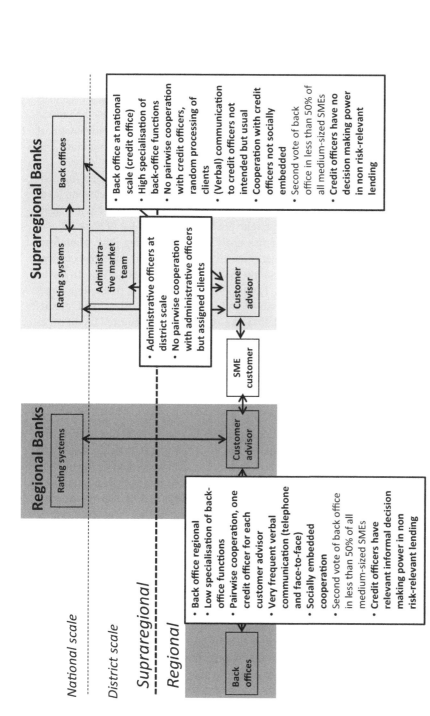

Figure 4.14 Comparing the back offices of savings bank 1 and big bank 1

Source: author's figure

does not intend there to be intensive communication between the two, in order to preserve detached risk analysis; nevertheless, some communication is usual, but remains socially unembedded. Therefore, customer advisors must face profoundly more difficulties in transmitting soft information to the credit officers at big bank 1 than at savings bank 1. Revealingly in this regard, big bank 1 organises its back offices for large SMEs in a way that supports socially embedded cooperation and the accumulation of knowledge, further indicating the disadvantage of the impersonal cooperation in the medium-sized SME segment of big bank 1 in terms of considering soft information.

Turning to decision-making power, formally the back-office department of savings bank 1 influences credit decisions only in cases of risk-relevant lending; hence, less than 50% of all borrower units need a second vote. Nonetheless, participant observation illustrated the relevant informal influence of back officers on credit decisions because of their risk analysis and reviewing jobs. Therefore, the market and back-office departments usually conduct credit decisions consensually. Less than 50% of all SME credit decisions need a second vote from the back-office department at big bank 1, too. These decisions are, on the one hand, the risk-relevant credits of more than €1 million and, on the other hand, credits with medium rating scores (PD ≥ 2.1%). If a second vote is required credit officers execute high decision-making power because an escalation procedure is not envisaged; otherwise, the back office has no decision-making power as it does not get involved.

4.2.4 Supervisors

Table 4.5 displays the hierarchical levels of savings bank 1 and big bank 1. The joint board of the savings bank's managing directors gains its decision-making power from the administrative councils that are, in turn, appointed by the municipal councils and the employees of the savings bank. At big bank 1, a joint-stock company under German law, shareholders elect the board of supervisors that appoints the managing directors. The joint board of managing directors (level 1) executes the power to change the organisation of credit granting and delegates credit decision-making authority to the different hierarchical levels. At level 2 the individual managing director executes less decision-making power than the joint board. Banks maintain the segregation of market and back-office functions from this level, as MaRisk regulates; hence, two directors execute power in lending, the market director (first vote) and the back-office director (second vote). Both directors delegate decision-making power to the lower levels. The market and back-office department heads decide in savings bank 1 at level 3. Big bank 1 applies a subdivision of power at this level, in line with its larger size. At level 4 team leaders execute higher decision-making authority than the customer advisor/credit officers (level 5). Before the allocation of competences between the hierarchical levels is compared (Section 4.2.4.2), Section 4.2.4.1 analyses organisation and communication between the hierarchies and shows the much longer functional distance to high-level supervisors in big bank 1 than in savings bank 1. Having

Table 4.5 Hierarchical levels of savings bank 1 and big bank 1

Responsible authority/Owner		Savings bank 1	Big bank 1
		Local authority	Shareholders
High-level supervisor	**Level 0**	Administrative council (loan committee)	Supervisory board
	Level 1	Joint board of managing directors (*Vorstand*)	Joint board of managing directors (*Vorstand*)
	Level 2	Managing director (market; back office)	Managing director (market; back office)
	Level 3	Department head (Mr Braun, Mr Baum)	Division head Market area head, department head
Team leader	**Level 4**	Team leader (Mrs Weber, Mr Mirow)	Team leader (Mr Holz)
Customer advisor	**Level 5**	Customer advisors (Mrs Hennecke, Mrs Friese, Mrs Kurz)	Customer advisors (Mr Maske)

Source author's table, sources: GB1D3, SK1D

said this, supervisors do not get involved in regular credit decisions concerning SMEs of the medium size class in the big bank, whereas comparatively small credit applications need supervisor approval in the savings bank. Section 4.2.4.3 generalises and concludes.

4.2.4.1 The communication with and functional distance to the supervisors

THE SUPERVISORS OF SAVINGS BANK 1

Supervisors at levels 1 through 3 are all located at the headquarters of savings bank 1. The managing directors occupy a separate and prestigiously furnished floor (SK1OIP01.10.12). The market director is also the CEO of the savings bank. At level 3, Mr Braun is the department head of the corporate customers department. Of all supervisors observed, only Mrs Weber is located outside the headquarters in her working group at the major branch of savings bank 1. All corporate customer back office functions are located at the headquarters of savings bank 1 where the department head Mr Baum has his office on the same floor as the SME credit officer team, headed by Mr Mirow.

Functional distance to the team leaders (level 4) is very short, in (micro-)geographical terms, at all observed teams of savings bank 1 (SK1MFPP05.11.13, SK1MFPP07.11.13, SK1MFPP14.11.13, SK1MPP19.11.13, SK1BSPP17.12.13). Mrs Weber's and Mr Mirow's offices are just next door to their teams' offices (see also Figure 4.6, p. 172). Nevertheless, the communication style between the observed customer advisor team and the back-office team differs. Communication between Mrs Weber and her team is very collegial using the informal *du*. The customer advisors easily address Mrs Weber for all questions (open door), and she also participates in private chats, e.g. during the morning coffee break (SK1MPP20.11.13). Mr Mirow communicates in a formal way with his team, he uses the polite form and closes his office door often. Personal differences between the two team leaders tend to explain the varying communication styles. Mr Mirow acts as an 'old style boss' and is in fact also older than Mrs Weber. Overall, the functional distance between Mrs Weber and her team is very short, because of the very high organisational (one team) and social embeddedness, as well as the very short (micro-)geographical distance.

Due to the remote location of the customer advisor team studied, functional distance to the market department head (Mr Braun), in geographical terms, prevents ad hoc face-to-face interaction, which savings bank 1 actually sees as a disadvantage. The market department has introduced a specific procedure to be well informed about the distant team. The customer advisors must first send all work instructions for their credit officers to Mr Braun's office (SK1MPP11.12.13), wherefore Mr Braun is informed about all new credit applications, including the applications that he does not need to approve. The SME customer advisor team located in savings bank's headquarters does not have to follow this procedure, indicating that geographical distance is perceived to hinder the flow of information in the savings bank.

The communication frequency of the customer advisors to level 3 and 2 supervisors is much lower than team leader communication. Six interactions of the customer advisor team with Mr Braun were observed during the one-month observation. Especially Mrs Weber very frequently contacted Mr Braun because she was dealing with a large client at acute risk of default (see 4.3.1.2). In the observed communications Mr Braun was not always instantly accessible because he was out of the office or engaged with other telephone calls. The customer advisors and Mr Braun know each other personally and communicate in the polite form but familiarly. Only Mrs Weber and Mr Braun address each other with *du*.

Four interactions of the customer advisors with the CEO were witnessed. These interactions included one telephone call between the CEO and Mrs Weber, where the critical client was discussed (SK1MPP19.11.13); the face-to-face watch list meeting (see Box 4.9, p. 200); and a joint meeting of the CEO and Mrs Hennecke at a customer's factory site to inspect a new production line. Here the CEO also called in advance to prepare the visit (SK1MPP25.11.13). CEO calls are not unusual for the customer advisor team, but the joint customer meeting of Mrs Hennecke and the CEO was in fact an event the team chatted about. The style of communication with the CEO is formal and friendly.

Three interrelated reasons for communication with level 3 and 2 supervisors were observed. Firstly, communication with the supervisors relates to the monitoring and treatment of borrowers at acute risk of default (see Box 4.9, p. 200). Secondly, supervisors are contacted to agree in advance on credit applications that need supervisor approval. And thirdly, communication accrues in the preparation of and at joint client meetings with the supervisors. We now discuss the communication for the latter two reasons.

According to the observation, customer advisors have three reasons – to avoid irritation of supervisors, to ensure reliability of credit assurances and to avoid wasting effort on unsuccessful credit applications – to agree credit applications with the supervisors in advance (see Box 4.10), although only one in-advance agreement with the supervisor was actually observed. Advance negotiations are rare in the savings bank because the experienced customer advisors know ex ante which credits will be approved, and which requests have no chance at all. Therefore, in practice the observed customer advisors conduct an initial screening of new credit requests on the basis of the documents and intuition or 'gut feeling'. This practice is rational in everyday business to avoid unnecessary effort but comprises a potential source of discrimination for certain credit requests, e.g. unusual business ideas, suspicious persons.

The one in-advance agreement observed related to an unusually low equity contribution for a property development project (see Box 4.8, p. 198). Mrs Hennecke had already negotiated the terms with the credit officers but was not pleased with the result. Therefore, she called her department head Mr Braun to inquire if he would support the unusual credit terms (SK1MPP10.12.13). As Mr Braun was out of the office, his assistant promised he would call back, as occurred the next day. Mrs Hennecke explained the offer she wanted to present and informed Mr Braun about the disagreement of the back office. Mr Braun proposed a compromise between the position of Mrs Hennecke and the back office.

Box 4.10   Reasons for in-advance agreements of critical credit applications

Finding agreements on credit decisions in advance of the actual credit application preparation is rewarding for the customer advisors for three reasons. Firstly, customer advisors avoid irritating the supervisors with the presentation of inadequate credit applications. The former credit officer of savings bank 1 expressed this reason:

F.F.:   And he then has an interest not to do this, because he saves work if it has no chance at all.

Answer: Precisely, well that is how it works, if he exactly knows that this credit volume lies in the competence of the team leader, department head or CEO, then he must be very sure that the case will not cause problems, because of course he has little interest in talks like how can you present me this case at all and the case will be rejected etc. Normally we should survey some days, but my assessment is that the cases that are presented will be approved

> by the supervisors in almost all cases. Because these are cases that just fit to the risk profile of the bank, this is everything that is just possible. I mean who wants to present a credit application to the CEO that will be rejected.
>
> (SK1MFIT02.09.13)
>
> Secondly, customer advisors promise loans to their clients in advance of the official credit decisions, so they must make sure that they are able to keep their promises, as their reliability depends on their assurances. Thirdly, compiling credit applications is costly and time-consuming, so bank employees make sure not to waste effort. In fact, customer advisors appoint credits verbally with customers before they process the credit applications. Accordingly, they assess clients that do not take approved loans or want major changes after approval as unreliable and (try to) charge processing fees for the revision work (SK1MPP02.12.13, SK1MPP09.12.13).

Joint customer meetings of the customer advisors and supervisors are a further occasion for communication and cooperation. Observations indicate that the savings bank schedules joint meetings for three reasons. Firstly, banks compliment the clients with CEO visits, which indeed certain clients expect (Geno2MIT23.02.14II). Mrs Hennecke and the CEO's visit to the firm with the new production line exemplifies this. The firm had sound financial records, had a relatively small loan at savings bank 1 and did not request a new credit; thus, the CEO only visited the firm as a tribute. Secondly, joint meetings are used to support the negotiating position of the customer advisors, i.e. support a negotiation on equal footing with the managing owners of SMEs (SK1BSPP19.12.13). The CEOs of savings banks tend to be regionally well known (GB1MIT25.09.13II) and their standing better equips them to negotiate with firms' top management. Thirdly, managing directors also visit distressed firms to form their own impression so that they need not only rely on the credit application for their approval decision.

Overall, the outlined interactions with the high-level supervisors indicate socially embedded cooperation, i.e. customer advisors of the SME size class and supervisors personally know one another, and solution-oriented interactions. Nevertheless, in contrast to the credit officer and team leader cooperation, supervisor interaction remains less frequent. High-level supervisors, especially the managing directors, are not involved in the everyday business of serving the clients but only become active for the reasons outlined above, which suggests a lower organisational embeddedness of customer advisors with high-level supervisors than with the credit officers and team leaders.

THE SUPERVISORS OF BIG BANK 1

As shown in the previous sections, customer advisors, the rating system and credit officers together have credit-granting authority of up to €5 million, and an escalation procedure is not intended officially. Accordingly, the supervisors only get involved in the unofficial escalation procedure. Here the team leaders (level 4 supervisors) are the first contact partners (GB1MIT25.09.13II). Like at savings bank 1, the team leader's office is located just next door to the offices of his customer advisors (Figure 4.6, p. 172). Communication between Mr Holz and his team is usual and often conducted in joint customer visits, as it is the job of the team leader to mediate between clients and customer advisors in case of conflicts:

F.F.:   How is it, a customer advisor has a customer at his desk and there are problems and then you can say I know there are problems in this sector, watch out, or is this seldom?

Holz: Well, that is rather seldom. It is more like this if you have, well I'm brought in by colleagues if they notice that there is some trouble internally. I know I would guess also even if I do not service the customer myself I know about 40% of all clients of my colleagues. Because it is important to sniff around, to know the customers, because if whatever sort of problems arise, then I am the primary person in charge of solving the problems. Because quite often it is like this, if it does not work between customer advisor and customer because there are critical topics, then I am the referee in a sense. Then it is of course better if I know the customer, rather than going to the customer the first time when the problems are there. This means I know all large customers, because I frequently join the colleagues, and also independent of my own customers I am certainly twice a week on tour with one of my colleagues.

(GB1MIT25.06.13I)

Level 3 supervisors are either located at the district (market area heads) or national scale at big bank 1. Direct communication of the customer advisors to these supervisors is unusual. Mr Holz, in contrast, maintains personal connections to other supervisors. The interviews indicated that he mainly needs these personal contacts for lending to large SMEs (GB1MIT25.06.13I, GB1MIT25.09.13II). Overall, the interviewed customer advisor and team leader of big bank 1 indicated that communication between customer advisors and high-level supervisors was rare for medium-sized SMEs, as high-level supervisors are not involved in credit decisions except for the unofficial escalation procedures.

4.2.4.2 The integration of the supervisors in the credit-granting process

As big bank 1 does not integrate supervisors in credit decisions to firms of the medium SME size class, this section reports on the integration of supervisors in the process of credit granting at savings bank 1 only. Here the supervisors' decision-making authority depends on the overall credit volume, the blank credit volume and the rating score of the firms (Table 4.6). The larger and riskier a borrower unit becomes, the more supervisors at higher level get involved in the lending decision. Nevertheless, the customer advisors always conduct the first

Table 4.6 The allocation of credit-granting authority of savings bank 1

Back office	Total credit volume	Blank credit volume	Market						
			Credit decision		Total credit volume	Blank credit volume and sound rating score	Blank credit volume and medium rating score	Blank credit volume and poor rating score	
			Second vote	First vote					
Level 1	–	Escalation procedure	Yes/no	Yes/no	More €2 million	More €1.5 million	More €1.5 million	More €1.5 million	Level 1
Level 2	Escalation procedure	From €1.2 million	Yes/no	Yes/no					Level 2
Level 3	From €250,000	Only in case of absence	Yes/no	Yes/no	€1.4 million	€900,000	€900,000	€900,000	Level 3
Level 4	Only in case of absence	No official competence	Yes/no	Yes/no	€900,000	€500,000	€300,000	€200,000	Level 4
Credit officer	No official competence	No official competence	Check	Yes/no	€400,000	€200,000	€50,000	€25,000	Customer advisor

(Numbers and limits marginally altered)

Source: author's composition deduced from SK1D

decision as they have the right to refuse credit requests in the first place. The bank does not further process such credit requests; consequently, supervisors do not receive information about them. One instance was observed where the request of a new customer was rejected by Mrs Weber after a detailed examination of the documents (SK1MPP04.12.13), indicating initial refusals to be rare. More often credit requests are turned down because no agreement on the terms was gained (SK1MPP28.11.13, SK1MPP03.12.13).

Table 4.6 summarises the allocation of credit-granting authority at savings bank 1. As discussed in the previous section, the back office only gets officially involved in credit decisions in case of risk-relevant lending. Here the back-office department head (Mr Baum) conducts the second vote. The managing director of the back office is involved with the escalation procedure, which savings bank 1 has so far never applied. In the market department the credit-granting competence of the customer advisors and team leaders (level 4) depends on the blank credit share and the rating score. In contrast to this, the credit-granting authority of high-level supervisors no longer depends on the rating score. Total credits of above €2 million have to be approved by the joint board of managing directors; ca. 100 borrower units of savings bank 1 exceed this limit.

Table 4.7 gives examples of the formal credit approval process at savings bank 1. In example 1, a firm wants to increase its current account credit. With the extended credit line, the total credits volume is €200,000 with a blank credit share of €50,000. Due to the firm's sound rating score the customer advisor grants this credit on her own authority. She has to order a credit application from her credit officer, who will write the credit application and review the calculation of the customer's ability to cover interest and principal payments. The credit application then needs to be signed by the customer advisor, and the credit officer will store the credit application in the basic file and prepare the new credit contract. After the contract is signed and, if applicable, additional documents have been sent to the credit officer (e.g. extended land charge entry), the credit officer will extend the current account credit in OSPlus. A very similar credit application with a poor rating score needs to be approved by the team leader at savings bank 1 (example 2 in Table 4.7), as the customer advisor lacks the authority to grant credit above €25,000 to firms with poor rating scores. Therefore, the team leader even needs to approve a small extension of a current account credit.

Example 3 of Table 4.7 illustrates a typical mortgage loan used by a property developer to purchase and renovate an apartment building. In this example the credit request also includes a current account credit of €100,000 as working capital and reserve for unexpected expenses. Here the credit needs to be approved by the customer advisor, reviewed by the credit officers and then approved by the team leader and finally the market department head. This is because the total credit volume exceeds credit-granting authority of the team leader. The back office does not vote because with €200,000 of blank credit volume the borrowing unit remains below the risk-relevant lending threshold. Example 4 of Table 4.7 illustrates a similar credit application, only the (calculated) collateral value of the property remains lower, leading to a higher blank credit volume of €300,000 that

Table 4.7 Examples of the formal credit approval process of savings bank 1

	Example 1		Example 2		Example 3		Example 4		Example 5	
	Back office	Market	Back office	Market	Back office	Market	Back office	Market	Back office	Market
Level 1		Accepted								Accepted / CEO (yes)
Level 2				Accepted		Accepted		Accepted	Department head (yes)	Department head (yes)
Level 3					Department head (yes)	Department head (yes)	Department head (yes)	Department head (yes)		Team leader (yes)
Level 4				Team leader (yes)	Credit officer (review)	Team leader (yes)	Credit officer (review)	Team leader (yes)	Credit officer (review)	Team leader (yes)
Credit officer /customer advisor	Credit officer (review)	Customer advisor (yes)	Credit officer (review)	Customer advisor (yes)	Credit officer (review)	Customer advisor (yes)	Credit officer (review)	Customer advisor (yes)	Credit officer (review)	Customer advisor (yes)
Customer	€20,000 extension of current account line (total credits €200,000; blank credits €50,000; sound rating score)		€10,000 extension of current account line (total credits €100,000; blank credits €50,000; poor rating score)		€1 million mortgage + €100,000 current account line (total credits €1.1 million; blank credits €200,000; sound rating score)		€1 million mortgage + €100,000 current account line (total credits €1.1 million; blank credits €300,000; sound rating score)		€1 million for new production line (total credits €1.5 million; blank credits €1.3 million; poor rating score)	

Source: author's composition

requires the back office's agreement (second vote) in addition to the approvals of the market department.

Example 5 of Table 4.7 illustrates a very risky credit application. The firm has a poor rating score and wants to invest in a new production line. With a blank credit share of €1.3 million, savings bank 1's losses would be profound in case of default. As the rating score has no impact on the credit decision-making authority of level 3 and 2 supervisors, the market managing director executes the power to approve the loan if the back office and the market department accept. This example clarifies that savings bank 1 has allocated credit-granting authority so as to prevent poor rating scores hindering lending. However, in cases of poor rating scores bank employees must justify credit decisions extensively and high-level supervisors have to approve the applications. Overall, high-level supervisors' power to influence credit decisions increases with the riskiness of the credit application in terms of total and blank credit volume as well as rating score, as they only have to approve riskier credits.

Alongside the credit-granting authority of the supervisors themselves, the question of the extent to which supervisors use their authority to influence credit decisions was addressed. During the course of participant observation, no exercise of influence by high-level supervisors was noted. In this respect, it is revealing how the SME customer advisor team reacted to the question about the influence of high-level supervisors:

> My question on the influence of high-level supervisors is directly related to cases where the CEO or head of department wants to grant credits and said a solution has to be found for this firm. In general, everything can be discussed with the supervisors, but it sometimes happens that they have an opinion. The customer advisors find out quickly if supervisors have an opinion, then they can no longer convince the supervisors. The only exception is the auditing, especially the external auditing by the regional savings banks association. External auditing is apparently used as an argument to influence supervisors' decisions.
>
> (SK1MPP16.12.13)

The fact that customer advisors referenced the question to cases where they are reluctant to lend but supervisors push for lending indicates the rarity of rejections by high-level supervisors. Two reasons tend to explain the more conservative credit-granting preferences of customer advisors compared to their supervisors. Firstly, as explained later, savings bank 1 has no incentive system at the individual level in the corporate customer department; thus, customer advisors receive no individual reward for lending. Secondly, high-level supervisors, especially the CEO, maintain contacts to regional politicians and the stakeholders of the regional economy. Savings bank 1 in general and the managing directors in particular therefore consider the effects of credit decisions for the regional economy in line with the public mandate.

During participant observation no case of political influence was directly observed but the customer advisors reported on two cases from the large SME team. Here regional politicians directly approached the CEO about lending to an existing firm and a start-up company, respectively. In both cases the CEO ordered an evaluation of the credit request from the large SME team which eventually led to rejections (SK1MPP16.12.13). This report from the customer advisors supports the assumption about the existence of political influence on the lending decisions of German savings banks (Gropp and Saadi 2015). Simultaneously, the report indicates that politicians do not cancel the formal process of credit decision making, i.e. dictate the lending decisions to savings bank 1, but are rather only able to enforce a detailed evaluation of credit requests.

4.2.4.3 Generalisation and systematisation: supervisors

In-advance agreements of critical credit requests with supervisors tend to be a widespread practice in the SME credit business, as all the other interviewed savings banks report similar practices to savings bank 1 (SK3MIT24.09.13, SK3MIT18.08.13, SK4MIT25.09.13, SK4MIT25.10.13, SK2MIP13.03.13). The following extract of the interview with the SME customer advisor of savings bank 4 exemplifies this but also indicates that not all her colleagues discuss credits in advance:

F.F.:   I have two final questions: how often do credits you want to grant get declined? Thus firstly because you have to re-negotiate them or you are not allowed to grant them at all.

Answer: Less often for both cases. I work like this, however this is not exemplary for the whole team: I look in advance who is the authorised decision maker. And if I see that is not only me from the market department, then I discuss the credit application with the market supervisor in charge in advance, before I present the final offer to the customer.

(SK4MIT25.10.13)

Concerning functional distance to the high-level supervisors, the market managing director of the small cooperative bank illustrated the big differences between small regional banks and big banks. He is aware of the differences because he has worked for a large bank before. The interview excerpt also indicates what proximity (short functional distance) is about from the director's point of view: knowing the customer advisors and the (important) clients by heart:

F.F.:   How would you describe proximity between the customer advisors and the managing directors? So what is proximity about for you?

Answer: Well quite simple, firstly you are on one floor, the managing directors of DZ-Bank sit on the 6th Floor of 51 in Frankfurt, yet he has several branches in Germany. I myself was in [other big German city], I never saw the directors. I think once one director was in [other big

German city], that was an event, there the yard was swept. This shows the significance or rarity of this event, this was really . . . there the king was coming and resided in [other big German city], there everything was done and there everybody clicked their heels, even the head of the branch. Like I said, I am the whole day in the regional bank, I talk with the people very often and e.g. our customer advisor for farming who also has big cases, these cases are always approved by the joint board of managing directors [. . .]. There I am, well I know the big cases, there I only get additional information, basically I know the top 30 clients of the bank. There you can wake me up at night, I know them with all key aspects, this is certainly something that no managing director of a big bank can say. We're that close.

(Geno2MIT23.02.14II)

As the managing director stated, for him short functional distance is not only about personal contacts between customer advisors and supervisors but also about being frequently involved in the lending business, i.e. organisational embeddedness, which leads to an accumulation of knowledge about the clients (a statement in line with the finding on functional distance to the credit officers). It simultaneously indicates that functional distance to high-level supervisors tends to be higher in comparison to the credit officer distance at savings bank 1 because of supervisors' minor involvement in the everyday credit business to medium-sized SMEs.

To systematise, Figure 4.15 illustrates the key findings of the supervisor comparison; differences between the studied banks are highlighted. Figure 4.15 includes the team leaders as distinctive actors because functional distance to them strongly differs from the distance to the high-level supervisors in both banks compared. The geographical distance of the customer advisors to the team leaders (level 4 supervisors) is very short at savings bank 1 and big bank 1. Very close cooperation between the team leader and her customer advisors was observed at the savings bank, whereas, according to the interviews, at big bank 1 close cooperation often takes place at joint customer visits.

The geographical distance of the observed customer advisor team to high-level supervisors is on the regional scale at savings bank 1. Customer advisors are personally known to level 3 supervisors, and managing directors and interact frequently with them, though the interactions are not on a day-to-day basis, indicating longer functional distance in comparison to the credit officers. The other interviewed regional banks confirmed that personal and frequent interactions with high-level supervisors are usual for regional banks. In contrast to this, level 3 supervisors and managing directors are located at a very long geographical distance to the customer advisors at big bank 1; personal communication remains the exception. Especially, ordinary bank employees have almost no access to managing directors in the big banks.

At big bank 1 supervisors do not become formally involved in credit decisions to SMEs of the medium size class because customer advisors, rating systems and

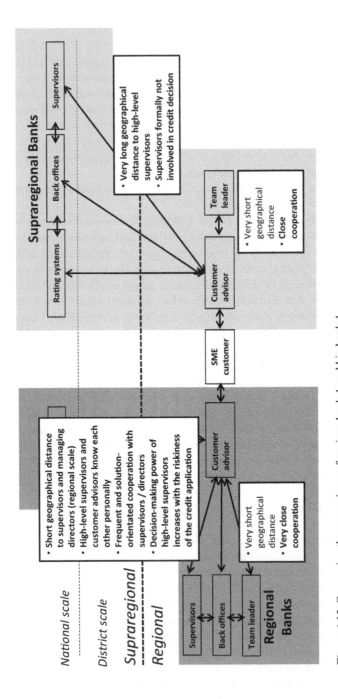

Figure 4.15 Comparing the supervisors of savings bank 1 and big bank 1

Source: author's figure

credit officers together possess credit-granting authority of up to €5 million, and an escalation procedure is not envisaged. In contrast to this, supervisors execute substantial decision-making power in savings bank 1, because high-level supervisors possess formal voting rights even for relatively small blank credit volumes, i.e. €200,000, if a firm's rating score is poor. Furthermore, the observation has indicated that supervisors potentially influence credit applications even if they have no formal voting right, as in exceptional cases they push lending in line with the public mandate of the savings bank. Considering the fact that no cutoff rating score exists at savings bank 1, formally the rating systems do not constrain the lending decisions of the high-level supervisors. In fact, poor rating scores do not even cut the credit-granting authority of high-level supervisors in terms of blank credit volume. However, as discussed in Section 4.2.2.2, credit approval to firms with poor rating scores needs a conclusive justification.

4.2.5 Indirect actors

This section introduces actors that indirectly influence the credit decisions of banks, i.e. actors who monitor the credit-granting processes, set guidelines and specify initiatives. Section 4.2.5.1 discusses banks' risk controlling and management responsible for the calculation of the lending limits and credit terms. Section 4.2.5.2 looks at banking auditing in charge of overseeing the rule conformity of the credit-granting process. Section 4.2.5.3 turns to the sales management and incentive system of banks, and Section 4.2.5.4 discusses the effects of the savings banks financial group on the credit-granting processes of savings banks. Bank regulation is not discussed in this section because the regulator's impact on the process organisation (e.g. MaRisk, see Box 4.7, p. 195) and the ability of banks to grant credits (e.g. SolvV, see Box 4.1, p. 159) have been discussed in the previous sections.

4.2.5.1 Banks' risk controlling and management

At savings bank 1, risk management and controlling is conducted by a special working group of the controlling department (SK1BSPP17.12.13). Here one or two employees monitor each of the three types of risk: default risk, market risk and operational risk. Mr Hauser calculates the default risk of savings bank 1's credit portfolio and explains the portfolio management (SK1BSPP08.01.14). The Finanz Informatik GmbH & Co. Kg provides credit portfolio data from which Mr Hauser calculates key bank portfolio indicators by using a commercial software tool (which is provided by the regional savings banks association). This is, on the one hand, the expected losses and, on the other hand, the unexpected losses of the credit portfolio. A factor to account for cyclic economic development and different values from the actual loan loss provisions are added to the calculated expected losses. Based on this calculation Mr Hauser and his team leader compile the quarterly risk report for the joint board of managing directors (SK1BSPP09.01.14).

Mr Hauser further uses the calculations to inform the credit risk strategy. As savings bank 1 has a high number of borrower units with large total credit volumes, the calculated unexpected losses are higher than savings banks' average. Therefore, the credit risk strategy states that these large credit engagements "shall not exceed" a certain percentage of the bank's overall credit volume (SK1D). In a similar way, the risk strategy sets a credit volume limit for the construction and commercial rental sector because of high exposure to the sector (SK1D). However, both limits were not nearly exceeded at the time of observation and the wording of the limit in the risk strategy is soft: "When increased risks are identified, suitable measures are to be introduced" (SK1D). Both pieces of evidence indicate that limits specified in the risk strategy have little influence on the everyday lending of the savings bank, especially in the segment of medium-sized SMEs.

Savings bank 1 determines the risk premiums, i.e. the interest rate intended to cover expected and unexpected losses, in a second calculation. The basic idea of the so-called risk adjusted pricing is that every credit should earn its total costs (Figure 4.16), i.e. the market interest rate and the operational cost of processing. Furthermore, the risk premium must be earned, which includes the expected losses and the cost of the equity capital (e.g. dividend payments) that banks must hold as provision for unexpected losses. Savings bank 1 calculates the risk premiums with another commercial tool running on Microsoft Access. Inputs of the calculation are expected and unexpected loss, interest structure curves and other information provided by the Finanz Informatik GmbH & Co. KG. Based on these calculations, savings bank 1 determines the risk premiums for different types of credits ad hoc and unfrequently; i.e. at the time of observation the risk premiums were based on two-year-old data (SK1BSPP09.01.14). The central services department specifies operational and overhead costs for the credit terms. The calculated credit terms are proposed to the joint board of managing directors and are decided upon in the

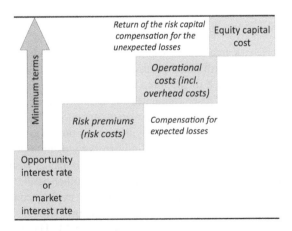

Figure 4.16 Risk adjusted pricing of credits

Source: altered from OLD17.06.13

terms committee. According to Mr Hauser, the terms committee does not 'blindly' decide the calculated terms but also respects terms' enforceability at the regional banking market and profit expectations (SK1BSPP09.01.14). Therefore, the calculated terms inform the appointment of the actual terms, but do not determine the credit terms of savings bank 1.

At big bank 1 the risk management and controlling departments influence credit terms and set limits. Mr Holz explained their impact and pointed out that limits from portfolio management hardly influence the medium and large SMEs segments:

F.F.:   Which departments are indirectly involved in the credit business; can you add more? I have thought about things like bank risk controlling, controlling, sales management etc.

Holz: If you see it like this, we have a controlling included that says okay we need to calculate every credit from the margin. In [big German city] there is of course a controlling instance, they say okay if risk class A at collateral class D you must talk of the minimum margin of C. This is of course regulated in [big German city], so we have them indirectly included, so to say. Then we have of course another risk controlling in [big German city], that says if risks of a certain portfolio class are very high, we don't want to have them anymore. I would say five years ago a limit was set on the construction sector. There I had a customer with €100 million credits, there it may be that risk controlling say okay hello we want to go down from €100 to €80 million, then this is not a real back office topic but risk controlling from [big German city], that can occasionally happen, but it is the exception.

(GB1MIT25.09.13II)

As the interview expert clarifies, one department of big bank 1 is in charge of the calculation of credit terms and another department conducts portfolio management. In contrast, Mr Hauser executes both jobs in savings back 1 alone, though with the inputs of the Finanz Informatik GmbH & Co. KG and the regional savings bank association.

Big bank 1 conducts credit portfolio management according to the PD and LGD of borrower units (Figure 4.17). The bank wants to increase the credit portfolio of customers with sound rating scores and LGDs below €100 million (section A of Figure 4.17). The portfolio volume of customers with LGDs above €100 million is to be held constant and reduced for those with LGDs above €400 million (sections B and C of Figure 4.17). Lending to customers with less sound ratings depends on the sector outlook. Credit engagements in section E of Figure 4.17 shall be increased in sectors with positive outlooks and reduced in sectors with negative outlooks. Credits in section D of Figure 4.17 must be reduced. Credits in section F represent all credit below the rating score cutoff limit of 3.6% and have to be reduced under the supervision of the intensive care unit. Lending to new customers below this threshold must not take place (GB1MFIP05.11.12).

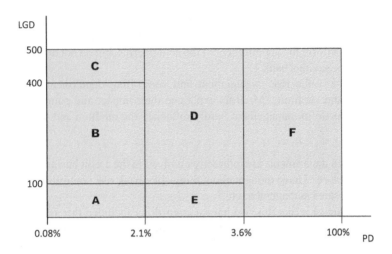

Figure 4.17 The credit portfolio segregation of big bank 1
Source: author's figure based on GB1MFIP05.11.12

Because of big bank 1's risk controlling and the general exclusion of certain credit businesses, the customer advisors cannot always satisfy the credit demands of their customers. Mr Holz explained:

F.F.:   For what reason have you not been able to fulfil customer demands that have clearly been directed to you? What are examples?

Holz: Partly things where the bank imposes restrictions, e.g. the financing of real estate for rental business. [. . .] And where we have general difficulties is the sector of renewable energy at the moment, simply because the prospects are not really clear. What is Merkel doing with this industry? Two years ago she simply turned off nuclear power stations but all the other things do not work well yet. These are topics where we say at the moment, the companies that are in this sector [. . .], there we have to fight from time to time, where we have also had to say to many customers, sorry this does not make sense at the moment.

(GB1MIT25.09.13II)

According to Mr Holz's statement, big bank 1 enforces sector discrimination which in fact impacts lending to medium- and large-sized SMEs of the industries concerned, i.e. rental business and renewable energy. The bank further restricts a range of other industries in cases of poor sector outlook, e.g. the steel sector and the construction sector at the time of the interviews (GB1MFIP05.11.12, GB1MIT25.09.13II). Furthermore, big bank 1 does not offer start-up finance because of the general riskiness of this business (GB1MIT25.09.13II). The bank also constrains certain other sectors, like the armaments sector, for reasons of corporate social responsibility and compliance (GB1MIT11.02.14). In total, and in contrast to Mr Holz's interview statement on page 226 the big bank's risk management in fact impacts lending to medium-size SMEs of the concerned industries as well as start-ups.

In the direct comparison of the risk management and controlling of savings bank 1 and big bank 1, the big bank enforces more and more restricted sector limits. Savings bank 1 does not enforce strict sector discrimination, i.e. does not prohibit lending to certain industries overall; start-up finance and financing real estate for rental are part of its everyday business. Due to its much smaller size, savings bank 1 enforces a lower credit volume limit. Nevertheless, the limit exceeds the credit volumes in the SME size class and the wording of the limit in savings bank 1's credit risk strategy is soft.

4.2.5.2 Banking auditing

Internal and external auditors review a random sample of banks' credit-granting and monitoring processes ex post (BaFin 2012a: AT 4.4.3) with the aim of securing rule conformity, i.e. to ensure that the employees respect the rules of the bank. Although auditors cannot directly influence credit decisions, actors are aware of the random audits and room for minor discretion in the interpretation of the rules exists (GB1MIT25.09.13II). Therefore, auditors' interpretations of the banking rules tend to indirectly influence credit decisions.

The internal auditing reports to the joint board of CEOs. As outlined in Section 4.2.2.2, internal auditing is intended to hinder customer advisors from manipulating the rating execution at big bank 1, as credit officers only review a limited range of rating executions (GB1MIT25.09.13II). In this regard, Mr Holz pointed out occasional divergent opinions between customer advisors and auditors as to whether the rules of the bank were applied:

> This is also a matter of opinion ultimately. The colleague stated in the rating that business has been constant, the number is just saved in the wrong place however. Then the colleague of the audit did not find the number and says you were not allowed to do this, well then you search together for the right number and then the matter is finished.
>
> (GB1MIT25.09.13II)

The external auditing also supervises the work of the managing directors, which becomes apparent at savings banks where the external auditors of the regional savings banks associations report to the associations. The CEOs of savings banks tend to be concerned about the standing of their savings bank in the association and consider the judgments of the external auditors (SK1BSPP19.12.13). In fact, savings bank 1' customer advisors stated that they use the external auditing as an argument to oppose politically motivated lending pressure of their high-level supervisors (SK1MPP16.12.13, see Section 4.2.4.2). This statement indicates the countervailing force of the external auditing to political influences on lending decisions.

4.2.5.3 Sales management and incentive systems

The sales management and incentive systems of banks are accused of provoking faulty financial advice to customers and causing high pressure on bank employees (Breisig et al. 2010, GB3MIO23.04.13II). Against this background, this section analyses the influence of the incentive systems on customer–customer advisor relationships. The banks studied use three kinds of targets to control their customer advisors in the medium-sized SME segment. Firstly, they specify volume targets, e.g. for new credit, net income or profit contribution (GB1MIT11.02.14, SK1MPP16.12.13). Secondly, banks control their customer advisors with specific product or product group targets, e.g. insurance or securities fee earnings, the number of new leasing contracts (GB3MIO23.04.13II, GB1MIT11.02.14). Thirdly, banks control the activities of their customer advisors; e.g. they specify how often the customers must be visited each year (SK4MIT25.10.13, GB1MIT11.02.14). Although three interview partners of the savings banks highlighted the profoundly higher sales pressure in private banks (SK4MIT25.10.13, SK1MFPP06.11.13, OSGITV01.03.13), the study of Breisig et al. (2010) points out that sales pressure is an issue for savings and cooperative banks, too.

Savings bank 1 does not apply an incentive system or award bonuses to its corporate customer advisors at the individual level, but only calculates target achievements for the department. Savings bank 1 controls for new credit business, revenue from commission fees (e.g. commissions from sales of products from partner firms of the savings banks financial group) and fees revenue (e.g. processing fees). Savings bank 1 executes no controlling of products or product types and activities in the corporate customer segment (SK1MPP16.12.13, SK1BSPP20.12.13). The bank adopts sales targets from its regional savings banks association; i.e. it takes the average sales of the other savings banks in its size class as targets. The corporate customer department met its new credit and fees revenue targets last year; the commission fees target was clearly missed (SK1BSPP20.12.13).

Participant observation demonstrates that the customer advisors of savings bank 1 try to meet sales targets despite the non-existence of individual-level incentives. In one case, Mrs Hennecke proposed a special term in a leasing offer, in order to earn commission fees, with respect to the bank's poor performance on the commission fees target (SK1MPP19.11.13). In this context, the customer advisors highlighted their limited influence on target achievement because sales depend on firms' demands. Nevertheless, they argue that they could gain extra business if they had sufficient time to serve potential customers quickly and helpfully, which is not always possible due to the high workload (SK1MPP09.12.13).

The implementation of sales management and incentive systems differs between the savings banks (OSGVIT16.04.13). Savings bank 3 defines profit contribution targets at the individual level and undertakes activity controlling on customer contacts (SK3MIT18.08.13). Savings bank 4 focuses on gross return and also defines activity targets for its SME customer advisors (SK4MIT25.10.13). In contrast to this, the incentive system of savings bank 1 specifies fewer targets (e.g. no activity targets) and does not control/reward individual performance. In fact, as the customer advisors of savings bank 1 also stated (SK1MPP03.12.13), savings bank 1's 'soft' specification of the sales management and incentive system tends to be the exception rather than the rule for savings banks. However, in interview the customer advisors of the other savings banks highlighted that the gratifications account for a small part of their income with little influence on their behaviour (SK3MIT24.09.13, SK4MIT25.10.13).

The sales management of big bank 1 controls for gross return of the SME customer advisors, which is the most important target (GB1MIT11.02.14). Sales management further controls for the sales of different product types (e.g. commodity securities), and activity targets are assigned (GB1MIT11.02.14, GB1MIT25.09.13II). The bank reports sales successes and targets in a reporting system, as Mr Maske explained:

> I have a reporting system I can look at and there is really revenue per cus-tomer, but also per customer advisor, I can retrieve this there. So I can really see by months how much revenue I have earned with the customers or how much money is paid to the bank. So the system is really good and then you can understand where the money came from.
>
> (GB1MIT11.02.14)

Big bank 1 centrally assigns identical sales targets for all SME teams. The team leader Mr Holz indicated that it is his job to mitigate between given targets and the regional conditions (GB1MIT13.02.14, GB1MFIP05.11.12):

F.F.: And the numbers are the side condition that of course. . .

Holz: The numbers are the side condition so it is of course like this, if our boss in [German big city] says the numbers in [your city] are crap anyway, I have to push the colleagues more for sales, then my mood is not the best, but I have to put up with this in a sense and occasionally I have to argue why it is like it is. Because our business is very cyclical, this is dif-ferent in private customer business. They are controlled on a very short-term basis; we are controlled long-term. If you have bosses who know the business they just let you do it for a while.

> (GB1MIT25.09.13II)

Corresponding to savings bank 1, big bank 1's customer advisors indicated their limited influence on actual sales because customer demand drives sales. Never-theless, the customer advisors are keen to stimulate certain demands, as Mr Holz and Mr Maske explained:

> Holz: Well, we are of course also assessed for which business we are doing, but this is solely by revenue and our customers are simply advised according to their demands ultimately, and they get the products that fit their demands. That you of course from time to time try to stimulate demands for certain

products where we think they are useful for clients, that is clear. But it is not as if I talk to my boss and he says okay you have not sold a credit this week now go for it, no we do not have this.

(GB1MIT25.06.13I)

F.F.:   When are you personally satisfied with your work?

Maske: If I go out of a meeting with the customer and it was a good discussion and I want to implement everything we have discussed. If this all works and maybe further along an add on is gained, that I can also do an additional hedging transaction, and if I can earn there also a couple of euros then I am satisfied and I go out with a smile on my face.

(GB1MIT11.02.14)

The interviews with big bank 1 indicate that, like for savings bank 1, sales follow the demands of the SMEs; thus, customer advisors have limited means to influence demands of clients. Accordingly, the bank has designed an incentive system that focuses on gross sales and only sets limited incentives for specific product types and activities. Mr Maske highlighted the responsibility customer advisors bear for gross sales and satisfied customers in the SME business. A detailed controlling of activities and products is not implemented in contrast to the private customer segment of big bank 1 (GB1MIT11.02.14).

Big bank 3 exemplifies a bank that has applied strong commission fees–oriented sales targets for medium-sized SMEs. This dissatisfied the former customer advisor interviewed: "I eventually said, if I had wanted to be an insurance agent, then I wouldn't have done a bank apprenticeship" (GB3MIO23.04.13II). He outlined in the interview how he dealt with sales pressure and how sales pressure can become a disadvantage for SMEs:

F.F.:   Did a dilemma ever arise because of sales pressure when advising customers?

Answer: Yes, okay there you have to, there everybody has to find a way for himself and also see what he can stand. Because I personally have always chosen only to sell what I can support. So I was above sales pressure. If the numbers in the insurance section were not sufficient then I did not care. There somebody can tell me 'you have to' but this I did not take as an argument to bamboozle the customers. However, there I had on the other hand the advantage that I was very strong in the credit business of my existing customer portfolio, therefore they could not blame me for missing targets in a way that would have had any consequences for me. Certainly there have also been some colleagues who have been pushed by sales pressure to sell certain products that did not really fit.

(GB3MIT29.05.13I)

As the former customer advisor of big bank 3 stated, pressing incentive systems have caused adverse advice for the medium-sized SME customers of his previous employer. Nonetheless, this interview partner (as well as the other customer advisors interviewed) pointed out that he had not advised his customers in an adverse way. Although contrary statements are not to be expected with the interview method, three factors indeed indicate the limited influence of sales management and incentive systems on the customer relationship. Firstly, the demand-driven SME business reduces opportunities to stimulate sales. Secondly, the financial literacy of SMEs tends to be higher than in the private clients segment. And thirdly, responding to these two facts, the studied regional banks and big bank 1 have set up the incentive systems to focus on gross sales instead of controlling for particular products; this restricts initiatives to sell inappropriate products. Nonetheless, the sales targets raise the incentive of customer advisors to stimulate certain demands of their customers and the non-existence of sales controlling on the individual level at savings bank 1 is something of an exception, also among savings banks.

4.2.5.4 Savings banks financial group and the Sparkassen Finanzkonzept

The different associations, firms and banks of the savings banks financial group influence the way savings banks conduct lending. This section outlines striking aspects of the savings banks financial group's influence on lending to SMEs by its member banks; i.e. it discusses products, information, guidelines and joint projects of the financial group.

Savings banks are able to offer their comprehensive choice of financial and insurance products only in cooperation with the firms and banks of their financial group, which strongly influences product terms and conditions. For example, Deutsche Leasing defines which assets are leasable, how the leasing underwriting process works and specifies the basic terms and gratification. Savings bank 1 is left to execute the rating of the leases and defines the terms based on the given basic terms (SK1MPP19.11.13, SK1MPP16.12.13). Furthermore, the financial group provides information and guidelines to the savings banks. For example, the Deutscher Sparkassenverlag publishes the sector reports and the DSGV frequently publishes information and guidelines via the intranet that also influence the corporate credit business, e.g. information about new fraud cases. Another example of the financial group's influence is the handbook service of the DSGV. The handbook of a savings bank regulates its process organisation. Savings bank 1 subscribes to the handbook service and receives draft versions of handbook changes, e.g. to comply with new regulations, that the bank adopts into its process organisation (SK1BSPP06.01.14).

Joint projects of the savings banks financial group foster the homogenisation of savings banks' process organisation. The savings banks financial group organises joint action with projects to develop new products, services, techniques and solutions for regulatory requirements (OSGVD). Projects consist of three phases (OITSGV16.04.13). In the development phase, the departments, firms and thematic working groups, i.e. groups of experts from the member banks, are responsible for developing new solutions/methods. In the pilot phase, selected member banks test the project results, and in the rollout phase results are offered and recommended for use to all member organisations. These solutions are rolled out via the intranet, and the association and its firms offer the necessary infrastructure (e.g. via the Finanz Informatik GmbH & Co. KG), tools (e.g. software, printed matter), consulting services and contact persons to help the savings banks with the implementation (OSGVIT16.04.13, OSGVIT30.05.13, SK1BSPP27.12.13). In this regard, one project which decisively influences SME lending was the joint development of the rating systems (see Section 4.2.2). Another project example is the *Sparkassen Finanzkonzept*, or savings banks finance concept (see Box 4.11). Thus, projects are an important instrument for developing and adopting new solutions/methods jointly in the savings banks finance group.

Via its products, information, guidelines and joint projects, the savings banks financial group influences the process organisation of its savings banks, and hence also lending, e.g, via rating systems. Through the cooperation economies of scale are increased in the financial group. As the outlined proceeding of the project development indicates, the financial group does not initiate projects top-down; projects are rather developed and tested bottom-up. Nevertheless, the savings banks financial group tends to standardise the process organisation of individual savings banks.

Box 4.11   The *Sparkassen Finanzkonzept*

The *Sparkassen Finanzkonzept* is a sales instrument developed by the savings banks financial group. The market strategies department of the DSGV promotes the *Sparkassen Finanzkonzept* and offers adapted concepts for the different customer segments, e.g. private customers, business customers, freelancers (OSGVIT16.04.13). The *Sparkassen Finanzkonzept* aims to ensure comprehensive consulting of clients, oriented towards their needs (Schüller and Goebel 2010). The *Sparkassen Finanzkonzept* illustrates the following hierarchy of needs appealingly as a pyramid (Figure 4.18): basic needs at level 1: services (e.g. payment transactions), liquidity (e.g. current account credits) and savings (e.g. investment funds); risk hedging at level 2 (e.g. insurances, commodity securities); investment at level 3 (e.g. investment loans); provision for employees and own use at level 4 (e.g. pension funds); international activities at level 5 (e.g. export financing); and succession arrangements at the top level (e.g. acquisition loans). The key instrument of the *Sparkasssen Finanzkonzept* is the so-called finance check questionnaire, which guides customer advisors to survey all the needs of the customers and their fulfilment in the consulting meeting. With this instrument, advisors should identify unsatisfied needs and offer fitting products accordingly. Savings banks have the option to apply the *Sparkassen Finanzkonzept* in combination with a customer portfolio management system (also offered by the DSGV) to manage sales occasions (OSGVIT16.04.13).

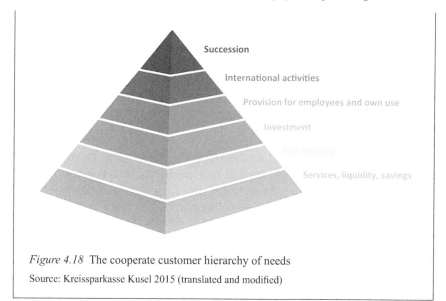

Figure 4.18 The cooperate customer hierarchy of needs

Source: Kreissparkasse Kusel 2015 (translated and modified)

In this context, the *Sparkassen Finanzkonzept* for business clients has the potential to strikingly heighten the standardisation of credit-granting processes as it aims to influence customer–customer advisor interaction. The *Sparkassen Finanzkonzept* guides the advisory meetings in order to guarantee a certain minimum quality of such meetings and to utilise cross-selling opportunities (Wemhöner and Grunwald 2008). According to the interview partner of the DSGV, ca. 66% of all savings banks use the *Sparkassen Finanzkonzept* for business clients (OSGVIT16.04.13). However, he explained on request that the customer advisors would not aggressively apply the finance check questionnaire, the key instrument of the *Sparkassen Finanzkonzept*, for every credit enquiry:

> Well yes, like I said you cannot rape the customers, thus not slavishly say so and there comes a customer and has a complex project to be financed and then I say okay let's have a sit down and firstly analyse for two hours, there the customer will say well I haven't got the time right now.
>
> (OSGVIT16.04.13)

Because of its high standardisation potential, the practical application of the *Sparkassen Finanzkonzept* was of interest during participant observation in savings bank 1. As this was not actually witnessed, the customer advisors were asked about their application of the *Sparkassen Finanzkonzept*. The daily protocol reports the following answer:

> I ask about the consulting questionnaires of the *Sparkassen Finanzkonzept*. Mrs Hennecke says that she fills in some questionnaires at the end of the

month, but they are only filed. Mrs Friese says that she used to take the questionnaires into the advisory meetings at the beginning. She actually knows the answers to the questions already, thus the customers think she is off-the-wall if she asks these questions. Mrs Hennecke also thinks that she can fill in the questionnaires by herself and because the questionnaires are only filed, there is no added value for the savings bank. For new colleagues the questionnaires may be helpful.

(SK1MPP09.12.13)

As the responses of the customer advisors of savings bank 1 indicate, the intended use of the *Sparkassen Finanzkonzept* as foreseen by the DSGV differs from its actual application by savings bank 1. The *Sparkassen Finanzkonzept* tends to have no influence on the customer–customer advisor interaction of the observed team. Having stated this, other savings banks may use the *Sparkassen Finanz-konzept* in a more mandatory way, as suggested by the interview results from savings bank 3. Here the bank deduces sales targets from the hierarchy of needs; i.e. the customer advisors are encouraged to sell products of every hierarchical need level (SK3MIT18.08.13).

At the district scale, the regional savings banks associations indirectly influence credit-granting processes in at least three ways. Firstly, by their auditing tasks and their law and regulation advisory work (see Section 4.2.5.2). Secondly, savings banks compare their earning and risk performances with their peers from the regional associations. As outlined above, savings bank 1 adopts its sales targets from the peer group of the regional savings banks association (GB1MIT13.02.14). Thirdly, the savings banks academies of the regional associations train the staff of savings banks. Besides the general job trainings, the academies offer specialized expert seminars for customer advisors, credit officers, restructuring and workout experts, etc. (OSGVIT14.06.13I, OSGVD14.06.13II). In comparison to this, the big banks conduct their banker training partly in house, but also purchase specialized trainings from external firms and universities and send their employees to (public) courses (OEIT30.08.13). Differences in the professional training of the contrasted types of banks potentially evoke varying evaluations of credit requests, an aspect which this investigation does not further discuss.

4.2.6 Deducing the total distance of credit decisions to SMEs

This section aggregates the empirical results of the comparison of the credit-granting processes between savings bank 1 and big bank 1. To this end, the section deduces total distance of credit decisions to SMEs of the medium size class graphically and numerically, as proposed in Section 2.4. Rather than repeating the findings of the previous sections, the section aims to present the key results at a glance, wherefore the rich qualitative empirical findings are grouped into distance and power classes. Section 4.2.6.1 classifies distance between the customer advisors and the other actors, and Section 4.2.6.2 outlines the classification of decision-making power. As explored in the previous sections, the decision-making

power of the actors strikingly depends on the characteristics of the borrowing units, i.e. rating score and total credit volume. Accordingly, Section 4.2.6.3
deduces and compares the total distance of credit decisions for borrowers with
different characteristics in terms of blank credit volumes and sound, medium and
poor rating scores.

4.2.6.1 Distance

Table 4.8 states the distance classification criteria and the classification. The criteria are partly deduced from the theory on distance and knowledge transfer (Section 2.2.3), and partly inductively driven from the empirical findings in order
to gain a discriminating classification. As the distance between actors does not
depend on borrowers' characteristics, the classification remains indifferent to the
characteristics of the medium-sized SME.[5]

The *customer advisor–team leader* cooperation of savings bank 1 is classified
as taking place at very short distance. Very high levels of social embeddedness,
including colloquial communication, frequent private chats and organisational
embeddedness, i.e. operating in the same (small) working group, justify the classification. Micro-geographical proximity and the resulting daily face-to-face interactions further enhance cooperation at a very short distance.

The *customer advisor–credit officer* pairs of savings bank 1 and the *customer
advisor–team leader* pairs of big bank 1 cooperate at a short distance according
to the classification. In the former case the very frequent and colloquial pairwise
cooperation and the profound natural dependency indicate high social and organisational embeddedness. Customer advisors and their team leader at big bank 1
also cooperate at a short distance; e.g. they are located in micro-geographical
proximity and frequently communicate personally. Nonetheless, the findings suggest that the distance of cooperation tends to be longer compared to the customer
advisor–team leader pairs of savings bank 1. Twice as many employees work
in the customer advisor team of big bank 1, and the team leader is officially not
involved in credit decisions to SMEs of the medium size class.

Following the classification criteria, the *customer advisor–SME customer* pairs
cooperate at medium (operational) distance in savings bank 1 and big bank 1.
Both banks strive to build strong relationships to their clients. However, organisational embeddedness tends to be rather low compared to the cooperation within
the banks, because SMEs do not belong to the bank organisation. Occasion-
related communication with customers becomes very frequent, but, on average,
communication remains medium-frequent in comparison to bank internal communication. The higher micro-geographical accessibility of savings bank 1's
customer advisors is not considered in this classification.[6] Within the bank organisations, the *customer advisor–high-level supervisor* pairs at savings bank 1
and the *customer advisor–administrative officer* pairs at big bank 1 cooperate
at a medium distance. These classifications are justified in comparison to the
much shorter *customer advisor–credit officer* distance in terms of social and
organisational embeddedness at savings bank 1, as no pairwise fixed cooperation

Table 4.8 Distance classes

Name	Numerical parameter	Classification criteria	Classification
Long distance	5	*Low social embeddedness* • No fixed contact persons • Persons not personally known • Little/no verbal communication *Low organisational embeddedness* • Different firms/departments • Little/no mutual dependency *Long geographical distance* • Supraregional scale • No face-to-face interactions	*Savings bank 1* • Customer advisor–rating system *Big bank 1* • Customer advisor–rating system • Customer advisor–credit officer • Customer advisor–high level supervisor
Medium distance	1.5	*Medium social embeddedness* • More then one fixed contact person • Persons personally known • Occasional verbal communication *Medium organisational embeddedness* • Different firms/departments • Mutual dependency *Medium geographical distance* • Regional or district scale • Occasional face-to-face interactions	*Savings bank 1* • Customer advisor–customer • Customer advisor–high-level supervisor *Big bank 1* • Customer advisor–customer • Customer advisor–administrative officer
Short distance	0.75	*High social embeddedness* • Few/one fixed contact persons • Persons personally well known • Frequent and colloquial communication *High organisational embeddedness* • Same firm/department • High mutual dependency *Short geographical distance* • Regional scale • Frequent face-to-face interactions	*Savings bank 1* • Customer advisor–credit officer *Big bank 1* • Customer advisor–team leader
Very short distance	0.5	*Very high social embeddedness* • One fixed contact person • Persons personally very well known • Frequent and colloquial communication • Frequent private chats *Very high organisational embeddedness* • Same department/team • Very high mutual dependency *Very short geographical distance* • Regional scale • Micro-geographical proximity (e.g. next door office) • Daily face-to-face interactions	*Savings bank 1* • Customer advisor–team leader

Source: author's table

exists, cooperation is less frequent and mutual dependency remains lower (see Section 4.2.3).

At savings bank 1 long distance only exists between the *customer advisor–rating system* interfaces according to the classification criteria as customer advisors can only influence the rating systems to a limited degree with soft information. The *Sparkassen Rating* and Risikosysteme GmbH develops and maintains the rating systems for all savings banks (at the national scale); therefore, savings bank 1 has no influence on the rating algorithms. *Rating systems, high-level supervisors* and *credit officers* cooperate at long distances to the customer advisors of big bank 1. The long *customer advisor–credit officer* distance represents a decisive difference to savings bank 1. Customer advisors have no fixed contact partners, the bank does not encourage personal communication, credit officers are not always known personally and the dependence of the credit officers on the customer advisors remains low (see Section 4.2.3.1). As will be demonstrated in the following section, the differences in customer advisor–credit officer cooperation represent one key driver for the long distance of credit decisions in big bank 1.

4.2.6.2 Decision-making power

Table 4.9 displays the classification criteria of decision-making power which have been determined with the aim of usefully discriminating. In addition to the official allocation of credit-granting authority, i.e. voting rights, the criteria also consider different informal and indirect means of influencing lending decisions. Informal influence relates to effective performativity of rating scores as well as credit officers and supervisors affecting customer advisors' credit decisions beyond their official authority.

At big bank 1 credit-granting authority depends on the rating score and credit volume, whereas at savings bank 1 the blank credit volume and hence collaterals also influence authority. It is important to note that the following section (4.2.6.3) only discusses credit-granting power in relation to the blank credit volume, for comprehensiveness reasons. In so doing, the representation tends to underscore the decision-making power of the customer advisors and team leaders of savings bank 1 as their authority also depends on collaterals.

4.2.6.3 Total distance of credit decisions

Table 4.10 reports the numerical calculation of credit decision distance to SMEs, i.e. borrowing units, with different characteristics in terms of rating score and blank credit volume. The approach behind the numerical calculation is discussed in Section 2.4. The comparison of the total distance values shows which of the two banks studied decides credits at a shorter distance to the SMEs under consideration of the borrower units' characteristics. The numerical parameters for the calculation are taken from Table 4.8 and Table 4.9 and represent the allocation of decision-making power and the difficulties to transmit soft information. Especially, the values for the distance classes are arbitrary. Ordinal in scale, the

Table 4.9 Credit decision-making power classes

Symbol	Name	Numerical parameter	Classification criteria
■	Almost exclusive decision-making power	100%	Only official vote or (almost) non-negotiable credit refusal power
■	High decision-making power	50%	First of more than one vote and high responsibility for the credit-granting process
■	Medium decision-making power	25%	Official (non-first) vote or first vote with medium responsibility for the credit-granting process
□	Relevant influencing power	10%	No official credit-granting authority, but relevant means of influence: • Compiling and checking of credit applications • Relevant power on official credit voters (e.g. boss) • Decisive information in the credit-granting process (i.e. effective performativity)
□	Indirect or very occasional influence	1%	No official credit-granting authority, but indirect or occasional means of influence: • Minor compiling and checking of credit applications • Relevant power on official credit voters that is very occasionally used • Important indirect influence (e.g. auditing)
□	(Almost) no influence power	0%	All other actors

Source: author's table

numerical results allow for rank-order comparisons. The following subsections compare total distance of credit decisions to SMEs with blank credit volumes of €100,000, €500,000 and €1.5 million for savings bank 1 versus big bank 1.

BLANK CREDIT VOLUME: €100,000

Figure 4.19 compares the credit-granting power of and distance between the actors in the process of credit granting to a borrower unit with blank credits of €100,000 and sound, medium and poor rating scores. For credits to SMEs with *sound* rating scores (PD ≤ 2.0%), the customer advisors execute exclusive credit-granting authority at both banks studied. Nonetheless, three actors tend to restrict the official exclusive authority of the advisors at savings bank 1. These are, on

Table 4.10 Numerical calculation of credit decision's distance to different types of SME customers

		Savings bank 1						Big bank 1						
		Customer advisor	Back office	Team leader	High-level supervisors	Rating system	Sum	Sum	Rating system	High-level supervisor	Team leader	Administrative officers	Back office	Customer advisor
Blank credit volume: €100,000														
Sound rating score	Power p	1	0.1	0.1	0.1	0.1	1.4	1.11	0.1	0	0	0.01	0	1
	Distance d	1.5	2	2.25	3	6.5	15.25	26.25	6.5	6.5	2.25	3	6.5	1.5
	p*d	1.5	0.2	0.225	0.3	0.65	2.88	2.18	0.65	0	0	0.03	0	1.5
	Total distance						2.05	1.96						
Medium rating score	Power p	0.5	0.1	0.25	0.1	0.1	1.05	0.88	0.1	0.01	0.01	0.01	0.25	0.5
	Distance d	1.5	2	2.25	3	6.5	15.25	26.25	6.5	6.5	2.25	3	6.5	1.5
	p*d	0.75	0.2	0.563	0.3	0.65	2.46	3.14	0.65	0.065	0.02	0.03	1.63	0.75
	Total distance						2.35	3.57						
Poor rating score	Power p	0.5	0.1	0.25	0.1	0.1	1.05	1.12	1	0.01	0.01	0	0	0.1
	Distance d	1.5	2	2.25	3	6.5	15.25	26.25	6.5	6.5	2.25	3	6.5	1.5
	p*d	0.75	0.2	0.563	0.3	0.65	2.46	6.74	6.5	0.065	0.02	0	0	0.15
	Total distance						2.35	6.02						
Blank credit volume: €500,000														
Sound rating score	Power p	0.5	0.25	0.25	0.1	0.1	1.20	1.11	0.1	0	0	0.01	0	1
	Distance d	1.5	2	2.25	3	6.5	15.25	26.25	6.5	6.5	2.25	3	6.5	1.5
	p*d	0.75	0.5	0.563	0.3	0.65	2.76	2.18	0.65	0	0	0.03	0	1.5
	Total distance						2.30	1.96						
Nedium rating score	Power p	0.5	0.25	0.25	0.25	0.1	1.35	0.87	0.1	0	0.01	0.01	0.25	0.5
	Distance d	1.5	2	2.25	3	6.5	15.25	26.25	6.5	6.5	2.25	3	6.5	1.5
	p*d	0.75	0.5	0.563	0.75	0.65	3.21	3.08	0.65	0	0.02	0.03	1.63	0.75
	Total distance						2.38	3.54						

(Continued)

Table 4.10 (Continued)

		Savings bank 1						Big bank 1						
		Customer advisor	Back office	Team leader	High-level supervisors	Rating system	Sum	Sum	Rating system	High-level supervisor	Team leader	Administrative officers	Back office	Customer advisor
Poor rating score	Power p	0.5	0.25	0.25	0.25	0.1	1.35	1.12	1	0.01	0.01	0	0	0.1
	Distance d	1.5	2	2.25	3	6.5	15.25	26.25	6.5	6.5	2.25	3	6.5	1.5
	p*d	0.75	0.5	0.563	0.75	0.65	3.21	6.74	6.5	0.065	0.02	0	0	0.15
	Total distance						2.38	6.02						
Blank credit volume: €1,500,000														
Sound rating score	Power p	0.25	0.25	0.25	0.25	0.1	1.10	0.87	0.1	0	0.01	0.01	0.25	0.5
	Distance d	1.5	2	2.25	3	6.5	15.25	26.25	6.5	6.5	2.25	3	6.5	1.5
	p*d	0.375	0.5	0.563	0.75	0.65	2.84	3.08	0.65	0	0.02	0.03	1.63	0.75
	Total distance						2.58	3.54						
Medium rating score	Power p	0.25	0.25	0.25	0.25	0.1	1.10	0.96	0.1	0	0.1	0.01	0.25	0.5
	Distance d	1.5	2	2.25	3	6.5	15.25	26.25	6.5	6.5	2.25	3	6.5	1.5
	p*d	0.375	0.5	0.563	0.75	0.65	2.84	3.28	0.65	0	0.23	0.03	1.63	0.75
	Total distance						2.58	3.42						
Poor rating score	Power p	0.25	0.25	0.25	0.25	0.1	1.10	1.12	1	0.01	0.01	0	0	0.1
	Distance d	1.5	2	2.25	3	6.5	15.25	26.25	6.5	6.5	2.25	3	6.5	1.5
	p*d	0.375	0.5	0.563	0.75	0.65	2.84	6.74	6.5	0.065	0.02	0	0	0.15
	Total distance						2.58	6.02						

$$\text{Total distance} = \left(\sum_n^1 p_n \cdot d_n \right) \cdot \frac{1}{\sum_1^n p_n}$$

P_n = percentage of actor (n)'s decision-making power
D_n = distance of actor (n) to SME customer
Numerical parameters taken from Table 4.8 and Table 4.9

Source: author's table, see Section 2.4 for the explanation of calculations

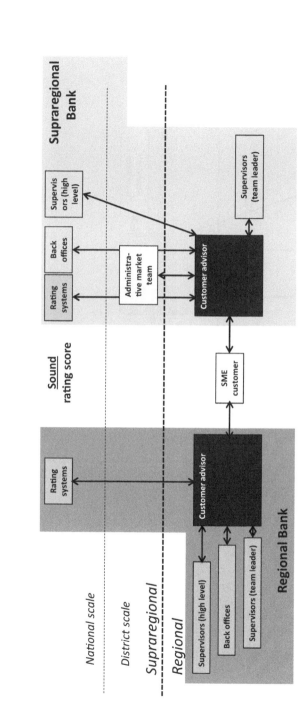

Figure 4.19 Distance of credit decision – blank credit volume of €100,000 and sound, medium and poor rating scores

Source: author's figure

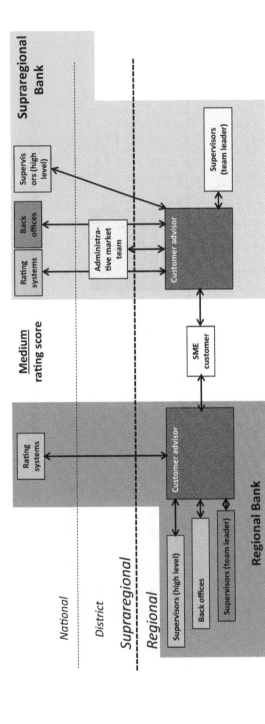

Figure 4.19 Continued

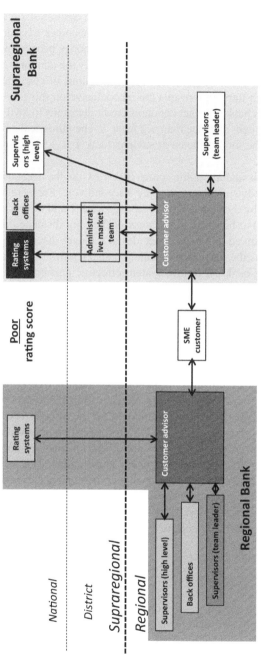

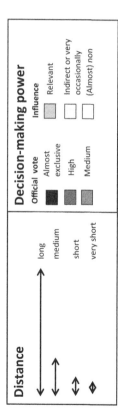

Figure 4.19 Continued

the one hand, the back officers, with their tasks of reviewing the calculations and producing the credit applications (Section.4.2.3.2), and, on the other hand, the team leaders and high-level supervisors who restrict authority by means of their influence on customer advisors' decisions, as indicated in Section 4.2.4.2. In contrast, the interview findings indicate that big bank 1's customer advisors face almost no restriction of their exclusive credit-granting authority because no back office reviews the credit applications for formal errors. Only the administrative officers are involved and potentially guide the credit decisions of customer advisors to a limited degree, yet interview results are inconclusive on this issue. Therefore, surprisingly, savings bank 1 in fact conducts credit decisions to SMEs with sound rating scores at a longer distance than big bank 1. The numerical calculation reflects this finding; the total distance at savings bank 1 is 2.05 versus 1.96 at big bank 1 (Table 4.10).

In case of borrower units with *medium* rating scores (PD > 2.0%), the decision-making authority of customer advisors is restricted by a second vote. Such credit applications must be approved by the team leader at savings bank 1 and the back-office team (at a long distance) at big bank 1. Because of the long distance difference between the actors involved, big bank 1 decides at a longer distance for medium-rated borrower units as the numerical calculation also confirms (2.31 at savings bank 1 vs. 3.57 at big bank 1). Rating system effective performativity tends to become an issue for medium-rated SMEs in both banks studied, as the PD must be taken into consideration in credit decisions.

A *poor* rating score (from PD 3.6%) of an SME customer does not cause a change in the credit-granting authority allocation of savings bank 1 compared to a medium rating score; i.e. the team leader's authority is sufficient to approve a blank credit of €100,000. In sharp contrast, the poor rating score leads to the almost final rejection of an application for an ordinary new credit by the rating system at big bank 1. The customer advisors have relevant informal means of influence because they provide the qualitative information for the rating process and discuss existing clients with the intensive care unit in cases of credit prolongation (see Section 4.2.2.2). Nevertheless, the strict cutoff limit in cases of poor rating scores causes the almost final rejection of credit applications. This is a profound difference to savings bank 1 where such credit applications in fact need neither back-office nor high-level supervisor approval, but only a sound justification for such lending is required (Section 4.2.2.2). Therefore, savings bank 1 preserves flexibility in lending to SMEs which are evaluated by the rating as being likely to default.

BLANK CREDIT VOLUME: €500,000

At savings bank 1, an SME with a blank credit volume of €500,000 and a *sound* rating score has to be approved by the team leaders and requires the second vote from the back-office department, while at big bank 1 the customer advisors alone approve such credits (see Figure 4.20). In fact, at the big bank credit volumes of up to €1 million count as non risk-relevant lending and need no second vote if the

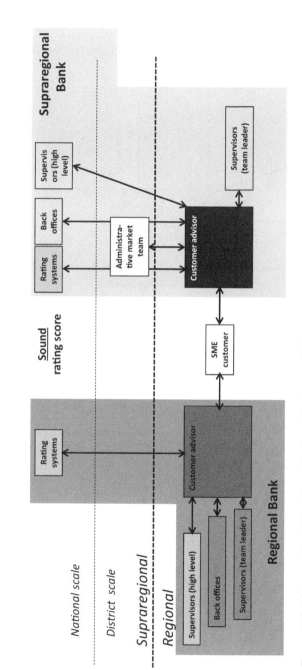

Figure 4.20 Distance of credit decision – blank credit volume of €500,000 and sound, medium and poor rating scores

Source: author's figure

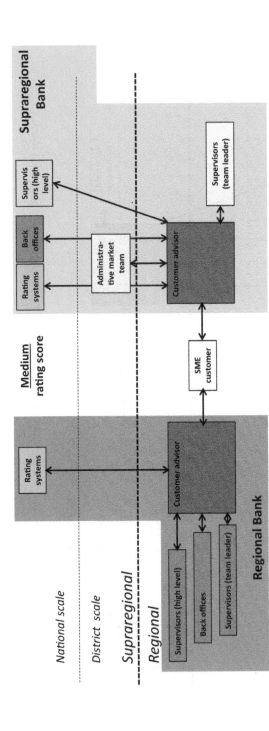

Figure 4.20 Continued

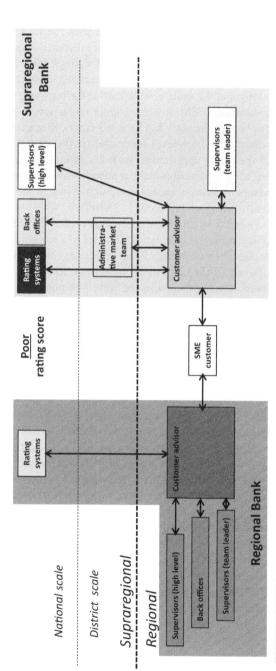

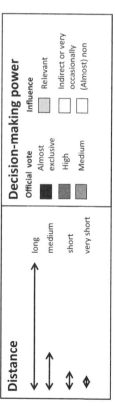

Figure 4.20 Continued

rating score is sound. Therefore, three human actors rather than one are involved. Only the effective performativity of the rating results indirectly diminishes the unrestricted lending authority of big bank 1's customer advisors for such a credit application. The numerical calculation in Table 4.10 also expresses the longer distance at which savings bank 1 decides. In fact, the 0.34 longer distance value represents the largest difference in distance to the detriment of savings bank 1. Accordingly, the distance of credit decisions to SMEs with sound rating scores of up to €1 million is substantially longer at the savings bank than at the big bank.

Total credit decision-making distance to SMEs with *medium* rating scores is longer at big bank 1 than savings bank 1, because big bank 1's back office conducts the second vote at a long distance. A high-level supervisor (in this case the department head) must approve the credit applications with his formal vote at the savings bank, too, as the team leader's decision-making power is insufficient. However, the high-level supervisors of savings bank 1 are much closer to their customer advisors than the credit officers of big bank 1. Therefore, with total distances of 2.38 (savings bank 1) and 3.54 (big bank 1) savings bank 1 decides at shorter distances according to the numerical calculation. In cases of *poor* rating scores the credit-granting power allocation of savings bank 1 does not change, as the scores do not restrict the authority of the high-level supervisors. In contrast, the rating system almost exclusively rejects new credits for firms with poor rating scores at big bank 1, due to the strict cutoff limit. Having stated this, effective performativity of the rating result potentially influences decisions-makers of the savings bank, as lending despite poor rating scores requires explicit justifications. Still the savings bank does not prohibit lending, as is the case in big bank 1.

BLANK CREDIT VOLUME: €1.5 MILLION

The CEO of savings bank 1 always has to approve a credit application from a borrower unit with bank credits of €1.5 million. Hence, total distance to SMEs with sound, medium and poor ratings does not differ (Figure 4.21). Similarly, the approval of the back office is always needed for credits of such volume at big bank 1. Because of the longer distance to the back offices of big bank 1 compared to the high-level supervisors of savings bank 1, the big bank always decides credits to medium-sized SMEs above €1 million at a longer total distance than the regional bank, according to the distance classification.

To sum up, this analysis identifies two cases where big bank 1 conducts credit decisions to SMEs of the medium size class at a shorter total distance than savings bank 1. These are borrowing units with total blank credit volumes of €100,000 and €500,000 and sound rating scores. The fact that the big bank's customer advisors execute exclusive credit-granting authority for borrowing units of up to €1 million in cases of sound rating scores explains the surprising finding. Having stated this, the functional distance of credit decisions to SMEs changes profoundly in relation to the rating scores at big bank 1, leading to distant credit decisions in cases of medium and poor rating scores due to the back-office vote or the rating score cutoff limit. In contrast, savings bank 1's total distance of credit decisions is shorter

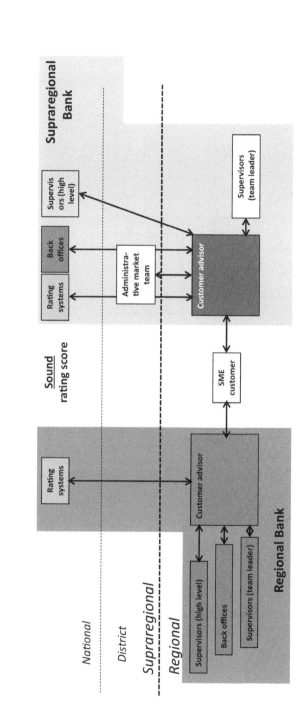

Figure 4.21 Distance of credit decision – blank credit volume of €1.5 million and sound, medium and poor rating scores

Source: author's figure

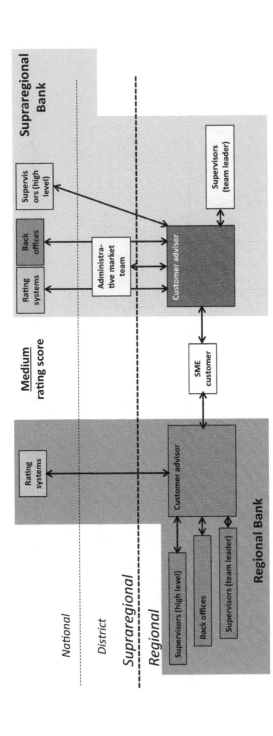

Figure 4.21 Continued

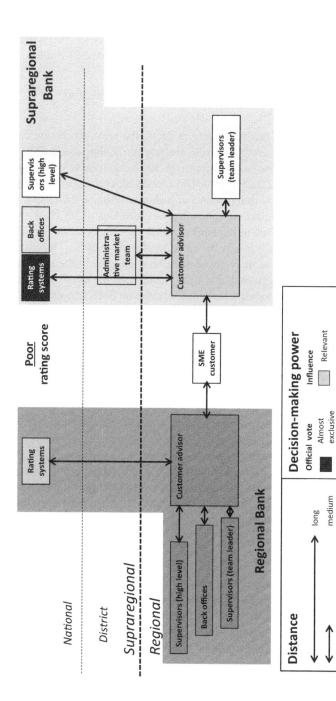

Figure 4.21 Continued

depending on the rating results, because all actors that execute official decision-making authority decide at very short to medium distances. Therefore, according to the considerations on distance and soft information, the regional savings bank tends to possess soft information advantages over big bank 1 only for SMEs with medium and poor rating scores or SMEs with credit volumes above €1 million.

4.3 The effects of the varying organisation of credit decisions at savings and big banks

Comparing the organisation of credit-granting in detail, the previous section has identified varying distances of credit decision making to medium-sized SMEs. In contrast to the widespread assumption that regional banks decide on credits at shorter distances (Section 2.2.2), big bank 1 in fact decides on SME credits of up to €1 million and with sound rating scores at a shorter distance than savings bank 1, the empirical findings indicate. Following the estimation of Mr Holz, the team leader of big bank 1, ca. 50% of big bank 1's SME customers are below this threshold (Section 4.2.3.2), which is why the bank decides about 50% of its credit applications at a shorter distance than would have been the case in the regional savings bank. Against this background, this section addresses the question of the effects of the (geographically) varying lending processes on SME finance. Gathering empirical findings on actual credit-granting processes, the section argues in essence that savings bank 1 maintains a shorter functional distance in lending when soft information tends to influence credit decisions most. Therefore, the regional savings bank maintains soft information advantages over the big bank studied, in line with the widespread assumption that regional banks gain informational advantages in lending to SMEs due to short distance.

The section is organised as follows: Section 4.3.1 presents four cases of financially distressed SMEs observed at savings bank 1, which illustrate how the actors cooperate in serving the clients. Section 4.3.2 brings together results about the interplay between distance and credit decisions. Section 4.3.3 discusses the willingness of banks to lend to financially distressed SMEs and compares bad debt of savings bank 1 and big bank 1. The findings indicate that the higher willingness of savings bank 1 to find solutions for financially distressed firms does not come at the price of increases in bad debt taking.

4.3.1 SME customer cases

This section follows the processing of four credit requests observed at savings bank 1. The customer cases have been selected because they are financially distressed SMEs, and thus illustrate the dealings of savings bank 1 with less sound clients. Section 4.3.1.1 follows Schmidt Solutions GmbH. The interaction of Mrs Hennecke and Mr Schmidt shows how close and knowledgeable long-term business relationships can become and demonstrates the large effort savings bank 1 is willing to invest in a financially distressed SME. Remarkably, the case also suggests that close customer relationships must neither come at the price of uncritical lending nor must they be unprofitable for the savings bank. Section 4.3.1.2 looks at Anlagenbau Mustermann GmbH, an SME with ca. 200 employees. In contrast to Schmidt Solutions, this customer relationship is distanced. Nevertheless, because of its regional embeddedness savings bank 1 gained decisive information about the company. The example of Retailer Kampfgarten illustrates the impact of the public mandate on the lending decisions of savings bank 1 (Section 4.3.1.3). The section also shows the negative impacts of the saving bank imperative to promote regional business on firms' long-term performance in line with the soft-budget constraint problem. Section 4.3.1.4 follows Wandland Immobilien GmbH and illustrates how personal interactions alter bank employees' evaluation of clients.

The customer cases were observed for (up to) six weeks, initially in the back-office department and later in the customer advisor team. At the time of writing (March 2015) no insolvency of the observed companies is known. Two firms, Anlagenbau Mustermann GmbH and Schmidt Solutions GmbH, have certainly stayed in business as their webpages confirm; the other two SMEs have no conclusive webpages.

4.3.1.1 Schmidt Solutions GmbH

With an annual sales revenue of ca. €1.5 million, Schmidt Solutions imports and processes consumer goods and sells them as a wholesaler; the firm thus needs a large amount of working capital. Mr Schmidt is the managing owner of the GmbH that overall operates quite profitably with acceptable indebtedness. Savings bank 1 is the *Hausbank* of Schmidt Solutions and provides a current account credit of €400,000 and a range of repayment loans from previous debt restructuring. The total credit volume of the Schmidt Solutions borrower unit exceeds the risk-relevant threshold because related firms and private members of Mr Schmidt's family also conduct business with the savings bank. Therefore, the department heads of the market and back-office department have to approve credit applications. As customer advisor, Mrs Hennecke has kept Schmidt's firm and private accounts for 10 years. Schmidt Solutions has debt with another regional bank that tried to take over the customer relationship a couple of years ago.

Mrs Hennecke describes Mr Schmidt as a very talented salesperson but with no interest in managing his business; i.e. he does not conduct sales or liquidity planning. At the time of observation, the client's liquidity was stressed for two reasons. Firstly, Mr Schmidt had high living standards, which used to be unproblematic because of the firm's performance. However, due to his divorce Mr Schmidt had to buy out his wife, who partly owned the firm, causing high personal drawings from the firm, rendering its liquidity critical. Secondly, just at this time the working capital demand of the firm increased because of changes in purchasing conditions and increasing sales. The rating result reflects the firm's double-faced financial situation. The basic rating score of Schmidt Solutions was sound (PD 1.3%), though the liquidity shortage caused extensive use/overdraft of the current account credit line, wherefore automatic warning signals caused rating score deterioration. Because of the downgraded rating score, Mr Flick – the credit officer in charge – needed to write a verbal explanation of the firm's financial situation for the annual disclosure (SK1MFPP15.11.13).

On 20 November 2013 the first interaction between Mr Schmidt and Mrs Hennecke was observed regarding a booked payment of €50,000 that Mrs Hennecke needed to approve because the firm's current account credit was almost totally taken up. Mrs Hennecke possesses decision-making power for overdrafts of up to €40,000 but set herself an overdraft limit of €10,000 for Mr Schmidt (SK1MPP20.11.13). As the booked payment exceeded the self-imposed limit, Mrs Hennecke did not approve the booking but waited for Mr Schmidt to call, which he did at midday to explain the importance of the booking. Mrs Hennecke, in turn, explained her disapproval and specified the amount of money Mr Schmidt had to transfer to the firm's account for her to accept the transaction. Before closing time, Mr Schmidt called and gave assurance of his booking of the necessary money, whereupon Mrs Hennecke approved the transaction, thus greatly exceeding her self-imposed limit. Mrs Hennecke justified her approval with her certainty that Mr Schmidt had arranged the money transfer, as he never lies to her and, in fact, a relative of Mr Schmidt transferred the necessary money the next morning.

In the following weeks bookings from either Mr Schmidt's firm or private accounts were on Mrs Hennecke's OSPlus approval list almost every day. In a range of instances, Mr Schmidt just transferred extra cash without communication; in other cases he discussed the booking with Mrs Hennecke on the telephone or face-to-face. For example, once Mr Schmidt approached Mrs Hennecke in her office with a wad of transfer slips and they discussed the order of transactions which she booked in the following days whenever sufficient money was in the accounts. Mr Schmidt highlighted Mrs Hennecke's superior understanding of his cash flow, and Mrs Hennecke reported, not without pride, that Mr Schmidt had already asked her to work for his firm as account manager. And in fact Mrs Hennecke reminded Mr Schmidt about upcoming payments, like the booking of his credit card and toll payments.

On 3 December 2013 Schmidt Solutions' account showed insufficient funds to settle an important foreign transaction which was due on this day and where Mr Schmidt had promised to transfer sufficient money. Mr Schmidt called and explained that he had handed in a cheque at the branch yesterday evening to transfer the needed money. Mrs Hennecke inquired about the cheque in the payment transaction department and other departments but did not find it. Convinced that the cheque had been lost in the bank's administration, Mrs Hennecke nevertheless approved the transaction trusting Mr Schmidt's statement. In the afternoon the payment transactions department informed Mrs Hennecke about the arrival of the cheque; a colleague at the counter had presumably delayed its posting (SK1MPP03.12.13). This incident indicates the trust of Mrs Hennecke in the integrity of Mr Schmidt, as she suspected an error in savings bank's administration to be more likely than a false statement by Mr Schmidt.

Despite the trustful cooperation, Mrs Hennecke criticised Mr Schmidt's management by highlighting the danger of his 'account keeping at the limit', as the day's protocol reports:

> If the customer cannot pay an important supplier or conveyance for instance, the firm is at risk of breaking apart, because important buyers or suppliers will cancel business relations.
>
> (SK1BSPP19.12.13)

To improve the liquidity situation, Mrs Hennecke, Mr Schmidt and Mr Schmidt's other regional bank negotiated changes in the credit structure. Mr Schmidt wanted an increase in his current account credit line or a restructuring of the firm's current account debt without a reduction of his current account credit line. Mrs Hennecke and the other regional bank also saw the need for restructuring debt but rejected an increase of overall credit volume. Though a further increase in debt would be justifiable according to the numerical cash flow analysis using the orientation values for living expenditures (see Section 4.1.2.2), Mrs Hennecke questioned Mr Schmidt's actual future ability to serve debt, primarily because of his substantial private expenses (SK1BSPP19.12.13). Thus, Mrs Hennecke wanted Mr Schmidt to create a realistic sales, profitability and liquidity planning and cut private spending accordingly. Furthermore, a factoring was discussed wherefore Mrs Hennecke appointed a meeting with Mr Schmidt, the other regional bank and the factoring expert of Deutsche Leasing for 6 December 2013 at the savings bank (SK1MPP09.12.13). As that day's protocol reports, the meeting failed to find a solution:

> The meeting with [Schmidt Solutions] has shown that he does not want to do factoring. He had expected that his current account credit would not be cut and that he would not need to undertake planning. Furthermore [the other regional bank] did not know that the customer had also assigned his advances to customers to savings bank 1 and this earlier than to [the other regional bank]. Mrs Kurz says that the first contract is the contract that comes first, hence the credits of [the other regional bank] are not collateralised by advances to customers. For Mrs Hennecke this is fair because the bank has muscled into her existing customer relationship. She has always told her back officer Mr Flick not to create a new assignment of advances to customers but to refer to the old contract, so that this contract is really older than that of [the other regional bank].
>
> (SK1MPP09.12.13)

Mrs Hennecke further reported that she noted how Mr Schmidt got angry at the meeting so she stopped asking critical questions. After the meeting she and Mr Schmidt chatted about the meeting. Both were amused by the young customer advisor of the other regional bank who performed as a 'professional businessman' but was not aware of his subordinated claims on the collaterals (SK1MPP09.12.13). Beside the cleverness of Mrs Hennecke, an experienced customer advisor, the meeting again indicates the close relationship between her and her client. It further suggests that Mrs Hennecke perceived the efforts of the other regional bank to gain 'her' client as inappropriate. After the meeting Mr Schmidt refused to enter new negotiations, and the firm's liquidity situation relaxed in the following days. Nevertheless, Mrs Hennecke was still certain that they could restart negotiations as liquidity would deteriorate again soon.

OSPlus repeatedly appointed Schmidt Solutions automatically for the watch list meetings (see Box 4.9, p. 200) because of the overdrafts and high current account credits usage. In preparation of the face-to-face meeting, customer advisors and credit officers must provide information about their clients and recommend actions to the supervisors wherefore OSPlus provides a questionnaire. The daily protocol describes the filling in of the watch list form:

> Mrs Hennecke used the input window 'other' of the form for each of her clients on the watch list. The window only permits 250 characters and for several cases this was not sufficient, so she used shortcuts and rewordings. We discussed what we can write. In the case of [Schmidt Solutions] I seemed to help her a lot wherefore she thanked me. We write that the firm is actually sound, the customer wants to increase his sales and stock in the next year. A negotiation about more liquidity (factoring) was called off by the client, because he does not want to undertake planning.
>
> (SK1MPP11.12.13)

The watch list meeting on 18 December 2013 produced the following results:

> The CEO was rather fed up [Schmidt Solutions]. Nobody other than the customer advisor team knows the customer personally, yet his family is known at the savings bank. It is suggested to lend the customer €200,000 privately, so that he can finance his divorce. However, Mrs Hennecke is against this decision, because the customer already does not have the ability to cover interest and principal payments. The CEO wants the customer to conduct planning etc. and has no understanding of his high living expenditures, because he himself is very thrifty according to Mrs Hennecke. The meeting result is that Mr Braun, the department head, will meet the client together with Mrs Hennecke.
>
> (SK1BSPP19.12.13)

Furthermore, Mr Schmidt had asked for a temporary €50,000 increase of his current account credit line (SK1BSPP19.12.13), so that the negotiations could restart as Mrs Hennecke had predicted.

The example of Schmidt Solutions shows how close customer relationships can become and how much knowledge customer advisors are able to gain in long-term relationships with clients. Despite her proximity to the client, Mrs Hennecke did not attempt to fulfil all of Mr Schmidt's financial requests, but rather refused the proposed extension of Mr Schmidt's credits to direct the borrower to sound long-term financial performance and thriftiness. In this context, the example also illustrates the effort that savings bank 1 invests in financially distressed firms as Mrs Hennecke dealt with the client almost every working day, involving substantial transaction costs. Having stated this, the example also indicates earning opportunities in serving financially distressed clients. The bank earns high interest payments from Mr Schmidt; i.e. he has to pay the standard interest rate of ca. 12% for his current account credit plus ca. 4% for overdrafts which he frequently uses. The actual default risk of the borrower tends to be lower than predicted by the rating score, as savings bank 1 is aware of financial support from Schmidt's relatives and the bank knows the financial situation of the relatives who are customers, too. Although this financial support cannot count as a hard guarantee, its reliability is nonetheless considerable as in the past the family has always helped out as a last resort.

The case of Schmidt Solutions demonstrates savings bank 1's ability to capitalize on soft information by identifying good quality borrowers (borrowers who will serve debt) among the group of SMEs with computed high default risk according to their rating scores. Considering the fact that the rating scores determine credit terms, i.e. risk adjusted price, banks which achieve superior monitoring of clients on the basis of soft information (not considered in the rating algorithms) gain extra profit. This extra profit potentially explains the profitability of the savings bank regardless of the substantial transaction costs it incurs with financially distressed SMEs.

4.3.1.2 Anlagenbau Mustermann GmbH

The medium-sized company Anlagenbau Mustermann belongs to a group of companies, employs ca. 200 people and produces investment goods in the municipality of savings bank 1. The savings bank is not the company's main bank but only provides a blank current account credit line of €1.5 million that the company rarely uses as it tends to be the most expensive credit line. Mrs Weber deals with Anlagenbau Mustermann despite the large size of the company due to the small total credit volume and receives BWAs and the annual financial statements from the professionally managed company unrequested. Further contacts have so far not been necessary. During observation, Anlagenbau Mustermann informed savings bank 1 about an upcoming liquidity problem because of a major decrease in orders. The company did not inform all of its banks. Mrs Weber assumed that they were informed because the CEO of savings bank 1 maintains close relationships to the regional boss of the trade union that Anlagenbau Mustermann was negotiating with about salary reductions and short-time work (SK1MPP03.12.13).

The CEO of savings bank 1 called Mrs Weber after she had conducted the first analysis of the firm's figure forecasts (liquidity plan, sales and profitability plan) (SK1MPP19.11.13). They appointed a meeting at the headquarters together with the credit officer, the market department head and the restructuring and work-out expert for the afternoon. The meeting ended without agreements on further action. Mrs Weber preferred to transfer the customer to the restructuring and workout team (SK1MPP02.12.13). Two reasons tend to explain Mrs Weber's willingness to hand over her customer. Firstly, Mrs Weber feared legal traps in dealing with this company in case of an insolvency proceeding as the company has four other creditors. Secondly, Mrs Weber's relationship to the company was distanced so she was not able to judge the seriousness of the crisis. Therefore, Mrs Weber added several warning signals (e.g. "ability to cover interest and principal payments at risk", "strong decline in orders") manually to OSPlus the next day (SK1MPP20.11.13). Still the warning signals were not critical enough for the watch list module to recommend a transfer to the restructuring and workout team, because the hard information (e.g. annual financial statements, account keeping) was sound and the deadline for the quarterly watch list meeting had been missed anyway (SK1MPP21.11.13).

On the same day, an inquiry from one of Anlagenbau Mustermann's other banks arrived. The standard form of the bank inquiry was inappropriate to the situation as the company was currently financially sound; it was the outlook that was poor. Mrs Weber ticked off "customer's financial situation is sound" and backdated the response to the day before the meeting at headquarters as she did not want to concern the other bank and cause a credit line withdrawal (SK1MPP20.11.13). This observation shows bank employees retain information in order not to compromise the financial situation of clients, as noted in Section 4.1.1.1.

Mrs Weber managed to arrange for the extraordinary inclusion of Anlagenbau Mustermann in the upcoming watch list meeting and therefore filled in the watch list module on 26 November 2013. She proposed an intensive care classification of the company without further constraints; a transfer to the restructuring and workout team was not justifiable in the current situation (SK1MPP26.11.13). On 2 December 2013, Mrs Weber and the expert from the restructuring and workout team conducted a long telephone discussion and a face-to-face meeting on the following morning to compile an e-mail requesting additional documents from Anlagenbau Mustermann (SK1MPP02.12.13); the company answered on 13 December 2013. Uncertain about the information of the documents, Mrs Weber forwarded the e-mail to the restructuring and workout team. The watch list meeting from 18 December 2013 ended without further action, as the daily protocol reports:

> In the case of [Anlagenbau Mustermann] nobody wants to take a stand, the restructuring colleague looks at his paper and says that they have already worked on this case. It is agreed to wait for the missing documents (i.e. sales and profitability planning for three years). Mrs Weber comments cynically that liquidity should actually last only until the end of the year, which is soon. From a telephone call with one employee of the company she found out that the company has industrial harmony and holidays now [termination of production] until the beginning of January. She has not received any demand

for additional liquidity and also did not want to ask about this, because she actually does not want to increase the current account credit line.

(SK1BSPP19.12.13)

The example of Anlagenbau Mustermann reveals the informational advantages and disadvantages of the regional savings bank. On the one hand, savings bank 1 received decisive information because of its, i.e. its CEO's, regional embeddedness. On the other hand, the example indicates the limited experience of savings bank 1 in dealing with financially distressed firms of Anlagenbau Mustermann's size class. Furthermore, the direct comparison to Schmidt Solutions shows how the much longer distance to the client meant Mrs Weber found it difficult to evaluate the financial situation of Anlagenbau Mustermann. In contrast, Mrs Hennecke's correct predictions document her knowledge on Schmidt Solutions' financial position. The cases Anlagenbau Mustermann and Schmidt Solutions consequently also show that the customer advisors interact at different distances with their clients.

4.3.1.3 Retailer Kampfgarten

Mr Kampfgarten owns a shop in a neighbourhood of savings bank 1's municipality. In the view of the customer advisor team his business concept is risky: the shop offers hire purchases to customers and keeps these credits in its books, i.e. the shop 'plays' consumer bank. Mr Kampfgarten has his business account with current account credit line as well as his private account and a mortgage at savings bank 1. As the total credit volume of the Kampfgarten borrower unit remains below €750,000, an annual financial disclosure is not required by bank regulations (Section 4.1.2.1), and Mr Kampfgarten does not disclose voluntarily. Mrs Kurz is the customer advisor of the client, having taken over from Mrs Hennecke due to disharmonies in the customer relationship.

At the time of observation, the liquidity situation of the shop was critical, causing Mr Kampfgarten to request an urgent €20,000 increase of his current account credit. As Mrs Kurz was on holiday, Mrs Weber had to replace her. She required the up-to-date annual financial statement and BWA from Mr Kampfgarten, who only provided the former document. In line with the risky business model, the shop's balance sheet disclosed a large amount of customer claims. Due to the uncertain recoverability of the claims, Mrs Weber excluded the claims for the evaluation so that the shop had almost no equity capital. On top of this, the profit and loss account reported a minor deficit in 2012, wherefore the shop lacked the ability to cover interest and principal payments on the basis of the 2012 data. Accordingly, Mrs Weber agreed with Mrs Hennecke not to increase the current account credit of the shop, to avoid over-indebtedness. Rather, they offered Mr Kampfgarten a private credit of €20,000 backed by his real estate where mortgage repayments have freed sufficient collateral volume (SK1MPP29.11.13).

In anticipation of Mr Kampfgarten's discontent with the offer, Mrs Hennecke ironically pointed out Mrs Weber's bad luck that Mr Kampfgarten needed a credit increase just when Mrs Kurz was on holiday. Mrs Weber called Mr Kampfgarten on 29 November 2013 to make the offer. The daily protocol reports:

> Mrs Weber conducts the negotiation with the customer via telephone. The customer is upset and says that savings bank 1 would leave a sound retailer out in the rain. Already in 2009 the customer had written a complaint letter to the CEO. Mrs Weber explains to him that the private credit is already a concession. The customer seems to accept this offer under protest.
>
> (SK1MPP29.11.13)

The example of Retailer Kampfgarten exemplifies the regional commitment of savings bank 1. The customer advisors managed to find an instant solution for the urgent liquidity need of this small shop; i.e. the whole business interaction was completed within one week, despite the firm's critical financial records and the limited cooperation of the managing owner. As noted in Section 4.2.4.2, the example also demonstrates the indirect influence of high-level supervisors in line with the public mandate of savings banks, i.e. the imperative to promote the regional economy. Even though supervisors do not approve small credits and thus will not receive information about the requests, the risk of customer complaints tends to affect customer advisors' actions. Mr Kampfgarten's complaint letter to the CEO from 2009 accused the savings bank, i.e. the customer advisors, of failing to provide support for regional business. As even an unjustified customer complaint tends to be a nasty affair for the customer advisors (SK1MPP28.11.13, SK1MPP02.12.13), they have an incentive to please their clients.

The Retailer Kampfgarten case also demonstrates the wariness of the SME customer advisor team. After all, the new credit was 100% collateralised by real estate. Mrs Weber justified her prudence with the fact that savings bank 1 must earn all losses in the credit business. A credit default of €20,000 consumes the interest earnings of a large-scale loan. Notably, the team did not manage to justify the credit extension on the basis of firm's future ability to serve debt but decided to grant Mr Kampfgarten a private loan. Thus, the most important lending criterion (future ability to cover interest and principal payments) was not met by Retailer Kampfgarten, and he received the credit because of sufficient collateral. This observation exemplifies the ability of collateral to outvote future ability to serve debt in exceptional cases, which contradicts the lending rule of no lending without the ability of repayment (Section 4.1.2.3).

Mrs Weber's lending decision tended to influence Retailer Kampfgarten's long-term financial stability arbitrarily as it promoted his over-indebtedness instead of promoting change being made to the inefficient business model. The handling of Retailer Kampfgarten is particularly surprising considering the example of Schmidt Solutions where the credit extension was rejected – although according to the hard information the future ability to serve debt was given – in order to support the firm's long-term financial stability. While the motives behind Mrs Weber's decision are open to speculation, it seems likely that her actions were influenced by the difficult managing owner and his inclination to complain to the CEO under reference to the savings bank's public mandate. Therefore, the observation suggests that the imperative of savings bank 1 to support the regional economy has arbitrary effects in some cases.

4.3.1.4 Wandland Immobilien GmbH

Mr Wandland works for a large organisation and further owns and manages a small property development firm. The Wandland Immobilien GmbH buys apartment houses, renovates them and sells off the freehold flats separately. A range of customers of savings bank 1 conduct similar businesses. Mr Wandland had founded a GmbH for his property investment, because of which the SME team rather than the private customer department is responsible for him. Wandland Immobilien GmbH owns ca. five properties and conducts business in a town within the *Ausleihbezirk* of savings bank 1 but outside of its municipality. Due to an unsatisfactory relationship with his old *Hausbank* (a neighbouring regional bank), he approached savings bank 1 to finance his new property investment. At the time of the observation the mortgage contract was signed, and the purchase payment was almost due. However, the back officer Mr Flick rejected the mortgage payout because Mr Wandland's old *Hausbank* refused to unblock a charge on the land from one of his other properties. Due to the high workload of the back office, Mr Flick did not detect this problem in a timely manner; i.e. he had delayed ordering the charge on the land clearance from the old *Hausbank* (SK1MPP19.11.13).

The example of Wandland Immobilien GmbH is informative because of the contrasting client assessments made by the customer advisor (Mrs Hennecke) and the credit officer (Mr Flick). Mrs Hennecke wanted to grant the mortgage, whereas Mr Flick preferred to withdraw the credit because of the issue with the charge on the land and other new information, as the daily protocol summarises:

- The project (purchase of a [apartment building]) is critical because of the poor location, which is why savings bank 1 demanded additional collaterals.
- The customer promised the collaterals, but the old *Hausbank* did not unblock them.
- The ability to cover future interest and principal payments on all objects is only marginally given.
- One of Wandland's accounts was under forced administration and debit notes were returned. Furthermore, he tried to a certain extent to conceal these facts wherefore the person is not trustworthy.
- For Mrs Hennecke the customer is very likeable and can explain the incidents.
- The feeling of the back office (Mr Flick) is that the mortgage is likely to get into trouble.
- Mrs Weber, who executes credit decision authority, says that if the mortgage actually gets into trouble after the warning from the back

office, then the market team has a problem and this absolutely rightly. Therefore, she advocates rejecting the mortgage.

- One other factor is that Mr Wandland is a new client and the business is relatively small and less profitable.
- Furthermore, the old *Hausbank* gave a rejecting bank enquiry, i.e. no information possible because of insufficient client knowledge, although the customer has high liabilities there; this bank enquiry astonishes savings bank 1, because as they later find out the customer had problems at the other regional bank, therefore a negative bank enquiry would have been appropriate (in this instance savings bank 1 would likely have rejected the credit request at the outset).

(SK1MPP19.11.13)

The differences in the customer evaluation tend to be explained by the personal impression Mr Wandland made on Mrs Hennecke; only she knows the client personally from two face-to-face meetings and a range of telephone calls. As the daily protocol outlines, Mrs Weber and Mr Flick further asked why savings bank 1 should grant a mortgage which is likely to get into trouble, e.g. payment delays, when the customer is new and not from the municipality of savings bank 1. Despite this negative evaluation, Mrs Hennecke continued to work on the case. She initially seemed to accept the rejection but changed her mind after talking to Mr Wandland. After this meeting Mrs Hennecke was convinced of Mr Wandland's integrity and believed his explanation that the old *Hausbank* treated him unfairly. She justified this conviction with her gut feeling (SK1MPP03.12.13). Two additional factors tend to explain the commitment of Mrs Hennecke. Firstly, savings bank 1 had already signed the mortgage contract and had never before withdrawn a confirmed credit. In belief of credit acceptance, Mr Wandland had purchased the property and faced profound legal problems if he failed to make the payment (SK1MPP09.12.13). Secondly, participant observation suggests that Mrs Hennecke felt personally unpleasant about informing Mr Wandland of the rejection, which would have been her task as customer advisor.

To advance this case, Mrs Hennecke called the old *Hausbank* to enquire about unblocking the land charge but the bank refused to provide information, invoking banking secrecy. Therefore, Mrs Hennecke re-approached the old bank with a permission letter from Mr Wandland and eventually managed to find a different way to gain the same amount of collaterals for savings bank 1. The daily protocol reports the codification of this solution:

Mrs Hennecke had called the [old *Hausbank*] and together with the customer she eventually persuaded the [old *Hausbank*] to unlocked parts of the collateral value. Furthermore, the customer delays one investment (in order to reduce the volume of the mortgage) and provides a smaller missing amount in cash on a money market account as additional security. Mrs Hennecke and I write the letter for the customer together. We summarise what Mrs Hennecke has agreed with Mr [Wandland] on the telephone. Mrs Hennecke wants the customer to sign the letter, so she is safe if it "explodes", i.e. if the [old *Hausbank*] does not keep to the agreement. We further specify an additional processing fee of €500, because a new credit application has to be written.

(SK1MPP09.12.13)

As the daily protocol reports, Mrs Hennecke applied an assurance strategy. She codified the results of the negotiation and made Mr Wandland sign it. The signed letter is not binding to the old *Hausbank*. Therefore, Mrs Hennecke increased the reliability of her soft information on the results of the negotiation with the signature in order to prove her successful negotiation of a solution in case the new credit contract fails again. After Mr Wandland signed the letter, Mrs Hennecke compiled the work instruction for Mr Flick, specifying the new mortgage volume and collateralisation (SK1MPP11.12.13). She further instructed Mr Flick to instantly request the unblocking of the land charge from the old *Hausbank*. During the negotiation, Mrs Hennecke kept Mr Flick and Mrs Weber informed. Both colleagues accepted this solution because the total collateralisation of the credit did not change with the new collaterals. All actors, including Mrs Hennecke, highlighted that they would not have forwarded the credit application if they had initially been aware of Mr Wandland's distressed financial situation (SK1MPP09.12.13).

The example of Wandland Immobilien illustrates discrepancies in the evaluations of customers between bank employees who personally know the clients and employees without personal contact. The customer case further indicates that personal interaction is able to alter customer evaluations; i.e. the honest impression which Mr Wandland made on Mrs Hennecke was one key explanation for Mrs Hennecke's willingness to continue lending. Having said this, customer advisors' aversion to communicating bad news to their clients, i.e. the withdrawal of the mortgage, also tends to explain Mrs Hennecke's behaviour. Finally, the Wandland Immobilien case indicates savings bank 1's positive discrimination towards existing clients and clients from its municipality. The strong engagement for Mr Wandland tends to be rather the exception than the norm.

4.3.2 *Distance and credit decisions*

Bringing together empirical findings about actors' interaction in the process of credit decision making, this section discusses the interplay of distance, information and credit decisions with reference to the customer cases described in the previous section. Section 4.3.2.1 discusses the empirical findings on the interplay between hard and soft information, functional distance and credit decisions. Against the background of the result that big bank 1 actually decides ca. 50% of medium-sized SME credits at shorter functional distance than savings bank 1, the discussion considers the implications for the widespread assumption that regional banks decide SME credits at shorter distances than supraregional banks. Sections 4.3.2.2 to 4.3.2.4 look at the role of geographical distance in credit decision making. As empirical findings indicate face-to-face interactions to be subordinated to organisational embeddedness for short distance between actors, Section 4.3.2.2 brings together empirical findings on the role of face-to-face meetings in SME lending. Section 4.3.2.3 turns to co-location and banks' regional embeddedness, and identifies co-location as one channel by which banks gain additional information for the SME credit business. Finally, Section 4.3.2.4 discusses the micro-geographical scale, i.e. bank branches, and indicates that micro-geography is to be considered as one aspect of operational distance capable of influencing lending.

4.3.2.1 Hard and soft information, functional distance and credit decisions

The customer advisors need soft information about their clients as inputs to the credit applications and to execute the qualitative rating module. However, soft information decidedly influences lending if hard information is inconclusive, participant observation indicates. The case of Wandland Immobilien, where the customer advisor's gut feeling about the integrity of the owner outvoted critical hard information (e.g. forced administration), demonstrates this. In a similar way, the evaluation of Schmidt Solutions is informed by soft and 'rather' hard information which the customer advisor had gained in a long and close business relationship. In interview the former credit officer of savings bank 1 confirmed this observation:

F.F.:   How important is soft information in practice really, thus where is it really important?

Answer: I think this is especially important if the hard facts do not allow a clear picture, thus there is the biggest relevancy of soft information really. This means if I have no worries with the hard facts, the ability to cover interest and principal payments is given, sufficient collaterals are there, then it is almost unimportant if the management is not particularly good, or particularly well educated etc. It is just the same if the credit application is hopeless. Everything that does not fit this black and white picture, there it is of course a big point if the managing owners are believed to be able to successfully repay the credits or not.

(SK1BSIT02.09.13)

As the interview partner stated, positive hard information tends to imply positive lending decisions and definite negative hard information, i.e. if the credit application is without hope, suggests credit rejection regardless of soft information. One case was observed at savings bank 1 where Mrs Weber rejected the credit enquiry of a new client on the basis of hard information from the application. Mrs Weber even refused a personal meeting because she did not want to raise the hopes of the client (SK1MPP04.12.13). As Mr Holz reported, big bank 1 frequently rejects (especially new) clients based on negative hard information (GB1MIT25.09.13II). Because of big bank 1's strict rating score cutoff limit, Mr Holz and his team do not take a closer look at credit requests that they believe will gain a poor rating score. This finding indicates the discouragement of the customer advisors' screening efforts by functional distance, as predicted in the Stein (2002) model (Section 2.2.2.2).

In a similar way to the observation at savings bank 1, the team leader of big bank 1 indicated the decisive character of soft information in cases of inconclusive hard information. It is the task of the customer advisors to decide if they consider the soft information to be sufficiently plausible to explain a client's negative hard information and to convince the decision-makers of the credit application:

Holz: At least once I am out there [at the premises of the customers], I also conduct a guided tour through the company if possible, which is also the most interesting aspect of the job.

F.F.:   I believe you.

Holz: This firstly and then there are the numbers. They have to fit of course. But if they do not fit the customer normally has an explanation for this. And then I have to decide for myself can I represent this, are the figures only so bad because of a special effect, can I explain this internally. Or are the numbers so poor and the customer cannot explain this to me plausibly, because the business model has no success. Then I cannot invest. As every credit is an investment of the bank.

F.F.:   And then you would argue in the credit application, for example, annual financial statement or BWA reports a negative trend but this and that?

Holz: But business model or client was able to acquire new customers, or is opening a new business area or could not gain profit because of restricted. . . , thus normally there are reasons.

(GB1MIT11.02.14)

Mr Holz's examples of information which explains negative hard information tend to be 'rather' hard information instead of soft information. For example, if an SME opens a new business area, contracts and other documents testify the activities in this area – though the appraisal of the documents is expensive for actors who are unfamiliar with the client. In this sense, decision-makers have difficulties to directly verify the information in the actual situation of appraisal, but verification by third parties is in principle possible, wherefore the information does not count as soft information. In contrast, as the customer cases show, the customer advisors of savings bank 1 transmit soft information like gut feelings and implicit guarantees of relatives to the credit officers and supervisors. The profoundly longer distance to the decision-makers, i.e. credit officers and high level supervisors, at big bank 1 potentially explains this difference from the savings bank.

When banks consider soft and 'rather' hard information firms tend to benefit. However, this information is also able to qualify positive hard information and prevent lending. Savings bank 1's information on Mr Schmidt's high private expenses which negated his future ability to serve debt (which was given on the basis of his financial records) exemplifies this. Similarly, Mr Holz stated that soft information is able to reject lending to firms with sound rating scores at big bank 1:

F.F.:   Does it also happen that you say to a customer with a super rating score we would rather not do business with you anymore?

Holz: We had this last year, recently there was a customer here who was tip top on the rating, but there the customer advisors and I did not have a good feeling about the person simply, there we said sorry there is nothing, because the discussions were always like that, the questions we posed, there you got the impression he was not very fit in his business. If there were questions about the sector, then he told us anything, where we had completely different insights, thus we said, that is overall not convincing. We said sorry then, here you get nothing.

(GB1MIT25.09.13II)

Mr Holz's report was about a credit decision from the previous year (the interview was conducted in September), which implies that at big bank 1 credit rejections made on the basis of soft information tend to be rare. Overall, participant observation and the interview results indicate the role of soft and 'rather' hard information in credit decisions as being decisive in cases of inconclusive hard information. As soft information is only able to influence rating scores to a limited degree (Section 4.2.2.1), SMEs with inconclusive hard information tend to be rated with medium to poor scores by savings banks as well as by big bank 1. Because of the distanced back-office team and the strict rating score cutoff limit, big bank 1 decides at a longer functional distance to SMEs with medium and poor rating scores compared to savings bank 1. In precisely these cases soft information potentially influences credit decisions most, indicating savings bank 1's superiority in soft information processing when it matters.

4.3.2.2 Face-to-face interactions

Face-to-face interactions are considered to be superior for the transmission of soft information, and Boschma (2005) and others point out their influence in reinforcing other forms of proximity (Section 2.2.3.3). However, as the customer advisor–credit officer pairs at savings bank 1 show, face-to-face interaction is subordinated to organisational embeddedness as a cause of the observed short distance of cooperation (Section 4.2.3.1). Observations and interviews find four occasions for face-to-face meetings in the process of credit granting. Firstly, face-to-'objects' meetings; secondly, face-to-face meetings to maintain personal contacts; thirdly, initial 'get to know each other' meetings; and, fourthly, face-to-face negotiations. The relevance of the four occasions in the process of credit granting is discussed in the following with a focus on the transmission of information.

The actual aim of face-to-'object' meetings is to come into contact with physical objects; i.e. customers deliver original documents to their banks, or the customer advisors visit their clients to sign lending contracts (GB1MIT11.02.14).

One other example is the property evaluations. The internal surveyors of savings bank 1 have to visit every piece of real estate before writing the property valuation report. Surveyors take the hard information about the properties, like cash flow, size, occupations, purchase price etc., from the documents. The observation of one survey showed that the surveyor inspected the rooftop and boiler room to identify apparent defects to estimate upcoming costs for renewals (SK1MPP27.11.13). Accordingly, information gained at these face-to-'object' meetings tend to be 'rather' hard as there is a need for direct encounters with the objects to gain and verify the information, e.g. condition of the property, validity of the document. After examination of the objects by one of its employees, savings bank 1 considers the information as reliable, making it unrestrictedly transmittable between the actors involved in the process of credit granting. This means, for example, that the collateral value of the evaluation report or the authenticity of a signature is not questioned after they have passed the initial evaluation of the bank.

Maintaining personal contacts through face-to-face meetings is a task of the customer advisors where gaining soft information is subordinated to reinforcing socially embedded cooperation. Customer advisors conduct these meetings with colleagues (GB1MIT25.09.13II GB1MIT11.02.14, SK1BSPP19.12.13) and clients. Big bank 1, big bank 3 and savings bank 4 have specified activity targets for face-to-face meetings with clients. The major aim of these meetings is to maintain contacts in order to initiate sales; the meetings also comprise information-related aims, like the annual ratings talks where the customer advisors explain the rating results to their clients (Middelberg and Plegge 2010). Savings bank 1 has no activity targets, but the customer advisors still conduct meetings to keep personal contacts. For example, before Christmas Mrs Hennecke conducted a face-to-face meeting with a manager where she also appointed the renewal of a credit line. Yet, the meeting was clearly motivated by the aim to maintain personal contact, as the contract agreement was undisputed and could have been conducted via telephone. Accordingly, the customer and Mrs Hennecke chatted about business and private matters and complemented each other with small Christmas presents (SK1MPP13.12.13).

Banks conduct 'get to know each other' meetings at the beginning of new business relationships and for larger new business, a range of interviewees stated (SK3MIT24.09.13, SK3MIT18.08.13, SK4MIT25.10.13, GB1MIT11.02.14, GB1MIT25.06.13I). For example, savings bank 3's customer advisors make clear: "well it always starts with a talk, you talk with the customer, what does he want" (SK3MIT24.09.13). At big bank 1, credit analysts, product specialists and several other actors (e.g. consortium partners) also participate in 'get to know each other' meetings in case of extensive credit decisions (large SME size class), though the initial meeting tends to take place between the customer and his advisors:

F.F.:   Do you meet with the whole consortium team, thus also with the competitors or is this unusual?

Holz: It depends on how far along the talks are. So the first meeting is normally always conducted between the company and the customer advisor. With [firm name] it was like this, they started in March or April with the first talks with big bank 1, I and the special department were there, thus we said you want to get there, that is what you want, this is about the structure. Then we conducted a talk in autumn, firstly only with the customer advisor side of all candidate banks so to say, these banks are in principle willing to join the consortium, thus firstly only on the side of customer advisors, though the one or other bank also brought along its back office, but this is not necessary, then from this so to say a catalogue of requests was given to the participating banks. There you introduce yourself and outline what you as a bank want to do basically and based on this a following meeting is then conducted with the back offices, with the specialists, then you have a big gathering. And after this there are actually no further personal talks but only talks via telephone conference, because for [firm name] there are banks, we from this city, then one from [other city], then one from [other distant city] and one from [other distant city]. Thus you do everything only by telephone, and you only have a further meeting after the credit approval, when the contracts are really signed, all other things are done via telephone.

(GB1MIT25.09.13II)

As the interview excerpt indicates, these initial meetings are important to get to know each other and to understand the client's demands. After the initial series of meetings, i.e. when actors know each other, face-to-face interaction becomes rare, Mr Holz pointed out, and explained this with the geographical distance of the actors involved. The participant observation at savings bank 1 shows that in existing customer relationships 'get to know each other' meetings are not mandatory for new credit requests as in a range of cases new lending was arranged via telephone and e-mail only. This observation suggests that the main function of initial meetings is in fact to 'get to know each other' rather than to exchange information on the credit request. Accordingly, savings bank 1 always interviews new SME customers face-to-face regardless of the size of their credit request.

Face-to-face negotiations are crucial for deciding on action in case of disagreements between the actors. Hard negotiations relate to price negotiation, credit decisions and restructuring and workout decisions (see also Section 4.2.1.1). They take place between firms' management and banks as well as bank internally (e.g. watch list meetings, see Box 4.9, p. 200). Even so, it was not possible to observe any of these negotiations because they were too sensitive; the participant observation recorded a range of hard negotiations indirectly as customer advisors reported after the meetings.

Arguably the key aim of such meetings is to transmit and verify soft information in order to agree on action. In line with the uncertainty of soft information's interpersonal reliability, the outcome of face-to-face negotiations is uncertain. One example of an action-changing meeting was the negotiation between Mrs Hennecke and her client Mr Wandland where Mrs Hennecke went into the meeting with the intention of communicating the credit rejection. However, Mr Wandland convinced her otherwise, so that she started searching for a solution to be able to grant the credit (Section 4.3.1.4). As the Wandland Immobilien example illustrates, the outcome of these negotiations is also uncertain for the bank employees. Therefore, Mrs Kurz felt uneasy about a renegotiation of terms with one customer in a face-to-face meeting as she feared she would give in to the client's demand (Section 4.2.1.1). Also the bank internal watch list meetings tend to exemplify hard negotiations. Here savings bank 1 decides how to deal with financially distressed clients. Before these meetings the actors exchange documents and fill in the watch list module of OSPlus; thus, available information is exchanged in preparation of the actual meetings. Therefore, arguably actors verify soft information at such meetings and collectively appoint action on the basis of all hard and soft information available.

To sum up, face-to-face meetings have several purposes and the transmission of soft information is only one among others such as initiating sales and reinforcing social embeddedness. Only face-to-face negotiations are usually conducted with the explicit aim of verifying soft information and agreeing on action in the process of deciding on lending. Accordingly, the outcomes of negotiations are uncertain also for the bank employees.

4.3.2.3 Co-location

As Section 2.2.3.3 outlines, co-location is associated with information advantages of firms. Bathelt et al. (2004) highlight, on the one hand, that co-location almost unavoidably delivers access to the local buzz, but on the other hand the quality of local buzz depends on the regional embeddedness of actors. The participant observation and the interviews identify co-location as one channel for information when lending to SMEs. The Anlagenbau Mustermann case represents the most telling example of this. Here savings bank 1's relationship to the local trade union was the reason the bank received the information (Section 4.3.1.2). The interview partners from the other regional banks comment on the relevance of co-location, but also highlight that this channel of information becomes relevant only in a few cases:

F.F.: Is there other market information, like national accounting, economic outlook, etc.

Answer: [. . .] you are of course always in discussion here; you are in discussion with the business consultants, with the colleagues, how this company develops and how that company develops of course.

(SK3MIT24.09.13)

F.F.: How does the difference in regional presence impact banks?

Answer: Yes, above all risk minimising I would say and of course this is the most important thing. Risk minimising in this way, that I have got a chance to see the object. And in this regional frame they also simply get information, thus they get information about borrowers, thus this implicit stuff.

(OSGVIT04.03.13)

F.F.:   Does something like regional knowledge, you said you are from this
           place you know a lot here, does this matter?

Answer: Also a little bit may be, well because everybody knows everybody
           somehow a little bit or the managing directors have more often contact
           and they know the customers, meet them like at Lions Club, Rotary,
           golf tournaments, these things. They come sometimes and have infor-
           mation that they give us.

                                                            (SK3MIT18.08.13)

All three interview excerpts indicate how co-location is useful to provide additional information about customers and their business, though the interviewed
bank employees make moderate claims regarding the frequency and relevance
of this information. The last interview extract outlines the managing director's primary role in maintaining contacts to regional actors. This role was also
observed at savings bank 1 where the CEO and other high-level supervisors not
only participate in private activities (Lions Club etc.) but are also members of
official regional groups (like the regional economy council and municipal business development agency), as well as attending events and conferences. Furthermore, with the administrative council the governance structure of savings banks
automatically connects them to regional politics, society and economy. The interview partners of savings bank 2 discuss the importance of being involved to gain
information and consider the bank's regional sponsoring as another instrument to
maintain regional relationships and get involved (SK2MIP13.03.132). Accordingly, the interview findings indicate that regional savings banks actively promote
regional embeddedness, i.e. being involved in their region.

Similarly, for Mr Holz, the team leader at big bank 1, regional presence is important in the SME business. Presence not only comprises personal meetings with
the customers but also being involved in regional affairs. Therefore, Mr Holz participates in the regional employers' association and the regional economic council, which is explicitly part of his job as regional branch manager of big bank 1
(GB1MIT25.06.13I). Revealingly, the customer advisor from big bank 3 –
the bank that finances SMEs without co-location – on the one hand stressed the
advantage of co-location for gaining information. On the other hand, he reported on
the development of close relationships to his geographically distant clients which
eventually replace relationships to local agents, i.e. co-located business consultancies:

F.F.:   Does regional anchoring also have advantages in sales?

Answer: Yes, you are, of course, closer to the individual decisions and to the
           stories of the people, if I – and it was like this at [big bank 3] – conduct
           everything at a distance of over 400 to 500 kilometres via telephone,
           then I depend on being provided with information from the customers,
           but there's no information from the surroundings.

                                                            (GB3MIT29.05.13I)

Let's say about 80% [of the customers have been conveyed] by agents, then
the agents, and that was also a phenomenon, slipped out of the relationship

after 10, 15 years, this means they were not close enough to the clients, and let them go and then they were totally in our hands.

(GB3MIT29.05.13I)

As the interview with big bank 3 indicates, close customer relationships are also able to develop across long geographical distances. Hence, co-location is not a necessary condition for relationship banking. Overall the empirical findings identify co-location as one channel by which banks gain information in the SME credit business, though bank employees consider such information as less decisive for most lending decisions. Banks actively promote regional embeddedness, i.e. get involved in the region to gain information.

4.3.2.4 The micro-geography of operational distance

Micro-geographical differences in the accessibility of the studied bank branches for the SME customers have been detected between savings bank 1 and big bank 1. As Box 4.4 (p. 171) sets out, due to the accessible branch design, clients are easily able to approach their customer advisors face-to-face, and indeed do approach them unannounced at savings bank 1. In contrast, customers must register at the counter before visiting their customer advisors at big bank 1. This section discusses the impact of the micro-geographical operational distance, i.e. accessibility, on the relationship between clients and customer advisors (see also Flögel and Zademach 2017).[7] The participant observation at savings bank 1 indicates that personal communication with clients is not always desirable from a bank employee's point of view for the following reasons:

- No interest in new business with certain clients. For example, one manager had performed badly in a property development project that was financed by savings bank 1. When he telephoned his customer advisor Mrs Kurz for a loan to develop a new property, she was very reserved and asked for many additional documents instead of offering to meet in person. Mrs Kurz indicated that she would be happy if the customer asked another bank to finance his project but was reluctant to reject him harshly due to concerns about compromising the existing loan contracts (SK1MPP02.12.13).
- No interest in the renegotiation of existing contracts. Personal negotiations with clients become emotional from time to time and always carry the risk of an uncertain outcome (see Section 4.3.2.2). Therefore, the customer advisors occasionally prefer to avoid personal encounters to prevent unpleasant verbal conflicts and render it less likely that they give in to the demands of the customers.
- Time constraints, i.e. the bank employees have not yet made an internal decision on how to act, or currently just have no time to interact with the clients (SK1MPP13.12.13).

The customer advisors of savings bank 1 are only able to avoid personal encounters in the case of telephone calls (SK1MPP04.12.2013) because of the micro-geographical accessibility of their branch. Often customers just pop into the offices (without prior announcement) and consequently make the customer advisors interact with them. Thus, the advisors are forced to interact with the clients and take a position. In the light of the uncertain outcomes of face-to-face negotiations and customer advisors' disinclination to communicate negative decisions to their customers face-to-face (Section 4.3.2.2), micro-geographical accessibility indicates to be a relevant aspect of the relationship between the customer advisors and SME clients. It restricts the ability of customer advisors to ignore the demands of their clients and may lead to more decisions in favour of the customers, as bank employees must consider the possibility of personal interactions with them. Against the background the inaccessibility of the customer advisors in the big bank sticks out as they have the ability to avoid spontaneous personal interaction, i.e. negotiations.

As already indicated, the architectural layout of savings bank 1's branch limits the feasibility of tactically avoiding spontaneous face-to-face interactions. Nevertheless, customer advisors try to manage the length and topics of the meetings with their selection of rooms. The following example illustrate this point: On one occasion a customer called and wanted to hand in his annual financial statements just before closing time. His advisor Mrs Kurz was not pleased because the customer was known to be talkative. The team joked that Mrs Kurz should avoid a talk in the meeting room because talking there would extend the duration of the discussion. To keep the interaction short, Mrs Kurz received her client in the counter hall and was back in the office within minutes – to the surprise of Mrs Hennecke (SK1MPP13.12.13).

Directing customers to the meeting room – and offering coffee, tea and biscuits – is an important tactic to extend the length of the meetings. In a similar way Mrs Weber closes her office door when she wants to conduct extensive discussions with her clients (her office contains a round table for meetings). Such selecting tactics also influence the topic of the talks because customer advisors can address critical and sensitive topics in the confidential environment of a meeting room; the restricted seclusion in an office that is shared by multiple customer advisors is less conducive for such conversations. As Mrs Hennecke pointed out, certain customers are aware of these placing tactics, especially Mr Schmidt refused to enter the meeting room because he knows that his extensive private spending will be addressed there (see Section 4.3.1.1). Therefore, Mr Schmidt would rather approach Mrs Hennecke unannounced in her office to discuss the settlements of his payment obligations. The shared office of the SME team was barely suitable for addressing critical topics because of the presence of the other customer advisors, ringing telephones, the risk of being disturbed by other customers and, not least, the presence of a trainee. It hence becomes clear that the confidentiality of sites influences the length and topics of face-to-face interactions.

At big bank 1, tactical customer interactions were not recorded, because no participant observation was conducted. The interviews with the big bank provide no direct indications in this regard, which is to be expected considering the sensitivity of the topic. Nevertheless, several comments indicate the way in which big bank 1 tactically interacts with its clients. Mr Holz confirmed that smaller customers tend to be served more slowly because customer advisors process the large deals first, which explains the relevance of segregation between large and medium-sized SMEs (GB1MIT25.06.13I). Other interview partners mentioned big banks' rigorous customer segregation and discrimination of less profitable clients (Geno2MIT23.02.14II, GenoZMIP12.09.14, GB3MIT29.05.13I). The SMEs interviewed in Handke's (2011) investigation also reported on the difficulty of gaining access to their customer advisors when they were considered less profitable by their big bank, indicating big banks' tactical handling of client interactions.

Overall, accessibility of bank branches influences the relationships between customers and customer advisors as it restricts advisors' ability to avoid personal encounters, which potentially leads to more decisions in favour of the customers. Accordingly, the micro-geography of bank branches is to be considered as one aspect of operational distance, indicating the longer operational distance to clients of big bank 1 in comparison to savings bank 1 with regard to micro-geography. Participant observation at savings bank 1 also made clear that the confidentiality of rooms represents another micro-geographical characteristic of sites that influences face-to-face interaction between banks and their clients. Recently, Zook and Grote (2016) demonstrated the impact of the micro-geographical scale on high frequency trading. The study in hand shows that the micro-geographical scale is to be considered in bank-based SME finance, too.

4.3.3 Credit-granting willingness to financially distressed SMEs and bad debt

This section discusses the empirical findings on the willingness of banks to find solutions for financially distressed firms, i.e. the willingness to lend (Section 4.3.3.1), and looks at the effects of credit-granting willingness on banks' credit portfolios. As Section 4.3.3.2 indicates, this willingness to support SMEs does not come at the price of higher bad debt.

4.3.3.1 Credit-granting willingness

Banks' willingness to find solutions for financially distressed SMEs of the medium size class depends on three dimensions that are independent of firms' actual financial situation, the empirical findings indicate. Firstly, banks are more willing to lend in close and long-standing customer relationships. Secondly, banks' assessment of the sector outlook influences their willingness to grant credits to firms from this sector. Thirdly, the economic importance of the SME for the region motivates the dual-purpose savings banks to grant credits to enterprises located in their regions (Figure 4.22). The sector and customer relationship influence willingness to grant credits at big bank 1, too, whereas the location of the SMEs tends

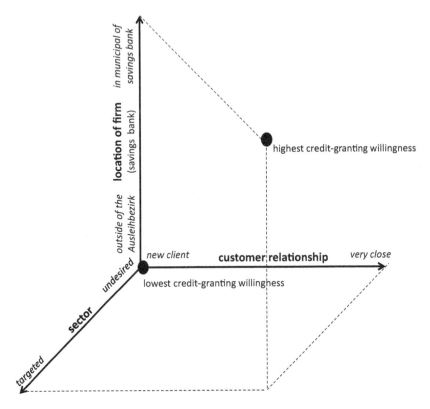

Figure 4.22 Credit-granting willingness of banks

Source: author's figure

to matter for the savings bank only. In the following the empirical findings on the three aspects are discussed.

In line with relationship banking theory, the proximity of the customer relationships impacts savings bank 1's willingness to find a solution for firms in critical financial situations (*x*-axis of Figure 4.22). On the one hand, this willingness relates to the soft-budget constraint problem; i.e. if banks reject (working capital) credit requests from existing clients with financial difficulties, there is a substantial risk of firm default. Therefore, savings bank 1 has an interest to find financial solutions to prevent the default of clients, as exemplified in the customer cases Schmidt Solutions, Anlagenbau Mustermann and Retailer Kampfgarten (Section 4.3.1). Consequently, if hard information identifies a critical financial situation, then savings bank 1 is more willing to lend to existing clients than to new customers; e.g. the only rejection based on hard information observed was a request from a new customer (see Section 4.2.4.2). On the other hand, participant observation further indicates that the duration and closeness of the relationship impact the willingness of the savings bank to lend for two reasons. Firstly, customer advisors develop attachments and feelings of responsibility towards their clients in close relationships which make it more difficult for them to make and communicate (face-to-face) decisions adversely affecting their clients. Secondly, in line with relationship banking theory, the scope and reliability of information in close relationships increase with time. This informational advantage enables customer advisors to handle clients' financial difficulties on an informed basis (see Schmidt Solutions, Section 4.3.1.1), which is restricted in distant customer relationships (see Anlagenbau Mustermann, Section 4.3.1.2).

Interview findings indicate similar conduct at big bank 1. Mr Maske reported on the personal attachment to clients in long relationships (GB1MIT11.02.14). Mr Holz stressed that they are willing to "push the credit through all authority" (GB1MIT25.09.13II) if they are convinced of a firm's future profitability regardless of negative hard information for existing clients. Nevertheless, as demonstrated, the process of credit decision-making restricts the ability of the customer advisors to do this for SMEs of the medium size class.

The sector of the SMEs has an impact on the willingness to grant credits at savings bank 1 and big bank 1 (z-axis of Figure 4.22), though the explanation for sector discriminations tend to differ. The sector discrimination of big bank 1 results from its risk controlling and assessment of the sector's outlook. Risk management has implemented strict lending prohibitions for certain sectors (e.g. renewable energy) and types of firms (e.g. start-ups); for other sectors, upper credit volume limits are defined (see Section 4.2.5.1). At savings bank 1, the relevance of the sector for regional development represents one important reason why the savings bank tends to be less willing to lend to the real estate sector, more precisely to speculative real estate developers, compared to all other sectors (SK1MPP28.11.13). Two reasons explain this discrimination. Firstly, the relatively high exposure of savings bank 1 to the real estate sector (see Section 4.2.5.1). Secondly, savings bank 1 perceives speculative real estate developers to be less important for regional economic development. The Wandland Immobilien case demonstrates why savings bank 1 has this perception (see Section 4.3.1.4). Mr Wandland speculates with real estate to increase his personal wealth. His firm has no employees. The rejection of a mortgage request from Mr Wandland would either imply that he needs to find another bank or that another investor would purchase the property, as a range of individuals and firms conduct similar businesses in the region.

In fact, savings bank 1 tries to slow down the active real estate speculation market and demands substantial equity contributions from real estate developers. Accordingly, the offering of so-called 'defence terms' to real estate developers with the intention to frustrate lending was observed several times (SK1MPP26.11.13). In this sense, the public mandate arguably motivates savings bank 1's discrimination of speculative real estate developers, as the bank perceives these enterprises as being less important for regional development.

The following excerpt from the interview with the former credit officer of savings bank 1 underlines the influence of the public mandate for savings banks' willingness to support regional SMEs:

F.F.:   From your point of view, are there relevant differences between savings and big banks with regard to SME finance? And I am now talking about bigger commercial customers, ca. from €100,000 up to €10 million.

Answer: Yes, I think there are big differences in the starting basis, all that is specified or not necessarily codified as a public mandate in a way and also the self-conceptions of these banks are different. I think that especially for savings banks the public mandate plays a big role. This mandate leads to the fact that a different view is selected for credit decisions, rather than the plain economic view. This means not only pursuit of profit and also, I don't know, risk minimising, but also other backgrounds like development, structural change in the region, preserving jobs, etc. These are motivations of the savings banks, and also of the cooperative banks, that differ to private banks [. . .]. A savings bank from [region x] has a very different connection to [region x] than a big bank [in region x] as big banks can just withdraw from this region etc. The savings or cooperative banks only have their market area, they have no alternative.

                                                            (SK1BSIT02.09.13)

As the interview partner pointed out, savings banks' public mandate and the regional principle together explain their willingness to support SMEs from their region, i.e. stressing the argument that savings banks have no alternative to doing business in their region, provoking a self-interest in regional development. Accordingly, a firm's location (*y*-axis of Figure 4.22) influences savings banks' willingness to lend, as they tend to be more obligated to lend to enterprises from their municipality (SK3MIT24.09.13, SK3MIT18.08.13, OSGVIT04.03.13). Nevertheless, participant observation revealed that regional savings bank 1 grants a range of credits within its much larger *Ausleihbezirk*. Even lending outside the *Ausleihbezirk* was observed, which is actually restricted by the regional principle. In these cases, the bank demands a written justification for lending elsewhere, which in one observed case was cultural affiliation to the firm (SK1MFPP15.11.13). Though lending is not restricted to its municipality, a preference for regional firms was obvious at savings bank 1, whereas at big bank 1 "regional does not matter" (GB1MFIP05.11.12).

Overall, the empirical findings suggest that savings bank 1 is most willing to find financial solutions for distressed firms in long and close customer relationships, from all sectors except the real estate sector located within its municipality. Although long and close customer relationships also tend to influence big bank 1's willingness to lend, the bank discriminates against sectors which are perceived to be risky, and regional economic considerations do not affect willingness to lend. Accordingly, the public mandate and regional principle provoke a willingness to support the local economy, suggesting savings bank 1 takes higher risks than big bank 1.

4.3.3.2 Non-performing loans of savings bank 1 and big bank 1

As the previous section showed, the public mandate and regional principle increase savings bank 1's inclination to lend to financially distressed firms, especially from its region. This greater willingness to lend, in comparison with the big bank, implies higher transaction costs (considering the effort involved in dealing with financially distressed clients) and higher rates of credit default. However, the qualitative findings also indicate superior screening and monitoring by savings bank 1, allowing the regional bank to capitalise on soft information advantages, potentially reducing credit default and bootstring earning.

As discussed in Section 2.1.2.2, empirical studies show that German savings banks do not underperform in terms of profitability or stability in comparison to their private peers (Ayadi et al. 2009; Beck et al. 2009; Behr et al. 2013). The ratio of non-performing loans to total credits represents an indicator of banks' credit portfolio performance (Christians and Gärtner 2014, 2015). Banks must publish these values in the annual pillar 3 disclosures reports, as Basel II regulates. Figure 4.23 reports the non-performing loan ratios of the corporate credit portfolio of savings bank 1 and big bank 1 in 2010 and 2013. The banks showed comparable ratios of non-performing loans in 2010 (5.02% for savings bank 1 compared to 5.37% for big bank 1) and outperformed the average of the savings

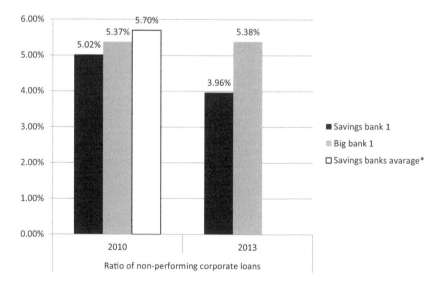

Figure 4.23 Ratio of non-performing corporate loans of savings bank 1 and big bank 1

* Cited in: Christians and Gärtner 2014

Source: author's figure from the pillar 3 disclosures of savings bank 1 and big bank 1 banks in 2010. In 2013 savings bank 1 showed a substantially lower ratio of non-performing loans than the big bank. A 1.05 percent point decrease of savings bank 1's non-performing loan ratio caused the superior performance. Therefore, this coarse comparison indicates a lower rather than higher proportion of non-performing loans of savings bank 1's corporate credit portfolio, despite its higher credit-granting willingness compared to the big bank.

When considering this finding, it is important to highlight that the comparison of non-performing loans is a coarse indicator for the success in screening and monitoring of the contrasted banks for two reasons. Firstly, the non-performing loan ratio reflects all (on and off balance sheet) corporate credits of the banks and not only lending to medium-sized SMEs. Especially for big bank 1, credits to smaller SMEs represent a minor proportion of its corporate loan portfolio. Secondly, non-performing loans depend on banks' allowance policies which potentially differ between savings bank 1 and big bank 1. Nevertheless, as lending to large companies is associated with lower PD compared to medium-sized SMEs, savings bank 1's lower proportion of bad debt in 2013 in fact suggests that the greater willingness to lend to financially distressed firms does not come at the price of amplified risk taking. As this study indicates, savings bank 1's superior ability to consider soft information in lending to financially distressed SMEs represents one potential explanation for the surprising result.

Notes

1 Savings bank 1 also asks for disclosure if the customers have business credits of more than €100,000 independent of the overall (business + private) credit volumes (SK1MFPP18.11.13).
2 The names have been changed.
3 To protect anonymity, this work does not report the precise nomenclature of big bank 1's rating scores.
4 Mr Holz's estimation includes the renewal of existing credits; the rejection rate because of poor rating scores tends to be higher for credit applications of new customers.
5 Minor differences can exist because the customer advisors who serve larger borrower units tend to interact more often with the relevant high-level supervisors, e.g. at joint customer meetings. Therefore, customer advisors that serve larger borrower units potentially operate at short distances to their supervisors.
6 Because the influence of lower accessibility on the customer–customer advisor interaction was not observed at big bank 1 (due to the methodological limitation of interviews) its impact on operational distance cannot be deduced.
7 Parts of this section are published in Flögel and Zademach (2017).

5 Conclusion

This ethnographic comparison scrutinises the widespread assumption that regional banks lend at shorter distances to SMEs than large banks and thus gain soft information advantages for credit decisions. Opening the 'black box' of banks' internal lending processes was necessary to advance our understanding of distance in the lending of modern regional and large banks, both of which use rating systems to conduct lending decisions and must handle tightened bank regulation. In essence, ethnographic insights surprisingly revealed that big bank 1, which was studied in-depth, had shorter functional distances when lending up to €1 million to SMEs with sound rating scores than the observed savings bank 1. Big bank 1's slim lending process organisation for smaller SMEs explains this unexpected finding, as the bank allocates unrestricted lending authority to the local customer advisors in cases of sound rating scores, whereas savings bank 1's CEO must approve credits of this size. However, participant observation at savings bank 1 demonstrated that soft information most strongly influences lending decisions when hard information about SMEs is inconclusive and that this inconclusive information causes inferior rating results. In precisely such cases, the savings bank makes lending decisions at shorter functional distances – in terms of organisational and social embeddedness as well as geographical distance – to decision-makers, thus enabling the consideration of soft information, in line with the widespread assumption. Observation of lending cases further suggests that savings bank 1 capitalises on soft information, which tends to reduce credit rationing to financially distressed SMEs and fosters profitable lending to such clients.

The remainder of this chapter is organised as follows. Section 5.1 outlines the key findings. Section 5.2 deduces practitioner recommendations, and Section 5.3 suggests further research directions.

5.1 Key findings

It is argued that distance hampers the transmission of soft information. Hence, regional banks – operating over short distances – obtain more soft information from their clients than large banks, and therefore gain information advantages which reduce credit rationing, especially to informationally opaque SMEs. Conceptualising from Stein (2002) and Alessandrini et al. (2009b), increasing operational distance is associated with declines in the screening and monitoring success of banks' customer advisors. Increases in functional distance influence supervisors' screening and monitoring success adversely and discourage the screening and monitoring efforts of the customer advisors (see Section 2.2.2). However, modern regional and large banks must comply with the same regulatory standards and accordingly apply centrally developed rating systems for SME lending in Germany. Furthermore, large banks can and do delegate lending authority to their local branches, and advances in ICT potentially obviate the necessity of short distances for the transmission of soft information (see also Flögel 2018). Therefore, the widespread assumption of regional banks' information advantages due to short distances in lending must be scrutinised.

The book in hand examined this widespread assumption by contrasting the actual credit-granting processes of regional and large banks by considering, among other actors, the rating systems as (asymmetric) non-human actors capable of shaping lending decisions. New realist ontology, the extended actor concept of ANT and the theory on the performativity of economics (MacKenzie 2006) proved useful for analysing banks' lending actor-networks and understanding the 'behaviour' of rating systems (Section 2.3). In particular, the empirical in-depth comparison of the regional savings bank 1 and big bank 1 collected two variables – decision-making power and distance – for the human and non-human actors involved in SME lending, thus specifying total distance. To this end, participant observation, i.e. a two-month, full-time internship, was conducted in the savings bank and the findings were compared to big bank 1, where six informative interviews with employees yielded detailed insights into the lending practices of a branch located in the same region as the savings bank. In addition, 34 interviews with bank employees of regional and supraregional banks and related experts were conducted, also to estimate the generalisability of findings from the in-depth comparison.

The direct comparison of savings bank 1 with big bank 1 shows that the greatest differences exist in the integration of the rating systems and supervisors/back officers in credit decisions to medium-sized SMEs (revenue: €500,000 to €10 million; total business credits of borrower unit: €100,000 to €5 million). Savings bank 1 does not reject a credit application from an SME solely on the basis of the rating score, rather the score only allocates decision-making authority; i.e. the greater the PD of a firm according to the rating result, the more supervisors at higher levels must approve the lending decision. In contrast, big bank 1 defines a strict rating score cutoff limit. SMEs with poor rating scores of PD 3.6% or worse will not obtain a new loan. Here the rating system finally rejects the credit applications of new clients, and the big bank has not designed an official proceeding to outvote the rating result (Section 4.2.2.2).

The allocation of decision-making authority at savings bank 1 implies that supervisors have to approve relatively small loans, e.g. €25,000 blank credit in cases of a poor rating score, and credit officers review the formal correctness of credit applications (including all rating executions). Accordingly, customer advisors do not decide on credits completely on their own. In contrast, big bank 1's customer advisors decide ca. 50% of the credit applications alone due to their unrestricted lending authority of up to €1 million, provided the SME's rating score remains below the threshold of PD 2.1%. In such cases the credit officers do not review the rating execution's formal correctness, though a small proportion of the cases are audited randomly ex post. The back-office team of big bank 1, centralised at the national scale, only gets involved in credit decisions about risk-relevant borrower units, i.e. SMEs with medium rating scores (PD ≥ 2.1% to < 3.6%) or with credit volumes above €1 million (Section 4.2.3.2). Supervisors are not officially involved in credit decisions for medium-sized SMEs. Due to these organisational differences, the credit-granting process for medium-sized SMEs is usually a collective affair at savings bank 1, whereas the customer advisors of big bank 1 evaluate ca. 50% of credit applications on their own.

Interestingly, the rating systems themselves tend to be comparable. Like large banks, all 417 regional German savings banks use the same rating systems, the so-called *StandardRating* for SMEs, provided by the Sparkassen Rating und Risikosysteme GmbH, an affiliated company of the DSGV located in Berlin. The *StandardRating* and the rating for SMEs of big bank 1 calculate the rating score on the basis of hard and soft information in different modules. As BaFin has approved both rating systems for IRA (thus admitting the calculated PD for the determination of regulatory minimum capital requirements), strong deviations in the rating results are not to be expected. Considering the relevance of hard and 'rather' hard information also in the so-called qualitative rating modules, soft information accounts for substantially less than 50% of the rating results. Two additional facts support the conclusion that soft information has a subordinated impact on the rating results. Firstly, as the customer cases have shown, soft information is often very context and firm specific, and thus resists evaluation by rating algorithms (Section 4.3.1). Secondly, it has been demonstrated that customer advisors manipulate rating inputs to generate scores above banks' cutoff limits (Berg et al.,2013). Because the verifiability of soft information is restricted, a high weight of soft information would make rating algorithms prone to such manipulation, contradicting their intended utility for banks' risk controlling and bank regulation (IRA).

With the in-depth comparison it becomes obvious that total distance in SME lending depends on the characteristics of the borrower units. Rating scores and credit volume influence lending authority allocation (savings bank 1 in addition takes collaterals into account), and hence determines which actors – at what distances – get involved in lending. Functional distance profoundly differs between the actors of the contrasted banks. Especially the close and intensive pairwise cooperation between the customer advisors (front office) and credit officers (back office) of savings bank 1 strikingly differs from big bank 1. Centralised in a German city, one back-office team conducts the second vote for all credit applications of risk-relevant medium-sized SMEs, no pairwise cooperation exists and credit applications are processed randomly in the big bank. Therefore, customer advisor–credit officer cooperation is organisationally and socially embedded at the savings bank, whereas big bank 1's slim process organisation restricts embedded cooperation, implying long functional distance. This, in turn, restricts the transmission of soft information to the back office and the accumulation of knowledge about clients and regions by the back officers. Interview results furthermore show the profound functional distance to high-level supervisors at big bank 1, though the supervisors are not involved in lending decisions to medium-sized SMEs.

Regarding operational distance, the study in hand has identified similar organisation of customer advisor–customer cooperation. Savings bank 1 and big bank 1 strive for *Hausbank* relationships and designate a fixed customer advisor for each SME client, with whom personal communication is usual. Both banks locate customer advisor teams in major branches only. However, the micro-geographical accessibility of the studied branches differs. Savings bank 1's branch design leads to the high accessibility of customer advisor offices, whereas in the big bank barriers hinder clients from approaching their advisors uninvited, potentially affecting the customer–customer advisor relationship (Section 4.3.2.4). Despite this nuanced contrast in operational distance, overall the most striking difference relates to functional distance to the back office of savings bank 1 compared with the situation at big bank 1. This difference only becomes decisive for risk-relevant lending decisions, because only then does the back office of the big bank execute the second vote. In this case, soft information usage tends to be constrained due to the profound back-office distance, whereas customer advisors in the savings bank cooperate in organisationally and socially embedded relations with supervisors and especially credit officers.

Participant observation supports the theoretical notion that short distance, in terms of organisational and social embeddedness as well as geographical proximity, eases access to (especially soft) information. Savings bank 1 codifies soft information in the credit application and in the qualitative rating module of the *StandardRating*. However, as soft information is per definition difficult to verify by persons who have not produced it, it is verified in personal communication and continuous interaction. Especially for critical and unclear (credit) decisions, savings bank 1 conducts face-to-face negotiations where the bank decides on action based on all the hard and soft information at hand. Furthermore, as the customer cases indicate, the bank employees are in close and frequent interaction when dealing with financially distressed SMEs. In this way the customer advisors, credit officers and supervisors know the critical cases by heart and consider soft information in credit decisions. Co-location is another channel by which banks gain information for the SME credit business; e.g. savings bank 1's contacts to the local trade union motivated a client to inform the bank about upcoming financial difficulties that were not revealed to all its creditors (Section 4.3.2.3).

To estimate the effects of the observed differences in the organisation of the credit-granting process one has to consider that clear positive hard information tends to imply positive lending decisions, and definite negative hard information suggests credit rejection regardless of soft information (Section 4.3.2.1). Thus, soft information decidedly influences lending if hard information is inconclusive, e.g. in cases of financially distressed SMEs. However, in precisely these cases big bank 1 is hampered in the consideration of soft information, as inconclusive hard information causes medium to poor rating scores, so that the big bank delegates lending decisions to actors at long distances. In contrast, savings bank 1 keeps distances short in such cases, thus permitting the consideration of soft information which can and does alter lending decisions about financially distressed firms, as the customer cases indicate. More (soft) information implies reduced credit rationing of banks according to the Stiglitz and Weiss (1981) model (Section 2.2.1.1). Savings bank 1's process organisation enables the selection of good borrowers among the group of SMEs with critical rating scores, whereas big bank 1's process organisation tends to hamper (medium rating scores) or exclude (poor rating scores) groups of borrowers from access to finance on the basis of their hard information. Therefore, the process organisation of the regional bank is associated with reduced credit rationing, indicating its superiority in terms of enhancing access to finance for medium-sized SMEs.

One may object to this conclusion by arguing that savings bank 1's process organisation comes at the price of lax screening and monitoring causing enhanced bad debt taking. However, the comparison of non-performing corporate loans in fact suggests the superior screening and monitoring success of the regional bank compared with big bank 1 (Section 4.3.3.2). One could also object that savings banks' process organisation comes at the price of increased transaction costs, considering the labour-intense supervision of financially distressed SMEs. This cost disadvantage of the regional bank implies competitive disadvantages especially for financially sound firms which do not profit from the reduced credit rationing of financially distressed SMEs. Paradoxically, the credit statistics show market share gains by the regional savings and cooperative banks at the expense of the big banks (Section 3.2.3) and a range of empirical studies indicate their profitability to be comparable with that of private banks (Ayadi et al. 2009; Beck et al. 2009; Behr et al. 2013). Two potential explanations for this paradox exist. Firstly, as the customer cases of savings bank 1 indicate, financially distressed clients pay considerable interest because of extensive current account line usage and the risk adjusted pricing of credit terms corresponding to the rating results. Banks that – based on soft information – identify good quality borrowers (borrowers who will serve debt) among the group of SMEs with critical rating scores are able to gain additional revenue from the risk premium of credit terms (Section 4.3.1.1.). Secondly, according to Handke's (2011) study on relationship banking in Germany, financially sound SMEs also tend to accept more expensive credit terms in anticipation of the implicit liquidity insurance for financial difficulties that is associated with regional *Hausbanks*. Therefore, the process organisation of savings bank 1 is potentially competitive with that of large banks in the long run.

In addition, one may point out the advantages of large banks in terms of sector and banking expertise, which, in turn, mitigates their disadvantage in soft information processing. This argumentation only applies to large SME clients of big bank 1 where the bank has designed a lending process that combines sector expertise, e.g. specialised back-office departments, with short functional distance (Section 4.2.3.3). However, the big bank withholds this credit-granting process from SMEs of the medium size class where no sector specialisation of the back office exists. Therefore, medium-sized SMEs tend to be exposed to the disadvantages of functional distance and increased credit rationing while benefiting to a limited degree from the advantages of the large bank.

Overall, the empirical comparison surprisingly revealed shorter functional distances at the big bank in approximately 50% of credit decisions because of the unrestricted credit-granting authority of local staff when lending up to €1 million to sound SMEs. Nevertheless, observations of soft information usage and credit-decision processes indicate that the regional savings bank is able to consider soft information when it most strongly influences lending decisions, i.e., when deciding whether to lend to financially distressed SMEs. The empirical findings suggest that savings bank 1's lending process organisation neither comes at the price of lax screening and monitoring nor is it uneconomical, as the bank capitalises on its soft information advantages when lending at short distances.

5.2 Practitioner recommendations

As the comparison between savings bank 1 and big bank 1 shows, the regional savings bank's lending process organisation is associated with reduced credit rationing, especially for financially distressed SMEs. Furthermore, according to the interview findings, other regional banks also tend to decide SME credits at a shorter functional distance than large banks when soft information becomes decisive. As Cowling et al. (2016) have shown for the UK, financially distressed SMEs have a higher demand for loans and are less likely to receive them, which underscores the relevance of banks' ability to lend to this type of client economically. Therefore, preserving or recreating a decentralised banking system, as proposed for the UK (Greenham and Prieg 2015; Bone 2016), is rational if SMEs' access to finance is of concern.

In this context, the customer cases illustrate the dedication of the dual-purpose savings bank to financially distressed SMEs, which the public mandate and the regional principle together condition (Section 4.3.3.1). Accordingly, short functional distance is not the only reason for the commitment of savings banks to financially distressed SMEs. Gropp (2016) accuses the German savings banks of lending to inefficient firms because of their politically motivated imperative to support the regional economy and suggests that this may hinder economic development in the long run because inefficient SMEs stay in business. On the one hand, the empirical findings support Gropp's (2016) argument, considering the customer case where savings bank 1 extended credits to the Retailer Kampfgarten though his business model was unpromising (Section 4.3.1.3). On the other hand, as exemplified by the case Schmidt Solutions, savings bank 1 critically examines the business and private situation of borrowers on the basis of hard and soft information and tries to direct clients towards sound long-term financial performance (Section 4.3.1.1). Hence, empirical observations identify opposing effects and make clear that the regional bank does not generally have laxer lending standards, as its lower level of bad debt also indicates. Further research is required to advance our understanding on the handling of financially distressed firms by regional, superregional, private and dual-purpose banks and to measure its effects on economic development.

To fully understand the persistency of decentralised banking in Germany, the specific national context must be considered. To name but a few context factors: the decentralised economic structure with its numerous SMEs, the specific corporate governance model (i.e. coordinated market economy) and especially the effect of the regional banking associations. German savings banks belong to the savings banks financial group consisting of numerous banks and companies under the umbrella of the DSGV, which gives individual banks access to services, techniques and knowledge that enable the realisation of economies of scale. To reiterate, the 417 savings banks are the market leaders in business lending, indicating the potential for economies of scale, and interview partners from both savings and large banks pointed out the competitiveness of savings banks' ICT for retail banking (Section 4.2.2.1) which the financial group develops for all members. The performance of the regional savings banks is to be seen in this wider context; hence, the establishment of regional banks in other national contexts – as proposed in the UK – tends to face challenging launch conditions.

Against this background, one may question whether large banks can learn from regional banks and establish credit-granting processes that encourage the consideration of soft information. On the one hand, big bank 1 delegates decision-making power to its local customer advisors. Hence, in principle, the bank would be able to mirror the lending process organisation of savings bank 1 and decentralise the back office to establish regional credit officer teams that cooperate pairwise with the customer advisors. In this way the credit officers would know the SMEs, customer advisors and regional context and thus be able to assess the reliability of soft information for credit decisions. On the other hand, a process organisation that completely decentralises decision-making power would hinder the managing directors' capacity to control large banks. Due to the small size of regional banks and corresponding short distances between the hierarchical levels (Section 4.2.4), the managing directors tend to be well informed about and influence critical lending decisions. Such short-distance base control is hardly possible in a large bank, suggesting the necessity of solid lending thresholds, like a strict rating score cut-off limit, to restrict risk taking. Having stated this, the design of banks' incentive schemes is one potential means to encourage decentralised decision-makers to successfully screen and monitor SMEs with critical rating scores.

Because of the current low interest rate environment, regional banks have to reconsider their business model in Germany. Low interest rates tend to reduce the profitability of the deposits-based lending business model of traditional banking, as conducted by the regional savings and cooperative banks. Regional banks are reacting with branch closures, mergers and the standardisation of processes to cope with low interest rates and tightened bank regulation (Atzler et al. 2014; Schreiber 2015; Flögel and Gärtner 2018). The standardisation of processes and mergers of regional banks are associated with extending functional distance, and branch closures amplify operational distance. As the results of this study indicate, long functional distance hinders soft information usage and potentially increases credit rationing to SMEs with critical rating scores. This is not to suggest avoiding necessary adjustments to changing market conditions, but decision-makers (e.g. CEOs, regional politicians) should be aware of the potential factors which enable regional banks to reduce credit rationing to SMEs in an economically viable manner. To this end, more research is needed to increase our knowledge of the causal relationships between distance, decision making and SME finance.

5.3 Future research directions

The geographical classification proposes the place of decision making – in short versus long distance – as one characteristic to distinguish between decentralised and centralised banks, because short distance is associated with enhanced access to information for banks (Section 2.2.2.2). However, Degryse et al. (2009) and others question the influence of distance for small firm finance – claiming the 'death of distance' – because modern banks are subject to similar regulation and apply rating systems for credit decisions (Gärtner and Flögel 2013; Dixon 2014). As this study has confirmed, regional banks do not always decide on SME loans at shorter distances than large banks. Nevertheless, they tend to decide at a short functional distance when soft information influences credit decisions about SMEs most. Therefore, the argument of information advantages for regional banks in SME lending holds its explanatory power for the geographical classification of banking systems, despite regulation and standardisation in retail banking. Accordingly, regional banks still possess the ability to decide on credits differently to large banks, and hence potentially increase the diversity of banking systems.

Because of the qualitative research design, the generalisability of the key results of this study is limited. The results from the four other regional banks indicate similar lending process organisation in general – i.e., the regional banks avoid rating score–based cutoff limits in the medium-sized SME segment – though thresholds in lending authority allocation differ corresponding to the different sizes of the banks. Findings for the large banks tend to be less clear as process organisation differs greatly between the SME size classes of the supraregional banks interviewed. Outcomes suggest that the profound lending authority of big bank 1's customer advisors tends to be specific because the bank has purposefully designed the slim lending process organisation to compete with regional banks for medium-sized SMEs. Further research on lending process organisation for different market segments and in other regional and national contexts is desirable to advance our understanding of decentralised versus centralised banking.

Ethnographic insights have shown the need to seek alternative variables and data sources to obtain more accurate functional distance variables, because metric distance to headquarters inaccurately captures customer advisors' difficulties in transmitting soft information up the hierarchy. Factors like rating score cutoff limits, pairwise cooperation with credit officers and the means and frequency of communication also need to be considered. The findings from this study could be used to design more accurate functional distance measurements, e.g. questionnaires for surveys and interviews, indicators from labour market statistics. In this context, Canales and Nanda (2012) use interview results to determine the level of decentralisation of banks to study its impact on credit terms, thus indicating that a combination of qualitative and quantitative data advances our understanding of such matters. More accurate functional distance variables would facilitate quantitative studies on distance in lending and allow consideration of the rating systems as one actor involved in the credit decisions of regional and supraregional banks.

Appendix

List of empirical data

Code name	Date	Data type	Specific characteristics of interview	Function	Sector/size	Position	Sex	Age	Geographical market orientation	Length in minutes
GB1D		D			Medium SME					
GB1MFIP05.11.12	05.11.2012	IP	2 interviewers	Credit officer	Large SME	Department head	m	30–50	Supraregional	115
GB1MIP11.09.13	11.09.2013	IP	Ad hoc interview	Trainee		Employee AD	m	20–30	Supraregional	25
GB1MIT11.02.14	11.02.2014	IT		Customer advisor	Medium SME	Employee	m	30–50	Supraregional	54
GB1MIT13.02.14	13.02.2014	IT		Customer advisor		Regional manager AD	m	30–50	Supraregional	101
GB1MIT25.06.13I	25.06.2013	IT	2 interviewers	Customer advisor	Large SME	Branch manager	m	30–50	Supraregional	60
GB1MIT25.09.13II	25.09.2013	IT		Customer advisor	Large SME	Branch manager	m	30–50	Supraregional	61
GB2MIP27.11.12	27.11.2012	IP	2 interviewer	Customer advisor		Regional manager	m	30–50	Supraregional	70
GB2OIP11.03.13	11.03.2013	IP	telephone interview	Historian		Bank historian	m		Supraregional	20
GB3MIO23.04.13II	23.04.2013	IP	Ad hoc interview	Customer advisor	Medium SME	Employee AD	m	30–50	Supraregional	20
GB3MIT29.05.13I	29.05.2013	IT		Customer advisor	MediumSME	Employee AD	m	30–50	Supraregional	55
GB4BSIT01.07.13	01.07.2013	IT		Risk manager		Department head	m	30–50	Supraregional	59
Geno1MIP28.01.14I	28.01.2014	IP	Telephone interview	Customer advisor		Managing director	m	50–70	Regional	25

(Continued)

(Continued)

Code name	Date	Data type	Specific characteristics of interview	Function	Sector/size	Position	Sex	Age	Geographical market orientation	Length in minutes
Geno2MIP23.02.14II	23.02.2014	IT		Customer advisor		Managing director	m	50–70	Regional	94
GenoZBSIT09.06.13	09.06.2013	IT		Risk manager		Employee AD	m	30–50	Supraregional	
GenoZMIP12.09.14	12.09.2014	IP	2 interviewers; 2 interviewees	PPP/project finance			m	30–50	Supraregional	40
OBCIP05.02.14	05.02.2014	IP	Telephone interview			Employee	m	30–50	Other	55
OBCIP23.10.13I	23.10.2013	IP				Partner	m	30–50	Other	73
OBCIT07.02.14II	07.02.2014	IT				Partner	m	30–50	Other	47
OBCPP17–18.10.13	17.10.2013	PP							Other	
OESGVD14.06.13II		D					m		Other	
OED 01.07.13	01.07.2013	D							Other	
OED03.06.13	03.06.2013	D							Other	
OED03.06.132	03.06.2013	D							Other	
OED08.07.13	08.07.2013	D							Other	
OED10.06.13	10.06.2013	D							Other	
OEIT30.08.13	30.08.2013	IT		Professor		Co-head of school	m	30–50	Other	86
OEIT30.08.132	30.08.2013	IT	Ad hoc interview	Professor			m	30–50	Other	26
OEPP03.06–24.06.13	03.06.2013–24.06.13	PP							Other	
OEPP30.08.13	30.08.2013	PP							Other	
OESGVIT14.06.13I	14.06.2013	IT		Teacher		Head of school	m	30–50	Other	50
OSGVIT01.03.13	01.03.2013	IT				Department head AD	m	70–90	Other	63
OSGVIT04.03.13	04.03.2013	IT				Bank historian	m	50–70	Other	88

ID	Date	Code	Role	SME type	Position	Sex	Age	Region	Rating
OSGVIT16.04.13	16.04.2013	IT	Manager for the *StandardRating*	Medium SME	Employee	m	30–50	Other	62
OSGVIT30.05.13	30.05.2013	IT			Team leader	f	30–50	Other	81
OLD17.06.13	17.06.2013	D						Other	
OLPP24.06.13	24.06.2013	D						Other	
OOIT01.03.13	01.03.2013	IT	Subsidised loans		Employee	m	20–30	Other	60
OSGVD		D						Regional	
SK1BSIT02.09.13	02.09.2013	IT	Credit officer	Medium SME	Employee AD	m	30–50	Regional	76
SK1BSPP02.01.14	02.01.2014	PP	Other					Regional	
SK1BSPP03.01.14	03.01.2014	PP	Other					Regional	
SK1BSPP06.01.14	06.01.2014	PP	Other					Regional	
SK1BSPP07.01.14	07.01.2014	PP	Other					Regional	
SK1BSPP08.01.14	08.01.2014	PP	Other					Regional	
SK1BSPP09.01.14	09.01.2014	PP	Other					Regional	
SK1BSPP10.01.14	10.01.2014	PP	Other					Regional	
SK1BSPP17.12.13	17.12.2013	PP	Other					Regional	
SK1BSPP18.12.13	18.12.2013	PP	Other					Regional	
SK1BSPP19.12.13	19.12.2013	PP	Other					Regional	
SK1BSPP20.12.13	20.12.2013	PP	Other					Regional	
SK1BSPP27.12.13	27.12.2013	PP	Other					Regional	
SK1BSPP30.12.13	30.12.2013	PP	Other					Regional	
SK1D		D						Regional	
SK1DDatenschutz		D						Other	
SK1DEBIL-Muster		D		Medium SME				Regional	
SK1DInfos für Gründer		D						Regional	
SK1DSatzung		D						Regional	
SK1MFPP05.11.13	05.11.2013	PP	Credit officer	Small SME				Regional	
SK1MFPP06.11.13	06.11.2013	PP	Credit officer	Small SME				Regional	
SK1MFPP07.11.13	07.11.2013	PP	Credit officer					Regional	
SK1MFPP08.11.13	08.11.2013	PP	Credit officer	Small SME				Regional	

(Continued)

(Continued)

Code name	Date	Data type	Specific characteristics of interview	Function	Sector/size	Position	Sex	Age	Geographical market orientation	Length in minutes
SK1MFPP11.11.13	11.11.2013	PP		Credit officer	Small SME				Regional	
SK1MFPP12.11.13	12.11.2013	PP		Credit officer					Regional	
SK1MFPP13.11.13	13.11.2013	PP		Credit officer					Regional	
SK1MFPP14.11.13	14.11.2013	PP		Credit officer	Medium SME				Regional	
SK1MFPP15.11.13	15.11.2013	PP		Credit officer	Medium SME				Regional	
SK1MFPP18.11.13	18.11.2013	PP		Credit officer	Medium SME				Regional	
SK1MPP02.12.13	02.12.2013	PP		Customer advisor	Medium SME				Regional	
SK1MPP03.12.13	03.12.2013	PP		Customer advisor	Medium SME				Regional	
SK1MPP04.12.13	04.12.2013	PP		Customer advisor	Medium SME				Regional	
SK1MPP09.12.13	09.12.2013	PP		Customer advisor	Medium SME				Regional	
SK1MPP10.12.13	10.12.2013	PP		Customer advisor	Medium SME				Regional	
SK1MPP11.12.13	11.12.2013	PP		Customer advisor	Medium SME				Regional	
SK1MPP12.12.13	12.12.2013	PP		Customer advisor	Medium SME				Regional	
SK1MPP13.12.13	13.12.2013	PP		Customer advisor	Medium SME				Regional	
SK1MPP16.12.13	16.10.2013	PP		Customer advisor	Medium SME				Regional	
SK1MPP19.11.13	19.11.2013	PP		Customer advisor	Medium SME				Regional	
SK1MPP20.11.13	20.11.2013	PP		Customer advisor	Medium SME				Regional	
SK1MPP21.11.13	21.11.2013	PP		Customer advisor	Medium SME				Regional	
SK1MPP25.11.13	25.11.2013	PP		Customer advisor	Medium SME				Regional	
SK1MPP26.11.13	26.11.2013	PP		Customer advisor	Medium SME				Regional	
SK1MPP27.11.13	27.11.2013	PP		Customer advisor	Medium SME				Regional	
SK1MPP28.11.13	28.11.2013	PP		Customer advisor	Medium SME				Regional	
SK1MPP29.11.13	29.11.2013	PP		Customer advisor	Medium SME				Regional	

Code	Date	Type	Format	Area	Organization	Position	Gender	Age	Scope	Duration
SK1OIP01.10.12	01.10.2012	IP	2 interviewers; focus group	CEO and human resources		Managing director, department head	m	50–70; 30–50	Regional	60
SK1OIP22.10.12	22.10.2012	IP	2 interviewers	Human resources		Department head	m	30–50	Regional	82
SK1OIP23.05.2012	23.05.2012	IP	2 interviewers; 2 interviewees	Human resources; public relations		Department head	m		Regional	
SK2MIP13.03.13	18.03.2013	IP	2 interviewers	Customer advisor	Medium SME	Department head	m	30–50	Regional	30
SK2MIP13.03.132	18.03.2013	IP	2 interviewers	Customer advisor	Small SME	Department head	m	30–50	Regional	30
SK2OIP13.03.13	18.03.2013	IP	2 interviewers	Treasury, marketing		Department head	m	30–50	Regional	35
SK2OIP13.03.132	18.03.2013	IP	2 interviewers	CEO office		Department head	m	50–70	Regional	30
SK2OIP18.03.13	18.03.2013	IP	2 interviewers; focus group			Department head	m	–	Regional	60
SK3MIT24.09.13	24.09.2013	IT		Customer advisor	Medium SME	Employee	m	30–50	Regional	56
SK3MIT18.08.13	18.08.2013	IT		Customer advisor	large SME	Employee	m	30–50	Regional	80
SK4MIT25.09.13	25.09.2013	IT		Customer advisor	large SME	Employee	m	30–50	Regional	64
SK4MIT25.10.13	25.10.2013	IT		Customer advisor	Medium SME	Employee	f	30–50	Regional	51

Source: author's table

References

Abberger, K.; Hainz, C.; Kunkel, A. (2009): Kreditvergabepolitik der Banken: Warum leiden große Unternehmen besonders? In: *ifo Schnelldienst* 62 (14), pp. 3–5.

Ach, J.; Heinrich, W. (2007): Sparkassen-Finanzgruppe: Geschäftsschwerpunkte der Landesbanken/Girozentralen. In: D. Bartmann et al. (eds.): *Knapps Enzyklopädisches Lexikon des Geld-, Bank- und Börsenwesens*. Frankfurt am Main, pp. 1–9.

Admati, A. R.; Hellwig, M. F. (2014): *The bankers' new clothes. What's wrong with banking and what to do about it*. Woodstock.

Agarwal, S.; Hauswald, R. (2007): *Distance and information asymmetries in lending* (Working Paper).

Aglietta, M.; Breton, R. (2001): Financial systems, corporate control and capital accumulation. In: *Economy and Society* 30 (4), pp. 433–466.

Ahnert, S.; Engel, M.; Rohleder, G. (2009): *Handbuch Firmenkreditgeschäft. Stuttgart.*

Alessandrini, P.; Presbitero, A. F.; Zazzaro, A. (2009a): Geographical organization of banking systems and innovation diffusion. In: P. Alessandrini, M. Fratianni and A. Zazzaro (eds.): *The changing geography of banking and finance*. New York, pp. 75–108.

Alessandrini, P.; Presbitero, A. F.; Zazzaro, A. (2009b): Global banking and local markets: A national perspective. In: *Cambridge Journal of Regions, Economy and Society* 2 (2), pp. 173–192.

Alessandrini, P.; Presbitero, A. F.; Zazzaro, A. (2010): Bank size or distance: What hampers innovation adoption by SMEs? In: *Journal of Economic Geography* 10 (6), pp. 845–881.

Allen, F.; Gale, D. (2000): *Comparing financial systems*. Cambridge, MA.

Altman, E. I. (1971): *Corporate Bankruptcy in America*. Lexington.

Altman, E. I.; Sabato, G.; Wilson, N. (2010): The value of non-financial information in small and medium-sized enterprise risk management. In: *The Journal of Credit Risk* 6 (2), pp. 1–33.

Ang, J. B. (2008): A survey of recent developments in the literature of finance and growth. In: *Journal of Economic Surveys* 22 (3), pp. 536–576.

Appleyard, L. (2013): The geographies of access to enterprise finance: The case of the West Midlands. In: *Regional Studies* 47 (6), pp. 868–879.

Arcand, J. L.; Berkes, E.; Panizza, U. (2012): *Too much finance?* (IMF Working Paper).

Arnoldi, J. (2009): *Alles Geld verdampft. Finanzkrise in der Weltrisikogesellschaft*. Frankfurt am Main.

Atzler, E.; Osman, Y.; Dorst, F. M.; Stock, O. (03.01.2014): Reginalbanken. Die Krise der Musterschüler. In: *Handelsblatt*. Online available at: www.handelsblatt.com/finanzen/banken-versicherungen/regionalbanken-die-krise-der-musterschueler/9281686.html, access 04.05.2018.

Audretsch, D. B.; Lehmann, E. E. (2016): *The seven secrets of Germany. Economic resilience in an era of global turbulence.* New York.

Ayadi, R.; Llewellyn, D. T.; Schmidt, R. H.; Arbak, E.; Groen, W. P. (2010): *Investigating diversity in the banking sector in Europe: Key developments, performance and role of cooperative banks.* Brussels: Centre for European Policy Studies.

Ayadi, R.; Schmidt, R. H.; Valverde, S. C.; Arbak, E.; Fernandez, F. R. (2009): *Investigating diversity in the banking sector in Europe. The performance and role of savings banks.* Brussels: Centre for European Policy Studies.

BaFin (2002): *Mindestanforderungen an das Kreditgeschäft der Kreditinstitute—MaK.* Rundschreiben 34/2002 (BA). Bonn.

BaFin (2012a): *Mindestanforderungen an das Risikomanagement—MaRisk.* Rundschreiben 10/2012 (BA). Bonn.

BaFin (2012b): *Minimum requirements for risk management—MaRisk.* Rundschreiben 10/2012 (BA). Bonn.

BaFin (2014): Jahresbericht 2014. Online available at: www.bafin.de/SharedDocs/ Downloads/DE/Jahresbericht/dl_jb_2014.pdf;jsessionid=C4F7505F358E79AC690EA C4B18D78175.1_cid298?__blob=publicationFile&v=2, access: 17.06.2016.

Bank for international settlements (2006): *International convergence of capital measurement and capital standards. A revised framework*: Comprehensive version. Basel.

Bathelt, H.; Glückler, J. (2003): Toward a relational economic geography. In: *Journal of Economic Geography* 3 (2), pp. 117–144.

Bathelt, H.; Henn, S. (2014): The geographies of knowledge transfers over distance: Toward a typology. In: *Environment and Planning A* 46 (6), pp. 1403–1424.

Bathelt, H.; Malmberg, A.; Maskell, P.; Malmerg, A. (2004): Clusters and knowledge: Local buzz, global pipelines and the process of knowledge creation. In: *Progress in Human Geography* 28 (1), pp. 31–56.

Baumeister, C.; Zademach, H.-M. (2013): *Financing GPNs through inter-firm collaboration? Insights from the automotive industry in Germany and Brazil* (MDW Working Paper 21).

Beck, S.; Scherrer, C. (2013): Varieties of capitalism. In: J. Wullweber, M. Behrens and A. Graf (eds.): *Theorien der internationalen politischen Ökonomie.* Wiesbaden, pp. 151–167.

Beck, T. (2012): The role of finance in economic development: Benefits, risks, and politics. In: D. C. Mueller (ed.): *The Oxford handbook of capitalism.* Oxford, New York, pp. 161–203.

Beck, T.; Demirgüç-Kunt, A.; Levine, R.; Maksimovic, V. (2001): Financial structure and economic development: Firm, industry, and country evidence. In: A. Demirgüç-Kunt and R. Levine (eds.): *Financial structure and economic growth. A cross-country comparison of banks, markets, and development.* Cambridge, MA, pp. 189–241.

Beck, T.; Hesse, H.; Kick, T.; Westernhagen, N. (2009): *Bank ownership and stability: Evidence from Germany* (Working Paper).

Beck, T.; Levine, R. (2002): Industry growth and capital allocation: Does having a market- or bank-based system matter? In: *Journal of Financial Economics* 64 (2), pp. 147–180.

Behr, P.; Norden, L.; Noth, F. (2013): Financial constraints of private firms and bank lending behavior. In: *Journal of Banking and Finance* 37, pp. 3472–3485.

Bellinger, D.; Castro, D.; Mills, A. (2004): *Data, information, knowledge, and wisdom.* Online available at: www.systems-thinking.org/dikw/dikw.htm, access: 16.05.2016.

Berg, T.; Puri, M.; Rocholl, J. (2013): *Loan officer incentives and the limits of hard information* (Working Paper).

Berger, A. N.; Cowan, A. M.; Frame, W. C. (2011): The surprising use of credit scoring in small business lending by community banks and the attendant effects on credit availability, risk, and profitability. In: *Journal of Financial Services Research* 39 (1–2), pp. 1–17.

Berger, A. N.; Demsetz, R. S.; Strahan, P. E. (1999): The consolidation of the financial services industry: Causes, consequences, and implications for the future. In: *Journal of Banking & Finance* 23 (2–4), pp. 135–194.

Berger, A. N.; Hansen, I.; Klapper, L. (2004): Further evidence on the link between finance and growth: An international analysis of community banking and economic performance. In: *Journal of Financial Services Research* 25 (2), pp. 169–202.

Berger, A. N.; Miller, N.; Petersen, M.; Rajan, R.; Stein, J. (2005): Does function follow organizational form? Evidence from the lending practices of large and small banks. In: *Journal of Financial Economics* 76 (2), pp. 237–269.

Berger, A. N.; Saunders, A.; Scalise, J. M.; Udell, G. F. (1998): The effects of bank mergers and acquisitions on small business lending. In: *Journal of Financial Economics* 50 (2), pp. 187–229.

Berger, A. N.; Udell, G. F. (2006): *A more complete conceptual framework for financing of small and medium enterprises*. World Bank (Working Paper, S3795).

Berndt, C. (2011): Märkte, Monster, Modelle—Kulturelle Geographien der Subprimekrise. In: *Zeitschrift für Wirtschaftsgeographie* 55 (1+2), pp. 35–49.

Betsch, O. (2005): Strukturprobleme in der Finanzindustrie. In: Z. Sokolovsky and S. Löschenkohl (eds.): *Handbuch Industrialisierung der Finanzwirtschaft. Strategien, Management und Methoden für die Bank der Zukunft*. Wiesbaden, pp. 5–19.

Beyer, J. (2002): Deutschland AG a.D.: *Deutsche Bank, Allianz und das Verflechtungszentrum großer deutscher Unternehmen*. Max-Planck-Institut für Gesellschaftsforschung (MPIfG Working Paper, 02/4).

Beyer, J. (2009): Varietät verspielt? Zur Nivellierung der nationalen Differenzen des Kapitalismus durch globale Finanzmärkte. In: J. Becker and C. Deutschmann (eds.): *Wirtschaftssoziologie*. Wiesbaden, pp. 305–325.

Bharath, S.; Dahiya, A.; Saunders, A.; Srinivasan, A. (2007): So what do I get? The bank's view of lending relationships. In: *Journal of Financial Economics* 58 (2), pp. 368–419.

Bijlsma, M. J.; Zwart, G. T. J. (2013): *The changing landscape of financial markets in Europe, the United States and Japan* (Bruegel Working Paper, 2013/02).

Boghossian, P. A. (2006): *Angst vor der Wahrheit. Ein Plädoyer gegen Relativismus und Konstruktivismus*. Berlin.

Bone, G. (2016): *Banking for the common good. Laying the foundations of safe, sustainable, stakeholder banking in Scotland* (A discussion paper by: nef, Friends of the Earth Scotland, Move your money, common weal).

Boot, A. W. A. (2000): Relationship banking: What do we know? In: *Journal of Financial Intermediation* 9 (1), pp. 7–25.

Boschma, R. (2005): Proximity and innovation: A critical assessment. In: *Regional Studies* 39 (1), pp. 61–74.

Bowker, G.; Star, L. S. (1994): Knowledge and infrastructure in international information management. In: L. Bud-Frierman (ed.): *Information acumen: The understanding and use of knowledge in modern business*, London, pp. 187–213.

Brämer, P.; Gischer, H.; Pfingsten, A.; Richter, T. (2010): Der öffentliche Auftrag der deutschen Sparkassen aus der Perspektive des Stakeholder-Managements. In: *Zeitschrift für öffentliche und gemeinwirtschaftliche Unternehmen* 33 (4), pp. 311–332.

Brassier, R. (2011): Concepts and objects. In: L. Bryant, N. Srnicek and G. Harman (eds.): *The speculative turn. Continental materialism and realism*. Melbourne, pp. 47–65.

Breidenstein, G.; Hirschauer, S.; Kalthoff, H. (2013): *Ethnografie. Die Praxis der Feldforschung. Konstanz.*

Breisig, T.; König, S.; Rehling, M.; Ebeling, M. (2010): *"Sie müssen es nicht verstehen, Sie müssen es nur verkaufen!". Vertriebssteuerung in Banken.* Berlin.

Breuer, W.; Mark, K. (2004): *Perspektiven der Verbundkooperation am Beispiel der Sparkassen-Finanzgruppen. Eine Analyse organisatorischer Strukturalternativen auf der Grundlage der Transaktionskostentheorie.* Berlin.

Brevoort, K. P.; Holmes, J. A.; Wolken, J. D. (2010): *Distance still matters: The information revolution in small business lending and the persistent role of location, 1993–2003* (Working Paper).

Brinks, V. (2012): Netzwerke(n) und Nestwärme im Coworking Space. Arbeiten zwischen Digitalisierung und Re-Lokalisierung. In: *Geographische Zeitschrift* 100 (3), pp. 129–145.

Bruff, I.; Horn, L. (2012): Varieties of capitalism in crisis? In: *Competition & Change* 16 (3), pp. 161–168.

Brunnermeier, M.; Crockett, A.; Goodhart, C. A.; Persaud, A.; Shin, H. S. (2009): *The fundamental principles of financial regulation.* London.

Bruns, B.; Henn, S. (2013): *Problem-centred interviews in sensitive contexts: Researching cigarette smugglers and diamond traders* (SAGE Research Methods Cases).

Bryant, L.; Srnicek, N.; Harman, G. (eds.) (2011): *The speculative turn. Continental materialism and realism.* Melbourne.

Bülbül, D.; Schmidt, R. H.; Schüwer, U. (2013): *Savings banks and cooperative banks in Europe* (SAFE policy papers 5).

Bundesanstalt für Arbeit (2014): Labor market statistics, special evaluation (unpublished database).

Bundesverband deutscher Banken e.V. (2014): *Homepage.* Bundesverband deutscher Banken e.V. Online available at: www.bankenverband.de/was-wir-tun, access: 13.05.2015.

Burgess, B.; Clark, J.; Harrison, H. (2000): Knowledges in action: An actor network analysis of a wetland agri-environment scheme. In: *Ecological Economics* 35 (1), pp. 119–132.

Burgstaller, J. (2012): Banks in disadvantaged areas. In: *Kredit und Kapital* 45 (1), pp. 51–70.

Butzin, A. (2013): *Knowledge dynamics in innovation biographies. A methodological and spatial perspective.* Marburg.

Butzin, A.; Widmaier, B (2016): Exploring territorial knowledge dynamics through innovation biographies. In: *Regional Studies* 20 (2), pp. 220–232.

BVK (2014): BVK-Statistik. Das Jahr 2014 in Zahlen. Bundesverband Deutscher Kapitalbeteiligungsgesellschaften. Online available at: www.bvkap.de/privateequity.php/cat/42/title/Statistiken, access: 04.05.2015.

Callon, M. (1998): Introduction: The embeddedbess of economic markets in economics. In: M. Callon (ed.): *The laws of the markets.* Oxford, pp. 1–57.

Callon, M. (1999): Some elements of a sociology of translation: Domestication of the scallops and the fishermen of St. Brieuc Bay. In: M. Biagioli (ed.): *The science studies reader.* New York, pp. 67–83.

Callon, M.; Millo, Y.; Muniesa, F. (eds.) (2007): *Market devices.* Malden.

Canales, R.; Nanda, R. (2012): A darker side to decentralized banks: Market power and credit rationing in SME lending. In: *Journal of Financial Economics* 105 (2), pp. 353–366.

Capelle-Blancard, G.; Labonne, C. (2011): *More bankers, more growth? Evidence from OECD countries.* CEPII (CEPII Working Paper, 2011–22).

Carruthers, B. G. (2013): From uncertainty toward risk: The case of credit ratings. In: *Socio-Economic Review* 2013 (11), pp. 525–551.

Cetorelli, N. (2002): *Life-cycle dynamics in industrial sectors. The role of banking market structure*. Federal Reserve Bank of Chicago (Working Paper, 2002–26).

Chick, V.; Dow, S. C. (1988): A post-Keynesian perspective on the relation between banking and regional development. In: P. Arestis (ed.): *Post-Keynesian monetary economics*. Alderhots, pp. 219–250.

Christians, U. (2010): Zur Ertragslage der Sparkassen und Genossenschaftsbanken in den strukturarmen Regionen Ostdeutschlands. In: U. Christians and K. Hempel (eds.): *Unternehmensfinanzierung und Region. Finanzierungsprobleme mittelständischer Unternehmen und Bankpolitik in peripheren Wirtschaftsräumen*. Hamburg, pp. 231–253.

Christians, U.; Gärtner, S. (2014): Kreditrisiko von Sparkassen in Abhängigkeit vom regionalen Standort und geschäftspolitischen Variablen. In: *Zeitschrift für das gesamte Kreditwesen* 67 (12), pp. 620–626.

Christians, U.; Gärtner, S. (2015): *Wo sind die profitablen Sparkassen zu finden? Ertragskraft, Kreditrisiko und Eigenkapitalausstattung der Sparkassen in Abhängigkeit vom regionalen Standort*. Herzogenrath.

Christophers, B. (2013): *Banking across boundaries. Placing finance in capitalism*. Chichester, Malden.

Clark, G. L. (2005): Money flows like mercury: The geography of global finance. In: *Geografiska Annaler Series B: Human Geography* 87 (2), pp. 99–112.

Clark, G. L.; Thrift, N. (2005): The return of bureaucracy. Managing dispersed knowledge in global finance. In: K. Knorr Cetina and A. Preda (eds.): *The sociology of financial markets*. Oxford, pp. 229–249.

Clifford, J.; Marcus, G. E. (1986): *Writing culture. The poetics and politics of ethnography: A School of American Research advanced seminar*. Berkeley.

Cole, R. A.; Goldberg, L. G.; White, L. J. (2004): Cookie-cutter versus character: The micro structure of small-business lending by large and small banks. In: *Journal of Financial and Quantitative Analysis* 39 (2), pp. 227–251.

Coleman, S.; Simpson, B. (2016): Ethnography. In: *Discover Antropology*. Glossary of terms. Online available at: www.discoveranthropology.org.uk/about-anthropology/glos saryofterms.html, access: 03.10.2016.

Commerzbank (2013a): *Annual report 2013*. Online available at: www.commerzbank. com/media/aktionaere/service/archive/konzern/2014_2/Geschaeftsbericht2013_AG_ EN.pdf, access: 03.02.2015.

Commerzbank (2013b): *Financial statements and management report 2013*. Online available at: www.commerzbank.com/media/aktionaere/service/archive/konzern/2014_2/ Geschaeftsbericht2013_AG_EN.pdf, access: 03.02.2015.

Conrad, A. (2008): Banking in schrumpfenden Regionen. Auswirkungen von Alterung und Abwanderung auf Regionalbanken. In: *Thünen-Series of Applied Economic Theory* (Working Paper No. 94).

Cook, I. et al. (2004): Follow the thing: Papaya. In: *Antipode* 36 (5), pp. 642–664.

Corpataux, J.; Crevoisier, O.; Theurillat, T. (2009): The expansion of the finance industry and its impact on the economy: A territorial approach based on Swiss pension funds. In: *Economic Geography* 85 (3), pp. 313–334.

Cowling, M.; Liu, W.; Zhang, N. (2016): Access to bank finance for UK SMEs in the wake of the recent financial crisis. In: *International Journal of Entrepreneurial Behavior & Research* 22, pp. 903–932.

Crang, M.; Cook, I. (2007): *Doing ethnographies*. Los Angeles.

Czycholl, H. (2008): Restschuldversicherungen: Urteil gegen Citibank. Kreditvertrag ohne ausreichende Informationen—Norddeutsches Ehepaar muss keine Zinsen zahlen. In: *die Welt*. Online available at: www.welt.de/welt_print/article2129651/Restschuldversi cherungen -Urteil-gegen-Citibank.html, access: 23.06.2015.

Deakins, D.; Whittam, G.; Wyper, J. (2010): SMEs' access to bank finance in Scotland: An analysis of bank manager decision making. In: *Venture Capital: An International Journal of Entrepreneurial Finance* 12 (3), pp. 193–209.

Deckers, M.; Goeken, M. (2010): Industrialisierung in Banken: Grundlagen, Fallbeispiele und Lessons Learned. In: *BIT* 2010 (2), pp. 29–42.

Deeg, R. (2001): *Institutional change and the uses and limits of path dependency: The case of German Finance* (MPIfG Discussion Paper 01, 01/06).

Degryse, H.; Kim, M.; Ongena, S. (2009): *Microeconometrics of banking. Methods, applications, and results*. Oxford, New York.

Degryse, H.; Ongena, S. (2005): Distance, lending relationships, and competition. In: *The Journal of Finance* 60 (1), pp. 231–266.

Delgado, J.; Sakas, V.; Saurina, J. (2007): Joint size and ownership specialization in bank lending. In: *Journal for Banking & Finance* 31 (12), pp. 3563–3583.

Deller-Schneil, N. (2012): *Zur Geographie des Kapitals. Das Finanzsystem als regionaler Wachstumsfaktor*. Bremen.

Demirgüç-Kunt, A.; Feyen, E.; Levine, R. (2013): The evolving importance of banks and securities markets. In: *The World Bank Economic Review* 27 (3), pp. 476–490.

Demirgüç-Kunt, A.; Levine, R. (eds.) (2001): *Financial structure and economic growth. A cross-country comparison of banks, markets, and development*. Cambridge, MA.

Deutsche Bundesbank (2010): *Statistik der Banken und sonstigen Finanzinstitute, Richtlinien und Kundensystematik*. Online available at: www.bundesbank.de/Redaktion/DE/ Downloads/Veroeffentlichungen/Statistische_Sonderveroeffentlichungen/Statso_1/ statso_1_02_monatliche_bilanzstatistik.pdf?__blob=publicationFile, access: 03.10.2016.

Deutsche Bundesbank (2012): *Bankstellenbericht 2012*. Online available at: www.bundes bank.de/Redaktion/DE/Downloads/Aufgaben/Bankenaufsicht/Dokumentationen/banks tellenbericht_2012.html, access: 15.01.2015.

Deutsche Bundesbank (2014a): *Banking statistics—November 2014*. Online available at: www.bundesbank.de/Navigation/DE/Publikationen/Statistiken/Statistische_Beihefte/ statistische_beihefte.html, access: 12.02.2015.

Deutsche Bundesbank (2014b): *3. Aktiva und Passiva nach Bankengruppen 2014*. Online available at: www.bundesbank.de/Redaktion/DE/Downloads/Veroeffentlichungen/Statis tische_Beihefte_1/2014/2014_12_bankenstatistik.pdf?__blob=publicationFile, access: 12.02.2015.

Deutsche Bundesbank (2014c): *Statistische Sonderveröffentlichung 5. Hochgerechnete Angaben aus Jahresabschlüssen deutscher Unternehmen*. Deutsche Bundesbank. Online available at: www.bundesbank.de/Navigation/DE/Veroeffentlichungen/Statistische_ Sonderveroeffentlichungen/Statso_5/statistische_sonderveroeffentlichungen_5.html, access: 03.06. 2015.

Deutsche Bundesbank (2015): *Statistiken*. Online available at: www.bundesbank.de/ Navigation/DE/Statistiken/statistiken.html, access: 03.06.2015.

DeYoung, R.; Glennon, D.; Nigro, P. (2008): Borrower—lender distance, credit scoring, and loan performance: Evidence from informational-opaque small business borrowers. In: *Journal of Financial Intermediation* 17 (1), pp. 113–143.

Diamond, D. (1984): Financial intermediation and delegated monitoring. In: *Review of Economic Studies* 51, pp. 393–414.

Die Welt (06.01.2003): Deutschland ist inzwischen der kranke Mann Europas. In: *Die Welt*.

Dixon, A. D. (2012): Function before form: Macro-institutional comparison and the geography of finance. In: *Journal of Economic Geography* 12 (3), pp. 579–600.

Dixon, A. D. (2014): *The new geography of capitalism. Firms, finance, and society*. Oxford.

Dörry, S. (2015): Strategic nodes in investment fund global production networks: The example of the financial centre Luxembourg. In: *Journal of Economic Geography* 15 (4), pp. 797–814.

Dow, S. C.; Rodríguez-Fuentes, C. J. (1997): Regional finance: A survey. In: *Regional Studies* 31 (9), pp. 903–920.

DSGV (2014): *Organigramm des Deutschen Sparkassen-und Giroverbandes*. Online available at: www.dsgv.de/de/ueber-uns/dsgv-aufgaben-und-ziele.html, access: 02.02.2015.

Egner, H. (2010): *Theoretische Geographie*. Darmstadt.

Elsas, R. (2005): Empirical determinants of relationship lending. In: *Journal of Financial Intermediation* 14 (1), pp. 1283–1316.

Engelen, E.; Erturk, I.; Froud, J.; Leaver, A.; Williams, K. (2010): Reconceptualizing financial innovation: Frame, conjuncture and bricolage. In: *Economy and Society* 39 (1), pp. 33–63.

Engerer, H.; Schrooten, M. (2004): *„ Untersuchung der Grundlagen und Entwicklungsperspektiven des Bankensektors in Deutschland (Dreisäulensystem) " im Auftrag des Bundesministeriums der Finanzen*. Deutsches Institut für Wirtschaftsforschung. Berlin.

Epstein, G. A. (2005): *Financialization and the world economy*. Cheltenham, Northampton.

Epstein, G. A.; Crotty, J. (2013): *How big is too big? On the social efficiency of the financial sector in the United States* (Working Paper).

European Central Bank (ECB) (2013): *Banking structures report*. Online available at: www.ecb.europa.eu/pub/pdf/other/bankingstructuresreport201311en.pdf, access: 03.10.2016.

Everling, O.; Langen, R. (eds.) (2013): *Basel III. Auswirkungen des neuen Bankenaufsichtsrechts auf den Mittelstand*. Köln.

Fendo, A. (2009): *Vom Umgang mit Vorschriften im Büroalltag. Eine ethnographische Studie*. Hamburg.

Ferraris, M. (2014): *Manifest des neuen Realismus*. Frankfurt am Main.

Fischer, K.-H. (2005): *Banken und unvollkommener Wettbewerb. Empirische Beiträge zu einer Industrieökonomik der Finanzmärkte*. Frankfurt am Main.

Fischer, K.-H.; Pfeil, C. (2004): Regulation and competition in German banking. In: J. P. Krahnen and R. H. Schmidt (eds.): *The German financial system*. Oxford, pp. 291–349.

Fletcher, M. (1995): Decision making by Scottish bank managers. In: *International Journal of Entrepreneurial Behavior & Research* 1 (2), pp. 37–53.

Flögel, F. (2015): The new realist ontology: Metatheoretical foundation for research of modern finance? In: *Zeitschrift für Wirtschaftsgeographie* 59 (4), pp. 230–242.

Flögel, F. (2018): Distance and modern banks' lending to SMEs: Ethnographic insights from a comparison of regional and large banks in German. In: *Journal of Economic Geography* 18 (1), pp. 35–57.

Flögel, F.; Gärtner, S. (2018): *The banking systems of Germany, the UK and Spain from a spatial perspective: Lessons learned and what is to be done?* (IAT discussion paper 18/1).

Flögel, F.; Gärtner, S. (2011): *Raumunternehmen. Endbericht an die Montag Stiftung Urbane Räume*. Online available at: www.iat.eu/files/raumunternehmen.pdf, access: 03.10.2016.

Flögel, F.; Gärtner, S.; Kulke, E.; Warland, M. (2013): *Die wirtschaftliche Stärke des kooperierenden Einzelhandels: Studie im Auftrag des Bundesministeriums für Wirtschaft und Technologie*. BMWi. Online available at: www.bmwi.de/BMWi/Redaktion/PDF/

Publikationen/ Studien/wirtschaftliche-staerke-kooperierenden-einzelhandel,property=
pdf,bereich= bmwi2012, sprache=de, rwb=true.pdf, access: 03.10.2016.

Flögel, F.; Zademach, H.-M. (2017): Bank branches as places of knowledge creation: Conceptual considerations and empirical findings at the micro-geographical scale. In: *Erdkunde* 71 (4), pp. 301–312.

Franz, M. (2010): The role of resistance in a retail production network: Protests against supermarkets in India. In: *Singapore Journal of Tropical Geography* 31 (3), pp. 317–329.

French, S.; Leyshon, A.; Thrift, N. (2009): A very geographical crisis: The making and breaking of the 2007–2008 financial crisis. In: *Cambridge Journal of Regions, Economy and Society* 2 (2), pp. 287–302.

French, S.; Leyshon, A.; Wainwright, T. (2011): Financializing space, spacing financialization. In: *Progress in Human Geography* 28 (4), pp. 798–819.

Friedmann, J. (1986): The world city hypothesis. In: *Development and Change* 17 (1), pp. 69–83.

Friedmann, J.; Wolff, G. (1982): World city formation: An agenda for research and action. In: *International Journal of Urban and Regional Research* 6 (3), pp. 309–344.

Froud, J.; Haslam, C.; Johal, S.; Williams, K. (2000): Shareholder value and financialization: Consultancy promises, management moves. In: *Economy and Society* 29 (1), pp. 80–110.

Gabriel, M. (2013): *Warum es die Welt nicht gibt.* Berlin.

Gabriel, M. (2014): Existenz, realistisch gedacht. In: M. Gabriel (ed.): *Der Neue Realismus.* Berlin, pp. 171–199.

Gabriel, M. (2015): *Fields of sense. A new realist ontology.* Edinburgh.

Gärtner, S. (2008): *Ausgewogene Strukturpolitik: Sparkassen aus regionalökonomischer Perspektive.* Münster.

Gärtner, S. (2009a): Lehren aus der Finanzkriese. Räumliche Nähe als stabilisierender Faktor. In: *IAT Forschung Aktuell* 2009 (8).

Gärtner, S. (2009b): *Balanced structural policy: German savings banks from a regional economic perspective.* Brussels.

Gärtner, S. (2009c): Sparkassen als Akteure der regionalen Strukturpolitik. In: *Zeitschrift für Wirtschaftsgeographie* 53 (1–2), pp. 14–27.

Gärtner, S. (2011): Die Zukunft von NewYorkLondonHongKong und CaymanJerseySchweizLichtenstein: Eine räumliche Forschungsskizze in Postkrisenzeiten. In: C. Scheuplein and G. Wood (eds.): *Nach der Weltwirtschaftskrise: Neuanfänge in der Region?* Berlin, pp. 49–83.

Gärtner, S. (2013): Varianten institutioneller Arrangements am Beispiel regionaler Finanzregime. In: O. Brand, S. Dörhöfer, P. Eser, O. Brand, S. Dörhöfer and P. Eser (eds.): *Die konflikthafte Konstitution der Region. Kultur, Politik, Ökonomie.* Münster, pp. 233–263.

Gärtner, S.; Flögel, F. (2013): Dezentrale versus zentrale Bankensysteme? Geographische Marktorientierung und Ort der Entscheidungsfindung als Dimensionen zur Unterteilung von Bankensystemen. In: *Zeitschrift für Wirtschaftsgeographie* 57 (3), pp. 34–50.

Gärtner, S.; Flögel, F. (2014): *Call for a spatial classification of banking systems through the lens of SME finance—decentralized versus centralized banking in Germany as an example.* (IAT discussion paper, 14/01).

Gärtner, S.; Flögel, F. (2015): Dezentrale Banken—ein Vorteil für die Unternehmensfinanzierung in Deutschland? In: *Geographische Rundschau* 67 (2), pp. 32–37.

Gärtner, S.; Flögel, F. (2017): *Banken und Raum. Zur Funktionsweise regionaler Banken.* Baden-Baden.

Gesetz über das Kreditwesen—KWG, in the version of 9 September 1998 (BGBl. I S. 2776), last amended by article 16 of the German Act on the implementation of Directive 2013/50/EU of the European Parliament—Gesetz zur Umsetzung der Transparenz richtlinie-Änderungsrichtlinie of 20 November 2015 (BGBl. I S. 2029).

Girtler, R. (2001): *Methoden der Feldforschung*. Wien, Köln, Weimar.

Goldsmith, R. W. (1969): *Financial structure and development*. New Haven.

Grabher, G.; Ibert, O. (2014): Distance as asset? Knowledge collaboration in hybrid virtual communities. In: *Journal of Economic Geography* 14 (1), pp. 97–123.

Granovetter, M. (1985): Economic action and social structure: The problem of embeddedness. In: *American Journal of Sociology* 91 (3), pp. 481–510.

Greenham, T.; Prieg, L. (2015): *Reforming RBS. Local banking for the public good*. New Economics Foundation. Online available at: www.neweconomics.org/ publications/ entry/reforming-rbs, access: 12.09.2016.

Gropp, R. (2016): *Financial intermediation, allocative efficiency and growth*. Lecture, Freiberg: 21.01.2016.

Gropp, R.; Saadi, V. (November 2015): Electoral credit supply cycles among German savings banks. In: *IWH Online* 11.2015.

Grote, M. H. (2004): *Die Entwicklung des Finanzplatzes Frankfurt. Eine evolutionsökonomische Untersuchung*. Berlin.

Hackethal, A.; Schmidt, R. H.; Tyrell, M. (2006): The transformation of the German financial system. In: *Revue d'économie politique* 116 (4), pp. 431–456.

Hakenes, H.; Hasan, I.; Molyneux, P.; Xie, R. (2014): Small banks and local economic development. In: *Review of Finance*. doi:10.1093/rof/rfu003

Hakenes, H.; Schmidt, R. H.; Xie, R. (2009): *Regional banks and economic development. Evidence from German savings banks* (Working Paper).

Haldane, A. G.; May, R. M. (2011): Systemic risk in banking ecosystems. In: *Nature* 469 (7330), pp. 351–355.

Hall, P. A.; Soskice, D. W. (2001): *Varieties of capitalism. The institutional foundations of comparative advantage*. Oxford, New York.

Hall, S. (2006): What counts? Exploring the production of quantitative financial narratives in London's corporate finance industry. In: *Journal of Economic Geography* 6 (5), pp. 661–678.

Hall, S. (2011): Geographies of money and finance I: Cultural economy, politics and place. In: *Progress in Human Geography* 35 (2), pp. 234–245.

Hall, S. (2013): Geographies of money and finance III: Financial circuits and the 'real economy'. In: *Progress in Human Geography* 37 (2), pp. 285–292.

Hall, S.; Appleyard, L. (2009): 'City of London, City of Learning'? Placing business education within the geographies of finance. In: *Journal of Economic Geography* 9 (5), pp. 597–617.

Hamburg, I.; Widmaier, B. (2004): Wissen und Wissensmanagementsysteme. In: B. Widmaier, D. Beer, S. Gärtner, I. Hamburg and J. Terstriep (eds.): *Wege zu einer integrierten Wirtschaftsföderung*, Baden-Baden, pp. 86–108.

Handke, M. (2011): *Die Hausbankbeziehung. Institutionalisierte Finanzlösungen für kleine und mittlere Unternehmen in räumlicher Perspektive*. Berlin.

Hardie, I.; Howarth, D. (2013a): Framing market-based banking and the financial crisis. In: I. Hardie and D. Howarth (eds.): *Market-based banking and the international financial crisis*. Oxford, pp. 22–55.

Hardie, I.; Howarth, D. (2013b): A peculiar kind of devastation: German market-based banking. In: I. Hardie and D. Howarth (eds.): *Market-based banking and the international financial crisis*. Oxford, pp. 103–127.

Hardie, I.; Howarth, D.; Maxfield, S.; Verdun, A. (2013): Introduction: Towards a political economy of banking. In: I. Hardie and D. Howarth (eds.): *Market-based banking and the international financial crisis.* Oxford, pp. 1–21.

Hart, G. (2009): Ethnography. In: D. Gregory (ed.): *The dictionary of human geography,* 5th ed. Malden, pp. 217–218.

Hartmann-Wendels, T.; Pfingsten, A.; Weber, M. (2010): *Bankbetriebslehre,* 5th ed. Heidelberg, Dordrecht, London, New York.

Harvey, D. (1982): *The Limits to Capital.* Oxford.

Havránek, T.; Horváth, R.; Valíčková, P. (2013): *Financial development and economic growth: A meta-analysis.* Czech National Bank (CNB Working Paper Series, 5/2013).

Hellwig, M. (2008): *Systemic risk in the financial sector: An analysis of the subprime-mortgage financial crisis.* Max Planck Institute for Research on Collective Goods (Preprints of the MPI).

Hellwig, M. (2010): *Capital regulation after the crisis: Business as usual?* Max Planck Institute for Research on Collective Goods (Preprints of the MPI).

Hesse, F.; Kuklick, C.; Pfingsten, A. (2012): *Der Einfluss der aufbau- und ablauforganisatorischen Gestaltung des Kreditgeschäftes auf den "Misserfolg" von Sparkassen* (Working Paper).

Hesse, H.; Cihak (2007): *Cooperative banks and financial stability* (IMF Working Paper).

Hilse, J.; Netzel, W.; Simmert, D. B. (eds.) (2010): *Praxishandbuch Firmenkundengeschäft. Geschäftsfelder, Risikomanagement, Marketing.* Wiesbaden.

Historische Gesellschaft der Deutschen Bank e.V. (2009): *Wünsche werden Wirklichkeit. 50 Jahre Privatkundengeschäft.* München, Zürich.

Hombach, B.; Schmidt, A. (2011): Interner Rating Ansatz aus Sicht einer Geschäftsbank. In: G. Hofmann (ed.): *Basel III und MaRisk.* Frankfurt am Main.

Höpfner, B. (2014): *CRD IV: New regulatory package for banks in force.* BaFin. Online available at: www.bafin.de/SharedDocs/Veroeffentlichungen/EN/Fachartikel/2014/fa_bj_1401_start_crd_iv_crr_en.html, access: 03.10.2016.

Horsch, A.; Schulte, M. (2010): *Wertorientierte Banksteuerung II: Risikomanagement.* Frankfurt am Main.

Ibert, O. (2007): Towards a geography of knowledge creation. The ambivalences between 'knowledge as an object' and 'knowing in practice'. In: *Regional Studies* 41 (1), pp. 103–114.

Initiative Finanzstandort Deutschland (2010): *Finanzstandort Deutschland Rating Broschüre.* Online available at: www.hwk-reutlingen.de/fileadmin/hwk/betriebsberatung_dokumente/rating_broschuere.pdf, access: 03.10.2016.

Jeck, M. S.; Bufka, J. (2004): Erfolgsfaktoren der Kundenbindung- Ganzheitliches Customer Relationship Management und ertragsorientierte Kundensegmentierung. In: B. Schäfer (ed.): *Handbuch Regionalbanken.* Wiesbaden, pp. 329–353.

Jiménez, G.; Salas, V.; Saurina, J. (2009): Organizational distance and use of collateral in business loans. In: *Journal of Banking & Finance* 33 (2), pp. 234–243.

Jöns, H. (2003): Von Menschen und Dingen: Konstruktive-kritische Anmerkungen zum (a) symmetrischen Akteurskonzept der Akteursnetzwektheorie. In: J. Hasse and J. Helbrecht (eds.): *Menschenbilder in der Humangeographie.* Oldenburg, pp. 103–144.

Jöns, H. (2006): Dynamic hybrids and the geographies of technoscience: Discussing conceptual resources beyond the human/non-human binary. In: *Social & Cultural Geography* 7 (4), pp. 559–580.

Kalthoff, H. (2003): *Zahlenwelten. Studien zur epistemischen Ordnung der Bankwirtschaft. Habilitationsschrift.* Frankfurt (Oder).

Kalthoff, H. (2005): Practices of calculation. Economic representations and risk management. In: *Theory, Culture & Society* 22 (2), pp. 69–97.

Kalthoff, H. (2009): Die Finanzsoziologie: Social studies of finance. Zur neuen Soziologie ökonomischen Wissens. In: J. Becker and C. Deutschmann (eds.): *Wirtschaftssoziologie.* Wiesbaden, pp. 266–288.

Kamp, A.; Pfingsten, A.; Liebig, T. (2007): Diversifikation oder Spezialisierung—Eine Branchenanalyse der Kreditportfolios der Banken in Deutschland. In: *zfbf* 57 (7), pp. 1–38.

King, R. G.; Levine, R. (1993): Finance, entrepreneurship and growth. In: *Journal of Monetary Economics* 32 (3), pp. 513–542.

Kirchner, S.; Beyer, J.; Ludwig, U. (2012): Wie viel Heterogenität gibt es im 'Modell Deutschland'? Zur Verbindung von betrieblichen Beschäftigungssystemen und Profilen der Innovationsfähigkeit. In: *Industrielle Beziehungen* 19 (2), pp. 211–235.

Kitschelt, H.; Streeck, W. (eds.) (2004): *Germany. Beyond the stable state.* London, Portland.

Klagge, B. (1995): Strukturwandel im Bankenwesen und regionalwirtschaftliche Implikationen. Konzeptionelle Ansätze und empirische Befunde. In: *Erdkunde* 49 (3), pp. 285–304.

Klagge, B. (2003): Regionale Kapitalmärkte, dezentrale Finanzplätze und die Eigenkapitalversorgung kleinerer Unternehmen: eine institutionell orientierte Analyse am Beispiel Deutschlands und Großbritanniens. In: *Geographische Zeitschrift* 2003 (3+4), pp. 175–199.

Klagge, B. (2009): Finanzmärkte, Unternehmensfinanzierung und die aktuelle Finanzkrise. In: *Zeitschrift für Wirtschaftsgeographie* 53 (1–2), pp. 1–13.

Klagge, B.; Martin, R. (2005): Decentralized versus centralized financial systems: Is there a case for local capital markets? In: *Journal of Economics Geography* 14 (3), pp. 387–421.

Klagge, B.; Martin, R.; Sunley, P. (2017): The spatial structure of the financial system and the funding of regional business: A comparison of Britain and Germany. In: R. Martin and J. Pollard (eds.): *Handbook on the geographies of money and finance.* Cheltenham, pp. 125–156.

Klagge, B.; Peter, C. (2009): Wissensmanagement in Netzwerken unterschiedlicher Reichweite. Das Beispiel des Private equity-Sektors in Deutschland. In: *Zeitschrift für Wirtschaftsgeographie* 53 (1+2), pp. 69–88.

Kneer, G. (2009a): Akteur-Netzwerk-Theorie. In: G. Kneer and M. Schroer (eds.): *Handbuch soziologische Theorien.* Wiesbaden, pp. 19–39.

Kneer, G. (2009b): Jenseits von Realismus und Antirealismus. Eine Verteidigung des Sozialkonstruktivismus gegenüber seinen postkonstruktivistischen Kritikern. In: *Zeitschrift für Soziologie* 38 (1), pp. 5–25.

Koch, T. W.; MacDonald, S. S. (2014): *Bank management.* Scarborough.

Köhler, P.; Bastian, N. (2011): Den Sicherheitslücken auf der Spur. In: *Handelsblatt*, pp. 6–7.

König, W.; Schamp, E. W.; Beck, R.; Handke, M.; Vykoukal, J.; Prifling, M.; Spathe, S. H. (2007): *Finanzcluster Frankfurt an Main: eine Clusteranalyse am Finanzzentrum Frankfurt/Rhein-Main.* Norderstedt.

Krahnen, J. P.; Schmidt, R. H. (eds.) (2004): *The German financial system.* Oxford.

Kreissparkasse Kusel (2015): *Sparkasse Finanzkonzept Firmenkunden.* Online available at: www.ksk-kusel.de/firmenkunden/ziele-wuensche-strategien/index.php?n=%2 Ffirmenkunden%2Fziele-wuensche-strategien%2Ffinanz-check%2Fuebersicht%2F, access: 05.02.2015.

La Porta, R.; Lopez-De-Silanes, F.; Schleifer, A. (2002): Government ownership of banks. In: *Journal of Finance* 57 (1), pp. 265–301.

Latour, B. (1987): *Science in action. How to follow scientists and engineers through society.* Milton Keynes.

Latour, B. (2005): *Reassembling the social. An introduction to Actor-Network-Theory.* Oxford.

Levine, R. (1997): Financial development and economic growth: Views and agenda. In: *Journal of Economic Literature* 35 (2), pp. 688–726.

Levine, R. (2002): Bank-based or market-based fiancial systems: Which is better? In: *Journal of Financial Intermediation* 11 (4), pp. 398–428.

Levine, R. (2005): Finance and growth: Theory and evidence. In: P. Aghion and S. N. Durlauf (eds.): *Handbook of economic growth.* Amsterdam, pp. 865–934.

Levine, R.; Loayza, N.; Beck, T. (2000): Financial intermediation and growth: Causality and causes. In: *Journal of Monetary Economics* 46 (1), pp. 31–77.

Leyshon, A.; Pollard, J. (2000): Geographies of industrial convergence: The case of retail banking. In: *Transactions of the Institute of British Geographers* 25 (2), pp. 203–220.

Leyshon, A.; Thrift, N. (1995): Geographies of financial exclusion: Financial abandonment in Britain and the United States. In: *Transactions of the Institute of British Geographers* 20 (3), pp. 312–341.

Leyshon, A.; Thrift, N. (1997): *Money, space. Geographies of monetary transformation.* London.

Leyshon, A.; Thrift, N. (1999): Lists come alive: Electronic systems of knowledge and the rise of credit-scoring in retail banking. In: *Economy and Society* 28 (3), pp. 434–466.

Leyshon, A.; Thrift, N. (2007): The capitalization of almost everything. The future of finance and capitalism. In: *Theory, Culture & Society* 24 (7/8), pp. 97–115.

Liberti, J. M.; Mian, A. (2009): Estimating the effect of hierarchies on information use. In: *Review of Financial Studies* 22 (10), pp. 4057–4090.

Lo, V. (2003): *Wissensbasierte Netzwerke im Finanzsektor. Das Beispiel des Mergers & Acquisitions-Geschäfts.* Wiesbaden.

Lockwood, E. (2015): Predicting the unpredictable: Value-at-risk, performativity, and the politics of financial uncertainty. In: *Review on International Political Economy* 22 (4), pp. 719–756.

Lucas, R. (1988): On the mechanics of economic development. In: *Journal of Monetary Economics* 22, pp. 3–42.

Ludwig, U. (2009): *Anatomie einer Pleite: Wie deutsche Senioren in der Lehman-Falle landeten. Spiegel Online.* Online available at: www.spiegel.de/wirtschaft/anatomie-einer-pleite-wie-deutsche-senioren-in-der-lehman-falle-landeten-a-612195–2.html, access: 23.06.2015.

Luintel, K. B.; Kahm, M.; Arestis, P.; Theodoridis, K. (2008): *Financial structure and economic growth* (Working Paper, E2008/3).

MacKenzie, D. A. (2006): *An engine, not a camera. How financial models shape markets.* Cambridge, MA.

MacKenzie, D. A. (2011): The credit crisis as a problem in the sociology of knowledge. In: *American Journal of Sociology* 116 (6), pp. 1778–1841.

MacKenzie, D. A.; Millo, Y. (2003): Constructing a market, performing theory: The historical sociology of a financial derivatives exchange. In: *The American Journal of Sociology* 109 (1), pp. 107–145.

Marshall, J. N.; Pike, A.; Pollard, J. S.; Tomaney, J.; Dawley, S.; Gray, J. (2011): Placing the run on northern rock. In: *Journal of Economic Geography* 12 (1), pp. 157–181.

Marshall, J. N.; Richardson, R. (1996): The impact of 'telemediated' services on corporate structures: The example of 'branchless' retail banking in Britain. In: *Environment and Planning A* 28 (10), pp. 1843–1858.

Martin, R. (1994): Stateless monies, global financial integration and national economic autonomy: The end of geography? In: S. Corbridge, N. Thrift and R. Martin (eds.): *Money, power and space*. Oxford, Cambridge, pp. 253–278.

Martin, R. (ed.) (1999): Money and the space economy. London.

Martin, R.; Klagge, B.; Sunley, P. (2005): Spatial proximity effects and regional equity gaps in the venture capital market: Evidence from Germany and the United Kingdom. In: *Environment and Planning A* 37 (7), pp. 1207–1231.

Maskell, P.; Malmerg, A. (1999): Localised learning and industrial competitiveness. In: *Cambridge Journal of Economics* 23 (2), pp. 167–185.

Mason, C. (2010): Special issue: Entrepreneurial finance in a regional economy: The case of Scotland. In: *Venture Capital: An International Journal of Entrepreneurial Finance* 12 (3), pp. 167–172.

Mattes, J. (2012): Dimensions of proximity and knowledge bases: Innovation between spatial and non-spatial factors. In: *Regional Studies* 46 (8), pp. 1085–1099.

Mattissek, C.; Pfaffenbach, C.; Reuber, P. (2012): *Methode der empirischen Humangeographie*. Braunschweig.

McDowell, L. (1992): Doing gender: Feminism, feminists and research methods in human geography. In: *Transactions of the Institute of British Geographers* 17 (4), pp. 399–416.

Merton, R. C.; Bodie, Z. (1995): *A conceptual framework for analyzing the financial system* (Working Paper, 95–062).

Meyer, C. (2000): *Kunden-Bilanzanalyse der Kreditinstitute. Eine Einführung in die Jahresabschluss-Analyse und in die Analyse-Praxis der Kreditinstitute*. Stuttgart.

Mian, A. (2006): Distance constraints. The limits of foreign lending in poor economies. In: *Journal of Finance* 61 (3), pp. 1465–1505.

Micco, A. M.; Panizza, U.; Yenez, M. (2006*): Bank ownership and lending behavior. Inter-American Development Bank* (Working Paper).

Middelberg, A.; Plegge, D. (2010): *Rating, pricing und EBIL in der Kundenkommunikation. Anregungen für die ganzheitliche Betreuung von kleineren und mittleren Firmenkunden inkl. EBIL und Rating*. Stuttgart.

Miller, D. (2004): Making love in the suppermarket. In: A. Amin and N. J. Thrift (eds.): *The Blackwell cultural economy reader*. Malden, pp. 251–265.

Minsky, H. P. (1992): *The financial instability hypothesis*. Levy Economics Institute of Bard Colloge (Working Paper, 74).

Mistrulli, P. E.; Casolaro, L. (2008): *Distance, lending technologies and interest rates* (Working Paper).

Mudd, S. (2013): Bank structure, relationship lending and small firm access to finance: A cross-country investigation. In: *Journal of Financial Services Research* 44 (2), pp. 149–174.

Müller, M. (2012): Mittendrin statt nur dabei: Ethnographie als Methodologie in der Humangeographie. In: *Geographica Helvetica* 67 (4), pp. 179–184.

Murdoch, J. (1997): Inhuman/nonhuman/human: Actor-network theory and the prospects for a nondualistic and symmetrical perspective on nature and society. In: *Environment and Planning D* 15 (6), pp. 731–756.

Murdoch, J. (2006): *Post-structuralist geography. A guide to relational space*. London.

Myrdal, G. (1959): *Ökonomische Theorie und unterentwickelte Regionen.* Stuttgart.

Nguyen, L.; Skully, M.; Perera, S. (2012): *Government ownership, regulation, economic development and bank stability.* International evidence (Working Paper).

Niestrath, C. (2006): Bonitätsbeurteilung durch Rating-Verfahren. In: *geldprofil* 6/06, pp. 12–16.

Nocera, G.; Iannotta, G.; Sironi, A. (2007): Ownership structure, risk and performance in the European banking industry. In: *Journal of Banking and Finance* 31 (7), pp. 2127–2149.

O'Brien, R. (1992): *Global financial integration. The end of geography.* New York.

Ouma, S. (2010): Global standards, local realities: Private agrifood governance and the restructuring of the Kenyan horticulture industry. In: *Ecological Economics* 86 (2), pp. 197–222.

Ouma, S. (2012): "Markets in the Making": Zur Ethnographie alltaglicher Marktkonstruktionen in organisationalen Settings. In: *Geographica Helvetica* 67 (4), pp. 203–211.

Ouma, S. (2015): *Assembling export markets. The making and unmaking of global food connections in West Africa.* Chichester, West Sussex, Malden.

Ouma, S.; Bläser, K. (2015): Räume der Kalkulation, Kalkulation des Raumes. In: *Zeitschrift für Wirtschaftsgeographie* 59 (4), pp. 214–229.

Pagano, M. (1993): Financial markets and growth. In: *European Economic Review* 37 (2–3), pp. 613–622.

Panzer-Krause, S. (2011): *Ohne Moos nichts los—KMU-Finanzierungen unter den Bedingungen sich wandelnder Finanzmärkte. Eine Untersuchung von Beziehungen zwischen Banken und KMU.* Hamburg.

Paul, S. (2011): Umbruch der Bankenregulierung: Die Entwicklung des Baseler Regelwerks im Überblick. In: G. Hofmann (ed.): *Basel III und MaRisk.* Frankfurt am Main, pp. 9–64.

Peia, O.; Roszbach, K. (2013): *Finance and growth: Time series evidence on causality* (Working Paper).

Petersen, M. A.; Rajan, R. G. (1995): The effects of credit market competition on lending relationships. In: *The Quarterly Journal of Economics* 110 (2), pp. 407–443.

Petersen, M. A.; Rajan, R. G. (2002): Does distance still matter? The information revolution in small business lending. In: *The Journal of Finance* 57 (6), pp. 2533–2570.

Pieper, C. (2005): *Banken im Umbruch. Strukturwandel im deutschen Bankensektor und regionalwirtschaftliche Implikationen.* Münster.

Pike, A.; Pollard, J. S. (2010): Economic geographies of financialization. In: *Economic Geography* 86 (1), pp. 29–51.

Pollard, J. S. (1999): Globalisation, regulation and the changing organisation of retail banking in the United States and Britain. In: R. Martin (ed.): *Money and the space economy.* London, pp. 49–70.

Pollard, J. S. (2003): Small firm finance and economic geography. In: *Journal of Economic Geography* 3 (4), pp. 429–452.

Ponds, R.; van Oort, F.; Frenken, K. (2007): The geographical and institutional proximity of research collaboration. In: *Papers in Regional Science* 86 (3), pp. 423–443.

Poon, M. (2007): Scorecards as devices for consumer credit: The case of Fair, Isaac & Company Incorporated. In: M. Callon, Y. Millo and F. Muniesa (eds.): *Market devices.* Malden, pp. 284–306.

Pukropski, U.; Kasprowicz, T.; Mayer, M.; Quinten, D.; Sommer, D.; Schabert, T. (2015): *Bankenregulierung im Umbruch. Teil 1: Von der Neugestaltung zur Anwendung (KPNG).* Online available at: https://assets.kpmg.com/content/dam/kpmg/pdf/2015/07/

Bankenregul-ierung-im-umbruch-teil-1-von-neugestaltung-zur-anwendung-KPMG-2015-neu.pdf, access: 12.11.2015.

Rajan, U.; Seru, A.; Vig, V. (2010*): The failure of models that predict failure: Distance, incentives and defaults* (Working Paper).

Rehfeld, D. (1999): *Produktionscluster. Konzeption, Analysen und Strategien für eine Neuorientierung der regionalen Strukturpolitik.* München, Mering.

Rehfeld, D.; Terstriep, J. (2013): Socio-cultural dynamics in spatial policy: Explaining the on-going success of cluster politics. In: P. Cooke (ed.): *Re-framing regional development. Evolution, innovation, and transition.* Abingdon, New York, pp. 274–294.

Riebell, C. (2006): *Die Praxis der Bilanzauswertung.* Stuttgart.

Riese, C. (2006): *Industrialisierung von Banken. Grundlagen, Ausprägungen, Wirkungen.* Wiesbaden.

Robinson, J. (1952): The generalization of the general theory. In: J. Robinson (ed.): *The rate of interest and other essays*, pp. 67–142.

Róna-Tas, A.; Hiß, S. (2008): *Consumer and corporate credit ratings and the subprime crisis in the U.S. with some lessons for Germany.* Wiesbaden.

Rose, G. (1997): Situating knowledges: Positionality, reflexivities and other tactics. In: *Progress in Human Geography* 21 (3), pp. 305–320.

Rousseau, P. L.; Wachtel, P. (2011): What is happening to the impact of financial deepening on economic growth? In: *Economic Inquiry* 49 (1), pp. 276–288.

Ruhkamp, S.; Frühauf, M. (2010): Heißer Herbst für die Bankenaufseher. Die neuen Regeln für die Geldinstitute nehmen Gestalt an. Für die deutsche Kreditwirtschaft steht einiges auf dem Spiel. In: *Frankfurter Allgemeine Zeitung* (206).

Rutten, R. (2016): Beyond proximities. The socio-spatial dynamics of knowledge creation. In: *Progress in Human Geography.* doi:10.1177/0309132516629003

Sachverständigenrat zur Begutachtung der gesamtwirtschaftlichen Entwicklung (2004): *Das Deutsche Bankensystem: Befunde und Perspektiven in: Erfolge im Ausland— Herausforderungen im Inland, Jahresgutachten 2004/2005.* Wiesbaden.

Sachverständigenrat zur Begutachtung der gesamtwirtschaftlichen Entwicklung (2008): *Das deutsche Finanzsystem. Effizienz steigern—Stabilität erhöhen. Expertise im Auftrag der Bundesregierung.* Wiesbaden.

Sapienza, P. (2004): The effects of government ownership on bank lending. In: *Journal of Financial Economics* 72 (2), pp. 357–384.

Sassen, S. (2001): *The global city.* New York, London, Tokyo. New Jersey.

Sawyer, M. (2014): *Financial development, financialisation and economic growth* (FES-SUD Working Paper Series, 21).

Schäfer, B. (ed.) (2004): *Handbuch Regionalbanken*, 2nd ed. Wiesbaden.

Schamp, E. W. (2009): Das Finanzzentrum—ein Cluster. Ein multiskalarer Ansatz und seine Evidenz am Beispiel von Frankfurt/ RheinMain. In: *Zeitschrift für Wirtschaftsgeographie* 53 (1–2), pp. 89–105.

Schamp, E. W.; Linge, G. J. R.; Rogerson, C. (eds.) (1993): *Finance, institutions and industrial change. Spatial perspectives.* Berlin.

Scheuplein, C. (2013): Eine empirische Analyse von Buyouts und Standortstrukturen der Private-Equity- Firmen in Deutschland. In: *Zeitschrift für Wirtschaftsgeographie* 57 (4), pp. 201–215.

Schmidt, R. H. (2009): The political debate about savings banks. In: *Business Review* 61, pp. 366–392.

Schmidt, R. H.; Bülbül, D.; Schüwer, U. (2014): The persistence of the three-pillar banking system in Germany. In: O. Butzbach and K. von Mettenheim (eds.): *Alternative banking and financial crisis.* London, pp. 101–122.

Schmidt, R. H.; Hackethal, A.; Tyrell, M. (2001): *The convergence of financial systems in Europe*. Johann Wolfgang Goethe-Universität (Working Paper Series: Finance & Accounting).

Schmidt, R. H.; Tyrell, M. (2004): What constitutes a financial system in general and the German financial system in particular? In: J. P. Krahnen and R. H. Schmidt (eds.): *The German financial system*. Oxford, pp. 19–68.

Schmidt, S. (2012): *Wissensspillover in der Wissensökonomie*. Münster, Berlin.

Schreiber, M. (2015): Ende der Kleinstaaterei. Immer mehr Sparkassen und Volksbanken fusionieren. In: *Süddeutsche Zeitung*. Online available at: www.sueddeutsche.de/wirtschaft/banken-ende-der-kleinstaaterei-1.3785722, acccess: 05.05.2018.

Schüller, R.; Göbel, R. (2010): Risikomanagement- Strategiegespräch mit dem Unternehmensmanagement. In: J. Hilse, W. Netzel and D. B. Simmert (eds.): *Praxishandbuch Firmenkundengeschäft. Geschäftsfelder, Risikomanagement, Marketing*. Wiesbaden, pp. 421–434.

Shin, H. S. (2009): Reflections on Northern Rock: The Bank Run that Heralded the global financial crisis. In: *Journal of Economic Perspectives* 23 (1), pp. 101–119.

Short, J. A.; Williams, E.; Christie, B. (1976): *The social psychology of telecommunications*. London.

Simpson, R. (2013): *The German Sparkassen. A commentary and case study*. London.

Sokolovsky, Z.; Löschenkohl, S. (eds.) (2005): *Handbuch Industrialisierung der Finanzwirtschaft. Strategien, Management und Methoden für die Bank der Zukunft*. Wiesbaden.

Solvabilitätsverordnung—SolvV, in the version of 06 December 2013 (BGBl. I S. 4168), last amended by article 1 of the regulation of 12 September 2016 (BGBl. I S. 2146).

Sparkassen Rating und Risikosysteme GmbH (2010): *Rating—Herausforderung und Chance zugleich. Ein Ratgeber für Firmenkunden über das Rating der Sparkassen-Finanzgruppe*. Stuttgart.

Sparkassen Rating und Risikosysteme GmbH (ed.) (2006a): *RatingCheck Markt und Produkte. Sparkassen Rating und Risikosysteme GmbH*. Stuttgart.

Sparkassen Rating und Risikosysteme GmbH (ed.) (2006b): *RatingCheck Planung und Steuerung. Sparkassen Rating und Risikosysteme GmbH*. Stuttgart.

Sparkassen Rating und Risikosysteme GmbH (ed.) (2006c)*: RatingCheck Unternehmensführung. Sparkassen Rating und Risikosysteme GmbH*. Stuttgart.

Sparkassen Rating und Risikosysteme GmbH (ed.) (2006d): *RatingCheck Wertschöpfungskette. Sparkassen Rating und Risikosysteme GmbH*. Stuttgart.

Stein, J. (2002): Information production and capital allocation: Decentralized versus hierarchical firms. In: *The Journal of Finance* 57 (5), pp. 1891–1921.

Steiner, C. (2014a): *Pragmatismus—Umwelt—Raum. Potenziale des Pragmatismus für eine transdisziplinäre Geographie der Mitwelt*. Stuttgart.

Steiner, C. (2014b): Von Interaktion zu Transaktion—Konsequenzen eines pragmatischen Mensch-Umwelt-Verständnisses für eine Geographie der Mitwelt. In: *Geographica Helvetica* 69 (3), pp. 171–181.

Stern, G. H.; Feldman, R. J. (2003): *Too big to fail: The hazards of bank bailouts. Federal Reserve Bank of Minneapolis*. Minneapolis.

Sternberg, R.; Litzenberger, T. (2004): Regional clusters in Germany—their geography and their relevance for entrepreneurial activities. In: *European Planning Studies* 12 (6), pp. 767–791.

Stiglitz, J. E. (1985): Credit markets and the control of capital. In: *Journal of Money, Credit and Banking* 17 (1), pp. 133–152.

Stiglitz, J. E. (2010): *Freefall. America, free markets, and the sinking of the world economy*. New York.

Stiglitz, J. E.; Weiss, A. (1981): Credit rationing in markets with imperfect information. In: *The American Economic Review* 71 (3), pp. 393–410.

Stolbov, M. (2013): The finance-growth Nexus revisited: From origins to a modern theoretical landscape. In: *Economics: The Open-Access* 7 (2013–2), pp. 1–22.

Svetlova, E. (2012): On the performative power of financial models. In: *Economy and Society* 41 (3), pp. 418–434.

Taboada, A. (2011): The impact of changes in bank ownership structure on the allocation of capital: International evidence. In: *Journal for Banking & Finance* 35 (10), pp. 2528–2543.

Taylor, P.; Beaverstock, J.; Cook, G.; Pandit, N.; Pain, K.; Greenwood, H. (2003): *Financial services clustering and its significance for London. Extended Report.* Loughborough University; Manchester Business School.

Terstriep, J. (forthcoming): *Innovation & Wissen: Zur Wirkung von Clustern auf die Innovativität von Unternehmen.*

The Economist (14.04.2012): What Germany offers the world. Germany's economic model. In: *The Economist.* Online available at: https://www.economist.com/briefing/2012/304/14/what-germany-offers-the-world, access 07.06.2016.

Theis, M. (2009): *Die Rating-Erstellung der Sparkassen: eine problemorientierte Analyse der Rating-Erstellung im Kontext individueller Entscheidungspräferenzen.* Frankfurt am Main.

Therborn, G. (2011): End of a paradigm: The current crisis and the idea of stateless cities. In: *Environment and Planning A* 43 (2), pp. 272–285.

Theurillat, T.; Corpataux, J.; Crevoisier, O. (2010): Property sector financialization: The case of Swiss pension funds (1992–2005). In: *European Planning Studies* 18 (2), pp. 189–212.

Thrift, N. (1994): On the social and cultural determinants of international financial centres: The case of the City of London. In: S. Corbridge, N. Thrift and R. Martin (eds.): *Money, power and space.* Oxford, Cambridge.

Titze, M.; Brachert, M.; Kubis, A. (2011): The identification of regional industrial clusters using qualitative input-output analysis (QIOA). In: *Regional Studies* 45 (1), pp. 89–102.

Tobin, J. (1984): On the efficiency of the financial system. In: *Lloyds Bank Review* 153, pp. 1–15.

Torre, A. (2008): On the role played by temporary geographical proximity in knowledge transmission. In: *Regional Studies* 42 (6), pp. 869–889.

Torre, A.; Rallet, A. (2005): Proximity and localization. In: *Regional Studies* 39 (1), pp. 47–59.

Turner (2010): What do banks do? Why do credit booms and busts occur and what can public policy do about it? In: Turner et al. (eds.): *The future of finance.* LSE report. London, pp. 5–86.

Uchida, H.; Udell, G. F.; Watanabe, W. (2008): Bank size and lending relationships in Japan. Organizational innovation and corporate performance. In: *Journal of the Japanese and International Economies* 22 (2), pp. 242–267.

Uchida, H.; Udell, G. F.; Yamori, N. (2012): Loan officers and relationship lending to SMEs. In: *Journal of Financial Intermediation* 21 (1), pp. 97–122.

Udell, G. F. (2008): What's in a relationship? The case of commercial lending. In: *Business Horizons* 51, pp. 93–103.

Udell, G. F. (2009): Financial innovation, organizations, and small business lending. In: P. Alessandrini, M. Fratianni and A. Zazzaro (eds.): *The changing geography of banking and finance.* New York, pp. 15–26.

Uzzi, B.; Lancaster, R. (2003): Relational embeddedness and learning: The case of bank loan managers and their clients. In: *Management Science* 49 (4), pp. 373–399.

Verdier, D. (2002): *Moving money. Banking and finance in the industrialized world.* Cambridge.

Vira, B.; James, A. (2011): Researching hybrid 'economic'/'development' geographies in practice: Methodological reflections from a collaborative project on India's new service economy. In: *Progress in Human Geography* 35 (5), pp. 627–651.

Vopel, O. (1999): *Wissensmanagement im Investment Banking: Organisierte Wissensarbeit bei komplexen Finanzdienstleistungen.* Wiesbaden.

Wallisch, M. (2009): Unternehmensfinanzierung durch Business Angels. Zur räumlichen Organisation des informellen Beteiligungskapitalmarktes in Deutschland. In: *Zeitschrift für Wirtschaftsgeographie* 53 (1–2), pp. 47–68.

Wemhöner, M.; Grunwald, T. (2008): Neue Wege für einen aktiven und ganzheitlichen Firmenkundenvertrieb in der Deutschen Sparkassen-Finanzgruppe. In: A. Schmoll (ed.): *Erfolgreiche Vertriebsstrategien im Firmenkundengeschäft. Konzepte—Praxisberichte—Lösungen.* Wien, pp. 31–52.

Willke, H. (1998): *Systemisches Wissensmanagement.* Stuttgart.

Windolf, P. (2005): *Finanzmarkt-Kapitalismus. Analysen zum Wandel von Produktionsregimen.* Wiesbaden.

Wójcik, D. (2009): The role of proximity in secondary equity markets. In: G. L. Clark, A. D. Dixon and A. H. B. Monk (eds.): *Managing financial risks. From global to local.* New York, pp. 140–160.

Wójcik, D.; MacDonald-Korth, D. (2015): The British and the German financial sectors in the wake of the crisis: Size, structure and spatial concentration. In: *Journal of Economic Geography* 15 (5), pp. 1033–1054.

Wray, L. R. (2010): *What do banks do? What should banks do? Levy Economics Institute of Bard College* (Working Paper, 612).

Yeung, H. W. (2005): Rethinking relational economic geography. In: *Transactions of the Institute of British Geographers* 30 (1), pp. 37–51.

Zademach, H.-M. (2009): Global finance and the development of regional clusters: Tracing paths in Munich's film and TV industry. In: *Journal of Economic Geography* 9 (5), pp. 697–772.

Zademach, H.-M. (2014): *Finanzgeographie.* Darmstadt.

Zademach, H.-M. (2015): Gutes Tun und Geld verdienen? Ethische Investments und nachhaltige Geldanlagen. In: *Geographische Rundschau* 67 (2), pp. 46–52.

Zademach, H.-M.; Rimkus, M. (2009): Herausforderung Wissenstransfer in Clustern. Neues Wissen vom Biotechnologiestandort Martinsried. In: *zfbf* 61 (6), pp. 416–438.

Zarutskie, R. (2006): Evidence on the effects of bank competition on firm borrowing and investment. In: *Journal of Financial Economics* 81 (3), pp. 503–537.

Zhao, T.; Jones-Evans, D. (2017): SMEs, banks and the spatial differentiation of access to finance. In: *Journal of Economic Geography* 17 (4), pp. 791–824.

Zook, M. A.; Grote, M. H. (2017): The microgeographies of global finance: High-frequency trading and the construction of information inequality. In: *Environment and Planning* 49 (1), pp. 121–140.

Index

Page numbers in *italics* indicate figures and in **bold** indicate tables on the corresponding pages.

For Product Safety Concerns and Information please contact our EU
representative GPSR@taylorandfrancis.com Taylor & Francis Verlag GmbH,
Kaufingerstraße 24, 80331 München, Germany

Printed and bound by CPI Group (UK) Ltd, Croydon, CR0 4YY

01/05/2025

01858450-0006